DIVINE MULTIPLICITY

TRANSDISCIPLINARY THEOLOGICAL COLLOQUIA

Theology has hovered for two millennia between scriptural metaphor and philosophical thinking; it takes flesh in its symbolic, communal, and ethical practices. With the gift of this history and in the spirit of its unrealized potential, the Transdisciplinary Theological Colloquia intensify movement between and beyond the fields of religion. A multivocal discourse of theology takes place in the interstices, at once self-deconstructive in its pluralism and constructive in its affirmations.

Hosted annually by Drew University's Theological School, the colloquia provide a matrix for such conversations, while Fordham University Press serves as the midwife for their publication. Committed to the slow transformation of religio-cultural symbolism, the colloquia continue Drew's long history of engaging historical, biblical, and philosophical hermeneutics, practices of social justice, and experiments in theopoetics.

Catherine Keller, *Director*

DIVINE MULTIPLICITY

Trinities, Diversities, and
the Nature of Relation

EDITED BY CHRIS BOESEL AND
S. WESLEY ARIARAJAH

FORDHAM UNIVERSITY PRESS ❖ NEW YORK ❖ 2014

Copyright © 2014 Fordham University Press

All rights reserved. No part of this publication may be reproduced, stored in a retrieval system, or transmitted in any form or by any means—electronic, mechanical, photocopy, recording, or any other—except for brief quotations in printed reviews, without the prior permission of the publisher.

Fordham University Press has no responsibility for the persistence or accuracy of URLs for external or third-party Internet websites referred to in this publication and does not guarantee that any content on such websites is, or will remain, accurate or appropriate.

Fordham University Press also publishes its books in a variety of electronic formats. Some content that appears in print may not be available in electronic books.

Library of Congress Cataloging-in-Publication Data

Divine multiplicity : trinities, diversities, and the nature of relation / edited by Chris Boesel and S. Wesley Ariarajah.
    pages cm. — (Transdisciplinary theological colloquia)
  Summary: "By putting religious pluralists, comparative theologians, and scholars of religious studies into conversation with theologians doing doctrinal work within the Christian trinitarian tradition, this volume generates critical and imaginative visions of divine and creaturely relations that can inform future theological, philosophical and ethical work in interdisciplinary, inter-religious and intra-religious contexts" — Provided by publisher.
    Includes bibliographical references.
    ISBN 978-0-8232-5395-1 (hardback) — ISBN 978-0-8232-5396-8 (paper)
  1. Trinity. 2. Christianity and other religions. I. Boesel, Chris. II. Ariarajah, S. Wesley.
    BT111.3.D58 2014
    231—dc23

2013006703

16 15 14   5 4 3 2 1
First edition

CONTENTS

Acknowledgments   ix

Introduction: The Whence and the Whither of "Divine Multiplicity" | *Chris Boesel and S. Wesley Ariarajah*   1

PHILOSOPHICAL EXPLORATIONS: DIVINITY, DIVERSITY, DEPTH

The God Who Is (Not) One: Of Elephants, Blind Men, and Disappearing Tigers | *Philip Clayton*   19

God's Vitality: Creative Tension and the Abyss of *Différance* within the Divine Life | *Eric Trozzo*   38

Polyphilic Pluralism: Becoming Religious Multiplicities | *Roland Faber and Catherine Keller*   58

INTERRELIGIOUS EXPLORATIONS: RELIGIOUS DIVERSITY AND DIVINE MULTIPLICITY

Abhinavagupta's Theogrammatical Topography of the One and the Many | *Loriliai Biernacki*   85

One and the Many: The Struggle to Understand Plurality within the Indian Tradition and Its Implications for the Debate on Religious Plurality Today | *S. Wesley Ariarajah*   106

Differential Pluralism and Trinitarian Theologies of Religion | *S. Mark Heim*   119

Spirited Transformations: Pneumatology as a Resource
for Comparative Theology | *Holly Hillgardner*   137

THEO-ANTHROPOLOGICAL EXPLORATIONS: QUEER GOD, STRANGE CREATURES, STORIED SPIRIT

Excess, Reversibility, and Apophasis: Rereading Gender
in Feminist Trinities | *Sara Rosenau*   153

Doxological Diversities and Canticle Multiplicities: The Trinitarian
Anthropologies of David H. Kelsey and Ivone Gebara |
Jacob J. Erickson   175

The Holy Spirit, the Story of God | *Sam Laurent*   193

DOCTRINAL EXPLORATIONS: TRINITY, CHRISTOLOGY, AND THE QUALITY OF RELATION

Absolute Difference | *Kathryn Tanner*   217

Multiplicity and Christocentric Theology | *John F. Hoffmeyer*   234

Divine Relationality and (the Methodological Constraints of)
the Gospel as Piece of News: Tracing the Limits of Trinitarian
Ethics | *Chris Boesel*   252

The Universe, Raw: Saying Something about Everything |
Cynthia L. Rigby   280

Notes   301

List of Contributors   347

ACKNOWLEDGMENTS

Given that this collection of essays emerged out of Drew Theological School's tenth annual Transdisciplinary Theological Colloquium, our acknowledgment of and thanks to those who have contributed to bringing this book to publication must begin with the Theological School's incomparable team of administrative assistants, Michelle Campbell, Maria Iannuzzi, Alma Tuitt, and Meghan Harnois, together with the very capable staff in Drew University's offices for housing, hospitality, and catering with whom they worked closely to ensure the success of the colloquium for which these essays were originally written. The amazing graduate student members of our planning committee, Holly Hillgardner and Sara Rosenau, were at the front lines of planning and organization from the conception of the colloquium's theme through to the last of the participants being safely delivered to the airport to catch their return flights home. The director of the series, Catherine Keller, was again at the helm of the entire process.

The Drew colloquium of 2010 was blessed with a rich table of thoughtful, adventurous minds and distinctive, creative voices. As with every colloquium in the series, invited participants were not limited to those who are asked to write and present essays for discussion. We also invited scholars, teachers, and activists working in pertinent fields of discourse to respond to the essays and contribute in various ways to the conversation. These included two scholars from Drew's College of Liberal Arts, Karen Pechilis, specializing in Hinduism and Asian religions, and Christopher Taylor, specializing in Islam and Islamic mysticism. Drew Theological School's comparative theologian, Hyo-Dong Lee, was joined by colleagues in the field, John Thatamanil and Michelle Voss Roberts. Also gathered around the table were theologians Serene Jones, Laurel Schneider, Peter Heltzel, and Jason Mahn, together with Rabbi Lawrence Troster, rabbinic scholar in residence for an interfaith coalition addressing environmental issues, and Callid Keefe-Perry, a graduate student at Colgate Rochester Crozer Divinity School. This table of conversation partners constituted the original audience for these essays, and the conversation that ensued in response to the essays no doubt contributed to their final versions which we have gathered into this book. And that process of "gathering"—and proofreading, and formatting, and proofreading again—was ably assisted by another team of Drew graduate students: Beatrice Marovich, Jacob Erickson, and Michael Oliver.

Finally, we want to thank our friends at Fordham University Press for their continuing partnership in the TTC series. A special thanks is reserved for Helen Tartar, for her inspired vision for and leadership in that partnership. We are also indebted to Thomas C. Lay, for his particular editorial guidance of this volume's journey to publication.

DIVINE MULTIPLICITY

Introduction: The Whence and the Whither of "Divine Multiplicity"

CHRIS BOESEL AND S. WESLEY ARIARAJAH

This collection of essays is the result of work undertaken on the occasion of Drew Theological School's tenth annual Transdisciplinary Theological Colloquium. Each fall, since the turn of the millennium, a relatively small cohort of scholars working in and around the fields of religion and theology have been invited to engage a specific theological theme of current interest. The object of the series is to bring together thinkers from a variety of disciplines who share a cluster of interests: a commitment to interrogating the ethical impulses and material effects of theological and religious discourse; an appreciation for the always surprising complexity of theological and religious traditions; and an interest in contemporary theoretical approaches to scholarship (such as postmodern, postcolonial and liberationist methodologies). This introductory chapter outlines the issues and questions that the scholars invited to Drew for the tenth annual colloquium were asked to reflect on and engage from their own concerns and commitments within their various disciplinary locations. Our hope is to provide sufficient context for the theological, ethical, and disciplinary issues and stakes involved in these essays to emerge in all their dicey yet promising complexity.

DIVINE MULTIPLICITY AND THE NATURE OF RELATION

The contributors to this volume were asked to think, write, and talk about plurality and diversity as they pertain to the nature of divinity and/or ultimate reality. What are the possible grounds—philosophical, theological, ethical—for conceiving (or not conceiving) of divinity, or ultimate reality, in such a manner? Similarly, what are the corresponding implications entailed for divine and creaturely relations?

Along the complicated and shifting boundary between philosophy and theology, the "one" of the ancient philosophical conundrum of "the one and the many" has traditionally been identified with the divine in theological discourse, at least in the West. This has left "the many" and "the multiple" to characterize cosmological reality in some way that is fundamentally distinguishable from the simple, unified reality of divinity. Consequently, all the philosophical difficulties entailed in the relation between the one and the many—unity and multiplicity, identity and difference, coherence and conflict—tend to get translated into the theological register of a God-world relation. And this gives rise to one particular line of questioning pursued in these essays: How exactly is the nature of the God-world relation of theological and religious discourse determined by the philosophical conundrum of the one and the many, especially in terms of the assumed normativity of the one in relation to or over against the many? Alternatively, what are the theological consequences of questioning the philosophically conceived reality of the one and its assumed normative power while simultaneously asserting—even positively affirming—the irreducibility of the many? And this, not only for the divine-creature relation, but for the nature and reality of divinity itself.

In a similar vein, along the boundary where the ethical is continuously passing into and distinguishing itself from the religious and theological, two related areas of concern determine much of the thinking undertaken in these pages. First, how do conceptions of divine reality vis-à-vis the question of the one and the many function to determine the nature of relations within the creaturely world? Concern over the nature of the relation between theological discourse and the materiality of socioethical relations has lately given rise to a critique of monotheisms (and less explicitly, though by implication, religious systems of nonduality) as complicit in monarchical, hierarchical, totalitarian, and exclusionary sociopolitical orderings of creaturely relations. The constructive moves accompanying this critique argue for certain theological conceptions of divine multiplicity as the much-needed remedy—to the extent that such conceptions entail an affirmation of radical relationality as constitutive of divine reality. Several essays explore the extent to which such theological conceptions (e.g., contemporary transformatory retrievals of the Christian doctrine of the Trinity) can be said to model and/or fund nonhierarchical, egalitarian relationality in creaturely life and thereby function as a resource for the just and sustainable ordering of that life.

The second ethically directed concern deals with the specific arena of creaturely relationality constituted by religious pluralism and interreligious relations. The translation of the philosophical one into a theological conception of divine reality in singular, simple, and universal terms—whether as the Ultimate, the Abyss, the Universal, or as the God of Classical Theism, Panentheism, Pantheism, or Deism (all self-consciously distinguishable from, for example, what is often perceived to be an insufficiently philosophical "God of Abraham")—implies that the vast multiplicity of religious phenomena are all related to the same fundamental and encompassing divine reality. Theological discourse about religious pluralism and interreligious encounter has, in this case, tended to focus on the multiplicity of religions as a natural part of the creaturely diversity of the cosmos: varying symbol systems as human cultural products that express different experiences and forms of relation to a single, unified divine or ultimate reality.

However, in response to a growing appreciation for the realities and dimensions of religious difference experienced through sustained, intentional, interreligious encounter, the assumptions about the singular and universal nature of divine reality often found in the discourse of interreligious dialogue have, at least in the West, been recently criticized as problematically entangled with—and expressive of—the imperialism of Western liberal discourse. The concern is that these assumptions cannot do justice to the real difference between religious systems and their practitioners, but instead constitute the imposition of fundamental assumptions of certain traditions and systems (e.g., Christianity and Greek philosophy) onto others. Consequently, as demonstrated by several essays included here, some scholars of religious pluralism and participants in interreligious encounter are debating whether a truly respectful and egalitarian relationality between religions and their practitioners requires that religious plurality not only be conceived in terms of the diversity of religions but in terms of the diversity of divine reality as well—for example, a divine reality entailing a certain plurality and relationality within itself, or a plurality of divinities or ultimate realities coexisting in some form as differences in relation.

INTERROGATING LIMITS, CONJURING VISIONS: TRINITIES AND PLURALITIES

The essays in this volume, each in its own way, interrogate and explore the opportunities for transformative thinking that the related clusters of philosophical, theological, and ethical questions articulated above open up, as well as the difficulties, limits, and contradictions that such transformative thought might encounter. Taken as a whole, this volume poses certain critical questions and suggests certain constructive possibilities regarding the extent to which trinitarian and pluralist discourses can be put into fruitful conversation with one another. On one hand, it interrogates the possibilities of trinitarian theology and its ethical promise with regard to divine and creaturely relationality by putting it into specific engagement with discourses of pluralism, diversity, and multiplicity. How do trinitarian conceptions of divine multiplicity open the Christian tradition to increasingly more creative and affirming visions of creaturely identities, difference, and relationality—including the specific difference of religious plurality? Where can the triadic patterning evident in the Christian theological tradition be seen to have always exceeded the boundaries of Christian thought and experience? How has it inhabited and determined other religious traditions' conceptions of divine and/or creaturely reality in ways internal to their own distinctive histories? Similarly, in what ways—and toward what ends—does the conception of divine multiplicity exceed, or need to exceed, the specific numeric identity of the "three"? Why three? Is divine (or creaturely) multiplicity by any other number just as theologically and ethically resourceful? More so? Less?

On the other hand, the volume interrogates the possibilities of discourses on the various dimensions and arenas of pluralism by putting them in a very particular context of pluralism and difference, that is, by putting them in conversation with concrete theological work not specifically pluralist or comparative, nor intentionally transgressive or heterodox methodologically or thematically. That is, we have placed religious pluralists, comparative theologians, and scholars of religious studies alongside theological and doctrinal work carried out within the (albeit broadly conceived) normative thread of a specific tradition (to the extent, of course, that this "within" is possible, given the questionable status these days of binary oppositions like inside/outside). What are the possibilities of a polydox discourse that entails both inter- and intrareligious encounters of difference? To what extent can it collect within itself a convergent diversity of orthodox, heterodox, postcolonial, process, poststructuralist, liberationist, and feminist sensibilities while avoiding irruptions of conflict, competition, or the logic of mutual exclusion? And again, in the midst of these crisscrossing lines of cohering and/or conflictual difference, as the case may be, what critical, imaginative visions of divine and creaturely relations might be generated?

Focusing on the concrete particularity of the Christian trinitarian tradition in relation to pluralist discourses has its obvious risks. A good number of the scholars in this volume representing the pluralist and comparativist side of the encounter are also to various degrees located in or working primarily in relation to the Christian tradition. Although this enables a sufficient amount of theological work within the general stream of normative trinitarian tradition as well as methodological and disciplinary diversity within trinitarian conversation necessary for real intrareligious as well as interreligious multiplicity, it undoubtedly creates an interreligious imbalance weighted more heavily in the direction of Christianity. Similarly, strictly with regard to disciplinary identity, the focus on substantive theological work within a particular religious tradition (and doctrine) means that although there is still a diversity of disciplinary identity here, it is for the most part a diversity tightly packed, as it were, internal to the field of theology: systematic, contextual, ecumenical, comparative, philosophical, pluralist. Bringing this less broad, more intimate, finely differentiated diversity together necessarily means that other fields and disciplines identified closely or loosely with the academic study of religion are sometimes underrepresented in this particular conversation.

Taking all this into account, it is clear we have taken an editorial gamble on the promise of what this rather specific species of diversity might hold: polydoxy inclusive of orthodoxy, pluralism with regard to pluralism. Ultimately, of course, the contribution of this volume to the issues and questions addressed here, and to the fields of discourse in which they are pursued, interrogated, and debated, will have to be judged by the volume's future (if it is to have one): by whatever future work, action, and commitment it gives rise to in the minds and lives of its readers.

DISCIPLINARY APPROACHES AND THEMATIC INTERESTS

We have organized this collection of essays according to what we felt were the most compelling commonalities in theme and discipline. Although both theme and discipline are not always the same, or related in the same way, in each of the essays gathered under a particular part heading, we looked for certain lines of resonance that seemed to generate a mutual attraction and constitute a shared if in some ways contested context.

Philosophical Explorations: Divinity, Diversity, Depth

Philip Clayton provides an ideal opening not only for this first section of essays, which work predominantly from philosophical grounds and with philosophical resources, but for the volume as a whole. Clayton's leading question asks how we might best construe religious plurality and pluralism to avoid subsuming, erasing, or otherwise transcending the reality of concrete differences in such a way that does an injustice to those inhabiting those differences. Clayton takes his lead from a critical appraisal of John Hick's work on religious pluralism, on one hand, and of contemporary theological projects that tend to reduce theology and religion to an ethical core or criteria, on the other. He proposes polydoxy as a philosophical and theological methodology that allows practitioners to be positively located within a concrete tradition in such a way that they can cultivate its "local" resources for the benefit—rather than the erasure or appropriation—of their various neighbors. Clayton's essay goes on to enact just such a cultivation of particularly Christian resources, employing Hegel and Whitehead (among others) to rethink the trinitarian inheritance in terms of what he feels to be the more open, capacious, and hospitable concept of "deep dialectics."

Eric Trozzo shares Clayton's desire to render diversity in such a way that avoids transcending and encompassing difference and multiplicity in a concept of a final unifying coherence. His essay focuses on the implications of applying such a nontranscending rendering of diversity to the very essence of the divine life. If we are serious, Trozzo insists, we must acknowledge that such a radicalized concept of diversity risks introducing conflictual tension into the nature of divinity, even to the extent of finding in that conflictual tension the sources of destructive forces we characterize as evil. Trozzo suggests that Paul Tillich's philosophical theology exemplifies a Christian attempt to acknowledge conflictual tension within the divine, but one that is ultimately qualified by a more fundamental commitment to harmony. Trozzo enlists the resources of medieval scholasticism, a sixteenth-century Lutheran mystic, and more recently, Friedrich Schelling and the postmodern philosophy of John Caputo to push beyond Tillich toward the limits of an unflinching acknowledgment of the "demonic" within the life of God that can simultaneously affirm a trustworthiness in the Christ symbol that is not eclipsed by the risks of a destructive divine nature.

The essay by Roland Faber and Catherine Keller begins by identifying a certain tendency toward colonization and appropriation in even the most well meaning and ethically driven discourses on religious plurality, especially in the West. They suggest that the ethical desire to affirm and celebrate plurality is often difficult to distinguish from forms of exoticism and "piracy," whereby an ever-widening diversity is continually gathered into a single "collection"—for example, a discourse—for the aesthetic pleasure of its "owner," the Western subject. To resist and counter this tendency, Faber and Keller propose a form of polyphilia as an emerging form of discourse. This love of multiplicity envisions plurality and difference as generative, exceeding any effort to "collect" diversity into a totality or unifying whole. Yet it also brings forward a generativity that is "sticky" (essentially connective and mutually constituting) rather than inherently conflictual, competitive, or isolating. Drawing primarily on the philosophy of Alfred North Whitehead in conversation with postmodern and postcolonial theory as well as various religious traditions of both East and West, Faber and Keller launch upon a polydox "experiment" self-consciously grounded independent of any distinct religious confession for the sake of providing resources for an emerging future of religious difference beyond competition or appropriation.

Interreligious Explorations: Religious Diversity and Divine Multiplicity
This part gathers together a collection of scholars from different disciplines addressing the issue of divine multiplicity as it is found in different religious traditions (predominantly Hinduism and Christianity). Some of these essays also focus—in different ways and from differing perspectives—on the explicit issue of religious difference itself.

Pointing to the dilemma posed by the one and the many within Western thought, and its constant temptation to return to the one over the many, Loriliai Biernacki turns to the thinking of Abhinavagupta, an Indian thinker and mystic in the Tantric tradition who lived from the latter part of the tenth to the middle of the eleventh century C.E. in Kashmir, India. Biernacki suggests that Abhinavagupta provides a possible way out of the dilemma of the one and the many through an interrelation between the transcendent and immanent as expressed in his grammatico-theology. Abhinavagupta proposes a structural template to explicate his theological cosmology through the modalities of the first, second, and third persons of grammar: the "I," the "you," and the "it." Biernacki's essay explores the trinitarian syntax modulating the interpenetration of grammatical persons as a means for bridging the boundaries between the one and the many. Giving an outline of Abhinavagupta's thinking, Biernacki holds that the structure of language as grammatological system reflects the division of the one into the multiplicity that becomes the subject, the object, and the relationship between them as the syntax of the sentence. In so doing, Biernacki suggests that Abhinavagupta's understanding helps us rethink the relation between the one and the many as a dialectic of language.

Taking one of the central themes of the volume head on, S. Wesley Ariarajah asks whether it is necessary to look to some form of divine multiplicity in order to affirm plurality in general and religious plurality in particular. Ariarajah explores this question by recounting the struggle over the one and the many within the Indian philosophical tradition. He argues that the plurality and multiplicity of the universe itself had not been an issue within the mainline philosophical traditions of India because most of them consider the universe as *maya*, an evolute that evolves and dissolves but has no *ultimate* reality in itself. According to Ariarajah, the Sankya system of philosophy insisted that the universe can be understood only in terms of the two realities, the material (*prakriti*) and consciousness (*Atman*) that finds expression in the multiplicity of souls, thus positing a radical dualism. The later Advita Vedantic system, by Sankara, challenges this position by arguing that the perceived plurality of the souls and the world can be understood within the singularity of an ultimate reality. Ultimately, Ariarajah's reading of Hinduism supports a wider argument that the major religious traditions have not historically posited multiplicity in the divine as a way to understand or explicate creaturely plurality and diversity, including the move early within the Christian tradition to the concept of Trinity. This argument then raises questions as to the grounds for, and viability of, contemporary interpretations that attempt to find antecedents and precedents for this move in the texts and logics of those traditions.

A systematic Christian theologian attempting to take the self-definition and self-description of other religious traditions and practitioners seriously, Mark Heim has made a substantial contribution to a trinitarian entry point into theology of religions. His essay here continues to explore, in creative conversation with other scholars in the field, his long held conviction that "the doctrine of the Trinity offers Christians the deepest grounding for an understanding of religious diversity as a positive gift." In the first part of the essay Heim does an in-depth analysis of the pluralist position, with additional dimensions brought into the discussion by David Griffin, John Cobb, and others, in response to the pluralist proposal originally made by John Hick. In the second part he responds to six difficulties that John Thatamanil identifies in the trinitarian approaches to religious diversity. He then goes on to make a critical assessment of Thatamanil's own alternate thesis, which proposes a heuristic philosophical trinitarianism derived from Buddhist-Christian-Hindu dialogue, the three elements of which are ground, contingency, and relation. While recognizing that this position rectifies the Christian overdetermination of trinitarian formulations by drawing on central elements from these three religions, Heim sees building an integrative perspective out of these three as "a metatheological project of the first order" that "will gravitate toward a philosophical mediation between them and ultimately above them." Heim reiterates his thesis that the theological resources distinctive to the Christian tradition offer the most viable way—both theologically and ethically—for Christians to engage and respect the self-understanding and self-definition of other religions and religious practitioners.

Approaching the religious symbol of the Spirit from the comparative theological perspective, Holly Hillgardner explores the capacity of this symbol to enrich and complexify thought about the one and the many across the religions. Hillgardner begins by noting the extent to which the reality of Spirit is witnessed in a countless variety of ways across religious traditions. In the light of the consistency with which this religious testimony articulates Spirit's manifestation of divine life amid and within creaturely reality as the flowering of creaturely diversity, Hillgardner proposes Spirit as broadly accessible and so especially apt symbol of divinity's relation to multiplicity for the work of comparative theology. This broad accessibility is, of course, partly due to the biblical and extrabiblical representations of Spirit by and in the various "universal" elements, such as fire, wind, or breath. Further, of the three elements, or "persons," of the Christian symbol of Trinity, Spirit may best lend itself to an understanding of divine reality that dwells in necessary partnership with the natural world in all its diversity. This integral partnership of Spirit and nature opens up a Christian space for conceiving of religious diversity. In support of this thesis Hillgardner engages in a comparative theological reading of Sankara and Catherine of Siena. Drawing on these two seemingly disparate religious resources—an early medieval Indian Advaitan Hindu and a fourteenth-century European Dominican Christian—she expounds four dimensions of Spirit that open the Christian tradition up and into the space of interreligious, comparative theological relation: Spirit as the matrix of creation; support for the logic of multiplicity; as interrelated love; and the destabilizer of static ontologies.

Theo-Anthropological Explorations:
Queer God, Strange Creatures, Storied Spirit

Here we have clustered together those essays focused primarily on the notion of divine multiplicity as, to varying degrees, resource for and/or symbolic, theopoetic expression of imaginative visions of creaturely diversity and the possibilities for relationality that they entail.

Taking Elizabeth Johnson's feminist revisioning of the trinitarian symbol as her starting point, Sara Rosenau identifies a certain limit in feminist theologians' efforts to create space for women and the feminine in Christian language for God. Although appreciative of the necessity and value of this work, she argues for the need to go beyond it. She identifies the emergence of an increasingly critical assessment of the limits of the term "woman" within feminist and womanist discourse, noting that "before feminists could get to 'right speech' about God," it seemed "they had to agree on how to speak rightly about 'woman.'" Rosenau follows Judith Butler's lead in disturbing the singular notion of "woman" through questioning and destabilizing the sex/gender divide, pushing beyond Johnson to a deeper multiplicity of divine imagery that would subvert the male/female binary of gendered language for God. To carry out this constructive move of deeper multiplicity, she borrows the metaphor of the nomad from Marcella Althaus-Reid, as the transgressing of borders within the rich terrain of the Christian theological tradition. In her nomadic reading of the trinitarian tradition and its feminist revisions, Rosenau employs the theoretical triad of excess, reversibility, and apophasis to queer "the limits of the category of gender in the godhead," creating theological space not only for women, but for nonnormative gender and sexual identities as well.

Beginning with the image of strange, hybrid creatures—biblical seraphim—Jacob J. Erickson professes to make an equally strange theopoetic proposal for theological anthropology. With recent critiques of anthropocentrism in environmentalist philosophy and ecotheology in mind, Erickson urges us to find new ways of understanding creatureliness in the midst of planetary relations to the divine. He suggests that engagement with conceptions of divine multiplicity entailed in the symbol of the Trinity can exceed the offering of a social program or an unveiling insight into the life of God. Rather, such engagement can tap into an apophatic unsaying—"a warm blur"—of the human and of our various constructed boundaries of creaturely life. "Talking Trinity in theological anthropology," Erickson argues, "can continuously deconstruct dangerous impulses of anthropocentrism." His essay goes on, then, to enlist the resources of recent work by David H. Kelsey and Ivone Gebara in theological anthropology, along with a variety of contemporary feminist voices, in order to queer the human creature in relation to the divine. Drawing on the Christian tradition that discerns "vestiges of the Trinity" within creation, Erickson's bringing of the strange seraphic nature of trinitarian relationality into focus reveals how the nature of those creaturely vestiges themselves—in both human and nonhuman vessels—takes on a strangeness that exceeds and decenters any strict anthropocentric view of creaturely identity and value. "What emerges is a divine relationality that illumines ecologically convivial, *queer* creatures—a blur of human, animal, bird, elements, and divine warmth— where the burning passion of seraphim in all of their suffering and ecstasy might more closely model a contemporary hope for a 'posthuman' vision of theological anthropology."

Similar to Hillgardner's essay in the previous section, Sam Laurent also taps into recent developments in the pneumatological vein. His essay explores the possibilities of a pneumatology of story, envisioning the trinitarian Spirit of the Christian tradition as the "paradoxically multiple story of God." No single transmission of a unified message, according to

Laurent, the pneumatological story *of* God inspires the diversity of our own stories *about* God through the irreducible multiplicity of divine reality that moves in and through it. Laurent suggests that the notion of Spirit as Story provides a conceptual framework for understanding both divine and creaturely multiplicity, not as challenge or predicament, but as the very structure of creaturely life with God: God's participation in our life constitutes a "diversifying of the world" that calls us into relations of divine and creaturely community. Drawing on the work of Eugene Rogers and Kathryn Tanner, Laurent employs their concepts of the paraphysicality and incarnationality of the Spirit to describe the fundamentally diversifying work of the Spirit within God's trinitarian engagement with creation. He concludes the essay by turning to Laurel Schneider's notion of the "narrative forms of truth-making" to flesh out an understanding of "the role of the incarnational Spirit in the diversity of religious views."

Doctrinal Explorations: Trinity, Christology, and the Quality of Relation
As the subtitle suggests, the following essays come from those working in some fashion as Christian systematic theologians, reading the Christian doctrinal tradition in engagement with philosophical resources, various theoretical discourses, and testimonies to contemporary experience, in order to articulate doctrinal themes and positions for the church that are both theologically faithful (depending, of course, on who gets to determine the criteria for faithfulness) and ethically relevant, particularly to concerns for justice.

"Yes, unity that stifles diversity can be suffocating," notes Kathryn Tanner, "but would a genuinely encompassing unity, comprehensive of all perfection in the highest degree, do the same?" She goes on: "Diversity can be enriching, of course, but what if this diversity were to include grossly unfair extremes of inequality in character or circumstance?" Having thus questioned any easy assumptions regarding unity and diversity as unproblematic ethical or philosophical values in and of themselves, Tanner frames her theological treatment of these two concepts and their interrelation with the observation that "apart from a more concrete discussion of particulars, I don't see much reason to favor (or be wary of) one or the other, on simply a priori grounds." She then engages in a detailed examination of the evolution of the doctrine of the Trinity in the Christian tradition and the eventual emergence of the complex way unity and diversity are held together within it. The evolution of the doctrine, of course, had to contend with certain Neoplatonic metaphysical presumptions: Oneness is the prior source of multiplicity; the divine is characterized by its simplicity in the context of nondivine multiplicity; diversity represents ontological devolution. Tracing the history of the struggle to reconcile unity and diversity within the classical tradition, Tanner dwells on the work of Pseudo-Dionysius, who suggests that the way unity and diversity complement each other in creation has a higher analogue in the way the two opposites come together in God. Because unity and diversity in God are unlimited and absolute, they go together. They are integrated in perfect harmony and are rendered perfectly compatible with each other. "Might it not be the case, then," asks Tanner, "that the imperfect character of difference within creation is manifest in the way diversity and unity remain in tension with each another?" She goes on to develop this idea by suggesting a picture of the intense relationality of trinitarian persons as it is affirmed in classical trinitarianism, precisely in its qualitative distinction from the limited possibilities of creaturely finitude. This picture suggests, in turn, a possible limit to the theological venture of finding in trinitarian relationality a directly applicable and inhabitable model for creaturely relations of difference.

John F. Hoffmeyer's essay also highlights some of the easy assumptions and pitfalls that can attend explorations of unity and diversity in relation to divine multiplicity. He calls into question a common pejorative assumption that identifies multiplicity with fragmentation. Hoffmeyer points out that fragmentation and the tendency toward disjointed "manyness" is not the only meaning of multiplicity. On the contrary, the etymology of "multiplicity" in fact works against such fragmentation. In his view, the Christian doctrine of the Trinity is a particularly potent instance of just such a conception of multiplicity. Not only does it mediate the dialectic of unity and multiplicity, it also moves that dialectic off the plane of abstraction in a distinctive way. According to Hoffmeyer, the primary evaluative question in considering the relation of unity and multiplicity in the doctrine of the Trinity is not "Unity or multiplicity?" but "What sort of unity and what sort of multiplicity?" Against the background of these contestations between unity and multiplicity, the abstract and the concrete, Hoffmeyer addresses what, in modernity, has been experienced as the problematically "concrete" nature of the Christological—pejoratively characterized as the christocentric—origins of the doctrine of the Trinity. Arguing that the development of the doctrine of the Trinity cannot be separated from the struggle to understand the significance of Jesus of Nazareth, he uses the parable of the sheep and the goats in Matthew 25 to suggest an understanding of Christ as the "decentering center." Hoffmeyer suggests that such an understanding may enable an affirmation of trinitarian identity and relationality that is distinguishable from what are taken to be toxic forms of unity. In contrast to what Jean-François Lyotard describes as the logic of the metanarrative, decentering the Christological center of trinitarian theology might open up a space of genuine encounter with "the other," including the religious other.

Primarily concerned with issues of theological method, Chris Boesel begins by noting that, for much traditional Christian faith and theology, the emergence of the doctrine of the Trinity is understood to be fundamentally a response to a "piece of news" about God's saving action in Jesus in the power of the Spirit. However, it is just this understanding that entails an intractable surd of exclusionary particularity, apparently limiting the potential of trinitarian resources to function as a site for a progressive ethics of relationality, especially with regard to religious difference and interreligious encounter. According to Boesel, the modern transformation of the nature of Christian doctrine into an instance of the general category of religious "symbol" can be seen as an attempt to allow the trinitarian pattern's innate resources of multiplicity and relationality the necessary generality to fund an inclusive affirmation of the integrity of other religious traditions. But, Boesel asks, does the gift of generality come with its own ethical cost? He then investigates the possible limits of this methodological shift from news to symbol. He does so indirectly, however, via an exploration of the admittedly exclusionary *theological* logic of Karl Barth's christocentric trinitarianism. Focusing on the specific quality of divine and creaturely relations required by Barth's particularist theological assumptions, Boesel proposes to discover surprisingly robust *ethical* logics of inclusion and commitment across difference—including religious difference—that may exceed the familiar (not to say unjustified) refrains of progressive critiques of orthodoxy, an exceeding that may, in turn, shed its own critical light on certain refrains of progressive theological constructions as well.

Cynthia L. Rigby examines the Christian theological struggle to relate to the classical trinitarian formula of "three in one and one in three" by means of a perichoretic relationality. While recognizing the liberal anxiety over the "hard" language of metaphysics and its accompanying desire to affirm multiplicity in the contemporary context, she sets out a number of arguments in the form of reflections based on concrete life situations as to why the trinitarian formula can still have deep meaning in our day. Rigby first laments the tendency to move away from metaphysics and metaphysical analyses in our concern to honor particularities, diversities, and multiplicities. She questions this tendency with the thesis that "metaphysical claims do not dishonor, but actually support diversities and multiplicities when the unities they espouse are known only by virtue of the indwelling of particulars." Rigby then explores how the struggle with the trinitarian formula can actually help us reflect on the three things we wonder about most: (a) perceiving the unperceivable; (b) acting as finite beings in a world full of contingencies; and (c) knowing and being known by others. She concludes by proposing that we "need to attend to reclaiming 'perichoretic possibilities,' if multiplicities and diversities are to be supported by simplicities and unities."

• • •

Finally, we have asked the contributors to begin their essays by reflecting briefly on the significance of the collection's theme. This idea emerged from the final wrap-up discussion of the Drew colloquium for which the initial drafts of these essays were written. At a critical point in that final conversation John Thatamanil asked about the "existential" reasons driving those gathered around the table to reflect on issues of the one and the many and divine multiplicity with such urgency, as if they mattered terribly for the well-being of our respective communities, both local and global, and of the planet itself. Thatamanil followed up with his own answer to this question: the profound contemporary anxiety in the West about "being" exhibited in the threat of so many arenas of conflict—economic, religious, political—in which "the other," the immigrant, the Muslim, is so readily and easily targeted for hostility and violence.

Not all of our contributors chose to address the personal context of existential urgency in the manner of Thatamanil's initial comments. Many of the introductory reflections simply serve as a more general introduction to the essay proper. Whatever the approach taken by our authors, we trust that those additional paragraphs will help readers more readily identify the possible relevance of what may initially appear to many—if the history of trinitarian theology in the Christian tradition can be taken as an example—as a very abstract and ancient debate, a tedious and speculative exercise not far removed from determining how many angels can dance upon the head of a pin. We have left the occasional references to the colloquium that occur in these paragraphs, as well as the essays proper, as witness to the dialogical nature of the work from which these essays have emerged.

We trust that Thatamanil's brief words of existential urgency referred to here—in their own way a fitting summary of the passions and concerns behind the work contained in this volume—will at least convince any such potential readers to turn a page or two, read a bit further, and, to borrow from Kierkegaard, "Judge for yourselves!" Beyond this, we would not be ungratified if the occasional reader experienced himself or herself addressed and compelled by a challenging and creative voice or two with which to think alongside in the pursuit of their own intellectual and (as the case may be) spiritual labors.

◆ Philosophical Explorations:
Divinity, Diversity, Depth

❧ The God Who Is (Not) One: Of Elephants, Blind Men, and Disappearing Tigers

PHILIP CLAYTON

The relation between theology and philosophy in the West should henceforth become one neither of apologetics nor of criticism, but as the word "partners" suggests, fellows seeking from distinct backgrounds to understand the complex world, and the over-arching universe, in which we all, jointly, live; and the mysteriously human, in which we all, jointly, participate.
—WILFRED CANTWELL SMITH, "Religious Pluralism in its Relation to Theology and Philosophy—and of These Two to Each Other"

The elusive dance of the One and the Many fascinated me throughout the years of doctoral and postdoctoral study in Germany. But this fascination was, for me, never an intellectual artifact or abstract mind-game. Even before teenage years hit, and long before any formal exposure to either mysticism or organized religion, it was already a dance I knew well. Admittedly without sophistication or much in the way of argument, but certainly with tenacity, I would tell friends that "if God is in everything then somehow, in some way, everything must be one."

My teenage conversion to Christianity, and the subsequent years at a conservative Christian college, certainly pushed any such intuitions back to the margins of my awareness. But as time passed, and the discomfort with the overly neat evangelical answers grew, these thoughts reasserted themselves. Dropping out of seminary, I stuffed my backpack with Sartre and Hermann Hesse and hitchhiked around Europe for half a year. In a bookshop in Cambridge I encountered Vedanta—the metaphysics and epistemology of the great Hindu philosophers—and was finally exposed to a conceptual framework worthy of those monistic intuitions. My Christian location never disappeared, but alongside it slowly grew the roots of vishishtadvaita, or qualified nondualism, a philosophy and practice that affirms both the One and the Many in fascinating consonance. Of course, these Eastern convictions and practices were bound to raise their own dilemmas for a Christian theologian. The reader will observe some signs of that particular dance of the One and the Many in the pages below, but I also hope that she will see signs of the harmonies it can produce.

You might ask: What worldly significance could one possibly draw from a mystical-metaphysical stance, such as the inherence of the Many in the One? From the beginning (and like many before me) I recognized the powerful implications this view has for ecological activism. They are, in fact, radical implications, clashing with the tepid cost-benefit analyses of the "resource management" approach but linking naturally with the "Deep Ecology" movement and the complete rethinking of the human-nature relationship that we owe to ecofeminist thinkers. (In fact, that rethinking will represent the telos of this chapter.) The liberationist thrust of my position on the Many and the One also lies just under the surface, although this particular essay does not explore those themes as explicitly as I have done elsewhere.

The more orthodox among my friends in process thought are sometimes unhappy with the understanding of unity-in-diversity that informs the Indian traditions, most classically in Ramanuja's work. It's true that Ramanuja does not affirm the symmetry of One and Many in the same way that Whitehead does; and on this point I am more Ramanuja's disciple. Yet the astute reader will discern more similarities than differences; there is more of Whitehead here than at first meets the eye.

Many authors now recognize how crucial it is to draw fruitful lines between the world's religious traditions. It's a project of spiritual practice, and of ethics and politics, as much as it is a theoretical endeavor. Work of this kind is not less but more important in the light of the highly specific and "located" nature of the project. This particular essay grows out of a lived and practiced experience of the harmonies between Vedanta and Christianity, between bhakti (devotion) and kenosis (self-emptying). To the author, at least, these are not abstract claims. I know them more as existential discoveries than as disembodied speculations. I can only hope that the reader will also be able to discern some hints of the deeply personal roots of these reflections since, known or unknown, it's from those deep roots that the position, and its author, derive their ultimate nourishment.

ARE ALL RELIGIONS ONE?

In the school of thought known as New Age, differences between religions were minimized and their unity was emphasized. In the end, it was said, all religions teach the same thing, for all call their adherents to lives of compassion in union with the divine reality. Stephen Prothero's book *God Is Not One: The Eight Rival Religions That Run the World—and Why Their Differences Matter*[1] offers an effective counterpoint to these claims. Instead of drawing attention to agreements between traditions, Prothero focuses on differences. His work offers a convincing demonstration of how world economic systems, and the lives of billions of people, are affected by the unique features of the particular religion or religions that dominate a given country, culture, or era. Human existence is molded by religious contrasts as much as by the differences between, say, the cities of Murmansk, Malabo, and Lhasa. Religious beliefs and practices determine a landscape, an "environment," no less than living north of the Arctic Circle, on the equator, or in a holy city high in the Himalayas.

Prothero's emphasis on the particular is not just theoretical; nor does it hold only for "those other" religions out there somewhere. His work speaks just as effectively, for example, to the analysis of American foreign policy. Throughout its history, the United States has vacillated between two extremes, both implicitly (and sometimes explicitly) violent. We sometimes assume that all other peoples really believe, deep down, the same things that we do. This allows us to project our own mores onto other people-groups in firm confidence that we know what they "really" believe better than they. At other times we seek to win them over (from their "inferior" belief systems) to our own. "The One True God" has been used, and still is, as a crucial weapon for accomplishing these goals. This is true whether the debates are strictly theological, or whether they devolve into that other trinity that has so strongly marked this nation's history: democracy, capitalism, and the American Way.

Apart from politics and foreign policy, the inner conviction of a final unity underlying all religions has also fueled a highly specific form of interreligious dialogue, one that, for many years, was viewed as the only acceptable way of discoursing between religions. Beginning in the 1960s, for example, leaders in the Buddhist-Christian dialogue sought to establish a deeper unity between their two religions.² This approach seemed quite natural at the time. In retrospect, though, one realizes that it depended on a rather unlikely claim: that the religion of the One God, who is fully and definitively revealed in his only Son Jesus Christ, is identical to the meditation-centered practices of Zen Buddhism; that a religion deeply influenced by the unique history and salvation stories of the people of Israel, and by their Near Eastern cultural context, is really identical with the deeply Japanese conception of Zen; that a religion that focuses on getting specific beliefs right is the same as a set of practices oriented toward release and *sunyata*, in hopes of achieving freedom from illusion (*maya*) and an extralinguistic awareness of the full interconnectedness of reality.

A particular theology (or, as Marx would say, ideology) had to be constructed to make sense of this and other forced marriages of unlikely bedfellows, and it was John Hick who finally supplied it. In *An Interpretation of Religion*³ Hick argued that the clear differences between conceptions of the Ultimate should be left behind as one ascends from merely contingent details to the Real itself. In the end, Hick claimed, the Real is one and unified; all the distinctions gradually fall away as one ascends to the all-encompassing One. Even the difference between personal and impersonal attributes, which so deeply influences particular religious narratives and sets of practices, is ultimately transcended and thus erased.

Not surprisingly, Hick was deeply influenced by Immanuel Kant. "The Real" for Hick is a sort of noumenal "X," like the *Ding an sich* in Kant's *Critique of Pure Reason*. Hence, all predicates that we ascribe to God are akin to the categories of the understanding that human minds project onto the Totally Other—they are, in the end, simply of no consequence. This might well strike the reader as a rather radical, even costly, measure to take. But one can see that it's going to take an extremely radical, even counterintuitive redefining of what is "really true" in religion if one wishes to say that Zen Buddhists and evangelical Christians are, in the end, "really saying the same thing" about the Ultimate.

Many of us today have the same kind of response to Hick's painting all religions with the same brush as Alasdair MacIntyre had to Kantian or "universalizing" approaches to ethics. *Whose Justice? Which Rationality?*, we might ask. The democratizing tone of this proclamation of unity is misleading—someone is going to win and someone is going to lose. In Hick's case, the losers will be religions with highly specific stories and beliefs, since (on his view) distinctive narratives can remain only if one concedes that they are ultimately false. Conversely, unifying, all-is-one religions (or, more accurately, the refined philosophical traditions within such religions) will emerge as the clear victors.

Of course, the other winner was Hick himself—together with those religion-transcending scholars of religion like himself who are happy, from the safe haven of American Academy of Religion meetings in expensive hotels, to proclaim ex cathedra where truth lies and does not lie across the wide expanses of the world's religions. And, as in classical Freudian psychoanalysis, the more that the (religious) clients deny the analysis, the more the analysts take this to confirm the accuracy of their diagnosis of religion. But *has* the unity-of-all-religion approach really spoken the final word about truth, falsity, and the Ultimate?

GETTING TO PLURALISM WITHOUT LEAVING BEHIND THE DIFFERENCES

Suffice it to say that I do not view Hick & Friends as providing the last word on religious pluralism. Yet how should one construe pluralism if it does not mean transcending difference? Since challenge begins at home, consider an example drawn from my own institution. Through an amazing consensus of administration, faculty, and board, Claremont School of Theology has launched a new interreligious university.[4] We are now partnering with two other institutions—the Academy of Jewish Religion of California and the Islamic Center of Southern California—to found the Claremont Lincoln University, where students from all three of our traditions will study side by side. All three institutions already train men and women for leadership positions in their own religion, since all of us believe we can better prepare students for religious leadership in today's world in a fully interreligious context. Discussions are already under way to incorporate Hindu and Buddhist institutions into the partnership as well.

If John Hick provided the philosophical basis for an interreligious dialogue that produced (because it presupposed) the unity of all religions, what will serve as the theological framework for this *new* form of interreligious partnership? Because theologies matter—both conceptually and politically—a gentle tug-of-war has begun at my home institution over how best to define this first-of-its-kind project. Three distinct groups (theologies or ideologies) have emerged. Because the same alliances and battles arise again and again in debates over religious pluralism today, it is worth taking a moment to describe them.

The Hickian contingent among us wants this new partnership between religions to presuppose the final unity of all religions. Their motives and arguments should already be clear by this point. Another group, seemingly opposite to Hick and yet deeply connected with his position in another sense, argues for leaving behind *all* theological pronouncements and turning to ethics instead. On this view, all humans with a functioning conscience recognize injustices around the world and intuitively know the right and healthy ways for humans to live individually and in societies. The raison d'être of religions is to help bring about more just and humane living conditions for all humans, and indeed for all living things. Religions can be particularly effective at "healing the world," that is, at motivating governments and groups to improve living conditions, remove injustices, and take the long-term perspective. After all, religions are "repositories of wisdom," with stories, narratives, and metaphors that have been honed over centuries to induce humans to rise above their selfishness. On this view, however, the various religious accounts of *sunyata* or *nirvana*, of Brahman, Allah, or God, are not really important as claims about reality. They matter only if they are effective at motivating change. Herein lie the parallels with Hick. For both the first and second group, particular beliefs that arise within particular traditions are of only secondary importance. They are transcended and left behind by a higher instance: for the first group, by "the Real" without attributes; for the second group, by ethical and political transformation.

The third group, to which I belong, understands the belief systems of the various religions to be an intrinsic and equally important part of their overall gestalt. Before defending this view, I must admit that such a view stands at odds with the zeitgeist, which is more clearly reflected in the first two views. Also, across the millennia differences between religious beliefs have divided human beings and have repeatedly been used as justifications for intolerance, small-mindedness, even mass slayings and xenocide. Competing truth claims have all too often been taken as signs of ultimate difference and unbridgeable gaps. Indeed, these gaps have often grown into fissures and chasms, and many a program of reconciliation and tolerance has gone crashing down into this abyss, never to be heard from again.

Yet there is a new wind blowing, call it "postmodern" or "poststructuralist" or "postcolonial" or what have you. In this new climate resources have become available that allow humans to live in peace in the face of religious differences—without needing to rend asunder, like flesh from bone, the vibrant practices of religious communities (flesh) and the beliefs that orient their thought and practice (bone). An earlier book describes the movement beyond relativism and absolutism to "polydoxy."[5] By this point detailed work has been done on theories of knowledge that make it possible to treat religious belief in radically different ways, theories of truth that allow for difference without negation or elimination, theories of religious identity that acknowledge hybridity without downplaying real distinctions, and religious politics that work out the pragmatics of this new understanding of religious believing. Although I cannot here reiterate all the underlying arguments and theories, they are presupposed in what follows. Building on this earlier work, I will defend the following thesis: A new form of theological reflection is emerging, one that draws deeply and without embarrassment on the distinct resources of each given faith tradition, including its scriptures and theological traditions, while engaging constructively with the scriptures and theologies of other religious traditions and with the global (geopolitical and ecological) context of discourse that alone makes this conversation possible. This relatively new form of comparative theology represents a project that remains internal to a given religious tradition while transcending it into a global discourse.

POLYDOXY AS METHODOLOGY AND AS THEOLOGY

You are presumably familiar with the famous story of the four blind men touching different parts of an elephant—one the leg, another the tail, one the trunk, another the tusk—and drawing four completely different conclusions about the kind of object they are encountering. That metaphor (which I assume has Hindu roots, though no one seems to know for certain) is most often used to support the ineffability of all matters of ultimacy and, hence, to downplay the need for theological reflection. Reminding us of our own (metaphorical) blindness and finitude, the speaker concludes, "When you talk of God or Brahman, you are like the blind man. The little inkling we have of ultimate reality, the little bit of it that we experience, misleads us as to the nature of the whole. But the whole itself remains always shrouded in mystery."

Perhaps. And yet . . . must we construe the need for silence and mystery to be in contradiction with the need for reflection, speech, analysis, and evaluation? Of course, as inquirers we *may* remain shrouded in our own blindness, unable to draw any valid inferences about reality from the bits of it we can grasp. But how could one know that this is our fate? The new comparative theologian engages in broader reflection not only to understand her own tradition, and not only for the sake of practice, but also in hopes of knowing something about what reality is and isn't. Let's look, then, at the regulative assumptions behind this type of inquiry and the reasons for engaging in it.

Before turning to theological or ontological reasons, we need to think for a moment about the epistemic situation of our day.[6] Once one has moved beyond foundationalist assumptions,[7] there is simply no way from *within* a tradition to determine its absolute truth. Internal certainty may determine one's beliefs subjectively or psychologically. Cultural upbringing may limit the number of "live options" to a few (or only one), leaving one with the sense that she "can do no other." But no valid argument conveys one from psychological certainty to absolute truth. In analytic philosophy Roderick Chisholm attempted to make that argument based on indubitable foundations; Alvin Plantinga and William Alston made it from "basic beliefs"; Moritz Schlick and Otto Neurath sought to ground objective knowledge on "protocol sentences." Theologians, for their part, have looked for foundations in religious experience, the internal consistency of the Bible, the alleged epistemic presumption in favor of testimony, and even in the fact that the Bible self-attests to its own veracity (e.g., 1 Tim 3:16). But no viable epistemological model exists that would carry one from any of these starting points to the truth of one's own beliefs, and certainly not in the sense of demonstrating the falsity of all other views.

In fact, discussions of rationality and justification have shifted in exactly the opposite direction. John Rawls argued for the necessity of a "reflective equilibrium," whereby the best that one can hope for is a balance among the opposing stances.[8] Jürgen Habermas has underscored the need for free and open communities of discourse, to which all persons have access irrespective of status, wealth, culture, gender, and so on, arguing that the *manner* of our discourse, and not merely the structure of individual arguments, is basic to any claims for its rationality.[9] And coherence theories, which may have been the dominant school in Anglo-American epistemology since the late 1980s, place primary stress on the "fit" between broad realms of human experience and reflection more than on the independent veracity of specific arguments.[10] Each of these approaches helps mold and defend the methodology of comparative theologies that are defended here.

In particular, the need now is to connect the quest for knowledge with the nature of interpersonal relations. This is an insight that the male-dominated analytic philosophy of the 1980s would not have reached without the sustained work of several generations of feminist philosophers, who pushed back against a number of the core assumptions of their colleagues. The newer discussion has yielded insights into the locatedness of all knowledge claims, corresponding to the situatedness of all knowers; the embodiedness of knowledge and knowers; the role of interests (epistemic and otherwise) in determining the outcome of the quest for knowledge; hybrid identities; the complex interrelations between thought and emotion; and, in general, the massive complexity of any attempt to acquire, formulate, and ground knowledge claims.[11] These are all insights traceable, primarily, to thinkers in or influenced by the feminist traditions. And what's the net result? We've reached not only the negative conclusion that knowledge is not acquired objectively by disembodied human agents, but also a *positive* awareness of the complex fabric of relationships that determines what counts as knowledge, who counts as holding it, and what count as good or weak arguments in its defense.

Discussions in Anglo-American philosophy of ontological standpoints that might justify (or even make sense of) this transformation in epistemology have been much rarer and tend to be less robust.[12] A few metaphysical schools, such as the Boston Personalists, have sought to understand persons as the basic units of reality in terms of which all else is evaluated, rather than viewing persons as derivative from, say, Hobbesian "matter in motion." Most philosophers, however, have followed the lead of thinkers such as Richard Rorty and John Searle, taking the worlds of meaning, social connection, and cultural relatedness as sheer human constructs, derived from nothing else beyond them.[13] Virtue ethicists such as Philippa Foot and Martha Nussbaum, working in the tradition of Aristotle's *Nicomachean Ethics*, have taken virtues, character, or values as de facto basics.[14] But they usually consciously eschew the project of presenting any sort of metaphysical justification for doing so. This links them with the second group discussed in the previous section.

As a result, theologians and religious thinkers have most often been the ones who attempt to provide some sort of ontological grounding for the newer, postfoundationalist theories of knowledge (and even here it's becoming increasingly rare to find deeper reflections of this sort). Yet in most of the religious traditions of the world it's very natural to tell stories and give accounts of this kind. For Buddhists to appeal to the Buddha's doctrine of Dependent Arising (*pratityasamutpāda*), or for Hindus to ground this connectedness in the final existence of all things in Brahman, is second nature—just as it is basic for Muslims to recognize the connection of all things through their source in the creative action of Allah, whose image and divine order are still present in all things.

For Jewish thinkers a bit more effort was required. The implicit panentheism of Moses Mendelsohn in the eighteenth century, which influenced nineteenth-century European Jewish thought, offered a philosophical framework for conceiving the dependence of all things on God. The panentheism of the Kabbalistic and Hasidic traditions similarly influenced the broader philosophical and cross-religious dialogue through scholars such as Franz Rosenzweig, Gershom Scholem, and (more controversially) Martin Buber.[15] For example, Franz Rosenzweig's argument in *The Star of Redemption* explains (justifies) healing the world through the web of connections between God, humanity, and the world, interpreted theologically as creation, revelation, and redemption.[16]

In the next section I concentrate on the Christian tradition. At first blush, it might look like Christianity would never be able to join that illustrious group of religions that can embrace plurality without compromising its own uniqueness. For example, whereas Buddhists emphasize the "interbeing" of all things (Thich Nhat Hanh) and Hindus celebrate the existence of all Atmān within the one ultimate reality of Brahman, Christians seem to be committed to a God whose transcendence implies that "he" must be sharply distinct from the natural order. Classical medieval predicates such as the aseity, immutability, and omnipotence of God suggest a deity who cannot change, cannot be swayed by others, and cannot share the responsibility for the final outcome with anyone else but himself. When you add to these conclusions the claim that God has been revealed once and for all in Jesus Christ, so that the resurrection becomes not only the center and high point but the culmination or even the end of all history, it begins to look as if there is rather less space for learning from other traditions here than elsewhere.

But here is where the earlier comments about new theories of knowledge become relevant. On the approach that I have been exploring, it's the task of each individual and group to explore the resources of their tradition—not in order to negate the contributions of the other traditions, but to ascertain their own particular contribution to what I've described as a common task and responsibility. A religious tradition is not an empire seeking to vanquish all others and leave them in ashes, nor is it a castle to defend against all comers; it is a field that must be tilled and cultivated by the local residents, so that its fruits can be made available to those who live elsewhere. What, then, might be the specific contributions of the Christian tradition?

RETHINKING TRINITY: DEEP DIALECTICS

The Christian publishing market is hungry for simple solutions and intolerant of complex theologies.[17] Still, occasionally it's valuable to see how deep the concepts and arguments actually go—even when relatively few are prepared to descend to the depths and even the most adventurous among us cannot remain there for long.

Since every approach needs a name, let's call this one Deep Dialectics. It begins with the traditional or orthodox assumption that the one God is plural and, for reasons we will explore, Three. Hence my title, "The God Who Is Not One." A commentator once quipped that philosophers and theologians apparently can't count beyond three, since across the world's traditions one finds logics of one (monisms), two (dualisms), and three (dialectics). Beyond that we find only "the many" (pluralism), as in metaphysical atomism. (Whether this truncated mathematics corresponds with reality or only reveals the numeric ineptitude of philosophers I leave to the reader to decide.) Since trinitarian theologies fall in the highest numerical category that philosophers countenance, they may be as complex as our field gets.

Trinity sounds fairly orthodox. But I'm afraid the orthodoxy of my approach ends there, for dialectical theologies have never been accused of being overly traditional. What happens when we look back at some of the early Christian heresies with these more sophisticated dialectical tools in hand? One quickly finds that old boundaries and exclusions are realigned, and new possibilities emerge.

A historicized ultimate reality, existing in intertwined dialectical relationships with finite agents, cannot rest in timeless immutability. To really be a part of the historical process, it must already have forsaken the "omnis" (omnipotence, omniscience) in favor of relational interconnectedness. As Marjorie Suchocki puts it, if "God spans all time . . . would it not be . . . that God likewise feels the effects of all finite entities? Would not God be the Supremely Related One?"[18]

Certainly one cannot accuse dialectical thinkers of a premature appeal to mystery. The more rationalistic (the more Hegelian) among them can be faulted for a premature closure of exploration, questioning, and open-endedness. But the tone changes as soon as one drops the necessity claims. If the only actor were the Absolute Concept (*absoluter Begriff*), then tensions between thesis and antithesis might indeed compel a logical motion to each new synthesis. But if the actors are you and me and other living agents, then there is simply no abstracting away from our own radical contingency. A moment's introspection suffices to show that, even in our most "logical" moments, our actions and decisions are the products of a far more complex (and beautiful) panoply of influences and coincidences than "pure reason" could ever contain. There are moments of fusion, of finding syntheses that overcome tensions, and *some* of these moments involve complex reflection. But even if you were to limit "dialectic" to the syntheses that you can reconstruct in your theories, and even if you could explain how you "transcend yet preserve" (*aufheben*) the tensions, even then you will not hear the purr of some underlying motor of necessity. Syntheses in which personal agents are involved simply do not work this way.

The same holds for the mysterious processes in which (theists believe) God is involved with an ever-evolving creation. New understandings are produced when the tensions between the divine envisagement and our own wishes and desires are overcome. But as long as God remains not *less* than personal, these syntheses must be noncoercive and the relationships consensual. Interpersonal understanding and insight constitute the best model we have.

If God evolves in, with, and through the process of cosmic history and the evolution of consciousness, then we find ourselves in relationship with a panentheistic divine, not a God outside of (and over) universal becoming. This evolving Relationship is universes apart from the deus absconditus, the absent God. It has no place for the distanced and perfected completeness that we derive from Greek aesthetics. It does not shy away from God's being affected by the world and thus embraces *patri-* (or *matri-*) *passionism* without reservation. (Other heresies also lie in the background of this analysis—Gnostic, Neoplatonic, and adoptionist—even though the full measure of their influence may not be visible in these pages.)[19]

BEYOND ALL DICHOTOMIES

The Dialectical Imperative is easy to state: *Challenge all dichotomies!* Or, in an alternative formulation: *Whenever you encounter a Two, become suspicious*. Twos often admit of resolutions, and they can only resolved within the framework of Threes.

Because Hegel takes such a long time to clear his throat, readers often miss the fact that one of the most fundamental conversions of a Two into a Three in his opus is the relationship between the finite and the infinite. His argument is not only beautiful on its own, it is also a *Leitfaden*, a guiding thread through the rest of his (often perplexing) writings. Actually, the core idea is simple: Only a false or "bad" infinite would exclude the finite. Any infinite that places the finite outside itself excludes the finite—in this case, our entire universe or multiverse with its trillions and trillions of stars—from itself. But if all these suns and their planets lie outside of God, they "limit" God, they remain the unincorporated Other (and, in the case of a universe, that's a rather massive limitation!). Limiting God, in turn, transforms God into a bad infinite—not something that any God would wish upon himself or herself. There is only one solution: God must contain whatever exists within God's self.

This theological model, the postdichotomous God, provides the model for undercutting a number of further dichotomies. The first one we encounter in interreligious dialogue is the old dichotomy between Same and Different. Viewed from the standpoint of the dialectical logic of inclusion, Same and Different do not confront each other as contradictories, as battling opposites. If even the infinite can and must include the finite within it, then pure sameness (identity) becomes impure. Each thing, or subject, includes its other within itself, and only through the inclusion of this other is it able to be that thing that we name it to be. Thus, Deep Dialectics leads inevitably to the affirmation of internal relations that we associate with

F. H. Bradley and reaches its culmination (so far) in the work of Alfred North Whitehead.

Deep Dialectics is rife with political implications, as should already be clear. As long as all identities are impure—as long as they exist only by always already including their "others" within themselves—then inclusivism is a deeper word than exclusivism, which is now unveiled as a metaphysical mistake. The politics of exclusion and "othering," so common in the United States (but not only here), rests not only on selfish self-affirmation but also on a philosophical error.

Next, Deep Dialectics suggests that the traditional dichotomy, "Does God exist *in* time or *outside of* time?" must be mistaken. Answering this dilemma is rather more complicated, and the options are legion. I side with Whitehead's dipolar solution, where God includes both an antecedent nature, consisting of eternal qualities that remain a part of the divine experience in every instant of becoming, and a consequent nature, which is the emergent product of the relations in which God is involved. To be honest, though, Deep Dialectics also spawns some dissatisfaction with the dyadic tendencies in the Whiteheadian response. What mediates between the two poles, which appear to stand in opposition, conceptually unmediated? The dialectical answer is simple, though perhaps not clearly enough formulated in the process tradition: God *is* not the two natures. Rather, God is that reality that emerges out of the dialectical tensions between them—an enduring or eternal nature, on the one hand, and a series of relations with and responses to other actual entities, on the other. God is neither the primordial nor the consequent nature, but the unpredictable and perhaps inconceivable union of the two.

The Christian tradition has similarly shunted back and forth between the dichotomous poles of necessity and contingency. Reaching perhaps its purest form in the Scholastic theologians, the dominant answer has been that God is the purely necessary One, whereas our existence is pervasively contingent. Whiteheadians know in their gut that this dichotomy must be wrong, but we have been rather less successful in demonstrating why it is wrong. In my view, the corrections point in two directions. Deep Dialectics suggests that there are constrained features in our own existence. *Contra* Sartre, in some respects we cannot help but be the persons that we are. Similarly, there are contingent aspects in the divine existence. God is an eternal concrescence whose experience is *not* only divine. God is a Becoming/Being whose experience incorporates—takes into itself—finitude and error and incomprehension and suffering and, yes, even sin. (Think of what it means that the divine being can contain within itself even separateness from God.) As Kierkegaard realized in *Philosophical Fragments*, once we are forced to reckon with the infinite becoming finite, it's hard to avoid some rather dramatic inferences. Finite agents and the One who enfolds the many both share both qualities: the metaphysical features without which we cannot conceive them and the evolving, responding experience that remains pervasively contingent because it is the product of inputs that, qua relational, do not lie fully within our own control.

The radical implications of this approach should by now be clear. In classical trinitarian thought, "God became man" through the incarnation of the preexistent Logos. For that tradition, Jesus was admittedly a man, though always uniquely two-natured. But primarily (i.e., theologically)—the careful balancing act of the classical creeds notwithstanding—he was a manifestation of an eternal and unchanging aspect of the everlasting God, known as the Second Person. From the perspective of Deep Dialectics, the Jesus Event comes to word in a somewhat different way: always triadic, never (merely) dyadic. Here the triad is Jesus—Christ—Event. The "God-Man" is the eternal contingency of the divine writ large. It is the radical claim that God is not afraid to link Godself to the open-ended, fundamentally unpredictable process of human personhood, the process of emerging persons. Moltmann writes boldly of "the crucified God": God also was affected, impacted, by the event of the cross.[20] In some mysterious sense, God too knew death. If one reads this "death of God" back into the "becoming flesh" of God, then the act becomes less pristine and rather more like a birth: bloody, painful, unpredictable, dangerous, and above all irretrievable. No matter what happens once the child is alive, this little squirmy, unpredictable thing is yours to love, to struggle and stay in relation with for as long as the both of you shall live.

OF TRIADS AND TRINITIES

There was a time when the primary task of the Christian theologian was to affirm that Trinity belonged to Christians alone. We conveyed this claim using the language of the unique self-revelation of God in Jesus Christ. Christians alone possess it, it was said, as the true comprehension of God's nature. All other views are inferior. Even the names of the Three pegged them tightly to our grid alone: not just God, but the One whom Jesus called Father; not just the child of God or the Logos or Creative principle, but this individual man Jesus, our guy, who had always already been God; and not just Spirit, but *the* Holy Spirit, the Spirit of Christ—*our* Spirit. This insistence on uniqueness and superiority rested in turn on a number of other, equally exclusive foundations: scripture as foundational, creeds as indispensable, apostolic succession from St. Peter, Thomas Aquinas as "the" theologian of the church, and so forth. In the modern period the threat of modern philosophy, and in particular Feuerbach, led to new forms of exclusion. We know them, for example, in the "Five Fundamentals" of the 1880s, or the "metaphysical presuppositionalism" of Cornelius Van Til, or perhaps even in Barth's "Nein" to natural theology and the *analogia entis*. Nothing in the Christian doctrine of God, the exclusivists held, could be derived "from below," from humanity, for in that case the whole doctrine of God would turn out to be a projection of merely human qualities onto the divine. Thus the Threeness of God had to come "vertically from above" (*senkrecht von oben*) in order to be valid.

But Feuerbach's fear simply cannot be eradicated. Even Barth, his great opponent, was in the end tarnished by the same brush. Once one admits that the dangers and limitations of human projections can never be avoided, a new and precious freedom emerges. We, the new theologians, now find ourselves free to borrow, to adapt, and to openly acknowledge our adaptations. If *all* that one ever accomplishes intellectually is a kind of bricolage, it's easier just to admit it up front and then to make your bricolage as beautiful and powerful as you can.

So likewise with triads and trinities. What if, instead of making The Holy Trinity something we own, a unique possession of our tradition, we interpret the *vestigium trinitatis* in the most radical form possible?[21] For those of us who are panentheists, who understand the world as somehow always already located within the divine, it's natural to see trinities wherever one looks, and not merely on one's own property.

Consider, then, the more radical thesis that *the Trinity just is this triadic structure*. Trinity may have existed first in God, but by grace it has extended its play throughout the natural universe, human creativity, and culture. Perhaps it's true that the ultimacy of the divine Trinity will be fully seen, felt, and experienced only eschatologically, according to the Christian hope that it will "draw all things unto itself." But once we have disowned it, we no longer have to worry about protecting its purity behind those old walls that rend heaven and earth asunder. We no longer have to ensconce Trinity within our tradition as its only right and proper home. Kenosis, self-emptying, extends even to the Trinity itself.

Consider the implications of such a kenosis. It is *tremendum et fascinans*, both frightening and freeing. In other works I have explored some of these implications for anthropology, human freedom, divine action, and the relationship between religion and science. Today I wish to emphasize its transformative role in binding Christianity heart to heart with other religions rather than ennobling the Church as their foe and vanquisher.

After all, triadic or dialectical structures pop up across the world's religions. The play of threes becomes less rigid and more fruitful once we stop asking the question whether a given three is "theirs" (and therefore needs to be overcome eventually by "ours"), or whether it is really "ours" (in which case we implicitly domesticate the others as "anonymous Christians," as Karl Rahner did). Once the "ours" and "theirs" have been dropped, theology flows more smoothly between the differences and the samenesses, not stopping to count its possessions along the way. Many authors in this book, and many more in other publications, are already engaging in this new form of comparative theology. It is an outcome devoutly to be wished.

There is one last, and even more radical, entailment to be explored, and with it I close. For Deep Dialectics, the very structure of the human person is triadic. One begins with a sort of potential self. That self externalizes. She finds her "others" in the world and the communities around her. Gradually, as she is able to incorporate something of those others within herself, her awareness (and her self) grows. She becomes, in classical parlance, a self-conscious subject. Now, Hegel's particular treatment of the Other has been soundly (and rightly) criticized, especially by Levinas. But once one relaxes the tight grip of "the System," it is not difficult to reformulate a post-Levinasian version that avoids that totalizing drive.

Once this final step has been taken, we are ready to draw the theological inferences. God no longer needs to protect "his" purity by holding the Other of the world carefully separate from "himself," entering her only on occasion to fulfill his specific purposes. The divine One is now understood as including all others within, rather than excluding them from, herself. (One thinks of Jesus' words, "No longer do I call you servants . . . ; but I have called you friends," John 15:15, RSV). Instead of servants, we become to God *das Andere seiner selbst*, the other of herself. God's self-knowledge is simultaneously changed by this new relationship. For Whiteheadians, this is a basic word: The divine experience, God's consequent nature, just is the incorporation of the experiences of other actual entities into the ongoing concrescence which is God.

If God's very experience depends on us as the others whom she gathers together into herself, knowing differently and existing differently as a result, then how can we do less in our relations with other religions? Why not, instead, view the once-competing religious traditions as the equally interlocked and interdependent others of *ourselves*? Our self-knowledge always remains incomplete until we learn from and incorporate these others in our own self-understanding. They are now the broader community on whom we are dependent in order to know who we are. This is not a move to domesticate or to erase difference. It is, ultimately, a kenotic move, one in which we recognize our need of them, both in their differences from us and in their similarities to us. Whatever healing and irenic voice Christian thinkers today may have to offer, we owe it in large part to their contributions. Whatever words we utter—even those words that are "about" our own tradition—we utter thanks to them and their voices. It behooves us, then, to listen well and deeply. This organic interdependence, this becoming-through-others, leaves scant place for triumphalism and exclusivism. I could no more proclaim my truth by dismissing them than I could take sole credit for the family that nurtured me and made me who I am.

DEDICATED TO A WHALE AND A DISAPPEARING TIGER

The "Red List of Threatened Species" is the most authoritative inventory of species at risk of extinction. Better known as the "Red Book," it is based on data collected by the International Union for Conservation of Nature (IUCN). On my last visit to their website, I started to develop a conscious relationship with a western gray whale named Flex.

> Meet Flex. Flex belongs to the highly threatened population of western gray whales. He has been tagged by satellite and tracked by scientists in the hope to discover the migration routes of the species and ways to better protect it from threats such as accidental entanglement

in fishing gear, underwater noise and exposure to spilled oil. The western gray whale is listed as Critically Endangered on the IUCN Red List of Threatened Species™. In 2010, its estimated population size was about 136 whales, including only around 30 mature females.[22]

Whether one views the Red Book in printed form or online, what makes it so powerful is that one is able to make eye contact with individual animals who are teetering on the edge of extinction—and with many whom we will never see eye to eye, because we humans have already killed the last member of their species.

I dedicate this essay to a particular tiger whom you can meet eye to eye online.[23] He is one of only 3,200 tigers who still live in the wild on this planet. Along with polar bears and bluefin tuna, tigers are now among the most threatened species in the world. In fact, tigers topped the "10 to Watch in 2010 List" of the World Wildlife Fund. (The others on the list are the polar bear, Pacific walrus, Magellanic penguin, leatherback turtle, bluefin tuna, mountain gorilla, monarch butterfly, Javan rhinoceros, and the giant panda.) The 2010 watch list was also the first time that *a full one-half* of the list named species that are directly threatened by global climate change.

Spend some time, eye to eye, with a disappearing tiger. Remember that the eyes of these others also coconstitute us. They, along with the human others and the divine Other, are part of the community that has formed us and on which we continue to rely. This is as true theologically as it is biologically. The story has not been told, and understood, until one learns to perceive the links between elephants and blind men, disappearing tigers, and the God who is not One.

God's Vitality: Creative Tension and the Abyss of *Différance* within the Divine Life

ERIC TROZZO

At times, there seems to be a choice set before Christian theology regarding how to understand those outside of Christianity: Either they are somehow in relationship with the God proclaimed by Christians, or they are not. This division is, of course, complicated by different understandings of who is inside of Christianity and who is outside, as well as the exact nature of the God proclaimed by Christians. Nevertheless, there can still be a sense of a choice between ultimate separation or ultimate congruity between religious traditions. A promising attempt to break up this either/or scenario is a move toward recognizing the multiplicity of the divine. That is, by claiming that there are many different facets of the divine, it can be held that different religious traditions cling to different facets of God without making the further claim that the religious truth of the differing religions must be the same ultimate truth to which Christians cling. In other words, there is not simply one ultimate truth but many. Therefore, the diversity of religious traditions is not merely a function of human society or worldly realities but, rather, a true reflection of diversity located within the divine itself.

Although this move of setting diversity within God and the divine life would seem to be a helpful position for cultivating mutual tolerance and perhaps even understanding, it also raises some difficult questions. For example, are there limits to God's diversity? Are there claims that do not reflect any ultimate truths? If so, who determines which ones are acceptable and which ones are not? Is everything relative? I suggest that we cannot know for sure that anything is not from God and, therefore, consider everything to be part of this divine multiplicity. Yet this would mean that even evil is part of God. Why should we care about this ambiguous everything called God, then? Is there anything for us to grasp that would give meaning or bring healing to the world? What Good News might Christianity have to proclaim? Is there a way to understand Christ as that aspect of the diverse divine in which we place our trust for renewal of the world? If so, can this be done while honoring both distinctively Christian theological traditions as well as giving space for other religious traditions to express a relationship with aspects of divinity that may differ (and perhaps even contradict) that to which Christians might cling? It is with these questions that this essay wrestles.

• • •

Whence does diversity come? That is, is diversity only a characteristic of the world, or is it inherent in divinity? Surely our answer to this vexing question makes a difference in how we understand the reality of religious diversity. The dominant assumption among Christian understandings of religious pluralism has been that the multiple religious traditions are a facet of the world rather than an aspect of the divine. Yet a growing number of theologians have recently been advocating a more radical strain of pluralism that suggests multiplicity is inherent in divinity.[1]

In this essay I wish to number myself among those who understand multiplicity to be part of divinity. Yet while doing so, I also wish to point out the riskiness of the proposition. As John Hoffmeyer has adroitly pointed out, not all multiplicity counts among what we might consider the "good."[2] Indeed, if we take seriously the possibility that multiplicity may reside within the divine life, then we must also take seriously the potential implication that aspects of the divine may not only differ from one another but may actually conflict. That could mean that there may be aspects of the divine that contradict who we understand God to be. Religious traditions other than my own may be rightly pointing to an aspect of divinity that directly contradicts something that I deeply love, and to which I rightly cling. Affirming multiplicity within the divine life does not equate to an easy agreement for all to live together harmoniously, even if it eliminates claims to any exclusive hold on truth.

It is one thing to consider that there may be positions we disagree with encompassed within the divine, but perhaps the even more challenging issue is whether (either intrinsically or emerging out of conflicting dimensions of the divine aspects bumping up against each other) something evil might be contained within, or arise out of, the divine. To deal with this possibility we need either some criteria for what sorts of multiplicities are in and which are out (that is, we need to figure out how to keep God purely good) or we allow for an ambiguous space within the divine as a site of conflicting tendencies—a space that may also, in fact, turn out to provide creative tension. On the one hand, coming up with a set of criteria to define God's goodness is a quintessential exercise in the projection of human assumptions upon the divine that cannot help but favor the structures of value that we bring with us to the task. On the other hand, one might ask whether an ambiguous space within divinity that may produce evil can still be consonant with a Christian understanding of the divine as trustworthy. It would seem that the concept of multiplicity within the divine leads us to a conundrum or aporia from which there is no way forward.

There is a tradition within Christian philosophical theology of positing difference within the divine that may prove to be helpful, however. It is a tradition perhaps best exemplified by Paul Tillich and the sources from which he draws. In this line of thought, residing within the divine are radically different aspects (called "polarities" by Tillich) that are held in tension. From this tension emerges creativity, and it is creativity that gives God vitality. In Tillich's configuration of opposition within the divine life, I suggest we see a construction that allows for true differences within the divine. At the same time, I wish to point to the ways that Tillich's thought also harbors a drive toward extrahistorical harmonization that may impede this impulse toward multiplicity in his theological construction. That is, unlike Tillich, I am willing to risk allowing what he would call the "demonic" into the divine life as worthwhile in order to allow novelty and diversity to have free reign there.

Looking into the intellectual lineage of theological and philosophical thought from which Tillich draws, then, I will suggest retrieving some of the dimensions in it from which he distanced himself in order to loosen the extrahistorical resolution of tensions. Specifically, I have in mind the medieval Scholastic understanding of the *potentia Dei absoluta* and the ways this doctrine was imprinted on Martin Luther's thought, even while he sought to challenge it. This premodern thread of thought can also be traced into modernity through Jacob Boehme to Friedrich Schelling, who in turn was a major influence on Tillich. To carry the discussion further into the postmodern realm, I suggest we add the thought of John Caputo into the mix as a means of constructing a theology of dynamic tension within an abyss that is not singular. Such a theology may affirm multiple dimensions within divinity, perhaps even introducing *différance* into the divine life. At the same time this theology attempts to hold onto the Lutheran tradition that finds Christ as worthy of our trust, even if the divine is ambiguous. Let us first turn, however, to Tillich's understanding of the divine life.

TILLICH'S POLARITIES AND THE DIVINE LIFE

In Tillich's description, God can be said to have different dimensions or even stages. On the one hand, there is a mysterious depth dimension to the divine as an abyss beyond being. At the same time, God is also the structure and ground of being. Tillich wishes to affirm God as both Ground and as Abyss, even though the two are in tension. Indeed, we see here a key element of Tillich's thought worth lingering on for a few moments before returning more specifically to his understanding of divinity: polarized dyads of "principles" or "potencies," such as individualization/participation or form/dynamics, for example, of which both poles are affirmed so that the dialectical tension between them brings forth reality.

Tillich's exploration of the polarity of form and dynamics in the first volume of his *Systematic Theology* exemplifies this dimension of his thought. Commenting on Tillich, Lewis S. Ford argues that "this particular polarity constitutes the nerve of [Tillich's] ontology."[3] Form is what makes something what it is. It is the tangible structure of an actual being. For Tillich, dynamics, in contrast, "is the *me on*, the potentiality of being, which is nonbeing in contrast to things that have a form, and the power of being in contrast to pure nonbeing."[4] It is the power of nonbeing to become being. He equates dynamics with "the chaos, the *tohu-va-bohu*, the night, the emptiness, which precedes creation."[5] Dynamics brings liveliness while form provides concreteness.

Although Tillich demonstrates how dynamics gives vitality to creaturely, and particularly human life, he finds it more difficult to apply the concept to divine life. As Ford notes, the polar relationship of dynamics with form has no analogy in the divine because of its formless incorporeality.[6] In order to find a space for the dynamic within the divine, then, Tillich turns to a trinitarian structure. "The divine life is the dynamic unity of depth and form," he asserts. "In mystical language the depth of the divine life, its inexhaustible and ineffable character, is called 'Abyss.' In philosophical language the form, the meaning and structure element of the divine life, is called 'Logos.'"[7] Rather than a Father, Son, and Holy Spirit trinitarianism, then, Tillich offers up God as the tension between the creative and unruly Abyss and the form-building principle of the Logos. God must be both and not reduced to either, he argues. Without the abysmal dimension, God ceases to be understood as active and living and instead becomes a static concept. The abyss unleashes possibility. Form or Logos, meanwhile, is necessary to bring potentiality to actuality and thus become the power of Being. We can see, then, that Tillich transposes the oppositional forces of form and dynamics into the divine life. If the abyss is understood to be the potentiality of being, it would then serve as the source of dynamics within the divine. It is a space of divine openness. The second person, meanwhile, fills the other half of the couplet as the divine form.

There is, however, a major provision to Tillich's transposition of these forces into the divine. Within the divine, he argues, the polarities remain in harmony rather than falling into contradiction. Here we find the role of the Spirit in Tillich's trinitarian structure.[8] The Spirit acts as the unity within the dyads. It brings the contrasts into harmony so that they are not literally opposing forces but, rather, a vibrant harmony. Tillich explains, "In religious language the dynamic unity of both elements is called 'Spirit.'"[9] The tension that holds the Ground and the Abyss together, then, is the Spirit. It works as the unity between the two poles. Its calming function teams with the static force of form in overcoming the abyss's negative energy so that the strongly oppositional clashes from which true novelty might emerge are mitigated. He is quite concerned with the negativity that might come from an uncontrolled novelty within the divine. He argues that every "not yet" within the divine life is balanced by an equal "already." "It is not an absolute 'not yet,'" he argues, because that "would make it a divine-demonic power."[10] Tillich, we might venture, had seen enough destructive forces in the trenches during his wartime experience that he had no interest in mixing the demonic into the divine. Thus, he insists that the negative is overcome in the process of being. The oppositions that make the divine lively for Tillich, then, are not truly part of the divine but rather perceived by us because of our finitude. Multiplicity, then, is not really part of divinity for Tillich.

A word is in order here about what Tillich means by the "demonic." For him the demonic is the dynamic drive within every being to overcome the limitations of form. That is, the demonic "is the form-destroying eruption of the creative basis of things," as he puts it.[11] It is a power of creativity that can be productive but also destructive because if form is completely destroyed there is no longer any existence. The demonic, then, is a nihilistic tendency within the creativity of being. Because it is a force of creativity it requires tension to be produced, and so the resolution of tension within the divine prevents the demonic from entering divine space. Thus, the overarching power of harmonizing unity known as the Spirit prevents the abyss from becoming a space of unpredictable potentiality and negativity.

Tillich's sense of transformation, then, is of an overcoming of negativity by the divine. He wants to preserve (in the divine) a space apart from the ambiguity of demonic distortion so that the divine is purely a source of healing rather than unpredictability. Tillich's abyss loses its dynamic edge within the divine beyond the confines of history. Tillich, in fact, resists attributing a distinction between the real and the possible (such as form and dynamic, respectively) within God, arguing, "in God as God there is no distinction between potentiality and actuality."[12] Rather, any talk of polarity within God is symbolic and not conceptual. "Tillich is seeking a middle course between two dangers," Ford maintains: "the threat to divine simplicity which a composition of polar elements would introduce, and the opposite tendency to throttle the life out of God by insisting upon a rigorous and strict unity."[13] Thus, to speak of God as living or dynamic cannot, for Tillich, be literally true. Of course, all speech about the divine is symbolic for Tillich and so not literally true. Yet on this point he urgently emphasizes the gap between language about the polarities of dynamics and form and the divine reality of unity that he wishes to safeguard. At the same time, he recognizes that dynamics are necessary as part of God, to avoid a static deity. Specifically, he is countering the Thomistic understanding of the divine life as pure act, arguing that "pure actuality, that is, actuality free from any element of potentiality, is a fixed result; it is not alive."[14] Thus, he turns to speaking symbolically about the polar oppositions within the divine. Tillich is attempting to walk a thin line here. The contemporary theologian John J. Thatamanil, in working with Tillich's thought, expounds upon the way Tillich wants to affirm the experience of God as living while holding that "God really is the ground of being as well as its depth and abyss. God's character as ground of the structure of being is neither provisional nor contingent."[15] For Tillich, Thatamanil continues, the polarities recognized in being can be applied to the divine life with one major provision: "In the divine life, these polarities remain in harmony and do not fall into contradiction as they do in nature and in human life."[16] Again, then, we see that harmony functions as the highest absolute within Tillich's understanding of God.

This elevation of harmony allows Tillich to retain the idea of opposition while relinquishing tensions within the divine that would threaten divine unity. He professes, for instance, "Within the divine life, every ontological element includes its polar element completely, without tension and without the threat of dissolution, for God is being-itself."[17] Tillich's argument leads Ford to conclude that Tillich "wishes to emphasize the ultimate unity in God of a subordinate multiplicity, the polarity of dynamics and form."[18] In this Tillich is not far from many trinitarian formulations that wish to speak of distinctions within God and are nonetheless held together within a single divine substance. Such unity for Tillich, the theologian Daniel J. Peterson has argued, "achieves its resolution as a unity of opposites purely in eternity," because the unity of dynamics and form cannot be sustained under the conditions of existence.[19] In other words, Tillich can see divine unity only from an eschatological viewpoint, outside of history.

Such an insistence on unity, I contend, seems somewhat artificial. At issue is the role of the divine as abyss for Tillich. Because the abyss is hemmed in by the overarching unity, its primary function is to safeguard the divine's elusiveness that defies containment in human language and concepts. Because, for Tillich, there can be no distinction within God between potentiality and actuality, God as abyss cannot contain the creative power of opposition. Tillich tempers the dynamic wildness of the abyss, I daresay, with his insistence on unity. The attempt to balance the two would seem to stifle dynamic creativity by relinquishing oppositional tensions necessary for creativity, allowing form the upper hand. Tillich's concern in allowing too much creativity, however, is that it would mean unleashing forces into the divine life that would mix the demonic into the divine. If that were to happen, the novelty produced by the dynamically vibrant divine may be good, but would just as likely be horrifically monstrous, and could annihilate being.[20] One may ask whether this insistence does not place God's goodness and God's unity above God's creativity and vibrancy. If so, does not such a focus on unity tamp down liveliness, excluding diversity and multiplicity from the divine by holding the divine life in a safe stability?

If the oppositional forces of abyss and nonabyss are present within the divine, however, a different picture emerges. To be sure, all sorts of unpredictability are unleashed. Who knows what will emerge from the potentialities of this God who is beyond simple definitions of good and evil? Not even God does. The divine is an open and chaotic system rather than a closed and ordered one. There is no guarantee, here, that being will overcome nonbeing in the end. Yet the complex divinity of abyss and nonabyss also can harbor the unexpected, or the longed-for but seemingly unattainable. It is a space of vivacious possible impossibility, indeed a space with the potential for the salvific healing of the world. The infinite unpredictability propels divinity beyond inert stasis. Tillich, in his *Systematic Theology*, resists a lifelessness that is too easily applied to the divine but stops short of fully letting loose energized opposition into divinity.

Indeed, through his appeal to a trinitarian structure in the first volume of his *Systematic Theology*, Tillich is attempting to articulate a sense of unity within diversity. God, he is arguing, must have different facets within the divine self that are not only different, but indeed so different as to be conflicting. Yet these oppositions are necessary for the vitality and creativity of the divine life. It is through the differences bumping up against one another that movement and newness occur. Here, I suggest, we could find the basis for a position within the range of what David Ray Griffin calls "differential pluralism."[21] That is, different religious traditions could be understood to key into different emanations of the multiplicity of the divine. These emanations can be truly different and lead to truly different understandings of divinity. Divinity cannot be reduced to any one emanation. Tillich's appeal to trinitarian language was designed to point to the inability of any one articulation to pin down divinity. For him, the purpose of trinitarian language is not to arrive at threeness. And so, conceivably, there could be an infinite number of different planes within the divine tugging at one another. Tillich uses dyads to draw out the tension within the dynamic pairing. Within this argument, his larger point is to affirm the multiple experiences of the divine that we have while insisting that these many experiences are held together within God. The Trinity is a way to speak of radically varying experiences of divinity. Might we use this sort of Tillichian trinitarian logic to think about a diversity of religious traditions that uniquely experience diverse aspects of the divine?

I think there are some strong possibilities in this line of thought. Yet, to get there, I first have some concerns about the role that Tillich gives to the Spirit in relation to the polarities within the divine. I fear that his "unity" through the Spirit merges into "congruity." Indeed, I wonder whether his resolution of tensions leaves us with only a mirage of diversity. In the end God is a unifying force that does not truly allow aspects of divinity to be ultimately different but only temporally so. Such a position mitigates the radical otherness of distinctive religious traditions. Thus, it brings us to the question of whether—within such a Tillichian framework—we can hold together diverse religious traditions that seek *different* dimensions of divinity in a unity that does not resolve, even extrahistorically, into a tensionless harmony but, rather, retains opposition within the unity of the divine. What would happen if we loosened the polarities within Tillich's thought from any need to be harmonized?

A TRADITION OF DIFFERENCE AND UNITY WITHIN THE DIVINE LIFE

Tillich, in fact, draws deeply from a tradition that holds that there are indeed such unharmonized opposing forces within the divine. Most obviously he is drawing upon his longtime engagement with the nineteenth-century German Idealist F. W. J. Schelling. Yet the Western debate about a difference within the divine can be traced back through Tillich's and Schelling's own Lutheran intellectual background to the sixteenth-century mystic Jacob Boehme and even to Martin Luther. Indeed, tracing back even further, we find the sense of a distinction within divinity to be part of medieval Scholastic discussions.

The discussion of polarities within the divine may remind us of the Scholastic distinction between the *potentia Dei ordinate*, or the concrete goodness of God's actual life, and the *potentia Dei absoluta*, or the unconstrained potential of divine possibility. These terms came into theological discourse in the early part of the twelfth century to describe God's capacity to do things (*potentia absoluta*), which God does not actually do because they are not within the divine nature (*potentia ordinate*). These are two modes of divine power in which the *potentia ordinate* marks a self-limitation by God on divine activity.[22] It was the English Franciscan William of Ockham who, in the early fourteenth century, devised a particularly influential solution to understand this distinction within the divine. Ockham argued that "regarding the distinction relative to the power of God, I affirm that God can do some things in basis of ordained power and other things in basis of absolute power." Thus, he affirms the distinction between the *potentia Dei ordinate* and the *potentia Dei absoluta*. In other words, there is a difference within God. Ockham continues, "This distinction is not understood as if there were two really distinctive powers in God, of which one is ordained and the other is absolute, because in God there is one and only one power which regards the external action (ad extra) of God, and that power from every point of view coincides with God Himself."[23] Thus we see the *absoluta* refers only to divine power, while the *ordinata* takes account of the divine will and actions. That is, God has the power to do many things that God does not will to do. In other words, in this Scholastic formulation, as for Tillich, there are seemingly different dimensions to divinity but they are ultimately unified. Nonetheless, the doctrine holds that God continues to have the power to disrupt the structured orders of the *potentia Dei ordinata*.[24] There is something like a creative tension within the divine that keeps it lively and elusive, with the potential to produce novelty that breaks through the expected structures of existence. At least in theory, then, this doctrine affirms the potential for conflicting elements within God, even as it also affirms that such opposition does not actually exist.

Luther, for his part, was haunted by the understanding that God's power exceeds God's desire for structure that he received from his training in the *via moderna* that grew out of Ockham's teaching.[25] In *On the Bondage of the Will*, from Luther's debate with Erasmus of Rotterdam, Luther suggests that there is a facet of divinity that is outside of God's revelation in Christ. Luther remarks, "That in God there are many things hidden, of which we are ignorant, no one doubts."[26] Luther distinguishes this hidden God from the God who is known in Christ, and holds that we must speak differently about this God. He writes:

> We have to argue in one way about God or the will of God as preached, revealed, offered, and worshiped, and in another way about God as

he is not preached, not revealed, not offered, not worshipped. To the extent, therefore, that God hides himself and wills to be unknown to us, it is no business of ours.[27]

We can see the imprint the distinction between the *potentia Dei ordinata* and the *potentia Dei absoluta* made implicitly in this discussion. The distinction between the God preached, worshiped, and revealed in Christ (in whom we trust) and the hidden God who is not preached, worshiped, or revealed echoes the two facets of the divine found in the Scholastic debates. For Luther, the hidden or abysmal God has the power to act destructively, but we trust that such actions are not within the divine will because of our trust in Christ. Yet lurking behind this trust is the potential that God's will may not be the mercy seen in Christ, but may in fact include our damnation and destruction.

Tillich was influenced by Luther's interpretation of this distinction. He explained that for Luther, "God's absolute power is like a threat behind these ordering rules [of the *potentia Dei ordinate*], like an abyss in which they may be swallowed up at any moment. We do not know exactly what the will of God ultimately is."[28] In adapting this discussion for his own *Systematic Theology*, then, Tillich interprets the *potentia Dei absoluta* as "a perennial threat to any given structure of things."[29] Here, he is discussing human constructions that structure being, and not Being itself, however. One might say it is an anarchic haunting that lies behind any human perception of reality. In this the *potentia Dei absoluta* differs from the demonic, which threatens structures with a nihilistic tendency toward nonexistence. The *potentia Dei absoluta* is an uncertainty in the world caused by the mysteriousness of the divine abyss, but it is not a contradiction or opposition within the divine itself. Here it would, again, seem that Tillich posits a tension or uncertainty within the world that is not present in the divine. What if, however, we applied this concept of the *potentia Dei absoluta* to the divine (as Ockham did) but without the further step of affirming that the distinction within the divine does not actually exist. If we affirm that a space of uncertainty lies within the divine, might we have a locus from which aspects of divinity (other than those trusted by Christianity) might emerge?

Adding to these distinctions between God's absolute potential and ordered potential is the dialectical sensibility that Tillich inherits from Boehme and Schelling. Boehme speaks of "principles" whereas Schelling employs the term "potencies," but the thrust of this intellectual lineage is that the creative potential of the divine is brought to life through the clash of opposing forces within the divine life.

The basic structure of the divine as containing the polarities of byss and abyss, or being and potentiality, respectively, and unfolding from the opposition between them underlies all of Boehme's work. Indeed, his conception of the unground, or the nothing that is also everything, cannot be separated from the entire arc of cosmic history.[30] Boehme's description of the emergence of multiplicity out of the unground was central to his thought. Every one of his mature writings devotes several crucial chapters to the topic. As he describes it, "This unsearchable, inconceivable Will without Nature which is only one, having nothing before it, nor after it, which in itself is but one, which is as nothing, and yet all things; this is, and is called the only one God."[31] This infinite God is beyond good or evil, or any other description, for that matter. It is utter stillness. It is not being, nor even intrinsically the foundation of being. It is, rather, absolute freedom and undeveloped potentiality.

Within the stillness of the unground there arises, through what Boehme calls the "mysterium magnum," a hunger to know itself. In this will, to be revealed to itself, differentiation arises in the unground. Through this will, Boehme says, "The Nothing finds itself to be something in itself."[32] Thus from the unground, through a complex set of processes, otherness was created and potentiality begins to burst into vibrant realities. Thus at this level real contradictions emerge, including the struggle between good and evil. As the commentator Edward Allen Beach notes, "One of Bohme's most daring conceptions was that God's emergence out of pure oneness into differentiated actuality required a confrontation with opposition."[33] Contrasts are necessary for creativity. Boehme thus distinguishes between what he calls the first and second principles, where the dark first principle is the abyss of negativity whereas the light second principle is more properly called "God" and can be understood as loving. The first principle is held within the second principle in order to maintain the creative tension.[34] The negative darkness of suffering, pain, and even evil are thus in a sense at the root of divine goodness, and vice versa. The negative attributes are necessary for the manifestation of the positive attributes of the divine. The darkness and the light, in other words, are inseparable, and indeed it seems that darkness is an essential piece of God's self-revelation. The oppositional abyss is a necessary component of divine life for Boehme, and indeed for the unfolding entirety of the cosmos. It is this dialectical sense of movement and vigor within the divine that made Boehme's thought attractive to various later groups, in particular the early nineteenth-century German Idealists. Indeed, both Hegel and Schelling were influenced by Boehme, and it is especially via Tillich's reading of Schelling that Boehme's thoughts were brought into contemporary Christian theological discussion.

In Tillich's reading of Schelling's later work, God is understood as the synthesis of such contrasts as inward-facing egoism (which is linked to wrath), and outward-facing love. That is, we see a continuation of the theme of opposition within the divine that we have already encountered through Boehme. God becomes a personal God through the overcoming of egoism by love. Because this process of overcoming happens within the divine life, Tillich notes that Schelling understands God "not merely [as an] eternal being, but rather eternal becoming."[35] That is, for God to be a living God there must be some type of movement or emergence occurring. Otherwise, a personal relationship with an abstraction of "a God who is so metaphysically remote" is at best pointless.[36] In Tillich's early writings, he seemingly approves of Schelling's God as becoming. Tillich then goes on to speak of two contrasting principles within the divine: the conscious and the unconscious. The process of the divine and indeed all life is "that unconscious existence may be raised to consciousness."[37] Tillich quotes Schelling's contention that there is a moment when God "separates himself from himself, opposes himself to himself,"[38] and that this is the beginning of consciousness within the divine. This opposition within the divine is done in order that darkness may be moved into light. For without opposition there is no life, just as we have seen in Boehme. The conscious God becomes the living God while the unconscious, irrational component of the divine is the unground. Indeed, the marks of Boehme's thought here are unmistakable. This irrational moment is the divine *"prius."* That is, it is what precedes the divine's being as God. It is the universal abyss that does not individualize itself and become comprehensible.[39] It is a component of the divine, but it is not God, who is living, conscious, and individuated.

Tillich's later emphasis on harmony within the divine life is explicitly a tempering of the Boehme/Schelling tradition of polarities within the divine. His criticism of both of them in his *Systematic Theology* is not that they introduce plurality into the divine, but rather, as Ford observes, their "overemphasis on the dynamics in God and for [the overemphasis's] consequent depreciation of the stabilization of dynamics in pure actuality. The power of being resident in divine dynamics must be affirmed over against pure identity [for Tillich], but not in any way which might threaten the perfect balance of dynamics and form."[40] As in relation to creativity and the divine as abyss, Tillich's concern is that following Boehme and Schelling in permitting oppositional forces into the divine life would mix the demonic into the divine, thereby opening the possibility of the monstrous.

Tillich, then, wishes to exclude the possibility of evil coming from God, but does he do so at the expense of also eliminating that which was not congruent with his understanding of Christianity coming from the divine as well? Might there, however, be room for some multiplicity within the divine to slip back into Tillich's concept of divinity—perhaps through his argument that "in God as God there is no distinction between potentiality and actuality"?[41] In the "in God *as God*" some space opens up for abysmal seepage. In the Boehmian/Schellingian tradition, the unground or first potency precedes God *as God*. God does not become truly God until the primordial nothingness is overcome and God emerges as a personal God. There is, then, a deep difference within the divine that allows the abyss to be untamed by unity. The abyss (at least symbolically) lies prior to God. Although a hint of this idea comes through for Tillich, by and large, he is unwilling to risk the instability that it introduces into the concept of divinity.

DIFFÉRANCE IN THE DIVINE LIFE?

How might postmodern discussions of *différance* aid in understanding the diversity, or even opposition, within the divine? Might we find a supplement to Tillich that helps loosen the eschatological drive toward harmony in his later thought? I suggest that a turn to the work of contemporary deconstructive thinker John D. Caputo might prove to be a fruitful avenue to pursue. In Caputo's argument for the "weakness of God," we find a challenge to the tendency to teleologically hem in the divine as well as a plea for a faith that can withstand the possibility of a monstrosity emerging from the future opened under the name of God. Indeed, Caputo's thought seeks to be a call to a risky faith.

Affirming a multiplicity within God that may be expressed in truly diverse ways by truly diverse religious traditions—and not the mere mirage of such diversity—is certainly an endeavor fraught with risk. It may be that it is the demonic (or something monstrous) that ends up being expressed through such a divinity. How are we to find anything that will sustain hope in the face of such an ambiguous divine? Can we employ an unharmonized oppositional abyss within the divine and still find God worthy of our trust? Or must the tensions be released within the divine life, so that all religious traditions must have a certain congruity in order to be authentic? To shift to more deconstructive vocabulary: Can we understand differing religious traditions as radically Other to one another, or must they be reduced to an ultimate sameness? Is there a space for irreducible difference, or even *différance* in divinity? If so, is there any hope that we might speak of unity in a meaningful way?

I suggest that, in the dynamic God suggested by the oppositional tradition I have just traced, we may find the resources necessary to construct just such a sense of divinity. Before getting there, however, let us take a quick detour through a few pertinent elements of Caputo's thought, particularly his employment of the Derridean use of the concept of *"khora."* In this discussion he draws on Jacques Derrida's understanding of *khora*, though there is no need to restrict the concept to this particular name. *Khora* is the placeless place of which it is impossible to speak, and yet which must be spoken of. The term *khora* originates in Plato's *Timaeus*, where it is used as a sort of formless space in which the Forms are nonetheless inscribed, though without proper existence.[42] In Derrida's usage, *khora* functions as a gap of unknowable negativity that prevents comprehensive knowledge and from which deconstruction and the impossible might spring. Derrida describes it as that which, "beyond all given philosophemes, has nevertheless left its trace in language."[43] It is a barren place that is wholly other. It is the indeconstructable space of *différance*, an abyss of meaninglessness.

Caputo differentiates between *khora* and the abysmal God. Each may be an abyss, or "tropic of negativity," he holds, but the two function differently. *Khora* is less than being, and harbors unpredictability. *Khora* cannot be good, and does not give—at least not generously.[44] Indeed, the monstrous may issue forth from it. Yet *khora* also functions to keep the future open and unknowable, beyond the reach of any extrahistorical schemes. The God of the abyss, on the other hand, is beyond being and a source of goodness for Caputo. The name "God," he contends in his peculiar jargon, is a "harbor for the event" of justice. It is a "weak call" to a messianic thirst for justice to come, a hope for righteousness in the world, but without a guarantee, or even a likelihood, that such justice will ever come. It is an abyss because it has no concrete being. But it is experienced as a haunting call to a hope that the impossibility of justice may indeed actually come. Both this God and *khora* are experienced as abysses, and so there is an undecidability to each of them. The two should, however, be understood as distinct. We see, then, a structure of a double abyss (or, Caputo might hasten to add, at least two abysses). Yet for Caputo, only one of these abysses can be identified with the divine. *Khora* is not God, he contends.

Despite its differentiation from God, *khora* nonetheless plays an essential religious role for Caputo in inspiring faith. Without *khora* there is no faith, he insists. There is an undecidability between *khora* and God, an impossibility of knowing for sure which is which. It is an aporia, and faith is the act of making an undecidable distinction between that which is God and that which is *khora*. If the distinction were decidable, there would be no decision, no room for faith—it would be an obvious choice in favor of the unambiguously revealed God. He writes, "Without *khora* we would know what we need to know, and we would not be pushed to the point of keeping *faith* alive just when faith seems incredible and impossible."[45] Faith, then, is a step forward beyond the impossible because of the undecidability between God and *khora*. Such faith does not overcome or get rid of *khora*. It must always remain for faith to remain.

If we turn to the Luther-Boehme-Schelling tradition, however, we find there that the different aspects of the abyss cannot be easily separated, in this good-God-and-indifferent-*khora* manner that Caputo proposes. Rather, both aspects are encompassed within the abyss of divinity. Indeed, rather than a double abyss structure, we instead find a complex abyss that has multiple dimensions, including the potentiality of Caputo's *khora*. Might bringing both of Caputo's abysses—the abysmal God as well as *khora*—into the God of unresolved tensions allow us to speak of a terrifyingly complex and chaotic holiness that inspires an uncertain faith, while drawing on Caputo to help us cling to a future that is not predetermined? Where we might find a God of oppositional abysses in which *difference* may flourish?

Can Caputo's conception of God as a weak call, one that keeps the future open, survive my collapsing together of God and *khora*, however? If the indifferent aspect of negativity is incorporated into the divine call, does it still call us to the justice to come, or might we end up resigned to an indifference to come? Caputo's God as a weak force *requires* a differentiation between God and *khora* so that we may decide for God and pray for justice to come. The Lutheran tradition of the unified abyss allows for no such decision. If we close the door to Caputo's sense of the weak manifestation of the open-ended messianic God, do we lose his fervent insistence on expectant participation in the call for justice as well?

We can retain Caputo's understanding of a weak God, I suggest, by taking a page from Luther's playbook and using a circuitous route. For Luther, facing God directly was unbearable and could not inspire trust. Yet through an experience of the cross and being met by Christ within it, Christ could be experienced as good and trusted completely. Through this experience God's fullness could be trusted, even if the ambiguity of the naked God could still not be borne. In a similar manner, we can understand "Christ," rather than "God" or "ethics," to be the name that harbors the promise of justice to come. Messianic longing can be understood as a longing for Christ. I am not here equating Christ with Jesus exclusively, but rather with the promise of that for which we long, with the "to come." The name "Christ," then, harbors an event of the impossible. The name God, meanwhile, serves as a harbor for both the event of Christ and the space of *khora*, thereby fusing what Caputo calls God and *khora* within a divine abyss that is more than one. We would thus have unpredictably unfolding multiplicity within the divine and yet also through Christ have an aspect of divinity that Christians might claim as trustworthy.

A MULTIPLICITY OF DIVINE POTENTIALITIES

Might we find, then, a structure that hearkens to Tillich's trinitarian description? That is, could we understand *khora* as the mysterious abyss of the First Person, and Christ as the promise of justice to come as the Second Person? Both are the abysmal spaceless space from which the "to come" emerges, but "Christ" is the "to come" for which we long and pray and in which we may place trust. This framing of Christ as the to-come is a rather abysmal Christology. It is a Christology of not-yet, as opposed to Tillich's Christology of an "already" that balances the abyss's "not-yet." I am suggesting, within divinity, a dynamic pairing of "not yets" within the abyss that is both one and not one—the irascible elusiveness of *khora* and the hopeful promise of Christ—in a tension that brings forth the "may be" out of the "already."

We have here a sense of divinity that is both abysmally focused and, at the same time, strangely Christocentric. Each of these characteristics presents a challenge for making sense of the religious diversity of the world. For example, how does an abysmal divinity relate to the actuality of the world? When pondering that actuality, meanwhile, must it be understood through the lens of the expectation of Christ? How do either of these issues further interreligious discussion? Let us take each in turn.

Does an abysmal focus merely invert the Thomistic tradition of the divine as *actus purus*? Indeed it might. This divinity of creative tension that I am suggesting does not create actuality, but rather potentiality. In this I wish to hearken to Boehme's scheme. The action of such a divine is to open ever more possibilities that may disturb the structures of the world. In this it is something like Tillich's understanding of the *potentia dei absoluta*. The divine is a promise, calling, or disruption that challenges the way things are and offers that things may be otherwise. Yet, like Caputo's "weak God," it does not possess agency. It cannot turn the potentiality it creates into actuality. It is a vibrant and creative force that *inspires* but does not *do*. Indeed, it is through this *inspiration* that abysmal potentiality connects with material actuality. Inspiration is traditionally the work of the Holy Spirit, and so I would suggest that it is through a conception of the Spirit that the divine potentiality might affect worldly actuality. The Spirit brings potentiality to bear upon the givenness of the world.

Might we understand the Spirit, then, in a way that acts as a concretizing and unifying dimension that does not insist on congruity? Certainly such a conception of the Spirit would entail a turn to the world as it is, in all of its human and more than human variety, rather than Tillich's extrahistorical Spirit. Indeed the Earth works well as a locus of interaction. As it spins through space and shifts seismically, it teems with the vibrations of the multiple bumping into one another. Yet it is not the Earth itself that I wish to point to as Spirit, but rather the suggestion that all lies under the hope and shadow of the "to come." In the ecological webs of the Earth what comes—be it justice or climate change—has a ripple effect on all to some degree. An instance of justice gives hope to all who long for it to come, just as the forces of climate change affects humans and trees and ocean currents. Preliminarily, then, might we understand the Spirit as the principle of interdependence in the face of the "to come"? In the Spirit what happens through, within, and by the religious Others matters to each because each helps to shape the shared actuality of the earth to come through its own particular view of the potentiality for the earth. Mutual discussion and critique might come, then, by bringing the contrasting understandings of that potentiality to bear on one another.

Are we not left, then, with the problem of attempting to fit the multiplicity of the world within the confines of a Christian construction, as Thatamanil has noted of other trinitarian constructions of religious diversity?[46] Even more, by defining "Christ" as the "to come" for which we hope, are we not setting up Christianity as the repository for all that is good within the divine, so that all others are merely drinking from the divine dregs? It may, perhaps, be helpful to draw on a form of the Lutheran understanding of Christ's *pro nobis* dimension here. There is an emphasis within Lutheran theology on Jesus' death being experienced as being "for us" that makes Christ trustworthy. In a similar fashion, I suggest that the healing and renewing potential for the world that is harbored in the name "Christ" is that dimension of the divine that has been experienced by the Christian tradition as being "for us" and thus makes Christ worthy of our trust. This *pro nobis* need not be understood exclusively, nor must "Christ" be. That is, the healing and renewing potentiality within the divine is for the entirety of the world and named by Christians "Christ." The name "Christ" may not be the only name under which such an experience can be harbored, nor is it the only dimension of the divine that may rightly be trusted. Other religious traditions may point to other emanations of divine potentiality that may be trustworthy. Indeed, some individuals may be able to trust multiple expressions of the divine and dedicate themselves to the potentialities for the world unleashed by each.

Yet at the same time I contend that every actuality has some degree of demonic potentiality mixed in with the divine potentiality. Potentiality is ambiguous. Hope in the "to come" is haunted by the possibility that the "to come" will turn out to be monstrous. Indeed even a quick survey of examples of violence and oppression within most religious traditions, let alone through the bumping together of different religious traditions, reveals the myriad ways that horrors come forth in the name of the divine. There may, in fact, be dark aspects of the divine that can never be removed from divine potentiality. We nonetheless hope that the potentiality of the "to come" for bringing healing, justice, righteousness, peace, and care is worth the risk. The wonders and joys of the world are harbored in the divine abysmal tension along with destruction and monstrosity, giving reason to hope despite the ambiguity harbored within the divine.

✦ Polyphilic Pluralism: Becoming Religious Multiplicities

ROLAND FABER AND CATHERINE KELLER

In a small wooden box concealed behind a sliding pane in his sleeping quarters Lord Hauksbank of That Ilk kept a collection of beloved "objects of virtue," beautiful little pieces without which a man who traveled constantly might lose his bearings, for too much travel, as Lord Hauksbank well knew, too much strangeness and novelty, could loosen the moorings of the soul . . . the silk handkerchief of a pagan goddess of ancient Soghdia, given to a forgotten hero as a token of her love; a piece of exquisite scrimshaw work on whalebone depicting the hunting of a stag; a locket containing a portrait of Her Majesty the Queen; a leather-bound hexagonal book from the Holy Land, upon whose tiny pages, in miniature writing embellished with extraordinary illuminations, was the entire text of the Qur'an; a broken-nosed stone head from Macedonia, reputed to be a portrait of Alexander the Great; one of the cryptic "seals" of the Indus Valley civilization, found in Egypt, bearing the image of a bull and a series of hieroglyphs that had never been decoded, an object whose purposes no man knew; a flat, polished Chinese stone bearing a scarlet I Ching hexagram and dark natural markings resembling a mountain range at dusk; a painted porcelain egg; a shrunken head made by the denizens of the Amazon rain forest; and a dictionary of the lost language of the Panamanian isthmus whose speakers were all extinct except for one old woman who could no longer pronounce the words properly on account of the loss of her teeth.
—SALMAN RUSHDIE, *The Enchantress of Florence*

Where religious pluralism becomes more common, one witnesses also—including, but exceeding, the will to interreligious understanding and therefore political peace—an appetite for the differences. We are accustomed—with reason—to worrying about the Western voracity of such appetite, about the risk of colonization and appropriation of the Other. This essay makes a strong distinction between interreligious piracy and the love of multiplicity; a polyphilia that may better resist competition and colonization than mere ethical ecumenism. Drawing, for this experiment, on our shared involvement in a Whiteheadian discourse, we propose a convivial polydoxy of "living together" mindfully and nourishingly. Generating a mutually constitutive multiplicity rather than a separative pluralism, difference is theorized as inherently connective. We hope this experiment, itself provisionally distanced from any separable religious confession or exchange, helps develop "skillful means" applicable in the multiplicity of contexts in which religious, theological, and philosophical thinkers find themselves stressed by alterity.

SACRED COMPLEXITY

In Salman Rushdie's satiric narrative of early modern global encounters, Lord Hauksbank of That Ilk is a free-floating cosmopolitan, a pirate admiral occasionally commissioned by Her Majesty. His "objects of virtue" seem to mirror and mock a postmodern desire for difference, its delight in multiplicity, its escape from simple location. After all, those of us who treasure religious diversity often delight in the gifts of other wisdoms. Though our initial motives may be socioethical, something more comes into play than strategic ecumenism or the hope for interreligious peace among difficult differences. The appetite for difference itself grows. Our pluralism deepens.[1] And it multiplies: Our pluralism is not one! This essay grew originally from an exploration of the plural resonances of several religious traditions with process theology, with its largely (but never exclusively) Christian base. We operate here at an experimental distance from any discrete confession. Something comes to light, we think, that is of value for those of us still practicing such confessions as well as those of us inhabiting more permanently postreligious places—whether or not one confesses to any Whiteheadianism! It displays how a certain approach to pluralism may develop a *taste for religious multiplicity itself*. So we focus, in this essay, not on the relations of process theology to particular religions, but on a Whiteheadian understanding of the *inherent multiplicity of religion—and of the religious character of multiplicity*.

But how, then, might we distinguish between an apparently growing attraction to religious multiplicity and the pirate admiral's collection of multicultural treasures? How might we value—in this exercise as two process thinkers—at once the beauty of spiritual bricolage and the justice of intercultural encounters, the wisdom of eclectic explorations and the integrity of particular traditions? Can we, with Whitehead's support, examine the multiplicity of traditions transforming the single tradition, indeed perforating the boundaries of its singularity? One of us might love, for instance, the neighborhood yoga class spliced with Zen teachings and led alternately by a young Muslim from Istanbul and an aging Jewish feminist. Rhythms of interfaith marriage, ecumenical Koranic study, Pentecostal Sunday mornings supplemented with a Wednesday evening Ashanti women's ritual, churches sharing building and soup-kitchen with synagogues, theistic respect for certain rigorous atheisms, ecological alliances with a Native American inflection—such routine hybrids ripple fluently through the expanse of a cosmopolitan life. It takes a sweeping hypocrisy to dismiss such a spectrum as "new age" or "syncretistic." But, then, what dividing line remains between the complex resonances collected in this book and Lord Hauksbank's cabinet of treasures? If the present endeavor implies a pluralism that many would call postmodern, does that make us pirates?[2] Is our taste for multiplicity perhaps still more symptomatic of the voracious Euro-American consumption of "too much strangeness and novelty"—whatever remains exotic after centuries of appropriation—than of ecumenical respect?

We could, of course, take the route of much responsible interreligious work. We could lodge ourselves within the clear boundaries of a religious identity and a cultural context, from which we reach out carefully to representatives of other religions. We might practice a *separative pluralism* in order to avoid the risk, or at least the charge, of appropriation of the religious other. Yet the very notion of "religion" is being contested by some scholars of religion, as indicative of a pristine sense of simple identity, externally related. It represses not only the obvious syncretism of much current practice, but also the internal complexity of the so-called great religions—not to mention the multiple sources of their orthodoxies. John Cobb, who blazed the trail "beyond dialogue" of such complexities as "Buddhist Christianity," is now calling the traditions *Wisdoms* rather than "religions."[3] The way of process theology, to enliven participation in specific spiritual communities and their deep institutional and textual traditions (as demonstrated in this book), could never confine itself tidily to any bounded identity. It proceeds on the presumption that a mutual participation, and indeed, transformation, issues from the contact between the Wisdoms; and that when process thought is involved, it is intentionally activating their internal complexities. It is the endeavor of this essay to emphasize these connective preconditions. In other words, the constructive proposals for the diversification of process theology within different Wisdoms form a matrix of "sacred interactivity" under, within, beyond, and between the traditional boundaries of religions. The process approach does not, then, settle for the pluralism—so prone to piracy—of many separate ones, but opts for a *relational pluralism*. If these traditions live, in fact, only in process and in interaction, then only such relationalism can actually disclose the concrete, contextual life of Wisdom traditions.

If the identities of these traditions are not fixed but fluent one toward the others, then neither can we presume that there will be any single identity of process theology, ready to impose its new paradigm upon all Wisdom traditions. Instead, we find that in their complex exchanges, process approaches and Wisdom traditions connect and disconnect within multidimensional flows of resonance. They may, we hope, release "sacred complexities," forming amid their meandering infiltrations and mutual contaminations unexpected and unsettling alliances. Energized by its relational pluralism, why would we attempt to formalize process theology into some new, orthodox, pluralism, ready-made for any tradition it engages? Instead, we find that a process sense of the plurality of expressions of the divine or the sacred within, between, across, and beyond religious traditions resists the deceptive unity of an already tamed plurality, of what Whitehead calls "a neat little system of thought, which thereby oversimplifies its expression of the world."[4]

Process pluralism goes all the way down. Instead of a tidy system that will handle the plurality of traditions from *the* process point of view we find that process theology, from the start composed of a variety of theological and philosophical influences, was itself always a multiplicity. Evolving from Whitehead's complication of physical cosmology with divinity, process theology assembled a dramatic diversity of modes of thinking.[5] And, as with Whitehead, this assemblage has always been experimentally interlinked with the labyrinthine multiplicity of the world's Wisdoms.

Although some of its routes were conceptualized within the context of Christianity, process theology never intended to become either the expression of *one* religion, or the articulation of wisdom *as* One.

On the contrary, remaining true to Whitehead's cosmological vision means to attend to the world as a polyphony of experiential and interpretive processes. Its pluralism reflects the vastness of an irreducible multiplicity of becomings. It thus heightens sensibilities toward the adventurous in human—and also in nonhuman—nature. As this pluralism discovers connective differences, it activates an experiential space of uncharted intensities and forms uneasy harmonies of "togetherness."[6]

Amid our varied religions, process pluralism has always valued the movement of the improbably wandering wisdoms. It has understood multiple influences as important instances of "concrescence" ("growing together") in, between, and across these traditions. Following Whitehead's intuition that process thought "seems to approximate more to some strains of Indian, or Chinese, thought, than to western Asiatic, or European, thought" as it makes "process ultimate,"[7] process theologies appeal to an eros of relational differentiation that reveals the divine, or the sacred, in *and* beyond religions, in *and* beyond all inherited identities.

Hence, when a process theology exceeds the orthodoxies of a massively Euro-Christian tradition, its intent is not to *supersede* any of these orthodoxies (and so merely mirror their competitive oppositions) but to highlight—in the light of a connective sacredness—their own fluency. Cobb's game-changing *Christ in a Pluralistic Age*, for instance, deconstructed—with the help of Buddhism—the unifying substance metaphysics of classical Christianity, yet did so as a way of receiving key features of the Nicene and Chalcedonian logos-Christology.[8] Whitehead himself discerned, in the classically unassimilable logic of the Trinity, the breakthrough of a "doctrine of mutual immanence" in a "multiplicity."[9] Such a gesture need not deploy the promising multiplicity of the Trinity in competition with a stereotype of Jewish and Muslim monotheism. Rather, this relational pluralism of process theologies might let the divine reveal itself, for example, as a variant of the "plurisingularity" of the name *Elohim*.[10] Similarly, rather than trapping Asian thought within a mere One or a mere Nothing, we discover among the living options of Buddhism the example of the beautiful play of multiplicity in the *Lotus Sutra*.[11] This many-folded matrix thus may be disclosed as theistic divine *and* a nontheistic sacred. Indeed "S/He/It" has been acquiring a singular multiplicity of names!

By embracing many elements of many orthodoxies—along with many of the others they exclude—such a polyphony certainly eludes any essentialist unity. But it also means to avoid the piracy of an appropriative pluralism. Not content to espouse an oppositional heterodoxy or a defiant heresy, this differential process understanding of a sacred interactivity offers, instead, what we may call a *polydoxy*—an inherently multiple teaching of the multiple.[12] It does not take the place of our various traditions of "right teachings" and "right practices," but rather tracks the differences that connect them. Hence, a process pluralism is a *sapiential* polydoxy from the start: It does not assemble a mere many, nor yet a pirate admiral's exhibition of stolen treasures. On the contrary, as the various chapters of this book demonstrate, it displays the folds of a wisdom that we find enfolded only in multi*pli*city: The *pli*, which makes the difference connective and opens the connections into difference.[13] A polydoxical multiplicity connects the folds one to another in the very act of valuing the otherness of the engaged Wisdoms. It honors that which interlinks, pleats, or braids the flows of their difference together; it encourages living the intensities that its differentiations release.

Pirates do not just disappear, however. Some become emperors. Others attack the empire's integrity. We seem to find ourselves in a historical period of renewed interreligious conflict and theocratic wills to power—largely variants on the sibling rivals of Abraham, vying with each other and with state secularism for dominance. Therefore, we consider the cultivation of this *taste* for "connective differentiation" and "differential connectivity" not only joyful and nourishing but also *necessary* for the planetary weal. Without it, the energy for a decolonizing ecumenism and for a pluralist ethic quickly dissipates. Of course, the postcolonial worry must remain: We may love those exotic others to death and appropriate their treasures. Hence, engaging sacred interactivity may only avoid separation or piracy by recognizing the *risk*, within the neoliberal globalism, of transgressive entanglements. In other words, a polydox multiplicity recognizes its harmonics not only as joyfully complex but also as uneasily com*pli*cit.[14] If a certain "postcolonial ambivalence" (Homi Bhabha) has com*pli*cated the discourse of liberation, it does not pretend it could return to an original purity of the native or the ethnic. Postcolonial theologies do not imagine either a founding or a final purity of a separated, socially just religious community.[15] Difference does not separate. It does not protect authenticity from piracy by restoring oversimplification and mutual exclusion. Once I begin to *feel*—to "prehend"—the other (how am I separate from him/her/it?)—have I not taken some of that difference into self, effecting an "other in self"?

Attention to complicity—the *tricky* ways we are "folded together"—does not suppress our taste for multiplicity. It holds it *responsible*. It releases the flows of resonance that make response possible. Yet, as the multiple engagement of process understandings of different Wisdoms is currently demonstrating, their multiple entanglement does not hinder, but in their "togetherness" encourages complex commitments across and among traditions. *This* taste for the multiple is what process thinking cultivates as the very manifestation of the "Divine Eros."[16] If we, living with these Wisdoms, become mindful of the sacred multiplicity that always already constitutes their own process, we may experience a love that instigates a relational pluralism and then nourishes it. We call this love—*polyphilia*.[17] In what follows we explore a process theory of multiplicities as "skillful means," in the irreducible uncertainty and the loving possibility of its becoming.

BECOMING MULTIPLICITIES

Polyphilia is not omniphilia, polydoxy not omnidoxy. When we consider relational pluralism as a complex landscape of sacred foldings, its activating transformations take the most concrete, contextual, and conflictual forms. In the past half century, an unruly crowd of theories and practices has complicated religious and theological study, and therefore also comparative studies in religion and theology. These studies have enmeshed the problems of the ancient Wisdoms in a plurality of competing issues (race/gender/sex/class/ecology) multiplied by cultures (traditions/nations/ethnicities/diasporas), all intensified by historic urgency. One might almost sympathize with various conservative recoils from this "multiplication" of indignantly politicized identities within and between the Wisdom traditions. Even more, one might (almost) understand why all these issues—race, gender, sex, class, and ecology multiplied by cultures, traditions, nations, ethnicities, and diasporas as addressing life or death for a critical mass of earthlings—have been kept at bay in the institutionalized forms of interreligious dialogue. The complications seem to multiply into a chaos of irreconcilable demands, accusations, and impossibilities. Nonetheless, the Wisdom discourses—the theologies—show signs (amid this entanglement) of a mysterious metamorphosis: polyvocal and promiscuous, haunting and queer, grounding and ungrounded, situated and planetary. A theological polydoxy answering to the manifold of Wisdoms does seem to be emerging. And for all the indubitable confusions, a certain coherence does seem to be evolving. We are all—in such a volume—learning to embrace its sources both within and beyond the history of relevant orthodoxies. But how will such an identity-engulfing polyphony hold together?

Its logic would not resemble that of an abstract order of pyramidal meaning. Polydoxy, unlike the orthodox self-understandings it intersects, clings together by a connective, a *sticky logic*: "To cohere" means, first of all, "to stick together." Inconclusive and becoming, this stickiness, this mutual entanglement, seems to reflect something about all our relations. It is that which is, by definition, hard to unify in thought—something luring us to seek new ways to understand "togetherness." William James first dubbed this something the "pluralistic universe," indeed, presciently, the "multiverse." "Pluralism lets things really exist in the each-form," he wrote, emphasizing the concrete particularities of the world. Everything concrete exists "at all times in many possible connexions which are not necessarily actualized at the moment." James thus originates, at the same moment, pluralistic reflection on religious experience and on the cosmos. "If the each-form be the eternal form of reality no less than it is the form of temporal appearance, we still have a coherent world, and not an incarnate incoherence, as is charged by so many absolutists. Our 'multiverse' still makes a 'universe' . . . through the fact that each part hangs together with its very next neighbors in inextricable interfusion."[18]

Ernesto Cardenal, the great Salvadoran theopoet, sets this cosmos in *verse*: "Why say universe, as if it were only one / and not pluriverse?"[19] The inextricable interfusion keeps crossing disciplinary boundaries. William Connolly, a Jamesian and Deleuzian (he calls himself a "Jamesleuzian"), intercepts the multiverse for the purposes of a political theory centered in the problem of religious and irreligious pluralism. The philosophy of a pluralistic universe, he writes, "suggests that human civilization is an event that might not have happened, and that it is most apt to survive if we attend to the fecundity, volatility, and complexity of interconnections in which it is set."[20] Such interconnections—political, physical, spiritual—may be evoking the pluralist coherence we seek.

Another metaphor for this "cohesiveness" would be the polyphony of an orchestra in concert—its logic is that of *sounding together* in the pluri-singularity of a matrix of experienced meaning. The polyphony is enacted as *symphony*—without a singular, sovereign conductor and without the imposition of a unified form and program. Indeed the emblem of Whitehead's plural "togetherness" is this "symphonic form" in which we obtain a "sense of multiplicity" of "the experience of unity, of multitude, of transition."[21] This concrescence is thus a "living together."[22] In its metaphysical form—as stated by Whitehead's Category of the Ultimate[23]—this conviviality appears as the creative togetherness of the process of the multiplicity of becoming. Of all of Whitehead's "tentative formulations of . . . ultimate generalities,"[24] this one offers a pluralistic coherence amid imperialist attempts of (philosophical, religious, or political) totalization and indifferent relativism alike. Its generation of the rhythms and harmonies of coherence explores mutually relative multiplicities in process—unification of multiplicities, multiplication of unities, and their resonance in a creative advance into the unprecedented. In such a sympathetic multiverse, *nothing* is ultimate—*except* the very concrescent cohesiveness of the polyphonic convergences and divergences.[25] We sound or live together as mutual surprises in a symphonic complexity.

Gilles Deleuze,[26] perhaps the most eminent philosopher to be deeply appreciative of Whitehead's symphonic pluralism, echoes Whitehead's infinitely variable connectivity in a "Harmony of Harmonies"[27] with a "polyphony of polyphonies." Transforming "harmonic closure to an opening onto a polytonality,"[28] its multiplicity avoids totaling One, the disjunctive Multiple, but also the pirate captain's collection of many ones. He draws on Whitehead's "play that diverges" and honorifically dubs his symphonic pluriverse—in allusion to James Joyce—the "Chaosmos."[29] In its nets and webs of bifurcating and moving, cohering and crisscrossing foldings, what "lives together" discloses itself as an event of heterogeneous connections. Its imperative is: "Be neither a One nor a Many, but multiplicities!"

As a multiplicity "doesn't begin and doesn't end, but is always in the middle, between things, interbeing, *intermezzo*,"[30] we are asked to become *from the middle*, always *in between*, in the rhythms, alliances, and resonances of our living together. In this "motley world,"[31] unity always appears as a *finite* fold of multiple relations. Nothing is fixed; nothing is perfect; nothing is forever; but everything is vibrating, living, and resisting false unifications that defy multiplicity and life. This polyphonic pluralism employs an ethos of undoing oppressive hierarchies (sanctified ultimates and eternal orders) by creating folds of difference. Conversely, the imperial desire for the One is the desire for death. It is guided by a conservativism that for Whitehead "is fighting against the essence of the universe."[32]

Does this resistance to the colonizing Oneness, this ethics of relational multiplicity, not also demand that pluralism exceed relativism? Wouldn't the latter, if it harbors an ethos, not foster the ethics of global piracy or, perhaps worse, of mutually indifferent locations? Especially against the mutual isolation of closed contexts, interrupted by acts of aggression, we emphasize the excess of the polyphonic harmonics and symphonic rhythms of "living together." This excess of connective cohesiveness is produced not by the quantity of its relata but by the folds of the connection *between* them. Because these connections are folds of difference, not boundaries of separation, they also always exceed any bounded context. A separative pluralism is always tempted to simply identify with its own local context and leave others to do the same. Such localism belies the tangled interdependencies of the multiverse. An effectual pluralism of differential foldings, however, will instead require us to transgress closed contexts as false expressions of relationless units. Our differential pluralism will understand multiplicity in its *transcontextual* valences, transgressive of the sealed boundaries of any single context, religious or cultural.[33] Its ethical claims must transgress the sealed boundaries of any single context, religious or cultural (your religious practice may justify a ritual sacrifice of animals repugnant to me but less violent than my carnivorous people's industrial practices; at the same time, it may not justify runaway growth in production of CO_2 or of population among developing nations). Without this *connective* appeal, no pluralism can develop right teachings and right action—from an Eightfold or a manifold path—whereby we persist in the transmutation of our quantitative pluralities into a qualitative planetary multiplicity.

Relational pluralism thus distinguishes itself from relativism in the cultivation of what we could call "strange attractions" toward the others, the neighbors, the strangers, the stranger neighbors, with whom we find ourselves in relation—personally or planetarily—even before we can "identify" ourselves in difference from them. But in so doing, we open, and are opened by, the *fold between self and other*, the margin of stickiness, *jeong*,[34] overlap, hybridity, miscegenation, contamination, vibratory interference. Here, we join the tricksters[35] and ancestral lures,[36] the intermediary spirits and between-figures, charting the sacred interactivity of those older wisdoms that were superseded by the "great world religions" (if this is not in itself already an imperialist simplification).

We are suggesting that it is only in the discovery of such constitutive or *prehensive relationality* that pluralism escapes from the banal plural of a mere many, or series of separate ones. This enfoldment, however, is never reducible to one. Each fold is enfolded—partially, contiguously, stickily, symphonically. Each fold is a universe of others, each likewise "holographically" enfolding universes and "cryptographically" instigating new universes. While this com*pli*cating condition gets necessarily simplified by orders of abstraction, preference, and justice, notice that even sim*pli*city—contrary to its classical connotation of pure unity—involves secretly a folding. The singular is already plural: "Being does not preexist its singular plural."[37]

The taste for multiplicity gives rise to a trust that changes the meaning of faith and the sacred. It can, perhaps, be most deeply cultivated *from within the mysteries* of the respective pluralisms possible to specific traditions—even to those traditions that, in the rise of the West, fused with the forms of theology and science least historically amenable to pluralism. To the extent that any of us are rooted in a historic religion, we work *with* its resources *of* and *for* complexity. To the extent that our Wisdoms remain entangled with the separating simplifications of their orthodoxies, we work "prehensively" *toward* their symphonic and sticky connectedness. Christian pluralisms cannot therefore long operate without Muslim, Hindu, Buddhist, or Hopi pluralisms. If these are embraced in a polydox alliance, they spread the recognition that multiple teachings are always already constitutive of any specifically chosen tradition. As the various Wisdoms also need enough coherence, however, they will inevitably create, anew, simplifications of abstraction, preference, and justice in order to both exceed the indifference and constrain the piracies of a hostile plurality.

The spiritual impulse to *become* multiplicities, then, arises from a transformation of oneness-*into*-manyness. Its conviviality becomes possible when we let go of any presupposed static and world-capturing sacred totality and its corresponding isolating contextualism of a oneness-*without-manyness*. In this transformation, we activate the enfolded multiverse that always surpasses itself, that unfolds differences in becoming and asks us to always enfold its community anew. Within and between Wisdom traditions, we risk the adventure of seeking the sacred interactivity in, between, across, and beyond those very traditions. But in invoking process folds of the divine, or of the sacred *in* multiplicity, we do not envision yet another—a "better"—religion. In the light of the war-ridden exclusivities of simple identities that create sibling rivalries the self-designated "great world religions" and the primordial ways not even recognized as religions, the appeal to become multiplicities within diversity and entanglement takes on an incarnate urgency.

As we envision this embodiment of relational and differential multiplicity, we affirm also that the sacred or divine *in* multiplicity can never be reduced to only *one kind of* experience and understanding. This is not just a matter of ecumenical generosity. Rather we may understand the sacred or divine in the Wisdom traditions to reveal itself *in* an irreducible polydoxy. Because it *is* the very sacred or divine activity of enfolding, this multiplicity will allow us to discern it not only *in* multiplicity, but also *as* sacred or divine multiplicity. With Whitehead, we suggest that, "the actuality of God must also be understood as a multiplicity of components in the process of creation."[38] And with Deleuze, as he muses on Whitehead, we affirm that the sacred interactivity is not that of "being a Being," but that which "becomes Process."[39] Desiring this divine *in* multiplicity inherently directs our pluralistic gaze toward a trust no longer driven by fear of becoming, difference, and flux, but filled with anticipation of the *mutual embodiment*, of the *inter-carnation*, of encounters, conjunctions, and interferences of Wisdoms. Whether we evoke the plurisingularity of *Elohim* or the manyness-in-oneness of the Christian Trinity or the sacred intertwining of *samsara* and *nirvana* in the Buddhist "co-origination" (*pratitya-samutpada*) or the complexity of the trickster of native religions, we prehend the *sacred folds* of multiplicity. "S/He/It," we might say, not only *insists on* multiplicity but *becomes as* its very interactivity—not as the one, not as the many, but as *the sacred or divine (in) multiplicity.*[40]

We (like all the authors of this volume) who speak from within specific and various spiritual traditions, in their development and in their dotage, find ourselves invariably "between"—enfolding ourselves in an enfolded pluralism. As with the pirate admiral, the moorings of the soul get loose. So much the better: polyphilia! We may be learning to move with a more fluent grace, with less need and greed, amid strangeness and novelty. We may, at moments, enfold a postcolonial ethics along with precolonial hints of wonder, evolutionary sciences of emergence along with religious narratives of creation, bodhisattvas along with Christ, the Bible along with the Lotus Sutra. In unfolding the mystery of this *enfolded divine (in) multiplicity*, our polydoxy may become *upaya*—"skillful means"—of the greater healing.

SKILLFUL MEANS

Might the multiple approaches to Wisdom-folds collected here offer a *pluralism of skillful means*? Maybe we should approach their multiplicity like the opening of the Chakras—healing through flow of potentialities folded down into ourselves. The folds we have blocked (our relations, our cultures) and their interrelations may not be allowed to express a reality of rigidly bound Ones—wounded and wounding in their enforced separations. For our bodies no less than our traditions, may the violence of the "engendered monsters" (of the enclosed totality of occupation or the multiple totalitarianisms of separation) be broken when we realize that the "states of things are not unities or totalities but multiplicities"? May we realize that the "many states of things (where each state would be a whole)" where "each state of things is multiple (which would only be an indication of its resistance to unification)" are but the illusion of the united or divided One? May we instead open, or unfold, the "points of unification, centers of totalization, points of subjectivation" so that "multiplicity grows from the middle like grass"?[41] Healing begins where elements become less important than what is the "between" of the elements—the many folds of relationships, inseparable from one another.

This is the Lotus Sutra's doctrine of *upaya*. Indeed, what rises off the pages of the Lotus Sutra, what billows and balloons and fills the reading gaze, is its multiplicity of multiplicities. These multiples multiply mountainously, vertiginously. These lists start with the great audience of Buddha on Holy Eagle Peak, an audience of millions: of so many *categories* of worthies, starting, strategically with individual *arhats* representing the very ideal about to be superseded. Women are named from the start—two famous nuns and their thousands of followers. Then the eighty thousand *bodhisattvas* and the tens of thousands of various kings and deities—*Indra* alone is accompanied by "twenty thousand children of heaven"—and such marvelous collectives as the dragon kings and the centaur kings and the wheel-rolling kings and each of their tens of thousands of followers. As all these collectives collect themselves along with the narrator, this healing truth about multiplicity is said: that every Buddha has been closely associated with hundreds of thousands of billions of buddhas in the past, fully practicing the way of the immeasurable *dharma* that is demonstrated by a polydox polyphony and held together through the infinite folds of the Buddha insofar as he has *"innumerable skillful means* to save living beings."[42]

The multiplicity of means is seen to be skillful by the infinitely *many* sentient beings and to be conducive to the recognition of the *one* truth of salvation. The Sutra of Innumerable Meanings, which classically accompanies the Lotus Sutra, names this truth of the relational multiplicity of becoming (*pratitya-samutpada*), namely, that "all *dharmas* were originally, will be, and are in themselves void in nature and form."[43] We can read their "oneness"—sought in T'ien-t'ai's teaching of the "three thousand worlds in one thought-instant"[44]—as code not for a simplifying, homogenizing unity, an annihilation of difference that assures the eventual collapse of the multiple, but instead as the *dynamic interdependence* of oneness-and-manyness: "The buddhas, the most honored ones, know that *nothing exists independently* and that *Buddha-seeds grow interdependently*. This is why they teach the One-vehicle."[45] In the Hua-yen tradition, again, this one-multiplicity appears as the "interpenetration of part and part" (*shih-shih wu-ai*) and of the "interpenetration of part and whole" (*li-shih wu-ai*) in which recognition we release the healing process of the many-in-one of every single event as one-among-many amid infinitely many events.[46]

Multiplicity as *mutual interdependence*, again, as articulated in the *upaya*, resonates with Whitehead's conviction that any conceptualization of "ultimate realities" demands *a creative process of healing* by which it "converts the opposition into a contrast."[47] Multiplicity as *mutual interdependence of part and part* is clearly reflected in Whitehead's profound contention that every happening (as it gathers itself from its relations) "repeats in microcosm what the universe is in macrocosm" such that it, at the same time, "pervades the whole world."[48] Multiplicity as *mutual interdependence of part and whole* reflects Whitehead's contention that, since there is no absolute context, there are no absolutely separated contexts either. Hence, the very environment of a polydox articulation of the sacred or divine (in) multiplicity must be polyphonic in nature, in order to be healing from occupations and separations. The world as a "whole," as Whitehead says, "is a multiplicity."[49] It is, in other words, a "community of actual things" in "an incompletion in process of production," a process that is healing because in it "no two actualities can be torn apart: each is all in all."[50] Such a relational complex meets the heart of the healing process of multiplicity: *Polydoxy demands polyphilia and polyphilia releases polydoxy.*

In *Religion in the Making*, Whitehead indicated such skillful means by evoking a threefold characterization of healing interdependence of the mutual enfolded plurality of Wisdoms *across* religious traditions. There is the complexity of religious experiences that in its specific expressions in multiple modes of living (values) and thinking (dogmas) as well as their mutual interpretation (metaphysics) necessitates a *mutual resonance* between them that cannot be reduced to only *one* true experience, religious teaching, or cosmological understanding.[51] In order to allow for each fold to remain valuable, the togetherness of the folds must remain open to ever-new modes of interference. In Whitehead's typology of religious interpretations of the interrelations of the sacred or divine interactivity within the world, again, he demonstrates the *mutual incompleteness* of the folds. The "Eastern Asiatic concept" of "immanence," the "Semitic concept" of "transcendence," and the "Pantheistic concept" in which "the actual world is a phase of the complete fact" that is the divine are complexly intertwined.[52] And in an unprecedented "contextualization" of the sacred or divine *within* a multiplicity of ultimate aspects of reality—the multiplicities of worlds, values, and creativity[53]—Whitehead points at the *mutual immanence* of every folding of the sacred or divine and, hence, at the intercontextual nature of a multiverse in becoming. As in James, this intercontextuality never yields an absolute standpoint. Rather, its healing capacity lies in its profoundly processual relationality by which all of our abstractions, simplifications, and justifications must always be refolded again and again so as not to block their enfolded multiplicity.

As these threefold means of interdependence—of resonance, incompleteness, and immanence—arise in Whitehead's subtleties of thinking, what every process *upaya* of multiplicity will recognize at one point or another is this: What connects *and* differentiates all processes is their profound *mutuality*. With Plato, Whitehead calls this the *khora*—"the medium of intercommunication."⁵⁴ As the multiplicity of *dharmas* in the Lotus Sutra, Whitehead's *khora* unfolds into the irreducible dimensions of a healing multiplicity in which polydox complexities never stabilize, but always generate new dimensions, contingent on one another and without any unified framework of deduction.

As this healing mutuality releases the sacred or divine *into* the finite processes of becoming, the *upaya* of the infinitely many buddhas reveal only *one* truth: Their infinite multiplicity can become healing only when they skillfully direct us toward a polyphonic harmonics of the mutual embodiment of the sacred or divine *with* and *within* multiplicity. And enfolding the multiplicity of Wisdom traditions in their respective mystery, we may be surprised by the "one" truth of the Lotus Sutra—the healing character of the manifold. Its polyphonic interdependence is not indifferently all-inclusive, however, but rather dislodges the assertion that the sacred or divine controls the world or that only *one* religion can be true or that in *all* religions it would be only *one* expression of the sacred or that all the religions are indifferently true. Against these obstructions, Whitehead with the Lotus Sutra awakens a taste for sacred multiplicity with its healing character in terms of images of concern, care, tenderness, patience, love, intimacy, and peace.

Whitehead's divine (in) multiplicity fosters *such* a multiplicity of folds—releasing their healing capacity only in their mutual resonance, incompleteness, and immanence among themselves (*shih-shih wu-ai*) and with the universe (*li-shih wu-ai*). From the "principle of concretion" in *Science of the Modern World* with its multiplicity of names⁵⁵ to the "divine event" in *Religion in the Making* vibrating between impersonal and personal modes (as pertaining to Buddhist and Christian orthodoxies alike); from the multiplicity of ultimate realities to the complex nature of "God" in *Process and Reality* with a multiplicity of poles and oscillations; from the multiple names of the sacred in *Adventures of Ideas* (initial Eros, final Fact, tragic Beauty, Supreme Adventure, Harmony of Harmonies, Love, Peace) to the "Deity" of *Modes of Thought* that mediates our experience of the corporality of the multiplicity in the universe—Whitehead immerses in a multiplicity of means skillfully arousing, always anew and differently, the healing multiplicity in us, in our religious traditions, and in the unfathomable universe.⁵⁶

Although process theologies have, in general, concentrated only on a few of these complex images of the sacred, they have developed a variety of openings for, and beyond, these images. Although some process theologies limited their inquiries to the explicit use of "God" in Whitehead, others dwelled in the multiplicity of ultimate realities as sacred. Although some sensed the need to engage with the Abrahamic orthodoxies, others found it more useful to resonate with the characteristic creativity and beauty of Eastern Wisdoms. In their "speculative imaginations"[57] process pushed toward an astonishing and transgressive multiplicity: from a divine "event" to a divine "society"; from a sacred "creativity" to a "divine matrix." Always, however, we should think that it would be fatal to the *healing* process of multiplicity that the Lotus Sutra suggests if we would become tempted to understand these images as a closed systematization of that which Whitehead only approximated in terms of "tentative formulations of ultimate generalities."[58]

Multiplicities of skillful means—as offered by Whitehead and process theologies—will have to *risk* these and other polyphilic *uncertainties—healing* uncertainties, as it were—in the midst of the closures of orthodoxies. As long as we sense in them the humble love for the poetics of the open universe in its infinitely many finite connections,[59] we will excite their healing capacities against monopolies of truth, separatism, or piracy. When we use these uncertainties *as upaya* and the *upaya as* healing uncertainties, we *can* resist embalming our religious lives in intracontextual blindness. When we approach the sacred in, and in love of, the very multiplicity of unique perspectives, these *skillful uncertainties* will excite the very *concrescence* of our "living together." By interrupting our captivity to our most beloved abstractions, they will release us back into the ethical and spiritual demands of a sustainable conviviality.

UNCERTAINTY AND COMPLEXITY

Whitehead's connective pluralism of the sacred (in) multiplicity, unfolding the Buddhist *upaya* of a healing multiplicity, will also *enfold* itself so as to arrive on the path of meditative silence at the mystery of its "one" truth. At a certain point, where differences of belief and orthodoxy become obstructive to our "living together," what we may call the "interreligious uncertainty principle" kicks in. Uncertainty, as we have suggested, is implicated in multiplicity, as multiplicity will unfold into uncertainty—both as humility and as excess.

Since there "is no 'control' that doctrine can place on divinity, especially in the theory-resistant multiplicity of divine immanence,"[60] we suggest that the uncertainty of multiplicity names that excess. But it utters it *apophatically*, that is, it speaks its unspeakability. The apophatic tradition is deeply rooted in the "world religions," and in profound ways in Christian orthodoxy, as negative theology. So, the *upaya* of uncertainty does not silence but overflows the orthodoxies, religious discourses, and theologies as a silence that honors the apophatic plenitude of the sacred (in) multiplicity.

As polyphilic planetarity calls for unprecedented attention to polydoxic uncertainty, it is not that suddenly one sells short one's own conceptual or doctrinal commitments to Wisdom traditions. It is not a sudden swerve into relativism. Nor is it a merely strategic pause, a polite silence until one can reassert one's own position more cunningly. Rather, the complexity of positionality here practiced—including the entire multiplicity of teachings—is, we suggest, itself rooted in a profound *nonknowingness* or exercised in the very *process of unknowing*.

It is here that the verbose process tradition, confidently unfolded from Whitehead's affirmative metaphysics, may better practice the gesture of negative theology.[61] Process thought has quite kataphatically emphasized the complex mutuality of God and the world, underscoring their coherence—and, hence, the creative production of multiplicities at the relational heart of reality. Just as for Whitehead "no entity can be conceived in complete abstraction from the system of the universe," all key notions, or metaphors, in a system of thought "presuppose each other." Yet Whitehead's very concept of "coherence" is, as we noted above, set forth in a quasi-apophatic gesture. For the resistance provided by concrete interrelations against mere separation of abstract terms does not mean that the signifiers "are definable in terms of each other. It means that what is indefinable in one such notion cannot be abstracted from its relevance to the other notions."[62] The unknown is not excused from relation!

Khoric intercommunication, in Whitehead, is the relational process of the *unprecedented*—the opening of, and to, the uncertainty as the unknowing of "identification." Like tentacles feeling out the unknown, Whitehead's polydoxic theopoetics leaves us on the shaken grounds of an apophatic uncertainty on which the sacred (in) multiplicity cannot be "identified" with either God or ultimate reality. For the latter also indicate multiple sites of our unknowingness. Whitehead's "coherence of the unprecedented" appeals to an uncertain *manifold* of complex differentiations, overflowing into unexpected creative relations.

Emitted from its special resonances with Whitehead's mutual immanence of the world and the divine, we have for some time been riveted to the *docta ignorantia*—the "learned unknowing"—of Nicolas of Cusa. This version of the mystical tradition, with its apophatic force field of uncertainty and its autodeconstructive unknowing of "identities," does not leave us with a valueless equality of orthodoxies, but with a polydoxy that values an enfolded pluralism of the unprecedented ways of Wisdom as folds unfolded into the overflow of a positive cosmology of boundless mutual complication.

Enfolded in Whitehead's "contrasted opposites"[63] of the multiplicities of the world and the divine in their movement toward mutual enfolding and unfolding is an anticipation of Cusa's *complicatio/explicatio* rhythm. This vision of mutuality marks, for us, a historical beginning for the theopoetic of relational uncertainty. *Complicatio* names this mystery as the *apophatic* infinity of the finite in which all relations are enfolded such that it is the enfolded potentiality (*posse ipsum*) of all folds. Cusa already realized that it is its very *unknowability*—its "coherence" as infinite complexity—that prevents us from knowing that the religious other is wrong. Resonant with Whitehead's "mysticism" as the "insight into depths as yet unspoken"[64]—as enfolding the *unprecedented*—Cusa extends this unknowingness of the *docta ignorantia* with unexpected "coherence" to all *enfolded* creatures. And yet, such is the manifold enclosed in the divine—as enfolded multiplicity—that it begins, with Cusa, to break up and out into the world. What is "complicated" in the infinite enfolds the finite and *unfolds* in the finite. It is not a one that is opposed to the many; it is folded out—as the divine *explicatio* itself—*in* and *as* multiplicity in all creatures.

In Cusa's cosmology of an acentric or omnicentric manifold, early modern science is germinating. He comes close to intuiting the connection of uncertainty to nonlocal entanglement that is at the cutting edge of quantum physics. Whitehead was already dimly aware of the uncertainty principle and energized by the quantum principle in his imagination of connective multiplicity.[65] In its reverberating relevance, it will instigate an epistemic humility that should, by rights, grow in proportion to the amount of information. As the theoretical physicist John Wheeler put it: "We live on an island of knowledge surrounded by a sea of ignorance. As our island grows, so does the shoreline of our ignorance."[66] There are parallels between the interactions of science with religion to that of one religion with another that we cannot pursue here, but they root inextricably in the founding impulses of process thought.

In a wider polydox teaching, with its polyphilic eros, this unfolding into the multiplicity is enriched in beauty and restrained in appropriation by an ethic of finite multiple embodiments. Each relation comes unfolded out of an excess of relation. It therefore enfolds all its relations, even the most overexposed, in unknowingness. The fold of relation itself is shadowed—which is not to say overshadowed—by unknowing. As in Judith Butler's later parlance: "Perhaps most importantly, we must recognize that ethics requires us to risk ourselves precisely at moments of unknowingness, when what forms us diverges from what lies before us, when our willingness to become undone in relation to others constitutes our chance of becoming human."[67]

It is by way of an ethos of learned unknowing that we may stimulate the healing capacity of Whitehead's "skillful means." In its enfolding and unfolding of the divine (in) multiplicity, its uncertainty leaves us with a profound "apophatic plenitude" in any meaningful approach to the Wisdoms. The contrast between "personal" and "impersonal" aspects of the sacred ("God" and "creativity" in Whitehead's parlance) becomes *theopoetic adventure*.[68] The contrast as it pertains, for instance, to the Abrahamic (God, Yahweh, Allah) and Indian/Chinese religions (*narguna brahman, tao, sunyata*), is familiar to Whiteheadian interreligious considerations—as is the sacredness of the world for indigenous religions or the inclusive relationality (*pratitya-samutpada*) as personal complication in Eastern traditions (Amida Buddha) and the impersonal complication of God in Western mysticism (Eckhart's "Godhead," Schelling's *Ungrund*).[69] The mystery of "the sacred or divine interactivity" will unfold only as long as we don't create orthodox animosities, but a healing uncertainty, a complexity of *upaya*, a complexifying opening of blockings of the flow of sacred multiplicity.

Instead of colonizing them into a stable supermetaphysic that identifies and coordinates Wisdoms, we understand these sacred adventures as *processes of unknowing* in which their contrasts theopoetically, for the greater healing, *gather* the enfolded complexity of "ultimate reality" differently in relation to the polydoxic heart of different Wisdom traditions. They constitute a "community of unfolding" the enfolded mystery of the divine multiplicity. Therefore, it will be the very medium of intercommunication in which, irreducible one to another, their relational differences form *healing constellations* with one another. The ecumenical consequences of this unknowing—within, across, and beyond Wisdom traditions—become revolutionary, indicating the path *not* taken in the West for interreligious dialogue, according to Simone Weil.

When Cardinal Cusa deploys the *docta ignorantia* against a Christian ignorance of its own ignorance, he produces an unprecedented knowledge. Cusa had taken part in a great ecumenical expedition to Byzantium. Then, in 1453, Mehmet took down Constantinople; migrants flooded Europe with tales of horror; and the Ottomans pushed on. The pope called for a new crusade. The cardinal opposed it. Within weeks of hearing the news, personally devastating, he wrote *De pace fides*—a vision of religious peace. It invents an argument for interreligious dialogue: In nuce, because we finite beings cannot "know" the truth, which is infinite, neither can we exclude the truth of other religions.[70] We have no excuse to force conversion or to war over belief. Connolly offers a postmodern analogue: "When you encounter unfathomable mystery in your faith in the right spirit, you may become inspired to appreciate corollary elements of paradox, mystery, or uncertainty at different points in other faiths."[71]

This is the "one" polyphilic truth of the mystery as it unfolds its healing capacity in its infinitely many *upaya*: that the infinitely enfolded mystery of sacred or divine multiplicity cannot be expected to be "the same" or a countable plurality of manifestations. Wisdom, we say, is not about the "repetition" of existing modes of knowing, but about *creative unknowing* into the multiplicity of a polydoxic plenitude of the ever-new arrival of the sacred or divine. Whitehead encourages us to plunge into this irreducibly creative process of "creative unknowing" by noting that the creative constitution of new foldings (contrasts), when they form ever-more complex syntheses, can never be reduced to simpler contrasts of opposites. As its complexity is *emergent* und thus uncertain, such a process of contrasting Wisdoms produces an *infinity of categories*; complexity produces always new constellations of ways to connect. Engaging Wisdom traditions, for process theopoetics, must be a process of *incompletion*—the *processual* rhythm of diffusion (*implicatio*) and differentiation (*explicatio*).⁷² The infinite potential of constellations of the complicated aspects of ultimacy can and will produce—and, in fact, has always produced—ever-new events with a *unique character of their togetherness*. Then its "sacred discourse" does not reflect a mere archaeology of Wisdom traditions—as if we know already their identity and number. Rather it must become sensible to the incredible capacity of the unprecedented *event* of the sacred in a creative multiplicity of Wisdom traditions. And these events are always events of stickiness, of the "concrescence" of "living together."

In a sense, this gesture *beyond* "dialogue"—much appreciated when performed out of the certainties of the "identifications" with one's own tradition and the "otherness" of the other traditions—is always an apophatic leap of faith—or is it the event of enlightenment? Whether or not it is said or unsaid to be such, this "third space" in which mutual transformation might occur can be symbolized with Whitehead's *khoric* "medium of intercommunication" or Cusa's "Spirit," the "connection itself." It implicates every relation in the "negative infinity" of divine *complicatio*, a sacred *plenitude of enfolded multiplicity*. As in Whitehead, this infinite cannot close off the multiplicity as an "infinity without finitude" or close down the multiplicity into a monistic whole. Au contraire, as Levinas pits "infinity" against "totality" and Whitehead proposes "infinity" only "*in* finitude," their mutual perichoresis is the unfinished, the indefinite, the indefinable *in the process* of enfolding and unfolding.⁷³

The ethical and spiritual "call" of the unprecedented sacred polyphony immerses our miseries of hate and fear into the light of our healing capacities to be called forth from the unknowingness of the mystery into the unknown fragilities of "living together" in religious peace.

POLYPHILIC PLURALISM

The process pluralism we suggest here is an enfolding and unfolding pluralism, a relational and differential pluralism in a process of ever-new constellations of complication and uncertainty—an uncertainty that is complex because it names a mystery that cannot detect the sacred without an inherent love for the manifold in which it is enfolded. If this process pluralism is not to devolve into the piracy of a mere raid on whatever exotic differences globalization has not yet exhausted, then the emerging complexity remains, always, a work of self-critique—always a suspension of our presumptions that serves as a constraint on a pluralism that intends to be a healing event. Only in this manner does the value of multiplicity activate an ethics and spirituality of radical interdependence.

But the apophatic moment of this mystical suspension, as we have argued, is just the backside of the *more*: the excess of meaning, life, difference, embodied in all our relations and the relations embodied in our differences. A mutual embodiment invoked in all our ultimates. No single incarnation contains it. And so, what *limits* our pluralism to an ethics of nonviolent encounter, intolerant of intolerance, exclusive of exclusion, disrespectful of disrespect, would be the very criterion of mutuality we have set forth. The sacred interactivity of Whitehead's cosmic Eros drives an alternative concept of power—if it should yet be named "power" at all—in process theology. Persuasion replaces coercion at the level of supreme purposefulness, but without any purpose of subjection. Love comes into play, as well. The pluralism we seek is not only discourse in the form of polydoxy, but life in the character of *polyphilia—the imitation of the sacred love of multiplicity*.[74]

Of course, the supremacy of "love" is dangerously deformed by the history of Christian dominance. Moreover, it can never pretend to the role of common denominator for the dialogue (nor can *any* references to metaphysical ultimates). Process pluralists, however, do not wait for a common denominator but engage in common projects in which conversations yield shared aims of mutual resonance, immanence, and incompleteness. The lure would be neither ground nor goal but means—skillful means (of healing) or medium (of intercommunication)—the affirmative expression of the *upaya* in its productive suspension of certainty. The uncertainty principle of interreligious discourse—from which unfold the dynamisms of the infinite emergent complexity—requires the motive force of *polyphilia*, the love of this polyphony of multiplicities. The process pluralism we propose will not always worship polyphilic love as God, but it will always worship God as polyphilic love. For we suspect that whenever a God *is* worshipped, the primacy of the love-attribute will be the best check against the rapacity to which his/her/its followers are tempted. This is the point: The negation, the constraint of polyphilic pluralism, is the backside of the affirmation.

This affirmation, experienced in the lovable achievements of novel harmonies and intense contrasts, motivates not only religious but political pluralism. The sacred or divine in the image of such polyphilic love reveals itself as a love that *activates* us toward the respect of the fragility of the differences within the political and spiritual world. The affirmation of its complex values in their differentiation will draw attention to ever-new experiences as profound religious impulse in the changing landscape of Wisdom traditions. The *love* of the appearances of a multifarious world will arouse a practice of caring fragility in our living together in its ecological complexity. Hence, we are seeing the surprising emergence of a "politics of love," as a mimicking of the language of biblical love, or of "agonistic respect," a subliminal paraphrase of love of the enemy. Seemingly nontheistic approaches to multiplicity, such as Deleuze's, in their own work yield another motivation *for* Wisdom: the mystery of multiplicity, a new spirituality of value and virtuality, reverberating from Cusa's *complicatio*. Its *ethical, political, and spiritual impulse* always to reverse the simplifications with which we coerce not only "others" issues a divine Eros of suspension of simplifications in seeking ever-new and ever-more-beautiful contrasts of complexity. Whitehead's "God" is an image of the insistence of such a love of the manifold. In such a manifold, it is for us to recognize polyphilia as the manifestation of the sacred or as divine revelation and to live its tenderness as if it is our lives through which it may never be lost.

In the radical practices of *bodhisattva*, compassion has already long entered into subtle contrasts with Christian love, offering a nonclinging wisdom to our calamitous Western passions, while drawing into Asia a prophetic politics. The Whiteheadian divine lure—seeking ever-skillful means—is the arousal of nonviolent modes of acting and thinking in a universe that in its vastness tends toward unprecedented intensities and ever-new harmonies with the tenderness of a compassionate valuation of the least of its folds. Yet the language of "God" would, from the perspective of such a God, itself be subject to both Western mystical negation and Asian impersonal sublation. For the *upaya* will never stop demanding of us fresh uncertainties and surprising connections. They cannot be stored in a treasure chest. Yet, they must be released not in the name of any divine or sacred or ultimate, but *in the name of the living* in the fragility of their lives. The figure we offer at this moment, hoping no pirate will use it, is that of a *polyphilic pluralism*.

◆ Interreligious Explorations:
Religious Diversity and Divine Multiplicity

◆ Abhinavagupta's Theogrammatical Topography of the One and the Many

LORILIAI BIERNACKI

The unconscious is structured like a language.
—JACQUES LACAN, *The Seminar of Jacques Lacan, III: The Psychoses*

For much of the world's history, what happens to most of us (that is, the many, the people) has actually been dictated by the one—a singular person as ruler. Countries were ruled by kings and only one could rule; brutal wars were waged over which claimant to the throne could seize the right to rule the many. Moreover, the idea of one to rule the many, monarchy, found its justification in the divine order of things. Just as the model of only one God ruling over the world ensured the stable order of the cosmos, so a single king ruling a people ensured a harmonious society, just as, to use a commonly cited metaphor, the head was ruler of the body's various parts. Even with the absolute sovereignty of a king, there was always, as with the body, a delicate interaction between the one and the many. The many, though ostensibly voiceless and subject to the will of the one, danced a dialectic waltz with the one ruler. A good ruler developed the skill to hear and address the needs of the many.

Yet, as our American forefathers intimately knew, the problem of kingship is that the one ruler too easily neglects the needs and subjective experiences of all those many others. The problem with one voice to rule us all is that no one voice is omniscient enough, expansive enough to address the subjective needs of the many. With this insight, something rather radical happened in the eighteenth century—the advent of democracy—the idea that all of us, the many, should in fact have a say over what happens to us. Yet even with that profoundly world-altering document of 1776 that stated that, we, the people have a right to a government, by us, for us and made up of us, the structure of our lives has been slow to shift out of the older model. In most areas of our lives, power devolves to a single person. Not only are most governments structured this way, most corporations as well have a single head, a CEO who calls the shots from high above. The students and employees of schools also follow the dictates of that singular authority, the principal. Ships and platoons in the military demand the subservience of the voices of the many soldiers whose lives are legally forfeit in battle to a single ruling voice, the captain, the general, the admiral. And, although this is changing in the twentieth and twenty-first centuries, historically the family has also been traditionally ruled by one voice, usually the father or patriarch of the family, the sole voice to decide the legal futures of his dependents. The abundance of vocabulary nodding toward the bodily head as authority reveals the indelible traces of our older world model.

Embedded underneath a vocabulary of heads and body parts as the relationship between the one and the many, a deeper drive is revealed, a desire to collapse the many within the one, the one somehow privileged as more true than the many. Perhaps our theological models and monotheism in particular point to some subtle psychological wiring in the human brain to prefer the simplicity of the one over the messiness of the many. Too many voices, like too many cooks, will lead us astray, will spoil the broth. Or perhaps, we harbor within ourselves a deep-seated fear that any real dominance of the many will lead to an ethical paralysis; an unwieldy relativism will reign where universal values will be lost, abandoned. Indeed, it is just this criticism that is leveled by conservatives in America today against a perceived new multiculturalism, the plurality of voices making up the many that is America. The call for a return to a patriarchal world, railing against a public space for voices that were not traditionally heard, those of women, of minorities, reveals perhaps less a mean-spirited desire to silence the many very different others in our public space than a palpable yearning for a more secure, less messy rule by the one. In some sense, the democracies of the twentieth and twenty-first centuries offer an experiment, a tumultuous rehearsal of the dialectical balance of power between the one and the many.

The question becomes then, how to find a way of integrating the voices of the many with our ineluctable pull toward the idea of the one. How might we derive a subjectivity for the many that can encompass both the lure of the one, with its clear simplicity, and the complex negotiations that the many demands?

• • •

Resolving the conundrum of the one and the many has not only been a compulsive dialectical dance for the Western imagination. Indian thinkers have also struggled with the divine and the world as two poles of a pendulum with philosophical traditions swinging from one to the other to prioritize a transcendent singular divine or a pluralistic worldly immanence, reflecting the one and the many. In an Indian philosophical context this dialectic oscillates from the perch of a nondualism that sees only an absolute formless *Brahman* as the sole reality of all existence, to a celebration of the multiplicities of a *Māyā* brimming with a bodied life entangling itself and all of existence in a philosophical Trinity of qualities, again, alternatively, from a loving *bhakti*, or devotion that sees God as the essence and substratum of the creaturely *jīva*, the individual soul, to an irrefragable dualism that mirrors the ineluctable longing and separation of creature and God. Uniting this twain is the skilled provenance of only a few Indian thinkers; one of the most notable is the eleventh-century Indian philosopher Abhinavagupta. An unwavering nondualist, Abhinavagupta's philosophical speculations underwrite a cosmology that is nevertheless multiple in its iterations and dynamic via his use of the three grammatical persons to bridge the One with the Many.

This essay presents an analysis of the interpenetration of the immanent and transcendent as an instantiation of the problem of the One and the Many in the theocosmological mapping of consciousness that Abhinavagupta proposes. Particularly, I suggest that one finds the mode of interrelation between the transcendent and immanent expressed through a grammatico-theology. We see a structural template underlying this theological cosmology through the modalities of the first, second and third persons of grammar, "I," the "You" and the "It." This essay explores the trinitarian syntax modulating the interpenetration of grammatical person as a means for bridging the boundaries between the One and the Many.

I suggest that the grammatico-theology that Abhinavagupta offers gets to the heart of the problem of the one and the many because language is the very instantiation and genesis of the problem. Language functions as a code, not simply mapping reality, but magically generative of the world. Abhinavagupta's grammatico-theology encodes the dialectic between the one and the many and with this, entails a radical departure from our normal understanding of the relation between subjectivity and objectivity. In his system, subjectivity, associated with the first grammatical person, the "I," functions as the heart of all existence. As the subject shifts from the powerful originary participation in the sense of "I" into the mode of the other as "you" and then into the object as the third grammatical person, the "It," the multiplicity of the world ensues. Abhinava's prioritization of subjectivity as being more real than the mode of objectivity upsets our Western conceptions of the world as objective fact, as Abhinava offers a decentered, language-oriented map of reality.

After introducing the topic, I will give a very brief introduction to the thinker whose system I draw from, the eleventh-century Indian philosopher and mystic Abhinavagupta, along with a short account of the antecedents of Abhinavagupta's system in the grammar tradition. Following this, I will discuss Abhinava's use of dialogue and the grammatical three persons as a linguistic model for mapping the relation between the One and the Many.

It has become something of a truism since Benjamin Whorf first proposed the idea in 1941, to suggest that language structures the modalities of identity insofar as it sets boundaries on what we can think.[1] Indeed, even in contexts such as the current conversation of which this essay is a part, what we can say about the divine, about the relationships between the One and the Many, is limited by the language that we use, with built-in predispositions that structure what we can imagine. We have an apophatic impulse to resist the boundaries that language imposes when it comes to thinking about God, and in this, a tradition that emphasizes that mystical experience and the divine remain ineffable, resilient against the cataloging onslaught of language. Abhinavagupta, a mystic, nevertheless takes a view that stands in contradistinction to the idea that the mystical experience eludes our best attempts to trap it in language. And he does not envision an idea of spirit as speaking a divine language in and through the oracular possessions of bodies.

Abhinavagupta's vision of language and the divine is a mystical configuration, enmeshing the two: language as divinity, language itself as the map of cosmos. Language affords a mystical creation of cosmos through the word, a logos, which is here *vāc*, speech, and a goddess, Parāvāk, the goddess of speech. The goddess of speech—as speech—does more than simply divide the chaos into being or order the messy stuff of reality into a coherence. *Vāc* generates new life from within, in a favorite metaphor, as secret code in the tiny seed of the banyan tree. Like this tiny seed as code containing a vast proliferation, so language, especially as secret mantra contains within it the entire vastness of the cosmos.[2]

In the oft-quoted phrase of Jacques Lacan's above, the unconscious is structured like a language; in Abhinavagupta's system, the divine itself is structured like a language. No doubt there are implicit homologies in our representations of the divine and the unconscious; one could read much of Freud, especially his *Future of an Illusion* as an attempt to make just this link and through it, reduce the idea of the divine to mere mapping of the unconscious. Yet, Abhinavagupta's system turns this reductionism on its head, suggesting that not only is the unconscious structured like a language, but also the conscious and all else in between, the world itself modeled on a vision of language, and language itself is the divine generative power of the universe. That is, not merely is the unconscious structured like a language, but reality itself is enmeshed in and exists as language.

ABHINAVAGUPTA

A little bit of background on Abhinavagupta: He lived, from the latter part of the tenth through the middle of the eleventh century, in Kashmir in India. Abhinavagupta was a Tantric, and a left-handed Tantric at that, which means that he understood divinity to be immanent and transcendent, as something to be attained here on earth, by humans, as *jīvanmukti*, liberation while still in a human body. It means also that he practiced some transgressive rituals, involving the use of sex rites and illicit substances, such as wine and meat. Indeed, in one of the rare personal depictions of an individual writer in India, we find his pen portrait, penned by Kṣemarāja, his student, depicting him with a cup of wine and women on each side of him.[3] As a Tantric, the sources that he relied on as scripture were not India's classical Vedas. Rather, they were a new set of texts, called the *Āgamas*, a set of new revelations proposing to meet the new challenges of the *kaliyuga*, the age of darkness, an age that spans through the medieval period up to today as well.

Although certainly not a requirement for a Tantric, and not even the norm for his Kashmir of the tenth and eleventh centuries, Abhinava was a monist, understanding all of reality to be encompassed within a single and unified, though dyadic principle, Śiva-Śakti. His philosophy might best be understood as a panentheism articulated in evolutionary and emanationist terms. The element of Śakti in this dyadic principle is dynamic, involved in the specificity of life, and generative; the element of Śiva is transcendent and free from all change. The two are irreducibly entwined, inseparable, operating as modalities of each other. Abhinava's incorporation of both the elements of transcendence and immanence lends to it the framework of a panentheism.

His panentheism carries an evolutionary component precisely because his philosophy hinges on reincorporating a dynamism into the notion of the divine via language as a generative principle. It is, in fact, this element of his philosophy that enables him to make a link between the absolute divinity as a purely transcendent being and the messy reality of becoming that ensconces our existence. That is, his panentheism is what allows him to go beyond the Vedantic nondualism of his earlier compatriot, the eighth-century Śaṃkara, to devise a nondualism that can embrace both the One and the Many. His philosophy is complex, and I will not have the space to discuss some of the key ideas of his system, such as *spanda*, the vibratory essence of the cosmos, a kind of eleventh-century string theory, or his notion of the rapture of wonder, *camatkāra*, that transports us beyond mundane existence. For my purposes here, these other ideas, the vibrational throb of *spanda* and the capture of the transcendent through wonder reflect back on the notion of a fundamental identity between the multiplicity of beings, from us ordinary individuals here at this conference, down to the merest insect,[4] and up to the supreme divine. The glue in his conceptual framework that girds together the divine as One and us as the Many is the grammatology of a magical linguistic transformation that seeps through and links both One and Many through the Word.

BHARTṚHARI: THE EARLIER THEOGRAMMATICAL TRADITION

The grammatico-theological tradition that I draw from derives from Abhinavagupta's understanding of the mystical language of the mantra, the tradition of the secret, magical word. However, this tradition begins much earlier than Abhinavagupta and reaches an extraordinary level of sophistication as early as the fifth century C.E., with the grammarian Bhartṛhari. In this tradition grammar takes on a profound soteriology, as the summum bonum of all spiritual endeavor. As Bhartṛhari tells us, "Through recourse to the study of grammar, one attains the supreme state of liberation."[5] Not a modest claim, for this school the study of grammar is salvific precisely because the supreme absolute, *Brahman*, is itself the word, *śabda tattva*. As Bhartṛhari puts it in the opening to his *Vākya Padīya*, one of the definitive texts for this redemptive school of grammatology, "The word is the absolute, Brahman; it is without beginning or end. It is the imperishable essence of being."[6] By understanding grammar, those rules that define the combinations of words, one is able to purify speech. That is, grammar is the cure for maladroit speech, and beyond this, it is through this cure that one finds the door to the final salvation, release from worldly existence.[7]

Notwithstanding the enlightenment promised by Derrida's science of "grammatology" as deconstruction, dismantling from within—one might venture, a metaphysical analogue of the movie *Alien*, nevertheless, in India at least, the enlightenment that grammatology promises is a constructive enterprise. Still, like Derrida's understanding of identity as inextricably embedded within the grammatological structure that contains it, the idea of the word as essence in Bhartṛhari's grammatology is also embedded within. It is immanently implicated in the construction of the world, via its articulation of the world. The word sets in motion the process by which the world is created. To continue on with Bhartṛhari's opening of the *Vākya Padīya*, he tells us,

> Through its existence as meaning it appears to manifest, and from this the world is set in motion. It [the word] is one alone. This is the teaching. Yet, different energies [fem.] reside in it. Even though it is indivisible, because of these energies it appears as divided.[8]

Language then, is both the essence and genesis of being. Moreover, even though it exists as a singularity, as "one alone," internally, the word contains within it different energies—and here these energies are understood within the tradition that Abhinavagupta elaborates upon as goddesses to whom one would appeal for aid. The One contains within it the Many, as goddesses who then generate the multiplicity of the many that constitute the world. This grammatological formulation of the word encapsulates the paradoxical conundrum that we are charged with addressing here at this conference, the relation of the One to the Many.

Śabdatattva is literally the principle, or archetype (*tattva*) of the word (*śadba*). In this sense, one discovers a resonance with the Western idea of the logos, even as the multiplicity of gendered energies strikes a dissonant chord with the Western formulation of the logos. A plethora of goddesses as energies, undifferentiated in the indivisible unity of the One might seem untoward, even blasphemous, in the framework of the logos, yet in this context, these energies function as the powers of the One, which enable its freedom and capacity to unfold into the diversity that is the world. In this, there is both identity of these energies and the One that is the word, and the elaboration, the sequential articulation of the word as it transforms into ordinary speech, enacting an evolution (*pariṇāma*) of language and of the world.

ABHINAVAGUPTA'S THEOGRAMMATOLOGY

Abhinavagupta expands on the earlier tradition of the grammarians, to fit it into his own Tantric world, rife with the complex coding of mantras, magical words that are repeated over and over in a ritual context with the goal of granting the reciter supernatural powers. Mantras are foundational for Tantric rites, forming the central basis of nearly every ritual occasion. Mantras were understood to be the sonic body of the deity; functioning performatively, they instantiate the power of the divine to effect physical transformations in the mundane world, causing the rains to come, warding away illness, granting one wealth.

The text that I primarily draw from here, the *Parātrīśikā Vivaraṇa* represents Abhinava's synthesis of the grammar tradition into a theology that melds grammar and goddess. This text is approximately a hundred pages in Sanskrit; it is a commentary by Abhinavagupta on a very short Tantric scripture, the Parātrīśikā, thirty-seven verses revealing the secret essence of the Trika, the three goddesses. The root text of thirty-seven verses is framed as a dialogue between the fierce Tantric god Bhairava and the goddess (*Devī*). In this root text, the goddess asks Bhairava to teach her the highest secret (*mahāguhyam*) by which one achieves magical powers, through a particular Tantric teaching called the teaching of the Clans (*kaulika*). Bhairava gives her the teaching, the secret highest knowledge of enlightenment, known as "*anuttaram*," literally, "the unsurpassed," including the secret mantra,[9] the magical formula associated with this teaching of the Trika. Abhinavagupta relates this teaching of the *Trika*, literally "the Three," as the teaching of Parāvāk, the Supreme Goddess of Speech seen through a modality of three perspectives, where deity unfolds into the three grammatical persons of speech, the I, the You and the It.[10]

Abhinavagupta's one-hundred-page commentary takes us far beyond what is apparent on the surface in this very short thirty-seven-verse root scripture. He understands the text through the lens of language, and he uses the dialogue as a way into his own profound philosophical contemplations on the interpenetrations of language in the world and the divine. Language in his exegesis is the intermediating link between the One as the divine and the Many as the world. In this he outlines four levels of language: (1) spoken words that we commonly understand as speech (*vaikharī*); (2) speech on a more subtle level, which is not spoken but which forms in the minds of speakers (*madhyamā*); (3) speech that is not yet articulated, but rather seen (*paśyantī*), and which operates as a conceptual structuring modality (this level of speech might be in some respects analogous to Judith Butler's understanding of language as structuring the very possibilities for our identities or Benjamin Whorf's idea that language limits the possibilities for what we can think);[11] (4) the highest and most subtle level of speech (*parā*, also *Parāvāk*, the goddess), which is the essential condition for not only communication, but even for sentience.

Elsewhere[12] I have argued that within an Indian context, mantras operate as a powerful, primogenial, and performative language, analogous in some respects to the performative coding functions of DNA, or computer code in our world. Like the transfer of information with DNA and computer code, this coding information acts as a template to effect the structures of our physical world. There is a performative aspect to the mantra, which makes things happen. In Abhinava's view, it is, in fact, the articulation of language as it operates on the objective plane of physical reality that actually causes the physical manifestation of the world. Yet mantras differ in one respect from binary and biochemical codes; they do not follow a merely impersonal operation of the laws of physics and biochemistry or mathematical computation. One finds, in addition in the idea of the mantra, an intentional agentive element. That is, language works because the goddess of speech, Parāvāk, Parāśakti, intertwines and penetrates into the essence of being and of beings, and generates the capacity for the transfer of information, for meaning to arise. As Abhinava notes,

> That [goddess] resides as the essence of what is known as hearing. By her own freedom she gives a sense of coherence as a meaningful whole to what is otherwise a collection of letters vibrating as a mass in a confused formless sequence. Without that, even as one hears the particular words, the words are submerged in a confused noise causing one to say in common parlance, "I don't hear."[13]

The goddess as speech becomes the subject hearing speech, and when she chooses, then words convey meaning; they have coherence. Not an automatic process, Abhinava's system entails a theological immanence at the heart of the process of communication.

This immanence is what makes it possible for the divine, as the One, to reflect itself in a variety of positions, as subject and as object. The structure of language as grammatological system reflects the division of the one into the multiplicity that becomes the subject, the object and the relationship between them as the syntax of the sentence. Abhinava's idea of language, along with the dualisms imbricated in any linguistic system, itself undergoes a rich metamorphosis into the living performative language of mantra, the magical word. Language naturally expands and evolves into the multiple positions that make up grammatical syntax. As such, it is both the essence and genesis of being. For our purposes, Abhinava's understanding helps us rethink the relation between the One and the Many as a dialectic of language.

THE DIALOGUE

As I mentioned earlier, as a nondualist Abhinavagupta's philosophy posits a single divine substratum for all of reality. Nor does he, like his earlier compatriot Śaṁkara, take the position that the multiplicity of the world is an illusion. Rather he uses language to mediate between the multiplicity and the One. In this case, the context of his exegesis on these thirty-seven verses offers for him a way to unpack this apparent paradox of the singularity of the divine required by a monist worldview in the face of the multiplicity of the world. In fact, the very structure of his scriptural source, these thirty-seven verses framed as a dialogue, demands the incorporation of multiplicity, the other as conversation partner. That is, from the outset, revelation posits an unavoidable duality in the very mode of the revelation, the dialogue.

In his exegesis Abhinavagupta tells us that the form of language as dialogue is the unfolding of language through the four levels, evolving from its original unity within the goddess as pure subjectivity, the "I" (*aham*). For communication to occur in conversation, in dialogue, there needs to be some point of contact, of unity. This point for Abhinava is the unity of consciousness as divinity, the "I" (*aham*) of the goddess on the level of speech as *parā*, the highest, most primordial, and undifferentiated level of speech. It entails a universality that is the essence of sentience and which is the secret link as the goddess that connects us all, allows us to communicate with each other. This speech, which is none other than a goddess, evolves to the grosser differentiated levels of speech through an act of grace, to *paśyantī* down to *vaikharī*, the level of gross physical speech, allowing the actual words of the text's dialogue. Thus, the dialogue is the unfolding of speech to the mundane level as an act of grace, which becomes the context for revealing the scripture's secret teaching, the revelation of *anuttara*.[14]

With this explanation, Abhinavagupta plays upon a pun. The secret revelation is the doctrine of *anuttara*, the "unsurpassed." Meanwhile, the revelation itself takes the form of a dialogue, of question and answer, as Abhinava notes, "*praśna-uttara*."[15] The goddess asks the "question," *praśna*, and the god Śiva replies with the answer, the Sanskrit "*uttara*." The answer is the revelation of the secret teaching, "*anuttara*." *Anuttara* means the highest knowledge, and it also happens to be the negation of the word *uttara*, as the prefix "*an*" in Sanskrit negates the word it precedes, just as in English, the prefix "un" negates what it precedes, as in "unavoidable." Thus Abhinava points out that the pun in the word "*anuttara*" indicates that this secret teaching is in fact, literally a "nonanswer." The "nonanswer" to the dialogue, he tells us, signifies a shift to a nondualism. As Abhinava explains, both the question and its answer are contained within the goddess, who is pure consciousness, an encompassing awareness. At the core, the give and take of dialogue gives way to a unity of the One that precludes the need for an answer; it is a "nonanswer" since it contains within itself both question and answer.

At the same time, even as it remains the One, Abhinava points out that the use of *"anuttara"* as the idea of the supreme also carries with it the implication of two because the very form of the word is the comparative. Thus the word "anuttara" carries a double function: Its meaning denotes the superlative form; at the same time the grammatical form itself suggests the comparative. Here, Sanskrit grammar forms the comparative by adding the suffix *-tara*, which we see at the end of the word *"anut-tara."* It would have been possible to instead use the superlative, the *-tama* suffix, in the word *"anut-tama,"* which would also mean the "unsurpassed," in the superlative. This is like the difference between the English words "greater" and "greatest," where the *-er* suffix is the comparative and the *-est* suffix is the superlative.

Abhinava discusses at some length the choice that the scripture of the goddess of speech takes to dub the highest secret teaching with a comparative form rather than a superlative form. This comparative form in the word *"anuttara"* indicates the presence of the other, since the very form by virtue of comparison inherently implicates the presence of a second, to whom the first is compared. Not so with the superlative form, he tells us. The superlative remains alone; the very form of the superlative lacks the other, as rival or counterpart.[16] Even with this, Abhinava is at pains to make it clear that the singularity of the One that the superlative implies is in no way missing from the use of the comparative. In this way, the grammatical form of the word *"anuttara"* implicates both the idea of the One and of Two. Perhaps we might profitably use here a maxim that Abhinava employs elsewhere—the eye of a crow—to understand him. The comparative form in a sense functions like the eye of a crow, which oscillates back and forth between two distinct representations.[17] This, for us, is a odd figure of speech; it derives from a bit of Indian folklore that supposes that a crow has only one eye, which moves alternatively from one socket to the other, back and forth, to encompass two very different perspectives via dialogue and comparison.

This sophisticated exegesis of grammar presupposes a kind of faith in the power of grammar to signify more than a merely conventional usage. In fact his use of a pun is not mere wordplay, but carries as well an instantiation of this doctrine of language as the structuring basis of the cosmos in this grammatico-theology. The pun demonstrates the power of words to reveal in their basic forms, as letters and syllables, the underlying order and meaning of the cosmos. Words are a template for reality; they act to convey the code of life, a kind of linguistic DNA. Their forms, grammatical and syllabic, carry profound clues to reveal the underlying nature of the universe. More than this, by knowing the secret syllabic codes which map the universe, one is able to manipulate the topography, to effect changes in the universe, since this code is capable of generating the shape of our physical reality. We will see this play out more precisely later with his mapping of the cosmos onto the alphabet.

GENERATIVITY

We should note one more point in Abhinava's explication of *anuttara*. Even as this secret highest teaching, the *"anuttara"* is a "nonanswer" to the question, since it signifies the singularity of the One, at the same time in an exuberant exegetical maneuver, Abhinavagupta demonstrates the generative power of language. In a gesture resonant of Barthes, indeed a kind of Barthean *S/Z* on steroids, Abhinavagupta gives us sixteen different meanings of the word *"anuttara."* These range from understanding *"anuttara"* as that perspective beyond which nothing is, because it is the unbarred, expanding, delight of wonder (*camatkāra*) in one's own self;[18] to the understanding that there is no liberation, enlightenment, because the world itself is not really in a state of bondage; to understanding *"anuttara"* as embedded in the essence of the mundane existence of everyday affairs; to understanding *"anuttara"* as that which cannot be limited or separated; to understanding *"anuttara"* as a timeless state in which there is no suggestion of motion or sequence.[19]

For our purposes here, we can glean from his treatment of *"anuttara"* an idea of language in this grammatico-theology as affording a bridge, seamlessly shifting between the one and the many, between a transcendent timeless vision and the mundane world. Language is inherently generative and perspectival, he demonstrates in his extravagant multiplication of meanings for words. Furthermore, he employs this technique throughout this text, again with the word *"kaulikasiddhi"* and with the word *"mahābhāgā,"* the word *"sadyaḥ,"* among many others, indeed, even for the word *"devī,"* "goddess." There is no single right way of interpreting a word. Instead, he offers a prism of meanings, each reflecting a different perspective. Together they form a richly dynamic and ever-expanding production of meaning. Language indeed, as goddess, as we might expect from a goddess,[20] is profoundly generative. The goddess of speech multiplies things. She causes the world to unfold precisely because she contains within her a generative power. As Abhinava tells us, "The highest secret [*anuttaram*] is the one from whose womb billions of infinite creations flow forth. As it has been said, 'from which this whole proceeds.'"[21]

THE THREE PERSONS

The expansion from the One into the vast multiplicity, this infinite number of creations which is the universe, occurs through the generativity of language. Moreover, the structure of language mirrors in its grammar the structure of the cosmos. In the structure of language as three grammatical persons, the "I," the "You," and the "It," we find the whole of the universe contained. Quoting from the *Tantrasamuccaya*, Abhinavagupta tells us, "The whole universe exists always, in every way immersed in the three grammatical persons, in the activities of the all-knowing down to the daily routine of worms."[22] Describing the essence of the Trika philosophy, Abhinava explicates.

> Indeed, everything in the world has the nature of the Three, of *nara* [the human], *Śakti* [the goddess] and *Śiva* [the god]. This is the form of the *Trika*, the Three. There, whatever is alone in its own nature situated solely in the form of insentience, that is chiefly the nature of *nara*, as for instance, in the statement, "a jar is standing [here]." This refers to the third grammatical person only, leaving aside (the first and second grammatical persons). When, however some thing is addressed with the word "you," even though it is still a thing, a "this," separate from the person calling it, then the feeling of "this" is veiled, covered over by the "I" feeling of the person addressing it. That is the form related to *Śakti*, the second grammatical person, as in "you are standing [here]." And here the meaning of the word "you," the second grammatical person is indicated in the process of address. That is, one gets the idea, "just as I am standing [here], so in the same way, this other also is here [hence, an idea of two]." With this, the freedom of wonder in the unbroken feeling of "I" is the form of the first person speaking. In the sentence "you are standing [here],"

the one who is addressed assimilates to the wonder of the unbroken "I" of the speaker. This he points out by the second grammatical person with the meaning of "you." This is the Goddess Parāparā, the Goddess of differentiation. Again, when there is the unbroken sense of wonder in the apprehension of the "I," complete in its freedom, without any dependence on another, as in the sentence, "I am standing [here]," that is the first grammatical person, which is the highest Goddess Parā.[23]

That is, Abhinavagupta's conceptual framework for classifying the various entities in the world divides along three categories of Śiva, Śakti, and nara, which are the grammatical first, second, and third persons. Each of the three grammatical persons marks a degree of subjectivity, thus generating a scale from the pure subjectivity of the first person to the condition of being an object designated by the third grammatical person. Sentience or life itself in this framework is the function of the subject, the first grammatical person. In a sense, one can see a similar notion in Descartes's *cogito ergo sum*, "I think, therefore I am." Descartes comes to be convinced of the reality of his own existence only by ultimately appealing to his experience of subjectivity. The "I am" derived from the subjective experience of hearing himself think is not such a far cry from Abhinavagupta's location of sentience in the unbroken sense of wonder that arises from the feeling of "I" (*aham bhāva*).

Yet the interesting irony of it is that Descartes's conceptual scheme, linked as it is with the scientific revolution, then enabled a systematic shift to a prioritization of the objective pole of experience. The method of science is a reduction of the other to object. The "objectivity" that guarantees the universality of science works also to destroy the innate life of the other precisely by making it into object. In contrast, Abhinava's privileging of the subjective pole of experience, the "I" as the "highest Goddess Parā," generates a mystical science, of ritual symbolic identifications. In this perspective, language does not simply describe reality. Rather, it creates reality through the power it engenders by subjectivity. The subjectivity inherent in the use of the magical language of the mantra is the method for a shift into multiplicity, the multiple instantiations of empathy as the "I" takes on the perspective of a wider world, enlivening the self and the world through the generativity that language enables.

The sense of "I," the first grammatical person, is in fact for Abhinava the very essence of what it means to be alive, to be conscious. It is subjectivity writ large. This sense of the first grammatical person is more than our quotidian understanding of grammar. Here, it entails the rapture of wonder and is none other than the highest goddess, the goddess of speech in her first stage as she evolves out of herself the creation of the world.

Grammar drives the system. In Abhinavagupta's formulation the linguistic comprehension of the world takes priority over any sort of nonarticulated objective fact. That is, there is not a world "out there" to which language corresponds, a mapping of words onto a reality. Rather, the primary locus of reality stems first from the linguistic frame. Words are primary, the more real phenomenon, and the objective world of things—what we usually think of in our factually dominated and fact-infatuated world as reality—this is for Abhinava less real, precisely because it drifts away from the sense of subjectivity.

Yet even with this demarcation of subject and object, the positions are not fixed. When we refer to a jar as "it," the jar takes on the position of the object. However, as Abhinava notes above, when the other, whether jar or person, is addressed as "you," then that other takes on some of the life of the "I-feeling" of the person talking. The "you" stands at an intermediate point, when differentiation is beginning, but where there is both the presence of subject and object. Nor is this process confined only to clearly sentient beings, humans, like ourselves. Abhinava tells us, "Even the lifeless third person, if it sheds its lifeless form can take on the first and second person forms. [For example,] 'listen, o stones' and 'Of mountains, I am Meru.'"[24] Here the stones, by being addressed in the second person take on the life of second person address. The second example he gives, "Of mountains I am Meru," is spoken by the god Krishna to the warrior Arjuna in the classic Indian text of the Bhagavad Gītā; here Abhinava tells us, the mountain takes on the "I" feeling of the first grammatical person, transforming it from object to subject. With this, its essential reality shifts from lifeless object to sentient subject.

Even though the "you" indicates the duality of two and a degree of separation, it displays only a partial separation. It also partakes of a sense of the rapt wonder that is the condition of being the subject. As such, both the "I" and the "you" sustain a freedom that comes with consciousness, a freedom that resists relative distinctions of bigger or smaller. This innate consciousness of the "I" and the "you" affords them a measure of universality. "He," "she," and "it" of the third grammatical person encode a gender in their grammatical forms, but not the first and second grammatical persons. The "I" and the "you" are both genderless; that is, they can partake of both genders.[25]

Elsewhere Abhinava notes that the first grammatical person also correlates to the singular. Unlike English, which contains only the singular and the plural, Sanskrit contains the singular, the dual, and the plural. Following an intuitive logic, Abhinavagupta explains that the second grammatical person, the "you," is correlated to the dual, and the third person is related to the plural. This classification again reflects the evolution from the One to the Many, with the singular associated with the One and the plural with the Many. Again, demonstrating the process that we saw above where the third or second person becomes absorbed in the rapt wonder of the "I" feeling of the first person, grammatically when the first person and the second or third person are together in a sentence, as in "you and I are standing here," the verb form (in Sanskrit) assimilates to the first person (with "standing" in the first person in Sanskrit). That is, the "I" has the capacity to absorb into its own rapturous delight whatever it touches. As Abhinava reminds us again and again, "Nevertheless, by contact with the strength of the Self, a person becomes equal to that [Self]."[26] That is, the subjectivity of the "I" has the power to transform whatever it contacts, bestowing life on the mere object or stone, through a participation in the life of the subject.[27] The power of the Self is in fact, its position of subjectivity.

In this context, one gets the sense that the operative paradigm is contagion. Like the epic story of Rāma whose mere touch, his toe stubbing the stone that is the cursed wife, Ahalya, causes her to come back to life, the rapt wonder of the "I" feeling powerfully slides into anything it can reach, granting life in the process. This idea is pervasive in the Indian context, illustrated especially in the pan-India concept of *darśana*, or vision of the deity. In daily Indian religious life, one goes to the temple to take the vision or *darśana* of the deity or one takes the *darśana* of a holy person. The mere vision entails a kind of contagious exchange by visual contact that transforms the person.[28]

For Abhinava, the transformation from lifeless object to sentient subject is possible precisely because "everything has the nature of everything."[29] This central maxim of his philosophy encapsulates the flow of consciousness, a flow that always proceeds from the point of grammatical subjectivity, which is the generative matrix. This map of the world is one where the "I" is the genesis that unfolds into the world. Language is what facilitates this, via the goddess of speech, Parāvāk.

Indeed, this goddess of speech, Parāvāk, is herself the "I," as the powerful performative language of mantra, in Sanskrit, *aham*. So we see,

> The powerful *mantra* of this visible world is the Goddess of Speech, Parāvāk. She is the *mantra "aham"* ["I"]. Her innate and spontaneous essence is the rapture of wonder [*camatkāra*]. As it is said, "all visible phenomena rest in the Self, which is the 'I'- feeling." This is a secret beyond all secrets.[30]

Encoded in the mantra *"aham,"* the "I," which is the goddess of speech, is the grammatical architecture of cosmogony. A kind of linguistic DNA, each of the letters of *aham*—the *"a,"* the *"ha,"* and the *"m"*—encapsulates, and indeed generates the unfolding of the world. The *"a,"* the first letter of the alphabet, signifies the power of transcendent Śiva, again recapitulating the first grammatical person. The *"ha"* signifies the second grammatical person. The letter *"ha"* in Sanskrit, called *visarga*, literally means "emission" and in this theogrammatical cosmology points to the emission of the world. This correlation derives from pronunciation. If one tries to say *"ha,"* one notices the breath coming out, standing in as the microcosmic equivalent of the macrocosmic creation of the world. In this case, the *"ha,"* which is the "you," designates the shift from subject as the subjective sense of I moves away from the self into the duality of the other, just as our breath, which is life, escapes our bodily form when one pronounces *"ha."* The letter *"m"* constitutes the third grammatical person, the objective pole of experience. In the *"m"* rests the objectified essence of the other, the crystallization of the many as inert object.

Moreover, the idea of "I" operates on more than one level. In its pristine consciousness as goddess of speech, the "I" enfolds within itself the whole that manifests as the world. It encompasses this whole as modes, the modes of subject, of subject as object in the notion of "you" and of mere object. The "I" exists as latent or manifest form in all three grammatical persons; whether the subjective pole or the objective pole predominates depends on the mode.

On the level of the microcosm, within the individual person, the process also operates as a replication, a kind of fractal repetition of the cosmic creation. Each moment every individual divides up and maps the world using these three grammatical persons. When an individual rests within the rapture of the "I," there is the sense of the fullness of wonder, a state of bliss, and a kind of momentary enlightenment.

On the less pristine level, the level of ordinary egoity, which is not in this system (and perhaps not in ours either) considered such a good thing, the merely egoic "I" (*ahaṃkāra*—"I-doing" rather than rather than *ahaṃbhāva*—"I-feeling") becomes a split self that mistakes the objective element, the third person in the letter "*m*" for the first person in the letter "*a*." In this case, the small-minded egoity of the *aham*, the "I" is constituted through the transformation of the initial pure subjectivity of the letter "*a*" in through the duality of "*ha*" and then into the objectified condensation of self into the "*m*," as *aham*, resulting not in the whole as harmonious release of creative proliferation of the world as the multitude but a constricted confusion of the subject and the object.

Thus, the word itself as mantra, mantra which is the goddess of speech, as the "I," *aham*, itself figures and effects the sequence of cosmogony, beginning with the first grammatical person and flowing outward into the proliferation of multiplicity that is the *nara*, the third grammatical person, the many that constitute the world. The world is created essentially linguistically, as an expansion outward from the position of subjectivity into the multiplicity of the object that is the world. This happens on both a cosmic level, as the action of gods and on the individual human level in every moment of thought, indeed, as we saw above, even for a mere worm. "*Aham*," spoken or recited, encapsulates and performatively reenacts this process. This is a great secret for this Tantric tradition, one linked to a ritual and performative exercise. It is also a great secret because it gives a code, the underlying mechanism that explains the grammatical constitution of the world as subject and object, linking creativity and even sentience to the grammatical relationship between subject and object.

MAPPING THE ALPHABET

The understanding of the alphabet as map and code of the cosmos figures all the way down to earth and water and the other elements, to sound and the ear, to the mind, the intellect, to time, and desire, up to the highest deity, Śiva. The letters of the alphabet function as a kind of secret linguistic code of reality, a kind of DNA that can be manipulated through mental repetition—which is to tap into the subject mode—to then effect changes in the material world, which exists in the mode of object.

Mapping the alphabet onto the world is no doubt a structuralist venture: the quest for the master code that can explain and generate all of life. Interestingly, Abhinavagupta's understanding of the system entails an already sophisticated displacement of the hubristic reductionism implicated in a structuralist map of the cosmos. As he maps the alphabet onto the categories of what exists, earth or sound or time, he draws in again a perspectival approach, based on the four levels of language. What on one level correlates with a particular letter, the "la," for instance, with the limiting power of time, on another level corresponds to the sense of taste in a counterreflection. This can occur because, as we saw earlier, "everything is the nature of everything." The very nomenclature, *bimba*, which means "reflection" and *"pratibimba"* which translates as "counterreflection" deflects away from a kind of positivist summary of the world. In this view, there are only reflections and counterreflections. This moves toward a perspectival appreciation where the mode of subject is the only real origin. As language evolves through the levels of speech, from the highest level to the level of gross speech, and as the mode of awareness shifts from subject to object, the perspective shifts, generating the multiplicity that is the world. Running through the whole as the thread giving life on every level as she shifts from mode to mode is the goddess of speech, who is the "I," the position of the subject.

. . .

What does it mean to understand grammar as the template, the code defining reality? It places us in a very different relationship to the world than that we are used to in a twenty-first-century Western existence. It pulls us away from a positivist view of reality into something more akin to a kind of virtual reality, where our mental states and mental constructions of reality lead the way. This grammatical metaphysics might be profitably compared with some postmodern thought, for instance, the postfoundational decentering of positivism that Derrida suggests. Yet this view comes with an unexpected theological twist that reinstates a kind of structuralist and incongruently magical view of the world. The priority that Abhinavagupta gives to the subjective pole of experience as a universal point of origin certainly offers a radically different center, yet it does not devolve into a relativism. We find instead a vision where speech begins as the One, as a goddess whose essence is subjectivity, the "I," and yet this One is able to both generate and link to the Many through subjectivity, since as Abhinavagupta tells us, "there is no speech that does not reach the heart."[31]

❧ One and the Many: The Struggle to Understand Plurality within the Indian Tradition and Its Implications for the Debate on Religious Plurality Today

S. WESLEY ARIARAJAH

Every summer, in the month of July, the Ecumenical Institute of the World Council of Churches in Geneva (Ecumenical Institute, Bossey) brings together a group of about twenty Christians, Jews, and Muslims for about three weeks to live and learn together. They are also given the opportunity to participate in one another's worship practices to the extent they are able to do so. To facilitate their interaction, a Jewish rabbi, a Muslim imam, and a Christian minister/theologian are each invited to speak on two mornings to the multifaith group about their respective religious traditions. During the last two years I was asked to carry the responsibility of "explaining" the Christian faith to this group. The expectation was that I would teach the Christian faith on the first morning and the history of the church, especially in relation to the Jews and Muslims, on the second! It is a wildly ambitious undertaking but a challenging and rewarding task for the presenters.

What is most challenging about it is that one had to explain the Christian faith to Jews and Muslims in the presence of Christians from many parts of the world and drawn from many traditions of the church (Roman Catholic, Orthodox, and Protestant). It had to be done in ways that do not offend the Jewish participants, some of whom are Orthodox Jews from Israel, and the Muslims, who have problems with Christians because (in the words of one of the Muslim participants), they have "distorted the story of Nabi Isa [Jesus] by calling him the Son of God and a member of the Trinity." Muslims would never accept the concept of the "Triune" or the formula of "One God—Three persons." For them, Trinity is a form of tritheism that Christians refuse to admit; and they have compromised the oneness of God both by attributing divinity to Jesus and by calling him the Son of God. Much of the discussion time is spent on the problem of Trinity. I am sure you must have guessed it—the folks who are most confused and upset at the end of my sessions are the Christians!

The attempt to deal with the doctrine of Trinity as the entry point to struggle with religious diversity is a late-comer within the theology of religions. The first, as in the case of the early writings of Raimon Panikkar, was the attempt to expand and enrich Christology in order to accommodate the reality of other religious experiences without compromising some of the basic Christian beliefs about Christ.[1] Karl Rahner, for his part, made a heroic attempt to expand and embellish church's ecclesiology to account for the salvific experiences within other traditions. Amos Yong and others have begun a possible pneumatological entry point to the theology of religions.[2] Those not happy with John Hick's pluralistic position, like David Griffin and John Cobb, have been offering positions that qualify Hick's pluralist perspective. Although all of them make significant contributions and new points of entry to the debate, it is no secret that those in the field are aware that we are yet to arrive at an adequate theological response to religious diversity that truly respects the reality of other religious traditions in their "otherness."

Some of the early efforts to deal with religious diversity by expounding the doctrine of Trinity were made by Gavin D'Costa and others. More recent attempts, like that of Mark Heim, are situated within the wider postmodern debate about plurality itself. I am sympathetic to Heim's intention to recognize the full integrity of religious traditions to the point of wanting also to respect different religious ends.[3] However, I am not sure whether the painstakingly detailed attempts at reinterpreting the trinitarian formula to posit divine multiplicity and to relate religious ends to them has had the desired effect of respecting the integrity of other religious traditions in their otherness. In my thinking, all attempts to read religious plurality within the structure of the doctrines of the church result in highly qualified inclusivism of one form or another.

Respect for any form of plurality, let alone religious plurality, has not been the strength of the Christian tradition. The lack of an adequate Christian "theology of plurality" remains the foundational problem for Christian theology, both for its own internal theological enterprise and its theology of religions. The burden of this essay, therefore, is not to question the seriousness with which the issue of plurality is approached in our theme of "the one and the many." Rather, I would raise and deal with two issues that are relevant to our discussion: The first is to question the pluralist interpretation of the Trinity, and to examine the assumption that the answer may lie in moving toward a theology of divine multiplicity. I want to argue that positing divine multiplicity is not necessary to developing a healthy and positive understanding of plurality and to respecting religious diversity in all its dimensions. The second is to examine the nature of "religious ends" (salvations, liberation, release, and so on) and to ask whether it is appropriate to look for divine multiplicity as a way to give them some form of ultimate significance.

As an unrepentant pluralist of the John Hick variety, I want to put forward a position that it is still possible for us to conceive a common destiny for all human life, as also for the cosmos, if we approach the issue of plurality from a different angle. I hope to do so by looking for clues and insights on "the one and the many" within the Indian philosophic tradition.

ONE AND THE MANY IN THE INDIAN RELIGIOUS/PHILOSOPHICAL TRADITIONS

Before plurality and diversity began to receive good press within the Christian/Western theological tradition in our day, India's tolerant approach to religious plurality and its capacity to hold a vast number of *sampradāyas* or religious strands/systems/philosophies under an umbrella has been a matter of surprise and even a puzzle to many Western scholars. It is difficult to dismiss the approach as uncritical acceptance of any and all religious teachings, because the tradition also displayed many internal disputes, debates, and disagreements on religious issues, resulting in a multiplicity of religious and philosophic traditions. In fact, too much romanticism about religious tolerance in India is misplaced; there were periods when "sects" such as Buddhism and Jainism were persecuted for moving away from Hindu orthodoxy and its social ordering around the caste structure. However, on the whole, the Indian tradition does honor the Vedic aphorism, "Truth is one; sages call it by many names." The Hindu tradition had its own struggle with the one and the many in order to arrive at this position and to practice it.

The Indian attempt to grasp the problem diversity is already found in the earliest written scriptures available to us, the Vedas and the Upaniṣads, which are also seen as foundational to all subsequent philosophical reflections that fall within Hindu orthodoxy. Despite the attempts within some of the Upaniṣhadic hymns to engage in systematic reflections on the question of diversity in order to arrive at a considered position, the overall picture constitutes a variety of insights on unity and plurality. As a result, most subsequent schools of thought (with vastly different and even directly opposite approaches to reality) claim the authority of the Vedas for the positions they developed.

In his well-known fourteenth-century *Compendium of all Systems*, Mādhava gives a summary of sixteen different systems known in his day.[4] He also grades them according to his understanding of their "philosophical value," beginning with the *Cārvākas*, the materialists, to whom he gives the lowest position, and placing Saṅkara's absolute nondualism, *advaita*, at the top. Mādhava's classification included many systems that did not necessarily engage in philosophical discussions. Eventually Indian classical thinking accepted six systems as orthodox, insofar as they draw the impetus for their reflections from the Vedas.[5] It is not my intention to engage all these systems in the discussion but to deal with two of them, *Sāṃkhya* and *Vedānta*, which have struggled most in relation to unity and plurality. I would also include a much later system of thought that arose in South India, *Saiva Siddhānta*, which attempted to give a third alternative that moved away from the dualistic/non-dualistic debate between Sāṃkhya and Vedānta.

Not surprisingly, the essential issues can be boiled down to a single question of the natures of, and the relations among, the Ultimate Reality (God), the universe (world), and human beings (souls), although, as will be seen below, existence of an Ultimate Reality as a separate category was contested in Sāṃkhya thought. Once the materialist position of the Cārvāka was set aside, Sāṃkhya had to explain the pluralistic reality of the world, and it does so by insisting that based on all the epistemological tools available to us there are only two entities that need to be recognized, namely, the reality of the material world, and some form of consciousness that is distinct and different from it. The first is *Prakṛti*, the source of all material existence, and the other, *Puruṣa*, the eternal state of consciousness that is unchanging and subsists in the multiplicity of souls.[6]

The plurality represented in the names and forms of the material world has not been the preoccupation within the Indian traditions; they invariably related to the question of singularity and plurality of ontological realities. The plurality and diversity within the material word is explained in Sāṁkhya, by resorting to the principle of evolution or a process of becoming, which, with some variations, is accepted by most of the other systems of Indian thought. Sāṁkhya holds that a primordial, undifferentiated reality, prakṛti (the basis of everything material) through a process of becoming, gets differentiated into a multiplicity of objects; these differentiated objects can also revert to their primordial state. Thus the world is explained primarily in terms of becoming.[7] The potentiality of prakṛti to evolve into such a diversity of objects is possible because of the complexity inherent in prakṛti. Even though it is simple when not manifest, it can, in the process of becoming, evolve into twenty-four *tattvas* or principles of different subtleties. Further, innate to the prakṛti are three constituent *guṇas*, or strands or component characteristics, that are in a state of tension within the primordial prakṛiti. The three guṇas, already speculated about in the Vedic literature, are *Sattva*, the template for balance, or equilibrium; *Rajas*, the template for expansion or activity; and *Tamas*, the template for inertia or resistance to activity. The diverse characteristics of the tattvas and the inherent tension between the guṇas are used to explain the enormous variety and plurality that constitute the material world.[8]

It is not my intention to expound the Sāṁkhya system, which is beyond the scope of our discussion. What is of significance is that for Sāṁkhya, as stated earlier, the plurality of the material world itself did not present a problem of unity and diversity because the diverse is none other than the evolution and differentiation of the primordial prakṛti. Sāṁkhya's position, in this respect, is consistent with the evolving contemporary scientific understanding of the universe as that which emerges and evolves from singularity, which is yet to be fully understood, defined, and adequately named.

Sāṁkhya, however, by recognizing the reality of consciousness as a separate entity from the material, had to work with a dualistic proposition. It is unapologetic about its dualistic perspective, but it gives predominance to the puruṣa over prakṛti as that which is necessary to provide the impetus for the evolution of prakṛti. The existential issue in Sāṁkhya is that the evolved prakriti and pure consciousness (souls) are intermingled. The souls need to be liberated from their bondage to prakṛti because their association with prakṛti hides their true nature as pure consciousness.[9] Patañjali's Yoga-Sūtra, the classical text on Yoga, was developed to enable the souls to liberate themselves from the binding character of prakṛti and enter the state of pure consciousness.

It is significant that Sāṁkhya did not see the necessity to delineate the third category, an Ultimate Reality, or God. The primary reason given is that while the reality of puruṣa and prakṛti are self-evident, there is no evidence to indicate that there is yet another reality to be recognized.

Some of the later schools of Indian philosophy were attracted by the basic structure of the Sāṁkhya system but felt that the system does not give an adequate answer as to the purpose of the evolution of the prakṛti and of the need of the souls (puruṣa) to liberate themselves from their association with prakṛti. The South Indian school of Śaiva Siddhānta deals with this issue by postulating three eternal categories, *Pathi* (Ultimate Reality), *pasu* (eternal souls), and *pāsam* ("evil")—a third ontological category that binds the soul from eternity, hiding its true nature, and preventing it from its identity and association with Pathi, the Ultimate Reality. This third category in Siddhāntic thinking is not the material world but some form of primordial corruption/evil/power of individuation, *malam*, which hinders the identity of the Pathi (God) and the souls. Siddhāntin holds that it is self-evident that, for reasons not known to us, the souls are in bondage to a power that corrupts and hides their true nature, which is its identity with Ultimate Reality. We know through experience that this bondage exists, argued the Siddhāntin, but we shall never know how or why. We also know, through experience, that souls are in different stages of liberating themselves from this bondage.

The souls can be helped to liberate themselves from this bondage only when they come to the realization of their true nature, and the futility of being associated with pāsam. But can this be achieved? At the heart of the Siddhāntic understanding is the conviction that the souls receive liberative knowledge only through experience, *anubhava*. The Pathi, out of its love for the souls, causes the universe to evolve, and endows physical bodies to the souls with faculties like sense organs, mind, will, and so on. The physical universe and the body enable the souls to have experiences, or anubhava. It is through the good and bad experiences accumulated over many lives that the soul is gradually led to the realization of the futility of its attachment to pāsam or the "evil" that separates it from God, and is helped to liberate itself from its bondage.[10]

Again, there is no need to expound the Śaiva Siddhānta system here, except to note that Meykaṇḍar, the founder of the system, argues that we cannot understand the purpose of the universe and human experiences without introducing a plurality of ontological categories. The system sees God, the souls, and a power of evil as eternal categories, but does not give any ultimate reality to the universe. Pathi (God) causes the universe to emerge, evolve, and to dissolve out of māyā, an evolute that has no reality in itself. Sāṁkhya and Yoga, with some qualifications, see the body and the material world as hindrances to the soul's liberation. But Siddhānta looks at the human body and the material world as those that are caused to become, out of the grace of God, for the benefit of the liberation of the souls.

These systems insist that we cannot understand the mystery of existence without positing a plurality of eternal categories. It is important to note that the affirmation of plurality is not about the universe, which, in this view, has no independent existence apart from God, who causes it to become. These traditions, while recognizing a plurality of ontological categories, refuse to move in the direction of attributing plurality or multiplicity to the divine in order to give credence to the plurality and multiplicity within the universe.

The quest to resolve the problem of the one and the many did not stay there. The most radical step in this exploration was taken by Saṅkara, who held that Brahman is the only reality there is. It is important to note that Saṅkara does not say that there is only "one" reality, and that is Brahman. Positing "one" allows the possibility of "many." In his thinking, the Ultimate Reality is beyond numerical considerations and can be spoken of only in terms of its is-ness. But since humans are so conditioned to think in numerical terms, he said that the Ultimate Reality is "not two"—*Advaita*. Brahman simply is. Nothing else is.

It naturally followed that Brahman cannot be objectified, described, or even talked about. Advaita therefore is apophatic in its approach to reality and insists that one can say only what Brahman is not (*nēti, nēti*, not this, not this). However, as a concession to our human limitations and the quest to know, one could speak of Brahman as the "only" reality there is. Again since humans long to know what this only reality is, a concession is given, and Brahman is said to be sat-chit-ānanda, commonly translated as "being," "intelligence," and "bliss." But the meaning and intention behind the

Sanskrit terms runs much deeper: "Sat" is the affirmation that Brahman "is" (and nothing else is). "Chit" is used to indicate that it is a form of "consciousness" that is beyond all forms of intelligence and consciousness that human thought can grasp. And "ānanda" denotes that Brahman is fullness in itself and needs no other reference to be itself.

Advaita, however, does not deny the "reality" of the world. Rather, it insists that the human soul (ātman) and the cosmos are all in the isness of Brahman. Brahman in itself, the sat-chit-ānanda, is Nirguṇa Brahman, and Brahman as perceived as the universe is Saguṇa Brahman. But only Brahman is.

Very often the Advaita system is misrepresented as denying the reality of the world or as not taking it with the seriousness it deserves. How much more real should the world be than being Brahman itself? I quote Anantanand Rambachan on this issue at some length here. According to Rambachan, the Advaita tradition

> neither equates God with the world nor, on the other hand, does it assert the world to possess a reality which is independent from God. Avoiding both positions, it admits that the ultimate reality, in its relationship to the world is a mystery and indefinable (*anirvacaniya*). Without undergoing any change or losing anything of itself, God is both the cause and the source of the world. It has its existence in God, without in any way limiting God. We may view the world in Advaita as the mysterious self-manifestation of God. It is not the infinite plus something else, but the infinite inexplicably appearing as the finite.[11]

He goes on to conclude:

> It is unfortunate that some interpreters of the Hindu tradition have used the world's dependent status to explain it away. It must be remembered that the world is deceptive and false only when we attribute to it an independent reality. This is indeed a false reality. When, however, the world is seen as the mysterious and indefinable creation of God, rooted in God and pervaded through and through by God, it is no longer deceptive, but a celebrative expression of God's unlimited nature. . . . It is not at all necessary, as some have felt, to deny all reality to the world, in order to affirm the oneness and indivisible nature

of God. We do not need to deny the many in order to preserve the one, if we positively view the many as the celebration of the one.[12]

What is intended in Advaita is that behind all the multiplicity of the world, and beyond all the experiences that one can have because of the world, stands a Reality that is the Ultimately Real, which includes the souls. One would enter this realization when one's ignorance (*avidyā*) or blindness to this truth is removed through contemplation and meditation.

Again my purpose here is not to expound the Advaita system or to discuss its strengths and weaknesses but to show its approach to the one and the many and draw its implications for our interest in divine multiplicity and complexity especially as they relate to the Trinity and religious plurality. Before drawing the implications of the Hindu thinking to plurality of religions I would turn to the question whether the doctrine of Trinity lends itself to a move toward divine multiplicity. To do this it is necessary to explore the reasons why Christian theology found it necessary to develop the doctrine of Trinity.

WAS THE DOCTRINE OF TRINITY DEVELOPED TO AFFIRM THE MULTIPLICITY AND COMPLEXITY OF THE DIVINE?

One of the difficulties I have had with Heim's position is the assumption that the doctrine of Trinity lends itself so freely to a more authentic pluralist position, not only in relation to this world but also in whatever is believed to lie "beyond" in terms of religious ends. It is, of course, possible for us to reinterpret the Trinity for our day, but one should wonder whether positing divine multiplicity was ever in the minds of those who developed the doctrine of Trinity in the first instance. In fact, it should be possible to argue that the exact opposite was the intention of the doctrine.

The development of the doctrine of Trinity, the controversies that surrounded it, and the many modifications made to the doctrine to meet objections and doubts as they arose are so complex that one cannot give a convincing argument for any one perspective on the Trinity. The Jewish tradition, out of which Christianity emerged and was embedded in its initial history, was strictly monotheistic. The Greco-Roman world in which its classical Christian theology was gradually taking shape was against all forms of dualism in the interest of preserving the oneness of the Ultimate Reality. Within Greek philosophy the Ultimate was absolute, the unmoved mover.

Parallel to this belief about God, christological debates and disputes were beginning to fall on the side of affirming Christ as fully human and fully divine. The traditions of the church had also begun to speak of the Spirit that fell on the apostles on the day of Pentecost as an experience of God. Do these affirmations, namely the divinity of Christ and of the Holy Spirit, lead to the necessity to conceive some form of diversity or multiplicity within Godhead? No, was the answer, and the concept of the Trinity was developed into a doctrine to protect the oneness of God. Despite these varied experiences of God, all authentic in themselves, God remains one, not many. That's the belief the trinitarian doctrine set out to protect.

The debate, however, did not stop there. Those who wanted to preserve the singularity of the Godhead, spoke of the Son as "begotten" and the Spirit as "proceeding" from the Father, subordinating the second and third persons, while refusing to admit that the concepts of "begetting" and "proceeding from" did involve some form of subordination. Arius could claim that if the Son was "begotten," then, "there was a time when the Son was not!" The concepts of "eternally" begotten and "eternal" procession were developed to deal with this problem. At the same time, those interested in protecting the "integrity" of the divinity of the second and the third persons of the Trinity began to give greater emphasis to the concept of "persons," carrying it beyond the original intentions of the word *persona* (mask, face, or expression) and spoke of the eternal communion of love between the three "persons" of the Trinity (perichoresis), positing a form of tritheism, but refusing to admit that this was the case. These denials, however, indicate that classical theology, while wanting to attribute divinity to Christ and the Holy Spirit, was not inclined to accept any form of plurality or multiplicity within the Godhead. Until process thinking began to make an impact, the classical doctrine of God was an uneasy marriage between the monotheistic God of the Jewish tradition (with one set of attributes) and the Absolute of the Neoplatonic thought (with yet another set of attributes). By insisting on the divinity of the Son and the Holy Spirit and claiming them to be coequal and coeternal, Christianity was, in fact, introducing a form of divine multiplicity. Yet, through its doctrine of Trinity it denied and sought to refute any hint of multiplicity within the Godhead, leaving the church in a state of theological confusion then and now. It is little wonder that at Bossey it was the Christians who were more confused about the doctrine than the Jews or the Muslims.

No religious tradition, including Hinduism, embraces multiplicity and diversity within Ultimate Reality; nor does the doctrine of Trinity in its original intention. One could, of course, posit plurality within Godhead today, but then it would be, in my understanding, a departure from the theological affirmations about God in the Bible and in the traditions of the church.

IS IT NECESSARY TO HYPOTHESIZE DIVINE MULTIPLICITY TO UNDERSTAND RELIGIOUS PLURALITY?

The interest in affirming diversity and multiplicity as the stuff of reality comes from two corners. The first is from some within postmodern scholarship who seek to move away from the excesses of modernist thinking. The affirmation of the affective, relational, and the relative and the celebration of plurality and diversity over against attempts to unify and control with some forms of grand narratives or metanarratives have, in fact, played an important role in freeing the human spirit and liberating areas of life that have been smothered by a purely rational and hierarchical approach to life. I have, however, considerable sympathy for the need for some forms of metanarratives as indispensable for life in community, but this is not the focus of our current discussion.

Does our attempt to respect the authenticity of religious traditions, and our awareness that religious ends are different from each other, require us to root them in some form of divine multiplicity? What fascinates me about the Advaita, as Rambachan argues, is its refusal to accept the "one" and the "many" as alternatives or opposites to choose from. Brahman *is*, and there is nothing else, and yet, Brahman can be experienced at one level of spiritual growth in its full diversity as the phenomenal world. And the world and all the experiences of plurality are not unreal, except in the sense that with spiritual maturity and in deep meditation one would discover that behind all the multiplicity lies divine singularity. In other words, it is singularity that is experienced as multiplicity, because the simple can in fact be experienced as complex and diverse until one is able to experience its true singularity.

It is far from my intention to argue that Advaita or any of the other systems of Indian thought has found the answer to the problem. There are, however, two lessons that one could draw from the Hindu tradition's approach to reality and to religious diversity. The first is that it is indeed possible to take diversity and multiplicity for what they are and to take them seriously without having to root them in some form of divine multiplicity. There appears to be a studied caution against giving ultimate significance to diversity, including religious diversity, for its own sake.

This arises from two interrelated convictions. First is that the Ultimate Reality, or the Divine, by definition, has to be beyond all human perception, knowledge, and comprehension. Moving away from an apophatic approach to speak positively about the Divine is a concession that humans give themselves. It is welcomed, but the truth that the Divine will always remain a mystery has to inform the way we think and speak about religious and philosophic traditions even as we embark on the all-important task of exploring the meaning of existence.

The consequence of this is that all religious and philosophical quests are legitimate and appropriate, but no religious tradition or philosophic system can claim to have arrived at the Truth. Therefore, there would, of necessity, be multiple definitions of the Divine and conflicting truth claims. Different religious traditions and various strands within religious traditions would set different goals and ends. Debate and disagreements over these truth claims and religious ends are also to be expected and are legitimate, for they push the boundaries of the exploration and are the signs of the seriousness of the religious quest. The Sāṁkhya system with its dualism, the Siddhānta, which holds on to three eternal categories, and the Advaita with its strict nondualism are parallel systems within Hindu orthodoxy, although there would be individuals and groups that would make claims of the superiority of one over the other. There are saints and sages within all these systems who claim to have attained the goals and achieved their ends that their traditions hold out, and yet, none of them can claim to have found the Truth. The "Truth" lies beyond all of them.

Thus, even though the goals and ends that religions posit and strive to achieve are serious and fulfilling to their followers, they remain penultimate in the larger scheme of things. I agree with Heim's contention that the religious ends are so diverse that we must take them seriously and not ignore their differences by subsuming them under any one religious end. The difficulty I have with his thesis is when he moves to give ultimate significance to the diversity of ends.

As a Christian, I have a symbol system for my religion with defined commitments and a goal that I seriously pursue. I cannot do otherwise because of the circumstances into which I was born and the factors that had contributed to the development of the symbol system I have embraced. Similarly a Jew, a Muslim, or a Hindu works within a symbol system with practices and goals that are taken seriously within those traditions. Yet, claims to have found salvation, experienced release, attained nirvana, and so on are penultimate in character, for they are still within the universe of human experience and formulated within given symbol systems.

The fact that religions are diverse systems with different ends does not necessarily mean that that cannot relate to a singularity that lies behind all ends, which may not correspond to any of the ends. All religious truths and experiences are relative, and so are all religious ends.

I believe that John Hick was right in insisting that religious traditions are valid in themselves and should be accepted in their diversity and otherness. The search for meaning within this diversity and the ethical quest to see the possibility of creative relationships within this multiplicity moved him to posit that these multiple religious traditions are all turned toward what he called the "Real." The real needs to remain undefined because it has to remain the Truth that is beyond all the truths realized in the different traditions. He never equates the Real to the God of the monotheists or to understand any singularity it may suggest as monarchical or totalitarian. Singularity does not necessarily mean monarchy; nor is plurality necessarily relational. Many who interpret and criticize Hick appear to miss the subtlety of his argument, or they create of him a "straw man" to argue with.

The pluralist position that Hick has proposed is by no means perfect, nor does it answer all the issues related to religious plurality. But it is still the best way forward to fully respect the diversity of religious traditions and to respect their respective goals. The proposition they all are turned toward the "Real" is based on the realization that none of the religious traditions, despite their deep differences with others on the path, goals, and ends, has been open to a multiplicity of ends to human life, nor has any of them found it necessary to expound divine multiplicity as a way to account for or understand diversity.

Differential Pluralism and Trinitarian Theologies of Religion

S. MARK HEIM

The intensity of my interest in this topic stems from the reality I see before me on a regular basis. As one student with a particularly varied family and personal background said to me, "I am the many I am trying to make one." The tradition of thought about these issues may be philosophical, but the situation on which it bears is increasingly personal and immediate. Pluralism is less and less a voluntary adventure. If it does not come with the conditions of our birth, it is hard to avoid on our life paths, whether one pursues rigorous education, success in the business world, work in government, vocations in medicine or social service. For all of these, pluralism has become part of the itinerary, implicit or explicit. With regard to religious diversity, I think particularly of individuals who—by virtue of a hybrid heritage, serial belongings, or chosen combinations of practices—address issues of pluralism not as an external prospect but an internal reality. The one and the many is a question of personal wholeness and integration. My seminary has developed a deep relationship with our neighboring rabbinical school, and this conjunction has attracted (or in cases unveiled) persons in both our communities with profound, sometimes tangled connections not only with both Jewish and Christian historical traditions, but with both of them as living identities. In this sense, our institutional partnership is only slowly catching up with lived experience.

Entire communities—and I think particularly of Christian congregations—have a somewhat similar dynamic. Some Christian congregations face these questions not solely or even mainly in terms of dialogue or mission with an external other, but in terms of how to understand and harmonize the reality of the elements of various traditions that already live within the experience of their members or as part of the community's practice. A church I recently visited may be somewhat unusual in offering tai chi and yoga as an explicit part of its own spiritual program—in this case, with a careful theological rationale about how it understands these to play a role in the Christian life. But even a Christian community that seeks to feed people only from Christian sources must find the way that it does so altered immeasurably by the necessary recognition that all involved (teachers and receivers) operate in knowledge, often very intimate knowledge, of other perspectives and options. It is increasingly difficult to imagine a vital faith identity that does not incorporate an implicit theology of religious pluralism as an integral feature. Questions of the one and the many are not subsequent issues related to the application of one's faith, or reserved for academic speculation about it. They are often the burning, existential focus of the formation (or possibility) of faith itself.

These concerns, the personal and the congregational, are very much in the front of my mind as I come to our topic. It is impossible to divide them from the even wider question of the interaction of varied cultures and faith traditions in our national society and in global affairs. Here, too, a philosophical abstraction has become an urgent matter of statecraft, international policy and effective governance. Whether it is U.S. policy makers who are concerned with national security or the leaders of popular political movements flowering in the Middle East who must consider new patterns for their societies, or social workers delivering health care in an immigrant neighborhood virtually anywhere in the world who must communicate across several cultures, the questions we have the luxury to reflect on here are set as a daily challenge.

At all three of these levels, the personal, the communal, and the social, theories of pluralism are hardly mere ideas. They are patterns of life and action. All the more important that they benefit as much as possible from every type of reflection that can inform and improve them.

DIFFERENTIAL PLURALISM AND TRINITARIAN THEOLOGIES OF RELIGION

The one and the many may be a hardy perennial topic for philosophy, but its urgency in our time comes from our conflicting existential responses to diversity. On the one hand, diversity is a threat and a problem—whether it is the demand for constant choice that individuals face in a wired age, the political challenges of multicultural societies, or the spiraling complexity of global economics where the permutations of connections between labor, markets, and capital escape not only the control of any single political unit but at times the conceptual grasp of participants. On the other hand, diversity is also often a favored solution to difficulties that vex us. Whether lagging educational attainment or economic inequality or social conflict, greater diversity is often part of the prescribed cure: a greater diversity among decision makers and in subject matter or schools of thought. In all these areas we seek a way between too high a level of resolution that compromises difference and too essentialist a notion of difference that blocks communication and accountability.

Issues of religious pluralism reflect the same dynamic. Religious variety is, at once, the germ of recurrent conflict and an enriched pharmacy of healing cures. Religious oneness in the form of jealous absolutism is a nightmare. Religious oneness in the form of unity and sharing is a blessed wonder. Insofar as religion serves many as the largest framework for conceiving the issue of diversity and unity itself, the topic of divine multiplicities has never had such practical importance. Trinity is the Christian avenue to understanding diversity in the divine. This essay focuses on trinitarian theology and, in dialogue with John Thatamanil, explores the extent to which this theology itself may be a genuinely interreligious project.

WHAT KIND OF ANSWER DO WE WANT?

Of course, discussion of the one and the many seeks to plumb the pattern of reality itself. But our theories are inevitably mixed with evaluative dimensions. How much diversity is enough and how much is too much for a valid metaphysic? How much oneness do we need? My own answers to these questions are developed extensively elsewhere, in a trinitarian theology of religious ends.[1] For the purposes of this discussion, I will summarize briefly what it is I want in a theory of religious pluralism. To use the word "want" suggests a certain bald subjectivity when, in fact, I think my views are very much grounded in evidence and subject to argument. Indeed, they have only arisen, for me, out of attention to both. But I use the word to frankly acknowledge that there is an irreducible evaluative dimension in such conclusions, and that views about religion inevitably have a religious dimension.

In regard to religious pluralism I want enough diversity to support the existence of true religious alternatives. It is the reality of this diversity that supports both the validity of conservative exclusivistic claims for "one and only" elements in a tradition and liberal claims that other faiths may contain truths and possibilities not present in my own. And I want enough unity to support the inclusivist hopes of the many religions, the conviction that there is a way to one tradition's religious end from within the path that leads to another's, even from a point far along that path. Such a conviction requires, at the very least, that the traditions themselves not be monolithic.

This requires enough diversity in reality or the divine to ground the validity of at least some religious paths precisely where they have contrasting views and intend different ends than Christian ones. I say "at least some" because no one could have sufficient knowledge to judge this matter for all religious cases. Yet some particular cases appear to merit that conclusion. So, for instance, Buddhist no-self teachings are different from Christian ones about the self, and the end such teachings support is different from a Christian end, but the first appears to me to be valid, and the second appears to be real. I think there is enough diversity in ultimate reality to back up that contention.

This indicates that, because Buddhist teaching and the Buddhist end are grounded in this way, both the universal intent of Buddhism and Buddhism's inclusivist reading of Christianity are valid in a sense that Christianity can acknowledge. That is, Christians can recognize the Buddhist path as a live option that no theological apologetic or philosophical argument can delegitimate at root. And Christians can recognize this for a Christian reason. Buddhist claims are irreducible because they are grounded in God. A trinitarian theology of pluralism is an account of how they are grounded in God.

So how much diversity is enough? Enough to support the different ends and the contrasting teaching of at least several religions. How much is too much? Diversity that makes religious ultimates independent and incommensurate, and therefore presumes that religious practices can be entirely isolated and pure, is too much. To affirm such a view would be to preclude the possibility of a universality that the religions, even in their differences, affirm. The Trinity itself can be thought of as a "divine multiplicity," as a kind of roster of incommensurable ultimates, to ground the diversity of religions in a variety of absolutes.[2] One manifestation of this would be to identify different faiths with different divine persons in the Trinity, religions of the first person, the second, or the third. But such an approach is not consistent with classical trinitarian theology's description of a God whose nature is communion. My view is that the distinctive religious ends are based not in separate persons of the Trinity, but in the various dimensions of the communion (the oneness) among the persons, which are manifest in the different dimensions of relation of the divine with the world. When Wesley Ariarajah expresses the imperative he sees to "conceive a common destiny for all human life and the cosmos," I fully agree with him in rejecting views that rule out such a destiny a priori, or that condemn even the desire for such a destiny (reflected in the specific inclusivist hopes of any religion) as oppressive.[3]

How much oneness is enough? Enough to fund contrasting religions' inclusivist readings and hopes, including the inclusivist hopes of a perspective like John Hick's, which sees the traditions not as secondary means to attain the primary end of one particular tradition, but as primary means to attain a condition intermediate among the aims of all. The limits on this oneness are set by its ability to fund *contrasting* inclusivist readings. I believe there is a common destiny for all human life, if that means that in the end all will be resolved in connection with one divine reality, according to one set of parameters with which the universe consistently abides, whether that is a Buddhist set or a Christian set or an Advaitan one or a Muslim one or some other not wholly consistent with any of these. But I do not believe that this consummation necessarily implies that there would be an identical condition for all humans involved in that destiny or that the humans involved in that destiny would agree about its character.[4]

With this summary of my particular approach, we will turn to the background of trinitarian theologies of religious pluralism, and thus to features shared both by my approach and Thatamanil's.

THE MOVEMENT TOWARD TRINITARIAN THEOLOGIES OF RELIGIOUS PLURALISM

Religious diversity is frequently framed by religious thinkers as a problem. One truth or revelation alone may offer a coherent picture of the world. The problem for adherents of particular religious convictions is to account for the existence and apparent power of other unrelated or even conflicting faiths. Theologies of religious pluralism (or their cognates) historically negotiate religious variety as a challenge to the validity of one universal faith claim. The problem for those who would maintain the validity of religion in general against naturalistic critiques is that religious diversity makes religion an inconsistent witness in its own defense and requires its apologists to face in many directions at once. The "pluralistic hypothesis" advanced by John Hick is a solution to religious variety as a problem in just this sense.[5] Diversity, in both cases, is a difficulty to be negotiated. In both cases, if pluralism is a virtue, the virtue resides in its role as a delivery vehicle for one product. It is an anonymous conduit to others of the benefits of a single tradition, an exquisite tailoring of cultural garb around the same spiritual content.

In much of the Western world, this intellectual perplexity is balanced by a cultural enthusiasm. Pluralism is not so much a problem as an opportunity. On the one hand, religious diversity is an enrichment of individual choice, responsive to our varying temperaments and personal aims and consistent with our assumptions of autonomy. Adherents of one tradition may covet all the benefits of others that can be added without subtraction or substituted at need where my own falters or offends. On the other hand, pluralism reflects our multicultural reality, in which society-shaping traditions from many settings seed the same neighborhoods and households. From this perspective, the only kind of unity that matters is that defined by the limits of a single lifestyle or chosen by a consensual community. That orientation chafes for those of any religion who aspire to see that religion embodied in a comprehensive human polity.

In the past, a "theology of religions" was likely the interest of only a minority in either the popular or academic worlds. Today, for many people whose religious identities are multiple or undetermined, an operational theology of religions may be itself a key core religious commitment, guiding openness to and selective appropriation of material from many religious sources. A theology of religions becomes not the instrument of a tradition but functions as an identity itself. If there is a problem here, it is not a felt threat from the fact of a variety of faiths, but a consumerist insouciance about helping ourselves to others' spiritual goods and filtering out that in any tradition that might inhibit our own interests.[6]

On the intellectual side, we have only begun to move from treating religious diversity as a problem to engaging it routinely as a positive resource.

Comparative theology is a major step in this direction, not the refinement of theories about religions but a regular practice of religious scholarship whose sources stem from different traditions.[7] I believe that trinitarian approaches to religious diversity represent a similar kind of movement. The key shared conviction, in my view, is that if the diversity of religions is in any way rooted in the diversity of the divine life itself, then the heart of the religions, their insights and realizations, become permanent parts of the content of Christian theology even though the privileged access to this content lies outside the traditional sources of Christian theology. The implications of this conclusion are enormous, though they are also as yet unclear and variously understood.

The recent turn among some Christian theologians to the Trinity as the key to the theology of religious pluralism may have been led, at first, by concerns of the first type mentioned above—most notably the question of salvation among those of various faiths. But it has been greatly reinforced by a related but distinct concern for the positive meaning of religious difference. I believe the doctrine of the Trinity offers Christians the deepest grounding for an understanding of religious diversity as a positive gift. Connecting the Trinity (the internal ground of diversity in Christian theology) with external religious pluralism seems to me a marriage made in heaven. But the renewal of trinitarian doctrine in both Catholic and Protestant Western theology (via Rahner and Barth) did not connect sooner with the upsurge in attention to the theology of religions precisely because it is only when the distinctive content of other traditions is viewed in a sufficiently positive light that theologians think to ground that content in the trinitarian nature.[8] As theologies of religion began to approach the traditions as bearing intrinsic value rather than playing strictly provisional or providential functions as delivery vehicles, Trinity came to the fore. A generically positive view of other religions is not sufficient for this purpose. It is only where the contrasts are themselves valued that this dynamic can truly develop.

A trinitarian theology of religions interprets religious pluralism. But the value of a trinitarian theology for this task becomes apparent only under certain understandings of pluralism. David Ray Griffin has helpfully argued that much recent discussion of "pluralist" positions too quickly centered on the views of certain authors. In doing so, a wider spectrum of options was obscured. What Griffin calls generic pluralism has two parts.

The first is a negative statement. It is simply the rejection of "Christian absolutism, the idea that Christianity is the absolute religion, the sole vehicle of divine salvation."[9] The second is a positive affirmation that there are religions "other than one's own that provide saving truths and values to their adherents."[10] Griffin notes that generic pluralism has often been conflated with only one of its subsets, what he calls "identist pluralism." This view holds that "all religions are oriented toward the same religious object ... and promote essentially the same end."[11] A group of influential thinkers (John Hick, W. C. Smith, Paul Knitter) who held that belief and also claimed the title "pluralist" set the impression that the two were identical.

The views of these authors have been tellingly criticized, in Griffin's view.[12] And that has led many to conclude that pluralism itself is invalid and to dismiss under the same heading positions with more legitimate claim to the label. The result is great terminological confusion, reflected in the fact that the people who bear the title meet the generic definition but reject any deeper, real pluralism, whereas John Cobb and I, and others with similar views, do not bear the label "pluralist," though in Griffin's view we merit it on both scores.[13] What the criticism of identist pluralism actually reveals is the need for a better pluralism. This is to be found, he suggests, in another subset of generic pluralism, "differential" or deep pluralism, which holds that "religions promote different ends—different salvations—perhaps by virtue of being oriented toward different religious objects." It is "pluralistic soteriologically and perhaps also ontologically."[14] Although the most prominent "pluralistic" writers may be identist, others are not.

It is my contention that rich trinitarian theologies of religion tend to arise precisely in the area where "differential pluralism" overlaps with that part of the spectrum of inclusivist theologies of religion that moves toward what we might call "differential inclusivism." That is, trinitarian approaches to religious diversity respond to the ironic lack of concrete pluralism in identist pluralist writers and to the banality of inclusivism when it affirms, in other traditions, only what can be found in one's own. There is an elective affinity between trinitarian theologies of religion and differential pluralism. They are both fueled by the recognition that what is true includes what is different.

I can illustrate this from my own learning in this area. In 1987 Raimundo Panikkar, who is the undoubted modern pioneer in relating Trinity to religious pluralism, took part in the manifesto publication *The Myth of Chris-*

tian *Uniqueness*. The common platform in that volume was "a move away from insistence on the superiority or finality of Christ and Christianity toward a recognition of the independent validity of other ways."[15] Virtually all of the other writers were what Griffin calls identist pluralists. Panikkar might make common cause with them on the rejection of Christian absolutism, but I sensed strongly in his essay an approach quite different from that of the others. Panikkar's vivid trinitarian themes, his insistence that *reality* is pluralistic, his entertainment of an eschatological outcome in which all would not be one—all these rested uneasily alongside the assumptions of other contributors. In contrast, in a book of critical responses to *Myth* that followed soon after, I was struck by the essays by Rowan Williams, Gavin D'Costa, and Joseph DiNoia (the first two focused on the Trinity and the last on the validity of religious difference). Like some of their co-contributors, they connected their desire to maintain a particular, universal Christian claim with a respect for the correlative kinds of claims in other religions. That is, they connected the value of concrete Christian difference for them with the value of other concrete religious difference to others. And they saw in the Trinity both a confessional Christian conviction and at the same time a Christian grammar for understanding that the uniqueness of Christ had to be located in, one might say limited by, a wider economy of God's relation with the world. When I read these books, it seemed clear to me that Panikkar, Williams, D'Costa, and DiNoia were onto something of profound importance that simply did not fit in the battle among identist pluralists, on one hand, and inclusivists and exclusivists, on the other, a battle that revolved ironically around a shared belief in a monodivinity with a single possible goal. Who is right about the one? But Panikkar and the others were asking instead, What does it mean to be separately right about the many?

At the time I thought that it might simply be a coincidence that these writers framed their thought in trinitarian terms.[16] But I came to see the logic in that connection: There is at the least an elective affinity between trinitarian thought and approaches that view certain dimensions of difference as fruitfully permanent.[17] In the same work, John Cobb explained his objection to the *Myth* project by rejecting what Griffin calls identist pluralism and arguing instead that religions may have different characters (what Griffin calls differential pluralism). He differed with the *Myth* writers first because he rejected the idea of a common essence to religion and second because he continued to make a certain kind of claim to the superiority of Christianity, though this was posed as a proleptic belief that Christianity had an unsurpassed ability to be positively transformed through dialogue with others.[18] These things nudged me forward in my criticisms of pluralist theologies (of the identist sort) and in the development of a trinitarian theology of religions.

RESPONDING TO CRITICISM OF TRINITARIAN THEOLOGIES

Those who pursue trinitarian theologies of religious pluralism are by no means of one mind. Given the complexities of Christian trinitarian theologies, it is no surprise that the various authors working in this area do not necessarily work from the same assumptions, even before they engage the religions.[19] All of the "in-house" differences between a more social or psychological, a more economic or ontological view of the Trinity that are in play in ordinary Christian theology are present here as well. And they are augmented by a range of new questions that arise from close readings of other traditions. For the purposes of this essay, I focus on John Thatamanil as a trinitarian theologian whose work is exemplary of that second dynamic (thinking Christian Trinity through the lens of other faiths), on his criticism of the existing trinitarian options and particularly on his evaluation of my own. In the wider spectrum of views we stand quite close together, with many shared assumptions and shared critics. I believe this commonality also allows us to explore some important nuances.

Thatamanil's recent stimulating work has brought some significant, if congenial criticism my way. I say congenial, because one could not hope for more appreciative and measured consideration. The experience is to my benefit, as we are essentially moving in similar directions, in a common search for a more adequate theology of religious pluralism. His comments warrant close attention, and this essay is at least a beginning of that conversation.

Thatamanil argues that all extant trinitarian approaches (mine included) are plagued by six difficulties.[20] I have reorganized these in two groups for the sake of discussion:

1. (A) Trinitarian approaches simply slot other religions into preexisting Christian doctrine and terms, already fully formulated without reference to them. (B) Other religions are misread or misinterpreted

in the process in (A). (C) Christian theologians have not thought to allow the insights of other traditions to revise and reconfigure their understanding of the Trinity itself.

2. (D) There is insufficient recognition of diversity *within* religious traditions, so that the whole of a tradition like Buddhism is reduced to some single quality. (E) Because of (D) whole traditions are reified as oriented toward different destinations (in my view, attaining different religious ends). (F) Trinitarian views are still claims to Christian superiority: We have attained trinitarian vision, but others manage only to access some portion of that ideal whole.

I will respond to the second cluster first. Thatamanil has put his finger on something that other readers have found problematic about my approach—and they have expressed that concern with great clarity—the concern that in so emphasizing the differential validity of religious traditions I reify them internally around a single end. The charge is that my affirmation of large-scale diversity among religions goes hand in hand with an internal uniformity in each one that tends to flatten out hybridity and ambiguity. The reality of multiple religious belonging or composite identity is ignored. The supposition is that I am saying religious ends come one to a tradition and those under the umbrella of one religion have but one option.

In my arguments that different religions have realized a relation with God through dimensions and to depths not common in the Christian tradition, I have tried explicitly to address the problems suggested in (D) and (E). It has been a common Christian inclusivist move to recognize strengths in other traditions lacking in Christianity but to maintain that virtually all these things can already be found within the sweep of Christian historical tradition and existing diversity, even if insufficiently developed. The diversity within Christianity is a sign of its comprehensiveness. Christian inclusivists likewise point to diversity in other religious traditions as the foothold for "points of contact" by which persons in those traditions can be led closer to true religion (thus bhakti devotion in theistic Hindu traditions is seen as a way station to the gospel). I simply underscore the fact that these phenomena are reciprocal among religions. No religious tradition is without the same internal richness and differentiated assessment of others. Wilfred Cantwell Smith, whose views I criticize in many respects, was surely correct in pointing to this deep permeability of historical traditions.

Indeed, all this is the premise for the heated internal debates that go on within religions, such as those within Hinduism and Buddhism, which Thatamanil knows so well. The assumption in all such debates is that at some point, *within* the language and terms of one cumulative historical tradition, it is possible to pass from the watershed of one religious project to another, toward a different distinctive end. My argument has never been that religions have firm boundaries or that an individual tradition draws all those within it in lockstep in a uniform direction. Rather, it is that those conflicts, changes of direction, and conversions that occur, both within and between traditions, have a point and are grounded in something real. The traditions exemplify in a rough, large-scale way the type of choice that is available everywhere in finer scale. One may go further and deeper in certain directions (and do so more expeditiously) by looking to where those paths have been most cultivated, in another "religion." But contacts of that sort only bring to flower what is always a feature of religions "alone."

In short, many seem to conflate the idea that religious ends are real (that Christians can attain communion with God, Buddhists attain nirvana, Advaitans attain moksha) with the idea that only one end is possible for those in a particular tradition. I hold the first but not the second. So the suggestion that people of multiple affiliations or of indeterminate confessional identity are somehow unimagined in my view is simply wrong. It is not impossible that some such combination could hit upon an ultimate religious realization unknown in previous history, so expanding human options. But even that would not alter the dynamic we are describing. Hybrid identities either specify a religious end and possibility distinct from those of their tributary components, or they represent an evolving stage toward the existing possibility associated with the components of one tradition. Very few of us are purely anything. But all of us are moving in some direction. The great traditions are prevailing breezes in their neighborhoods and communities. Every craft advances at some angle to the wind, and some tack against it, even to another landfall. If reification means believing that a complex of beliefs and behaviors is connected with one kind of religious realization and another complex with a different one, then I am guilty of reification. If it means believing that everything that happens under some ostensible religious label (of any sort) has the same outcome, then I am certainly not.

A criticism often raised against my view (though not by Thatamanil) is that while under a more traditional Christian theology it seemed most humans had been born spiritually disadvantaged, with the saving knowledge of Christ denied them by geography, I introduce a mere variant on that theme. Under my approach cultural location becomes the same kind of virtual spiritual destiny, albeit now those in distinct historical traditions are consigned to a range of various positive ends rather than to hell. Location would decide which one of the several religious ends could be sought and attained. But from what has been said above it should be clear that this is not the case. People in every setting have differential options, which might never involve outward conversion or any ostensible conflict of grand traditions. One might live in an entirely Hindu or Muslim culture, but there are always choices about what kind of Hindu or Muslim to be, heretical options, the opportunity to bend toward or away from the dominant path before you. From such small ripples larger-scale changes in traditions may occasionally come, but they always are of significance for individuals or subtraditions. Precisely because major religious traditions dispose of what Thatamanil calls repertoires of elements, which include many that also feature in other faiths, it is possible to assemble the elements in a way that points toward the characteristic end of another path. People with hybrid identities or multiple practices operate in this same space. Whether understood in a Buddhist way (the incrementalism of rebirths) or in a Christian inclusivist one (where the direction of the spiritual intention within its context is fulfilled in the next life), this freedom is real.

Which leads to the question about Christian superiority. Thatamanil says that trinitarian theology carries an apologetic temptation to suggest that Christianity surpasses others' monolithic perspectives with one that is polyphonic and encompassing. Looking through the trinitarian lens, the Christian concludes that others are only partially, and secondarily correct. I do not rule out ideas of "superiority," Christian or otherwise (on that more below). But the charge is at least misstated. It sounds as though Christian trinitarians claim to be the only ones who take account of the full range of important phenomena, whereas other religions have narrower vision and are left with some truncated, lesser repertoire. But this is not at all what I have written, or think. Precisely because within any great religious tradition there is the kind of variety we just remarked upon, it is also true that the profound sources within those traditions take account of the experiences or arguments that give rise to that variety. Again, granted the differences in proportion and emphasis, it is not that different religions have fewer "pieces" to play with. It is that they put them together in different ways. The Advaitan or Madhyamaka readings of things are undeniably encompassing and polyphonic in every reasonable way by their lights. And there, the "polyphonic" character of the Trinity or Christian salvation registers as no superiority, quite the contrary. "Trinity" is the name for the way that many Christians have put together certain varying factors whose significance in Christian life could not be denied, whether those factors are experiential (experiences of the divine in spiritual subjectivity, in personal encounter, and in the presence of the natural world) or descriptive (God represented in Jesus of Nazareth, God as known in the Hebrew scriptures, God as revealed in created intellect) or economic (God as creator, redeemer, sanctifier) or ontological (God as Source, Word, and Spirit). Other religions have different integrating visions. In certain branches of Hinduism *nirguna Brahman* and *saguna Brhaman* are likewise ways of "saving the phenomena," in which various elements that figure in religious life within the tradition are ordered in a particular way. So too with the skillful means in Buddhist tradition according to which conventional truth and ultimate truth, wisdom, and compassion are ordered.

A claim for the Trinity over against these other possibilities is not a claim that they have left some possibility entirely out of consideration or a claim that they do not effectively lead their adherents to the goal they promise or a claim that people within the tradition that uses those categories cannot migrate to Christian salvation through the less-traveled paths within them. It is a belief that Trinity more truly describes the actual nature of the integration of these factors, and an evaluative conviction that the religious end made possible through participation in that mode of integration is the richest human end. In those respects, I believe in the superiority of "Christianity," though what I indicate by that term is something subsistent in the historical tradition of that name and seeded through others.

This takes us back into the first cluster of issues that Thatamanil raised. These had to do first with the trinitarian framework for religious pluralism being a completely a priori Christian one, insufficiently shaped by sources in other religions, and second with other religions being deformed to play their role in the trinitarian scheme. On the initial count, I can offer a somewhat suspect subjective observation that in the development of my own thought in this area, it has hardly seemed to work that way in practice. Trinity had figured in my understanding of Christology, but otherwise it hardly had a central role in my theological thinking. It was the substance of the religions that led me into a much fuller understanding (or reunderstanding) of the Trinity. It was studying the religions that actually sent me for the first time to the Trinity as a serious locus of theological construction. I can substantiate this with the somewhat embarrassing testimony of my first book in this area, where the Trinity merited two passing entries in the index.[21] Rather than using a settled trinitarian doctrine to frame the religions, it was my growing study of the religions that sent me back to investigate the Trinity. Whatever resources may exist in the recesses of Christian tradition in regard to the doctrine, it was certainly a novel and significant revision for me to begin to conceive of relations among the persons of the Trinity as including dimensions of emptiness and nonduality. Or to consider that God's relation with the world would function in these dimensions. Or to revisit the Incarnation in that light. It was difficult for me to force-fit religions into a robust off-the-shelf trinitarian theology because I did not have one prior to my encounter with religious diversity. I also think that one good test of whether religions have been deformed by our treatment of them is whether there are those within these traditions who find our thought useful in their own terms. It is encouraging to me on this front that there are some examples of Buddhist and Hindu thinkers who find my work a useful partner in their own reflections.[22] But this may not be entirely responsive to Thatamanil's point, for he is certainly right that the Trinity as Christianly understood gets priority in my reflection. This is not a bug but a feature.

As to religions being deformed when viewed in trinitarian terms, our disagreement may rest in different aspirations. My hope would not be that those in another tradition would agree with the framework in which a Christian interprets them, but that they would recognize themselves descriptively as the ones engaged by the interpretation, not least because it is their testimony that it is based upon. I remain somewhat unclear what Thatamanil means in positing a vision of the Trinity in which various traditions would be as it were equal contributors. The value of a quite particular Christian trinitarian theology of religions is that it explicitly stands parallel to other traditions' integrative principles. No doubt, it subsumes their traditions in a pattern that is not their own. But it also offers the internal Christian justification for why other religions can make exactly the reciprocal move. Madhyamaka emptiness and the paradigm of ultimate and conventional truth, or Advaitan nonduality and the related categories of *maya* and *nirguna Brahman*—these can be cogent alternative readings of the material that makes up Christian confession. And a trinitarian theology such as I have advanced gives Christian reasons to regard those readings as grounded in reality in such a way that their encompassing visions cannot in principle be displaced as error or their ends dismissed as unreal. Precisely because of the historical dominance of Christian theological discourse, a "multireligious Trinity" runs the risk of blurring this important point. The less transreligious the Christian trinitarian discourse is, the more evident it is that there are other characteristically religious ways of putting together the one and the many that stand formally on the same ground. Into those others the Christian Trinity and its elements are no doubt (to Christian minds) somewhat force-fit. But this situation preserves both the sting and the rich promise of difference.

A trinitarian construct that lies too much between the religions can too easily appear to stand above them. This has been my concern with Panikkar's treatment of the Trinity, with which I think Thatamanil's approach has much in common. Panikkar famously argued that the structure of reality itself is trinitarian in form. On one hand, this had the air of a formally inclusivist imposition of Christian terms. The groundbreaking aspect of his work was that he took his cue from the most strongly contrasting visions of the ultimate in various religions. He maintained that it is only a "trinitarian concept of reality which permits us to at least indicate the main lines of a synthesis between these three apparently irreducible concepts of the Absolute."[23] Yet in preemptively recruiting the various religions' views into the one structure of reality, he could also seem to demote them each from making the same kind of interpretive claim. On the other hand, Panikkar so loosened his notion of Trinity from relation with the historical Jesus and so emphasized that the Christian doctrine was but one relative way of apprehending this reality that for many Christian observers it was questionable whether the term remained Christian at all. This meant that actual Christian trinitarian thinking remained virtually unaffected by this grand vision.

Our discussion bears as well on the question that is often raised about views like mine that grant this much importance to religious difference. Thatamanil touches on it in his concern over the reification of otherness. If as trinitarian my view threatens to subsume all into a Christian mold, as differentially pluralist (in Griffin's terms) it threatens to "privilege diversity at the expense of relation."[24] The danger Thatamanil sees is that distinct religious ends imply a radical incommensurability between religions and devalue interreligious learning. This is a genuine concern where different religious ends are funded with an actual plurality of ultimates. In that case each religious belief and realization would be vertically integrated, as it were, with its own metaphysical referent. There would be no evident reason why the pursuit of one should intersect intelligibly with the pursuit of another. There is perhaps a tendency in this direction in Griffin's development of John Cobb's process thought, where the three ultimates are God, creativity, and cosmos. But a trinitarian theology as I have outlined it is nothing if not a rationale *for* communication and intelligibility among the faiths since, to put it simply, Christians have no separate dimension or channel of relation with the divine completely to themselves. The source of the various ends all rest in God, and the supreme referents of each find a unity there.

This has been an attempt to clarify some matters in Thatamanil's reading of me. It has not begun to address Thatamanil's alternative positive thesis on its own terms. He proposes a heuristic philosophical trinitarianism derived from Buddhist-Christian-Hindu dialogue, where the three elements are ground, contingency and relation. This approach rectifies the Christian overdetermination of trinitarian formulations by drawing on central elements from these three religions. The categories name, at the same time, dimensions of the divine life and also of the very structure of reality itself. Griffin's approach tends to connect the religions with appropriate categories in Whitehead's metaphysics (which then play the a priori role an established model of the Trinity might play in other cases). Such connections can be fruitfully suggestive. But the nature of the religious ultimates and their relations have been predetermined by the systematic definitions of God, creativity, and cosmos and their relations as described by Whitehead. In Thatamanil's case, rather than correlating the religions with philosophical categories he takes the categories directly from the religions themselves and extrapolates philosophical correlatives for Brahman or Sunyata or logos. To my mind this is a much more promising strategy.

Yet my suspicion is that it will prove a recursive process. To build an integrative perspective out of these three is a metatheological project of the first order: It will gravitate toward a philosophical mediation between them and ultimately above them. For I doubt that there are any integrative strategies not already more characteristic of one of these traditions, or some other one. It is not just that Advaita focuses more on "ground" in Thatamanil's terms and Christianity on "contingency" and Buddhism on "emptiness." It is that Advaita takes account of contingency and emptiness (careful account) by means of ground—not just as a supreme object or value, but as the integrative principle that gives place to these other factors. Contingency is not some alien emphasis, it is comprehended as the *maya* of Brahman. So too with Madhyamaka use of emptiness to affirm the place of contingency and ground in its worldview. Conventional perceptions have their truth, and that truth is positioned in relation to ultimate wisdom. In other words, the religions are the kind of project we are always trying to construct about them. Observers may disagree over whether the evenhandedness that is Thatamanil's noble ideal is attainable. My hesitation is that even success in this effort may be a pyrrhic achievement.

However, this suspicion may overweight the philosophical end of Thatamanil's project. It is undeniably theological as well. Where I look to "grow" the Trinity incrementally outward toward its root connections with other religions, Thatamanil is testing the limits of its conceptuality. His heuristic "Trinity" is one where at least these three traditions' visions are granted equal space in the divine life. It is a kind of experimental placeholder for a conception and a practice, neither of which can actually be specified. What would a (still Christian) Trinity be like that had realized to the fullest extent its openness to Advaita and Madhyamaka? This would presumably be recognizably one with the Trinity that had likewise realized the same kind of openness to Islam and Judaism (or to Theravada and bhakti). We don't know what it would mean for the ultimate to be a Trinity of Brahman, Sunyata, and logos, particularly if "Trinity" still carries Christian assumptions that these three are coeternal, coinherent, and asymmetrically related. To attempt to answer this question is Thatamanil's comparative theological project. It is an exciting one. Without it, and until others have undertaken its like, we will not know how far from the limits of this complex unity we have conducted our conversations.

Spirited Transformations: Pneumatology as a Resource for Comparative Theology

HOLLY HILLGARDNER

Come, Holy Spirit,
bending or not bending the grasses,
appearing or not above our heads in a tongue of flame,
at hay harvest or when they plough in the orchards or when snow
covers crippled firs in the Sierra Nevada.
I am only a man: I need visible signs.
I tire easily, building the stairway of abstraction.
—CZESLAW MILOSZ, "Veni Creator"

In some well-meaning concepts of interreligious interaction, "the many" seem to be valued in their embodied diverse traditions only to be ultimately collapsed into a metaphysical "one." To use the ubiquitous metaphor of the mountain whose one summit can be reached by many paths, many-ness gets displaced by the one peak of the mountain. Avalanche! When the peak cannot support the many, the manyness sliding off the mountain subverts the valuing of difference toward which embodied diversity tellingly points. After all, the logic goes, why should a devotee of one religious path bother with studying the fine points of another religious path if the differences between them are ultimately not meaningful and will be collapsed? Why not just live peacefully with each other, if difference does not ultimately matter?

Comparative theology answers that difference does indeed matter, and its methodology of juxtaposing religious traditions in creative ways uncovers space for identities, ideas, and categories to come apart and come together in endless meaningful permutations. Differing and coalescing and differing again in unique ways—a microcosm of the ontological oscillation of the many and the one—religious streams of thought converge, divert, recombine, dry out, and overflow. Like shifting waters, religious traditions shape each other through a fluid, organic difference-in-relation, and in this essay, I highlight some incarnational, connecting aspects of Spirit that support such a difference-in-relation. For those working in the Christian tradition, the symbol of Spirit can bolster thinking about the oscillating relationship of the many and the one as Spirit—part of a many-in-one and one-in-many Trinity herself—manifests in her countless earthly varieties. Through the creative workings of Spirit, diversity—religious and otherwise—flourishes as manifestations of divinity.

A comparative theological ethos involves taking other religious traditions seriously, seriously enough to undertake detailed study of religious tradition(s) other than one's own and reflect in the light of this study on one's own religious tradition(s). In this way, comparative theology explicitly values the manyness or multiplicity of creation as it manifests in the practitioners, ideas, and living contexts of the religious traditions studied. With few exceptions, Christianity, through its monotheistic emphasis on the one and its often exclusionary interpretation of who has access to that one, has historically resisted honest, reflective, transformative engagement with other religious traditions. Comparative theology can promise something different, that is, a notion of relational difference that does not apotheosize either the one or the many but instead opens up multiple pathways for them to relate in embodied ways. Relational difference thus sustains a comparative theology that does not abstract or annihilate the particularity of religious traditions, while nurturing a comparative theology that can reveal and create solidarities and other collaborations among religions.

THE SPIRIT OF COMPARATIVE THEOLOGY

Forgotten and menial in pneumatological neglect over the centuries, Spirit often ranked as the Cinderella of the Trinity in Christian theology. The poor, unprivileged, female relation of the wealthier, favored, and male Father and Son, Spirit was ignored as she anonymously went about her nameless work. Since then, in theology's "pneumatological turn," we have seen her liberating possibilities as she escapes the confines of her step-mother's kitchen, continuing her workaday creative activities out in the open in the wide world. In addition, a graceful gravity has settled on past notions of a noncorporeal Spirit, instead locating Spirit as a "grounding" energy in the sensuous, passionate life of the world.[1] When this Spirit cleaves to the earthly quotidian nature of life in the world, embodied, liberative, and, most importantly for this essay, comparative theology can flourish. Spirit, when conceived of as concretizations of the divine reality, encourages interreligious encounters that can both embrace solidarities and protect particularities.

I argue in this essay that comparative theology based in the Christian tradition functions more coherently and fruitfully by embracing a relational pneumatology as a primary resource for its crucial work, and I adumbrate how the symbol of Spirit creates religiously plural possibilities that respect difference both as a philosophical value and as a worldly reality. The symbol of Spirit possesses two interrelated advantages over other symbols for a Christian theology that opens itself to other wisdoms. (1) Among the elements of the Christian Trinity, Spirit may best lend itself to an understanding of divine reality that dwells in necessary partnership with the natural world in all its diversity; that is, this integral partnership of Spirit and world opens up a space for conceiving of religious diversity. (2) Spirit also serves as a broad and accessible religious symbol for thinking about divinity within the world's religious traditions, to which the biblical and extrabiblical representations of Spirit as universal elements such as fire, wind, or breath can witness.

Spirit also allows two primary and ambitious goals of comparative theology to flourish: (1) peaceful understandings and meaningful solidarities without sacrificing particularity amongst religious traditions and (2) the promise of constructively vital theological transformation as a result of studying two or more religious traditions in creative, faithful ways. With these aspirations in mind, I suggest four interrelated ways that spirit functions toward the realization of a comparative theology of difference-in-relation: spirit as a matrix for creation, spirit as support for a logic of multiplicity, spirit as the energy of interrelated love, and spirit as destabilizer of static ontologies.

RELATING THEOLOGY OF RELIGIONS AND COMPARATIVE THEOLOGY

By providing epistemological and ontological space for the fluidity required by related yet differing identities, ideas, and categories, the symbol of Spirit allows for the transformational possibilities of comparative theology. After years of comparative work as a Catholic theologian who concurrently reads both Christian and Hindu texts, Francis Clooney attests to his need "to write in accord with [his] current sense of the hyphen in Hindu-Christian Studies." For him, the hyphen no longer denotes just a potential bridge between the two fields of study, but a "deep mingling" that refers to one complex field.[2] When one is rooted in a tradition that consciously places itself in committed dialogue with another tradition, one abides in this hyphen that allows for deep, ongoing, and faithful transformations of faith and practice. According to the "Statement on Comparative Theology" from the 2006 American Academy of Religion Conference, "in a theology that is comparative, faith and practice are explored and *transformed* by attention to the parallel theological dimensions of one or more other religious and theological traditions" (italics mine).[3]

Before discussing our four elements of a pneumatology that opens more space for difference-in-relation in comparative theology, I will briefly examine some gifts and limitations of contemporary comparative theology's precursor, theology of religions—that awkwardly named twentieth-century branch of theology that attempted to make Christian theological sense of non-Christian religious traditions. As this thinking developed, theologians who embraced other religious traditions in one way or another increasingly employed the Holy Spirit for their unorthodox argument that there *is*, in fact, salvation outside the church. In their projects to convince fellow Christians of divine reality within non-Christian religions, inclusivist and pluralist theologians of the religions such as John Hick, Karl Rahner, and Paul Knitter employed the symbol of Spirit for the freedom, flow, and universalism that the Spirit's movement connotes.[4] The mysterious nomadism of the Spirit of John 3:8, in which "the wind blows where it chooses, and you hear the sound of it, but you do not know where it comes from or where it goes," nourished these modernist projects of interreligious inclusivism and pluralism.

The inclusivist and pluralist theologians of the religions largely succeeded in their project: a subsuming inclusivism, if not a full pluralism, gradually became the predominant viewpoint of mainline Christianity. Nonetheless, even with the help of pneumatology, movement toward a fuller pluralism that did not collapse manyness proved arduous, as the ontologies and epistemologies that provided the fixed foundations for much of this theology could not spaciously accommodate the desired plurality. In other words, the means did not well support the yearned-for ends. Even if pluralist theologians could claim an ethical high ground, the actual tenets of a static ontology and limited options for an epistemology of multiplicity stymied efforts toward a pluralist Christian theology that valued difference both philosophically and pragmatically. For example, much of this interreligious theology assumed monolithic theological categories, such as the self, salvation, and the religious ultimate. Born from the Western Christian theological tradition, these categories could not stand up to the particularities of the religions themselves or emerging poststructuralist accounts of subjectivity and postmodern critiques of ontotheology.[5]

Critics of theology of religions exposed pluralism as a hegemonic discourse that could not live up to its own claim to be truly plural. Suppressing differences in favor of locating essential similarities, pluralists often inadvertently created totalizing systems that transcended any notion of valuing multiple, specific religious perspectives. As a result of these dilemmas, critics circled from all sides. Postmodern critics cried, "Contradiction!" Traditionalist critics added the charges of relativism and nihilism. Space that had been painstakingly carved out for transformative interreligious encounters had to be vigorously protected against attack by multiple camps while the modernist foundations of much theology of religions shook and creaked.

Contemporary progressive constructive theologies have inherited a hard-fought ethos of religious pluralism, and this inheritance, along with the postmodern tendencies in today's academy and the realities of living in an interconnected and religiously diverse world, has contributed to an openness to the ethos of the comparative theological task. In fact, David Tracy suggests that "any theology in any tradition that takes religious pluralism seriously must eventually become a comparative theology."[6]

Here I expose my agenda: What theological elements can we identify and nurture to sustain this comparative ethos? In the hope that comparative theology will continue to find a widening and welcomed space within theology (as it has at Drew University's Transdisciplinary Colloquia, for which this essay was written), I propose robustly relational pneumatologies as crucial elements for a commodious axiological openness and interconnectedness that supports multiple kinds of difference.

The symbol of Spirit performs crucial work toward opening spaces for transformative interreligious encounters, but it does not do this through theological moves explicitly designed to create space for religions other than Christianity, as the modernist theologies of religions attempted to do. Instead, as the symbol of Spirit widens the spaces available for multiplicities and diversities of all kinds, it organically accommodates religiously plural possibilities. I do not here suggest that such a pneumatology is the only way to nurture a comparative theology of difference-in-relation, but only that the symbol of Spirit may serve as one way to encourage the further burgeoning of a transformational and transforming comparative theology.

FOUR CHARACTERISTICS OF SPIRIT FOR A COMPARATIVE THEOLOGY OF DIFFERENCE-IN-RELATION

What I am aiming for is a comparative theology of difference-in-relation; that is, one that recognizes relationality as integral to difference that is not always utterly and ultimately transcended. Toward this end, I perceive four ways that the symbol of Spirit functions toward a comparative theology of difference-in-relation. Again, these include Spirit as a matrix for creation, Spirit as support for a logic of multiplicity, Spirit as the energy of interrelated love, and Spirit as destabilizer of static ontologies. As I have pondered the role of the Spirit for a Christian interreligious praxis of transformation, the pneumatologies of Catherine Keller, Laurel C. Schneider, and Peter C. Hodgson have greatly influenced my thinking. Interestingly, none of these theologians identifies as a comparative theologian, but each of their pneumatologies proves to be a tremendous resource for those who do and for those who might yet feel lured into this field.

Spirit as a Matrix for Creation

First, Spirit flows between and among all elements of creation. Spirit has a long tradition of being associated with relationality, specifically as the love relation between the first and second persons of the Trinity. Often, however, theology has focused its attention on this relationship at the expense of emphasizing Spirit's countless, integral relationships with the world. Going further, Spirit does not merely relate to everything in the world, but exists as the web of relationship itself, the many-in-one and the one-in-the-many. For Hodgson, Spirit does not represent one element in a network of all interrelated things, but instead constitutes the network itself: pure relationality.[7] Keller writes of relational Spirit as "material energy," and this material energy exists as the *in-between* of the world and the divine, "the relation of relations." This relation connects the interdependencies of the divine reality to the interdependencies of the created world.[8]

Conceiving of Spirit as the matrix of creation creates possibilities for relations to exist among seemingly incompatible religious traditions. Spirit, relationally construed, can draw religions together without needing to compress them into some sort of amalgamation. For example, in a comparative theological experiment relating concepts of grace in Hinduism and Christianity, a matrix of Spirit would allow room for comparative work that protects and preserves difference in relationality. Instead of futilely pushing to create religious conceptions of grace that alleviate all tensions between Hinduism and Christianity, a matrix of Spirit anticipates a transforming relationality in difference. Difference, as the French deconstructionists remind us in their double entendre, *différance*, defers the meaning of difference. In this deferral, potential signifiers of grace multiply, options for understanding grace comparatively can then expand in creative and as of yet unimagined ways.

Spirit as Support for a Logic of Multiplicity
Second, in its esteeming of embodied difference, Spirit epistemologically engenders a logic of multiplicity that does not drown out differences. Instead, in this logic of multiplicity, differences are accentuated as they are brought by Spirit into relation with one another. In concert with Gilles Deleuze, Keller describes this relational Spirit in terms of "differentiator as connector: thus this spirit will not transcend or obliterate differences; rather differences are intensified precisely by being brought into relation."[9] For Schneider, Spirit makes incarnations possible—not only the incarnation of Jesus, but the countless incarnations that happen every day in the world; thus, Spirit "comes to body, to being, differently every time, in ev-

ery instance of creation."[10] In this logic of multiplicity, these Spirited incarnations lead her to embrace a Derridean ethic of "impossible exchange," in which no singular, unique entity ultimately can be valued over another singular, unique entity, an ethic with significant implications for diversity of all kinds.[11]

As mentioned previously, modernist theologies of religions tended to subsume religious difference into rigid Westernized categories. The pneumatological esteeming of difference creates space for difference that does not need to be imperialistically categorized. As Schneider succinctly states, "Bodies occur and make difference real."[12] The fact of difference allows an acceptance, even an embracing, of a pluriverse with many truths. As material energy, Spirit does not ethereally disconnect from the world, because Spirit simply cannot exist without the mediator of nature.[13] In its trinitarian mystery, Spirit provides Logos a body, and this is the body of creation.[14] As such, Spirit reminds us about the ways we are implicated in each other: Ready or not, our interreligious interactions with each other thus shape each other.

Although Spirit has often been set in opposition to bodies in a spirit/body dyad, embodied Spirit offers radical alternative possibilities. When aligning Spirit with multiple and varying bodies, and when perceiving these bodies as the only way that Spirit happens, then Spirit, by Spirit's very nature, flows through creation indiscriminately. Schneider warns that theologians must not limit Spirit to "disembodied ecstasies or to carefully controlled substances of sacrament or liturgy."[15] She describes how the logic of the One, with its drive toward noncontradiction and simplicity, tempted religious traditions to create nonpermeable boundaries of identity, such as exclusive rituals, to stave off anxieties about the traditions' own tenuous survivals. Schneider suggests that, while invoking God as the source of exclusivity, perhaps people are really making claims on God instead. Maybe jealousy and fear that God might love "indiscriminately, without propriety" fuels religious exclusivity.[16] In other words, what havoc would result if God loved the other, even loved one's own enemies? Of course, this fear runs against the ethical claim that religious traditions often make: to love the neighbor and the stranger. This tension leads us to consider the Spirit's potential as the energy of interrelated love.

Spirit as the Energy of Interrelated Love
The Augustinian tradition has understood Spirit as love itself, but specifically as expressed in the bond between God the Father and God the Son, as well as between God and Christians. Pushing this tradition further, Hodgson describes Spirit as an emergent figure, a social reality that emerges as God and the world interact with one another.[17] In this pneumatology, Spirit cannot exist without the world, because Spirit is not a preexisting "person," but only emerges in and through the world's relations. The love that God experiences together with *all* of the world, not only with an exclusive set of humans or species, catalyzes Spirit's growth and movement.

Provocatively, Schneider identifies the Spirit of interrelated love as "divine promiscuity."[18] In these two redolent words, she suggests diverse and free embodiments of the divine reality, as well as a divine love so overflowing and excessive that the divine reality could never exclusively wed itself to one religion or to a singular incarnation. As Christians aspire to love as God loves, love assumes a "posture of openness to the world as it comes to us, of loving the discordant, plenipotential worlds more than any desire to overcome, to colonize, or even to 'save' them."[19]

Spirit, as a matrix of loving relationships, no longer legitimizes the unjust hegemonies of the world but undermines them with a different kind of interconnecting power, one perhaps better described as material energy.[20] In the relationality that holds elements together while valuing difference, Spirit contains the energy to decolonize the dualistic and hierarchical relationships that have functioned to hold Christianity in higher esteem than other religious traditions.

Spirit as Destabilizer of Static Ontologies
Last, Spirit destabilizes static ontologies and in the process, destabilizes the distinction between the divine subject and created object. In its radical relationality, suggests Keller, Spirit "breaks the Trinity out of its doctrinal self-enclosure in the metaphysics of substance."[21] This constitutes one of Spirit's most important tasks, as breaking out of this metaphysics of substance is essential for opening up space for difference. As pure substance, immovable, one, and wholly other, the divine reality cannot change, cannot assume multiplicity, and cannot truly exist as constitutively and lovingly related with creation. Spirit, as fluid and intrinsically relational, al-

lows for an ontological multiplicity that recognizes, values, and sustains difference.

As the presence of the divine life in the lives of creatures, Spirit makes more porous the once seemingly solid distinctions between God and creature. With respect to philosophical concepts of God as ultimate subject and creation as ultimate object, the necessary, indiscriminate presence of Spirit in creation begins to destabilize the boundaries between subject and object. Furthermore, when one conceives the Spirit as not fully autonomous, but instead as dependent on creation in order to emerge or to become, then the ontological structure of the subject as the one that acts and the object as the one that receives loses its coherence. Boundaries become blurred as divinity and creation relate interdependently.

SPIRIT AS SUPPORT: A COMPARATIVE EXAMPLE

Pneumatologies that exhibit the four characteristics I have just described gracefully perform interreligious work. These pneumatological characteristics organically permit difference and allow a transformative comparative theology to happen coherently, imaginatively, and faithfully. In order to illustrate the ways in which these four characteristics of Spirit might support a specific work of comparative theology, I will employ an example, a comparative project that reads Sankara and Catherine of Siena together in order to shed light on questions of theological anthropology. In this specific task of Hindu-Christian comparative theology, I will examine how the four elements provide justification for the comparative task itself as well as offer methodological coherence for some of the project's key moves.

Spirit as a Matrix for Creation: Catherine and Sankara

Spirit as a matrix for creation helps the comparative theologian hold everything together without compressing differences into unified systems that extinguish all mystery and difference. For example, in my comparison of Sankara and Catherine, I explore the idea of an unknowable, apophatic self in each theologian's theology, but with an understanding that the idea of (S)elf means very different things to an early medieval Indian Advaitan Hindu, to a fourteenth-century European Dominican Christian, and to me.

The first question often asked of a comparative theologian about a particular project involves the choice of the subjects of comparison. Robert C. Neville has argued persuasively that comparative theology must rigorously construct and test its categories so as not to fall prey to a latent religious imperialism that subsumes differences.[22] Conceiving of Spirit as a matrix of creation encourages the Christian comparative theologian to choose boldly and experimentally in the light of the connectedness of all things, but spirit as a matrix of creation can never be used as an excuse for sloppy comparisons. In the matrix of spirit, responsible yet intuitive categorical experimentation can take place. At the same time, the matrix of spirit attests to the real consequences of our relationality that has often resulted in domination, colonialism, and other unjust practices; therefore, conscientious, rigorous, detailed study is necessary in order to work responsibly in two or more religious traditions. Although some subjects of comparison have more fruitful potential than others, ultimately, nearly all subjects of comparison, responsibly and knowledgeably construed, can have constructive potential under this model.

Spirit as Support for a Logic of Multiplicity: Catherine of Siena and Sankara
For comparative theology to have transformative value, those doing the comparing must, at the very minimum, begin with openness to the possibility of truths in religions other than their own. If no openness exists, then why would a Christian care what an eighth-century Hindu, such as Sankara, has to say about what it means to be human and in relation to the divine? This question goes to the heart of the comparative theological enterprise. When Spirit becomes inextricably connected with bodies of different kinds, in ways that perceive these bodies as the only way that Spirit happens, then Spirit flows promiscuously and indiscriminately through these multiple bodies. These bodies, be they Christian or Hindu in this case, then provide light on the theological questions guiding my comparative project.

In interreligious dialogue and some kinds of comparative theology, participants often place priority on discovering and articulating similarities among religions. Although bridge building of this sort will always have an important place, comparative theological work in the light of the embodied difference of a logic of multiplicity does not value commonality at the expense of difference. For example, as I explore a shared metaphor of "abiding in the self" in Sankara and Catherine, I look for differences in each writer's explication of this metaphor, hoping to perceive theological anthropology in fresh, life-giving ways. When working with embodied difference that supports a logic of multiplicity, I no longer need to know with certainty that a similarity exists at the heart of the universe, a One Truth into which all concepts must neatly fit. I remain free to be guided by Clooney's comparative ethic of a "patient deferral of issues of truth."[23] Now I can engage with Sankara's brilliant concept of the Self as Brahman, for example, without a need to change it or deny it to accommodate a preconceived idea of truth. Instead, I can encounter new concepts as ideas that may shed light on how the self abides in the divine.

Spirit as the Energy of Interrelated Love: Catherine of Siena and Sankara
The "patient deferral of issues of truth" prized in comparative theology must be held in tension with theology's responsibility toward the marginalized. Although the creative tension between the religious traditions under study must be consciously prolonged, ultimately a constructive gesture may need to be ventured. The methodological freedom to compare diverse subjects in creative ways requires the caveat that some topics are more likely to aid in the struggle for a more just world than others; thus, when reading Sankara and Catherine together, I keep my eyes open for ways that I can most responsibly engage theological anthropology. Remembering spirit as the energy of interrelated love allows me to examine how the self, differently conceived of by Sankara and Catherine, can become aware of itself as integrally related with others. In both thinkers, I notice that in the self's contact with the divine, the divine gives birth to an understanding of the self as not able to be autonomously known.

Catherine uses the image of a cell (or room) within a cell to think about the relation between the knowledge of God and the knowledge of the self. She writes, "This cell is really two rooms in one, and while you are in one you must at the same time be in the other."[24] In its emphasis on dwelling in both cells simultaneously, this image points to self-knowledge as inextricably connected to knowledge of God: One may come to know something of the self as one comes to know something of God. Sankara, for his part, insists that the Self does not exist ontologically; there is no such thing as the individual, autonomous self. Even in the "unenlightened" individual, Self is really Brahman; one just does not know it. A liberated person knows that the Self is unknowable because liberated persons know only the vastness of Brahman and in nonduality, the vastness of the Self.

In traditional readings of Sankara, upon Self-realization, the world, including the Self, disappears. Only Brahman remains. The limitations of this soteriology for liberated embodied action in the world leads me to explore some less traditional readings of Sankara that allow for the world to remain real, even after Self-Realization. Here, one risk of doing comparative theology emerges. Since one optimally comes to the task with an open mind toward other religious traditions but also with some cherished theological convictions, how great is the tendency to misread other traditions? How real is the threat of revisionist hermeneutics in support of one's own enculturated goals and values? To avoid these temptations, Michelle Voss Roberts suggests that comparative theologians must identify and then argue for the values that they represent rather than assume their universal appeal. For example, in studies that compare Advaita and Christian worldviews and their implications for ecology, liberationist comparative theologians would need to argue the case that certain world-denying interpretations of Advaita may obscure the responsibility to take care of earth and that religious persons of both faiths need to take this responsibility seriously.[25] This kind of comparative theology does not embrace an anarchic equalization of all differences or a stabilized hierarchy of dualisms but a third space of justice-seeking difference-in-relation.

Spirit as a Destabilizer of Static Ontologies: Catherine of Siena and Sankara
In my comparative project, the destabilizing tendencies of Spirit allow me to see possibilities for a different kind of theological anthropology, one inspired by a cautious nondualism in Catherine of Siena. I only began to discern this nondualism when I read her alongside Sankara's nondualism of the Self and Brahman. Traditionally, Catherine's emphasis on self-knowledge has been read as a continuation of the Augustinian tradition of knowing oneself and knowing God as the two primary spiritual tasks, but as I read some of her primary images along with Sankara, I may then entertain new readings of her images, for example, an image of the sea and of her reflection in that sea. Catherine returns repeatedly to the image of the "cell of self-knowledge" as a home in which to abide. For her, this abode becomes a place where her desire for the divine opens her self wider than a traditionally bounded self, taking her deeper into the mystery of fluid, interpenetrating, divinizing relationships with others and the divine Other.

The embracing of destabilization proves valuable for comparative theology to help explain the boundary slippage that often occurs in comparative projects. Rita Gross, a scholar of Buddhism, offers the helpful metaphor of the comparative mirror that blurs the boundaries of identities and categories. This mirror reflects "practical and religious alternatives that we would be unlikely to imagine on our own."[26] In the mirror, we learn to see ourselves phenomenologically as representing only one of many religious alternatives in the world. If we practice looking into this mirror, we begin to see the poverty of perspective that would result if we took only our own traditions seriously, and our own reflections change as we begin to see ourselves and others more fully. Scholars of religion, who claim to have expertise in this problematic category of "religion" and who live, teach, and write in this diverse world, have a responsibility to learn from traditions not their own. As I read Sankara to help correct my poverty of perspective, I find that my own religious categories become destabilized. Categories of (S)elf, God, world, and other shift, blur, and expand with possibilities.

TOWARD TRANSFORMATION

Contemporary comparative theology has expanded pluralist possibilities. Instead of merely undergirding the eternal destiny of the religious other or making crowded room for the religious other in a Christian system, comparative theology gives the religious other space to transform the *very content* of Christian theology. The realization of justice-oriented interreligious solidarities calls for the support of both a truly pluralistic, relational ontology and a fluid epistemology of multiplicity. In its relational, embodied, manifold, interdependent, and destabilizing modes, the symbol of Spirit gracefully meets the challenges of a transformative comparative theology of difference-in-relation.

Theo-Anthropological Explorations: Queer God, Strange Creatures, Storied Spirit

Excess, Reversibility, and Apophasis: Rereading Gender in Feminist Trinities

SARA ROSENAU

The lines we draw are invitations to cross over and that crossing over, as any nomadic subject knows, constitutes who we are.
—JUDITH BUTLER, *Undoing Gender*

Admittedly, reflection on the complexities of the "one and the many" in God can take on a kind of abstruseness when compared to the material injustices of everyday life: global poverty, war, and environmental degradation to name a few. Even if it is presumed that the "one" has a relationship to state power and the expansion of empire or to unity at the expense of difference, the question remains how meditating on the "many" really makes a tangible difference to the material lives of women.[1]

Feminist discourse, however, has long asserted that the personal is political. That is, how we understand the private sphere of self and family has everything to do with how, in the public sphere (community, state, nation, and world), we understand the distribution of goods, conflict, or our relations with the nonhuman world. To that end, much of feminist discourse has questioned the association of the "one" with an autonomous rational (masculine) singular self, asserting a more complex web of interrelations in its place. Put another way, feminist discourse pries open the "one" to make room for the "many": At the very least it aims to make space for at least two, for the difference of woman.

Following this logic, I find the Christian Trinity has a certain affinity with the feminist project because of trinitarian stubbornness against one and even two. The Trinity is always gesturing generously toward more, toward three at least. Whether we conceive of human life as modeled after the Trinity or caught up in the Trinity, such diversity in God's own "person" makes a difference for difference. That is, the Trinity holds some transformational promise for how we can think more clearly about *ourselves* as "many," as constituted by both the many stories of our past and by our relations with others. Judith Butler, whose work I utilize below, has been especially articulate about the interrelationship between the "I" and the "you." She writes, "One might say, reflectively, and with a certain sense of humility, that in the beginning I am my relation to you . . . given over to a 'you' without whom I cannot be and upon whom I depend to survive."[2] Conceiving of ourselves and the Divine as "many" might help us rethink an array of interrelations, including intimate partners, family configurations, and our larger community. Still, does this manyness also hold a promise for helping us rethink justice on a material plane? Might such things as property ownership and unequal distribution of food or health care also be challenged in the reconfiguration of the self as many? Such questions underscore the ties between feminist theories of subjectivity and a concern for material flourishing.

The generosity of the trinitarian three can also illuminate new ways of understanding gender, which is one goal of this essay. Feminist reflections on gender have recently been pried open beyond the two. The biologist Anne Fausto-Sterling has argued that the social construction of two sexes is really just that, a construction, when considered next to her statistical estimate that 1.7 percent of all births are intersex babies, babies born with some combination of both male and female genitalia.[3] Theoretically, Judith Butler has continued to question the utility of theorizing only two genders, especially in psychoanalysis. "Why can't the framework for sexual difference itself move beyond binarity into multiplicity?" she asks, posing the question to feminist theorists who, while theorizing sexual difference, simultaneously reinforce the binary of two genders. This aspect of Butler's work might even be said to represent her mourning for the cultural loss of a "third" gender.[4]

Moving from two genders to three and beyond is not simply an intellectual exercise to disturb categories that to many of us seem quite natural. This work is critically important for transgender persons who do not identify with the gender assigned to them at birth and struggle to make the journey toward expressing themselves fully as the other gender. Similarly, genderqueer individuals do not feel comfortable with either male or female labels and, rather, understand and express their gender identity in a more undefined or fluid way. In either experience, getting beyond the two is not a casual journey; it is often a matter of life and death. A 2009 FBI report on hate crimes found that "the LGBT community suffers from violent hate crimes at levels that are more then eight times their percentage in the population."[5] Further, violence against transgender individuals and discrimination in jobs, housing, health care, and social services render transgender individuals the most economically and socially vulnerable population in the lesbian, gay, bisexual, transgender, and queer family.[6] But doesn't God, who crosses over from one to two to three, from male to female and beyond, offer us something of a promise, even an ethical mandate, in the face of this suffering?

STILL STRIVING FOR RIGHT SPEECH ABOUT GOD

Elizabeth Johnson's *She Who Is* was a landmark study in feminist theological work on the Trinity.[7] At the heart of Johnson's work is the great mystery of the Divine; drawing on classical theology she asserts, "God as God, ground, support, and goal of all, is illimitable mystery who, while immanently present, cannot be measured, manipulated, or controlled."[8] Although acknowledging the inevitable partiality of human speech about God, Johnson nonetheless searches for what she calls "right speech" about God while denouncing the long tradition of "exclusive God-talk," speech about God as (only) male. Such speech, Johnson argues, has functionally produced both the metaphorical and literal exclusion of women.[9] Johnson's work aims to broaden the metaphor, to speak rightly of God using female images. Her goal is to shift the focus away from "undue emphasis on any one image, since pressing the multiplicity of imagery shows the partiality of images of one sex alone."[10] Johnson hopes her labor will contribute to a "new whole" where speech about God creates an "imaginative and structural world" that supports the inherent dignity of all human beings, male and female.[11]

Nearly two decades later we must confess that Johnson's vision of this "new whole" has not been achieved. Women still, as Luce Irigaray has said, "lack a God to share, a word to share and to become."[12] What can account for the deferment of Johnson's dream? Although it is unpopular now in some academic circles to speak of "the patriarchy," the sheer cultural force of over two thousand years of male imagery for God cannot go unnoticed. Another factor, however, has been the now well-rehearsed conflict within feminist theory over the limits of the term "woman." African American feminist scholars have continually needed to reassert the underlying racism in feminism's call for solidarity among women by pointing out that this vision for women's liberation is articulated from the vantage point, and to the advantage, of white middle-class women.[13] Trying to account for a more pluralistic understanding of woman, feminists in the tradition of continental philosophy have worked to theorize "woman" as multiple.[14] Rosi Braidotti, for example, connects the destabilization of the feminist subject to the problem of speech when she writes, "In feminist theory one *speaks as* a woman, although the subject 'woman' is not a monolithic essence defined once and for all but rather the site of multiple, complex, and potentially contradictory sets of experiences, defined by overlapping variables such as class, race, age, lifestyle, sexual preferences, and others."[15] So, in other words, before feminists could get to "right speech" about God, they had to agree on how to speak rightly about "woman."

One epicenter for the quake in feminist theory that disturbed a singular notion of woman was the destabilization of the sex/gender divide. This divide had helped feminists theorize gender as a cultural construction but had left untended the complex intersections of gender and sexuality. Judith Butler is the most notable scholar to question this binary in order to create a space for queer identity and gender variance. Butler argues that subjectivity, including gender *and* sex, is a cultural script written on the body, one continually constructed through *performative* gestures and other bodily acts.[16] Therefore, neither sex nor gender can be safely stabilized. A central goal of her landmark text, *Gender Trouble*, was to demonstrate "how nonnormative sexual practices call into question the stability of gender as a category of analysis."[17]

Some feminists have grieved the loss of the stability of the category of "woman," specifically its political importance. Others have worried that queer studies has effectively eclipsed feminist theory with its utopist vision of the end of gender. Butler, however, has maintained, helpfully I think, that "there is no story to be told about how one moves from feminist to queer to trans" because none of these stories have ended, but continue to be told in "simultaneous and overlapping ways."[18] For Butler, the theoretical convergence of feminist, queer, and transgender theory does a specific kind of work, one that continues to undo the presumed separation of various political identities while keeping the material and psychic suffering of (nonnormative) individuals in view.

For feminist trinitarian thinking, I argue, this invitation to convergence is a renewed opportunity to push at the limits of the category of gender in the godhead, and thus to open up, to use Johnson's words, "imaginative and structural worlds" still creating space for (diverse) women, but also making room for nonnormative gender and sexual identities within and beyond the constructions of male/female. So, in continuation of Johnson's project of right speech about God, this project "press[es] the multiplicity of imagery" even further, beyond Johnson's initial goal of "equivalent imaging of God in religious speech" toward a deeper multiplicity that subverts the male/female binary altogether.[19] Here I aim for what Janet Martin Soskice has called a "baffling of gender literalism" in the godhead.[20]

Thus, I aim to reinterpret, or read queerly, Johnson's *She Who Is* in order to forestall a certain "closure" of gender that takes place in this important feminist theological re-visioning of the Trinity. I queer Johnson's reading of gender in the Trinity with the methodology and metaphor of the nomad. Marcella Althaus-Reid has called this a "melancholic nomadism," or the mourning of "all the early closures of meaning in Christianity."[21] Thus, the queer theologian takes up the practice of wandering through the history of theological conversation identifying and transgressing borders. Johnson's own methodology has some nomadic qualities, as she explores (and mourns) the tradition in search of right speech about God for women. But the nomad keeps traveling: "Borders of thinking are crossed. Borders of prayer are crossed. Body-borders. God may cross God's own borders too."[22] This essay rereads Johnson's Trinity with the theoretical tools of excess, reversibility, and apophasis in order to cross the border of gender even further than Johnson attempts. All three of these nomadic tools aid the theological traveler in interpreting God's crossings while disrupting gender's closure of meaning. This triad of excess, reversibility, and apophasis is helpful in baffling gender literalism while also illuminating how gender is always and already baffling us. Thus, this essay pushes feminist trinitarian work beyond the goal of a balance between male and female imagery of God and toward imagery that overwhelms and undermines our presumed knowledge of both God *and* gender. Finally, following God across these borders returns us to ourselves. I will conclude with some meditations on gender in theological anthropology, contemplating our experiences of gender as creatures created in the image of the triune God.

TREADING NOMADICALLY ON ORTHODOX LAND

Method and history often go together, and here it will be important to expand on how a method of nomadic wandering aids feminist interventions into both historical and constructive theology. Theories of the nomad and border crossing have been important themes for feminist theory more generally. Gloria Anzaldua and Rosi Braidotti have both theorized a new epistemology that reflects the multiple intersections of identities, challenges binary thinking, and creates new pathways of thought. Toward this goal Anzaldua proposes the *new mestiza*, privileging the spiritual and cultural knowledge of those whose identities are constructed at multiple intersections. The *new mestiza* rejects binaries and lives with ambiguity, making a creative "leap in the dark" in order to forge new stories, symbols, and values. Anzaldua writes, "*Soy un amasamiento*, I am an act of kneading, of uniting, and joining that not only has produced both a creature of darkness and a creature of light, but also a creature that questions the definitions of light and dark and gives them new meanings."[23] With the metaphor of a creature from seemingly opposite worlds, darkness and light, Anzaldua explains how her identity both emerges from contradiction and questions and transcends the contradiction. Anzaldua's *new mestiza* emerges at the crossroads of race, sexuality, gender, spirituality, and culture.

Similarly, Braidotti describes the *figure of the nomad* as a "polyglot," one who has no mother tongue but is always moving in-between languages and cultures, and one who even desires and seeks this in-between state. Even monolingual people, however, can be understood as in-between because "the truth of the subject is always in between self and society . . . from the moment you were born, you have lost your 'origin.'"[24] Thus, border epistemology exposes, in a way, the falsity of all "origins" or "centers," including those of the "self." Braidotti is cautious, however, about associating the nomad simply with nonlocation, a privilege that is often marked by upper-class status and whiteness. Instead, the nomad is one who intentionally resists "hegemonic and exclusionary views of subjectivity" while performing an identity "made of transitions."[25] Therefore, in a way similar to that of Anzaldua, Braidotti finds in the nomad's politically oriented consciousness a "potential for positive renaming, for opening up new possibilities for life and thought, especially for women."[26] We will return later to nomadic subjectivity, exploring how nomadic feminist trinitarian thinking connects to theological anthropology. Here suffice it to say that both the *new mestiza* and the figure of the nomad transverse and transgress established borders, a movement that contributes to women's resistance.

We can apply these themes of resistance to binaries, disruption of origins, and creative reconstruction of identity and politics to historical and constructive feminist theological projects. Following Braidotti, Jenny Daggers encourages a feminist theological method of "nomadic consciousness" that disrupts any notion of "a single orthodox centre" through continuous travel.[27] Although often overlooked, Daggers traces a legacy of feminist engagement with orthodox themes, citing Elizabeth Johnson as a prime example.[28] Johnson takes a nomadic trip through the Christian tradition, reclaiming aspects that have been repressed and lost, particularly to the detriment of feminine symbols and names for God. In doing so, Johnson opens the tradition onto itself, claiming a more multiple center for theological language and, thus, making inroads into long-standing closures in the godhead. I agree with Daggers that feminist theology must both claim and continue its engagement with orthodoxy. My intuition, however, is that theological nomadism must not simply disrupt Christian orthodoxy in the name of gender, but must also disrupt and reconstruct the very meanings of gender. Otherwise, our nomadic disruptions achieve new openings theologically but simultaneously keep social and psychic borders intact. Thus, this essay further employs a nomadic method that travels not only into ancient and recent explorations of the doctrine of the Trinity but also into the slippery definition of gender itself. Such nomadic travel, by feminist theologians, can help forge "new routes towards the heart of the Christian tradition" while disturbing the notion of any single heart.[29]

SPIRIT AND EXCESS: SHE WHO IS MORE THAN SHE WHO IS

Excess is our first nomadic strategy for reading the deployment of gender in Johnson's Trinity. Excess is mourned by the nomadic theologian as a casualty of our attempt to draw strict boundaries around concepts. Not surprisingly, language about the third person of the Trinity, Spirit, flirts with excess. Johnson draws on excess to describe Spirit as both experienced by human beings and yet exceeding every experience. For in the diversity of human experience of Spirit "language about the Spirit consistently breaks the boundaries of neat codification or one single metaphor."[30] Spirit breaks through language, but also through space and time. In the wonder of nature, in the intimacy of relationships, and in the resistance of human communities to injustice Johnson understands Spirit as "drawing near and passing by, shaping fresh starts of vitality and freedom."[31] The excess of Spirit is captured metaphorically in scripture by the elements of fire, water, wind, and light. The effects of the elements are felt, but Spirit also has a boundlessness that cannot be contained.[32]

Johnson's feminist critique is that Spirit's excess has been neglected and repressed in Christian doctrine and practice. She argues that Catholicism has confined Spirit's work to institutionally sanctioned activities, such as ordination, and displaced the work of the spirit unto the Virgin Mary and the pope.[33] Protestantism, in contrast, has privatized Spirit's work, restricting it to personal salvation or revelation.[34] Doctrinally, Johnson emphasizes that the action of Spirit is also minimized in the triune relation, as Spirit is named as a neglected third after much theologizing about Father and Son has already taken place.[35] In addition, despite strong scriptural support for feminine metaphors for Spirit, including *ruah*, *shekinah*, and *sophia*, this metaphorical language for Spirit has been forgotten. Johnson concludes that the sublimation of Spirit's work in the world mirrors the marginalization of "women's work" in the home, church, and world.[36]

Where Johnson identifies Spirit with excess, and the repression of excess in the service of (male) church power, she does not explicitly connect excess and gender. Excess is an apt tool for describing how we can identify the social norms of gender, but these identifications never quite encompass all that gender is. I call myself a "woman," but inevitably my daily inhabitation of the identity "woman" does not meet the normative standard, my gender practice exceeds the norm that it approximates. As Butler has aptly written, "The body is that which can occupy the norm in myriad ways, exceed the norm, rework the norm, and expose realities to which we thought we were confined as open to transformation."[37] This is why, as Butler has shown, the practice of drag works as a critique of gender; when one gender imitates the other in an exaggerated way, it brings into relief how all gender is a kind of performance. We are all doing drag when we are doing (our) gender(s). Often it is our speech about gendered action that betrays the excessiveness of gender. This is because of a certain inevitable slippage between actions and what it is possible to say about them. This slippage is the queer theologian's tool for crossing the binary border of gender; for the more gender is "policed," the more borders there are where slippage occurs.

This slippage between action and speech about gender is evident when Johnson returns to the tradition to offer a critique of the eclipse of female imagery of Spirit and retrieve Sophia. She identifies one site of repression in the writing of Philo of Alexandria, a first-century Jewish philosopher. Although Philo is often understood to have been influenced by Platonic philosophical categories, he can also be viewed as a unique producer of Middle Platonic thought, one that takes seriously Jewish scriptural interpretation.[38] From Johnson's feminist standpoint, however, Philo is problematic because he represents an early example of how feminine Wisdom, or Sophia, is usurped by the masculine Word, or Logos. I argue, however, that this view of Philo misses a chance to tease out the excessive slippage in Philo's gendered account, and thus the chance to queer it.

Johnson acknowledges that in Philo's writing Sophia and the Logos are a "complicated affair," but she takes issue with his ultimate conclusion that the Logos is superior to Sophia.[39] She gives this quote by Philo as an example:

> For pre-eminence always pertains to the masculine, and the feminine always comes short of it and is lesser than it. Let us, then, pay no heed to the discrepancy in the gender of words, and say that the daughter of God, even Sophia, is not only masculine but father, sowing and begetting in souls aptness to learn, discipline, knowledge, sound sense, and laudable actions.[40]

Johnson rightly is suspicious of Philo's condemnation of Sophia "because of her female characteristics."[41] Although it would be hard to argue that Philo affirms Sophia here, this passage does demonstrate how unwieldy and excessive gender is for Philo. Here Philo has competing senses of faithfulness to the scriptural accounts of Sophia's actions and to his (Platonic) understandings of femininity and masculinity. His compromise is to restrict Sophia's immanence, letting only her son, the Logos, be active in the historical world.[42] Still, Sophia demonstrates the excessiveness of her gender, slipping into active roles similar to Word while also retaining her feminine name and pronoun. Philo tries to tame her excess by transforming Sophia into a masculinized father so that she can sow and beget. But, while struggling with her pronoun, in other writings Philo takes pains to locate Sophia with the Logos in the heavenly realm and retain her active stance as a co-creator. He names the Logos and Sophia similarly as "oldest," the "beginning," and the "firstborn."[43] Interestingly, then, both Sophia and the Logos share a space in the godhead, even though Sophia has to be masculinized to get there. Although some feminists, including Johnson, have found this abhorrent, we can also read Philo's "butch" Sophia as a kind of queer victory. That is, Sophia's gendered excess slips away from both Philo and Johnson; she remains stubbornly in the godhead as a divine female-father or a dyke-mother to her son, the Logos.

Although this reading of Philo tempers forceful claims of misogyny leveled by early feminist critics, it allows for other interpretations of Philo's intent. For, as the Talmudic scholar Daniel Boyarin has pointed out, Philo himself represents a queer place in the Jewish tradition. Philo's account of both Sophia and the Logos as active with God in the beginning and present in the earthly realm runs counter to strict understandings of Jewish monotheism. Boyarin argues that Philo's work reveals that at least "for one branch of pre-Christian Judaism there was nothing strange about a doctrine of *deuteros theos*," or a "second" God that was also compatible with the doctrine of monotheism.[44] This practice, Boyarin reasons, was not only the result of philosophical and scriptural interpretation but also of the struggle of worshiping communities "to connect a transcendent Absolute with the world and humanity."[45] Thus, Philo's Logos and Sophia cross each other, signaling the excess of both gender and Spirit as they exchange duties in the godhead and transgress the borders between Jewish monotheism and Christian trinitarianism.

Explicitly turning to the excesses of gender would help Johnson in her constructive recovery of Spirit-Sophia. Johnson struggles with articulating Spirit-Sophia's actions in terms of human deeds. For although she wants to pursue "understandings of the Spirit of God that cohere with women's experience of the holy," she is also wary of associating particular actions with only one gender, especially actions tied to social roles that have been repressive to women.[46] For example, Johnson uses metaphors that draw on women's experience: "Like a midwife she works deftly with those in pain and struggle to bring about the new creation (Ps 22:9–10)."[47] However, she is more careful when she names Sophia-Spirit as love and gift. Although she aligns the mutual love of Spirit-Sophia with "the model of relationship most prized by feminist thought," an understanding of Spirit-Sophia as gift must not simply perpetuate social expectations that women give at the expense of their own personhood. Gift, Johnson argues, must be "contextualized within the broad horizon of freedom."[48] Spirit's relational love is not simply one of dependence at the expense of freedom, she reasons. Rather, relationality and freedom are co-essential to each other. Although Johnson does not cite excess here, ultimately she does claim that the actions of the Spirit cannot be categorized neatly into stereotypical masculine or feminine terms. The mystery of God as manifested by Spirit exceeds these understandings.[49]

The Trinity itself is also helpful in describing the excessive slippage between being and action, and our speech about both. In the Trinity, no "person" in the godhead is restricted to one particular role. Each might be ascribed a role—God as creator, Christ redeemer, and Spirit sent out into the world—but each is excessively more then one role. This is because the three are also one, and therefore each does what the other does: Spirit-Sophia creates and saves even as she is a loving presence in the world. The excess of each person pushes against the desire to draw a clear line from the name of the person to the person's essence or the actions that might follow. In this way, the three persons of the Trinity are nomadic travelers within and among each other, not only pressing the limits of the borders among them, but also crossing into each other in ways that simultaneously strengthen and obliterate the idea of the border. Borders are both defined and defied where two (or three, or more) meet, like the merging of a river into the ocean or the seemingly distinct colors of a rainbow made from the bending light of the sun.[50]

Although, certainly, the Christian tradition has repressed feminine imagery of Spirit, even the counterbalance of Spirit-Sophia does not encompass or complete our description. Our speaking about Spirit is never finished because we know, even as we speak, that the Spirit of the triune God is more than this. As Soskice writes, "God is not lacking gender, but more than gender—to which our human experience of gender and physicality feebly but none the less really points."[51] The "more" of gender in the godhead is an excessive more, a more that spills over to us, for does not our performance of gender's excess mirror God's, crossing over and exceeding the boundaries of our name for it?

JESUS AND REVERSIBILITY: SHE WHO IS HE / HE WHO IS SHE

A second nomadic strategy for interpreting gender in the Trinity is reversibility. If excess emphasizes the theological nomad pushing at the border, reversibility is the nomad traversing back and forth across this border. Although excess was, for Johnson, an implicit strategy, reversibility has been key for feminist theologians in the recovery of Jesus-Sophia. Johnson turns to the gospels, especially the gospel of John, to reconstruct a "prehistory of Jesus as the story of Sophia."[52] In particular, John's prologue identifies Sophia as present with God in the beginning, active in creation, descending from heaven to be among the people, and rejected by some while giving life to others.[53] In the rest of John, Jesus' ministry mirrors the wisdom tradition. Like Sophia, Jesus is identified as Torah and his interactions with the symbols of bread, water, and wine follow Wisdom's actions in Proverbs.[54] Finally, both Sophia and Jesus are associated with saving activities, calling people toward a path of right instruction, truth, and life.[55]

By understanding Jesus as "Wisdom's child, Sophia incarnate," Johnson and other early feminist scholars interrupt an association between Jesus' historical male identity, something Johnson does not dispute, and the sacralization of his maleness as an essential aspect of his saving quality.[56] This sacralization has detrimental effects on theological anthropology when a "particular honor, dignity, and normativity accrues to the male sex because it was chosen by the Son of God himself for the enfleshment of incarnation."[57] To disrupt the spiritualization of male superiority, Johnson first returns to the biblical text. Although the Prologue of John is the muse of reversibility, it is also an enemy because of the way that the Logos and the Father-Son construct seem to subsume the role of Wisdom.[58] The figure of Christ is further masculinized in later centuries when he takes on the Greco-Roman role of head of household and is crowned king of the empire.[59] However, even in the figure of the "imperial Christ" Sophia is not entirely subsumed: She becomes a feature of the fourth-century christological controversies over Christ's divinity, where Christ's association with wisdom was used to argue for his divinity.[60] Ultimately for early feminist theologians, reversing the male symbol for Christ with a female one provides a counterbalance for this story of male superiority because it "breaks the stranglehold of androcentric thinking that circles around the maleness of Jesus."[61]

In terms of gender theory, however, the recovery of the feminine symbol from masculine repression is not the end of reversibility's task. Rather, this theoretical tool is one that complicates a strict delineation between the two gender constructions. Regarding the work of reversibility, the literary theorist Shoshana Felman writes, "The substitutions of woman for man and of man for woman, the interchangeability and the reversibility of masculine and feminine manifests a discord that subverts the limits and compromises the coherence of each of the two principles."[62] In this subversion, conventional femininity is exposed as that which simply assures the masculine symbol of his proper superiority, thus loosening the bonds of a strict delineation between the two. The femininity and masculinity that emerge in reversibility's wake align with the nomad's path, as they are symbols "constituted in *ambiguity*," formed "in the uncanny space *between two signs, between* the institutions of masculinity and femininity."[63] With the deployment of the intentional or unintentional strategy of reversal, masculinity and femininity are still at play, but with radically different results, as domination and submission give way to a truly queer mutuality. Taking reversibility seriously, we might spin Rosemary Radford Ruether's famous question "Can a male savior save women?" to ask, "Can a female savior save a man?" For what man is this Jesus who is Sophia enfleshed? What woman is this Wisdom who incarnates as Jesus?[64]

Johnson's reconstruction of Jesus-Sophia resources the fluidity of gender symbols, drawing especially from the wisdom tradition. However, with the tool of reversibility, Johnson could more explicitly argue for a subversive gender symbolism for her Christology. For example, one of Johnson's main goals in her reconstruction of Jesus-Sophia is to offer a theological anthropology that does not valorize one gender over the other. She also wants to avoid the idea that males and females are simply complementary. Johnson's solution, in part, is to argue for a theological anthropology that accounts for the diversity of human characteristics, including gender but expanding to race, economic status, culture, and so on. Broader diversity, Johnson hopes, will help move "beyond the contrasting models of sex dualism" to a "multipolar anthropology."[65] Johnson's "multipolar" vision, however, downplays gender in a way that detracts from Johnson's overall project. Rather than saying that "Jesus' sex is simply an intrinsic part of his own identity as a finite human being," the tool of reversibility would allow Johnson to argue that gender is, in fact, *crucial* to a newly conceived theological anthropology, but in a way that subverts conventional understandings of gender.[66]

Read through the lens of reversibility, I would argue that Johnson's Jesus-Sophia does more to reframe and subvert gender in Christology than she acknowledges. By interpreting Jesus' maleness through the lens of Sophia's femininity, Jesus' masculinity is subverted and transformed by the wisdom narrative. He preaches her love for justice and peace and adopts her desire to bring all of creation under her care. As Sophia, Jesus' ministry is inclusive of women as they "befriend, economically support, advise, and challenge" him, keeping vigil with him at his death and announcing his resurrection.[67] In parables, Jesus-Sophia takes on multigendered divine roles: "a shepherd searching for a lost sheep, a woman looking for her lost coin, a father forgiving his wayward child, a baker woman kneading yeast into dough, a mother giving birth."[68] Theologically, Johnson argues that Jesus-Sophia's mission is one of gender reconstruction. The cross is interpreted as "the self-emptying of male dominating power in favor of the new humanity of compassionate service and mutual empowerment."[69] Further, this inclusive reading of Jesus' ministry fits more seamlessly with the Christ-symbol, which is not modeled on a narrow understanding of Jesus' maleness but on "multiple redemptive role models" within the person of Christ.[70] In Johnson's reconstruction certainly "the typical stereotypes of masculine and feminine are subverted," as she says. This subversion, however, offers more then a situation in which "gender is not constitutive of the Christian doctrine of incarnation."[71] Rather, reversibility offers a way that gender remains constitutive of doctrine and is revolutionized therein.

Thinking reversibility and the Trinity offers a similarly "ambiguously constituted" masculinity and femininity. Whereas meditating on the excess of gender reveals how God is more then gender, reversibility brings gender into the godhead in a refigured way. Although we use gendered metaphors to describe how God relates to us, these metaphors are not a statement about essence. God is only *like* a laboring mother or a forgiving father. In the second person of the Trinity, however, gender is concretized in Jesus' historical male identity. But rather than affirm something ontological about maleness in the godhead, Jesus' association with the wisdom tradition queerly introduces a female presence within the godhead as well.

Rather than contemplating God's gender, what is perhaps more important is how our own understanding of gender is transformed in relationship to God. This is what Sarah Coakley finds in the work of the Cappadocian theologian Gregory of Nyssa (c. 330–c. 395). Gregory utilizes the tool of reversibility as he describes how the soul seeks the divine. At first, the soul is like a bridegroom seeking the bride of Christ, Sophia. However, as the soul progresses in relating to the Divine, it leaves behind intellectual knowledge of God and enters a more receptive, even erotic, state. In this stage, Sophia is Christ the *bridegroom*, pursuing a reunion with the soul who is now understood as the bride. Both the "persons" of God the Father and Spirit are understood by Gregory to be the bridegroom's mother. Coakley writes that for Gregory "gender stereotypes must be reversed, undermined, and transcended if the soul is to advance to supreme intimacy with the Trinitarian God; and . . . the language of sexuality and gender, far from being an optional aside or mere rhetorical flourish in the process, is somehow necessary and intrinsic to the epistemological deepening" that such desire for God entails.[72] Relying on Gregory, Coakley utilizes the reversibility of gender in the godhead to argue against a literal understanding of the social Trinity. In the same way that gender cannot be captured in one person of the godhead, so is each person not distinctly separate in relation to the other. For the three are also one. Further, in thinking of humanity's relationship to God, Gregory's work underscores that "the 'persons' of the Trinity are always being reconfigured and reconstructed as the soul advances to more dizzying intimacy with the divine."[73] Coakley's work with Gregory of Nyssa demonstrates how even ancient orthodoxy utilizes the tool of reversibility, thus disrupting gender stereotypes and providing queer understandings of gender in the human-divine relation.

One of the valuable gifts that Johnson gives us is an account of Sophia's crossing into each person of the Trinity, bringing a reformulated femininity to each and, likewise, disrupting the seemingly solidified masculinity that theological history has bestowed on the three. Sophia's crossing over sets the masculine symbols for God on their own nomadic voyage. Both feminine and masculine symbols co-inhabit the godhead, and yet travel across borders together. Where is she when we say "he"? When we recover the repression of "she," isn't he also transfigured? Because Sophia refuses to be associated with only one person, but is infused in each, she opens up a neglected space for women to see aspects of their own understanding of gender reflected in the godhead. But where sexuality intersects with gender, we see that our own bodies and desires complicate both masculine and feminine symbols for God. Does God's gender change as we pursue God with more intense desire, or does the gendered reversibility at work in God change us?

GOD AND APOPHASIS: SHE WHO ISN'T

Apophasis is the third nomadic strategy for reading gender in the godhead. If excess points to an overflowing at the edges of our concepts of male and female and if reversibility points to the intermingling of the two, apophasis goes right to the heart of the construct and finds nothing there. For as much as God is more than gender, encompassing both male and female symbols and reversing them, God is also not gendered at all. This points to the apophatic dimension of our gendered language about God; as soon as we say something about the male and female images and the Divine we immediately feel we must qualify it, or modify it. In apophatic discourse this is called "unsaying," for the only language that captures what we mean about God and gender is the language of the negative, saying what God is not. Apophasis is at the heart of Johnson's project, as she understands feminist theological interpretation of the Divine as "discourse about the mystery of God."[74] From classical theology she is especially beholden to the doctrine of divine incomprehensibility, or the otherness of God that our finite reality cannot capture. This is not God withholding God's self from humanity but is the inability of a single "human concept, word, or image, all of which originate in experience of created reality, [to] circumscribe divine reality."[75] God's mystery also draws the worshiper into deeper communion with God as she realizes "an unfathomable depth" to that mystery, "a vastness of God's glory too great for the human mind to grasp."[76] As Gregory of Nyssa noted, and as Augustine also said, it is therefore more appropriate to pursue God with our love rather than cognitive knowledge.[77]

Apophatic theology is a helpful tool for Johnson as she denounces the literal use of male language about God, a literalness that represses mystery. In Johnson's understanding, God's mystery belongs to the very essence of God. Paraphrasing Augustine, she writes, "Human minds can never exhaust that livingness: if you have understood, then what you have understood is not God."[78] In her discussion of Johnson's use of the apophatic, Catherine Keller argues that Johnson's denouncement of a literal understanding of God as masculine is itself an apophatic move, an attempt to unsay what has been said about the divine. Keller writes, "Apophasis in its own terms would be more aptly called the exposure of theological *idols*—the unsaying of divine attributes inasmuch as they mistake finite constructions such as gender for the infinite."[79] The proper response to divine incomprehensibility is not silence or a literal naming of God, but many names. "The tradition of the many names of God results from the genuine experience of divine mystery, and acts as a safeguard for it," Johnson writes.[80] In her discussion of the first person of the Trinity, Johnson is especially critical of the theological importance placed on God as father while God as mother has been neglected. Johnson cites Aquinas's reliance on Aristotle's outdated biology placing the male as the active principle in conceiving new life while the female ranks as the inferior passive principle. Thus, God as mother giving birth to creation is a metaphor that would "demean the dignity of God."[81]

In her critique of the metaphor of father and her reconstruction of Mother-Sophia, Johnson does not approach the possibility of the apophasis of gender itself. Like the incomprehensible mystery of God, gender is also mysterious. Catherine Keller has helpfully noted that feminist theory of gender has been approaching a "mysticism of 'knowing ignorance'" parallel to apophatic theology.[82] Within the history of second- and third-wave feminism, and feminist theology more specifically, Keller identifies four folds of gender theory including gender, race, sexuality, and multiplicity. Each of these has contributed to "a certain undoing of gender" moving toward an "apophasis of gender" itself.[83] Keller is respectful of Johnson, citing her work as an early, and largely unrecognized, example of feminist apophasis. But Keller gently argues that an undoing of gender does not necessarily contribute to the historical silencing of women. Rather to unsay gender is to affirm its dense mystery.[84] Like God, gender has many names, or folds, which we are only beginning to articulate.

Multiple workings of the apophasis of gender can be identified in Johnson's work as she attempts to recover positive images of Divinity for women. First, she is clear that the openness of human beings to freedom and responsibility demonstrates how "human beings are dynamically oriented toward fathomless mystery."[85] Thus, our experiences and our ability to be self-present are marked by an infinity that is beyond our full comprehension. This interpretation of theological anthropology in the image of God's mystery underscores the apophatic dimension of our nature as human beings.[86] Although not explicitly, Johnson affirms that because women are made in the image of an infinitely unknowable God, the experience of being a woman is also diverse, if not boundless.[87] Still, she resists staying with this point for too long as her project ultimately argues that mystery need not negate cataphatic speech about God, but instead inspires it: "Through women's encounter with the holy mystery of their own selves as blessed comes commensurate language about holy mystery in female metaphor and symbol, gracefully, powerfully, and necessarily."[88] In this way, the mystery held within the *Imago Dei* allows women to claim a self-understanding in opposition to the oppressive structures of dominant society and, in turn, positively name God with images supportive of the freedom and mystery of women.[89]

Still, an apophatic understanding of gender can strengthen positive speech about God as Mother-Sophia. This is because, as might be expected, positive names for the Divine using male or female metaphors inevitably slip toward gender stereotypes, some even harmfully. In exploring the wisdom tradition in Proverbs, for example, Johnson presents Wisdom as characterized by the feminine example of a nurturer. In order to balance this, however, Johnson "unsays" even this feminine quality with what might be termed masculine qualities: wisdom as a powerful ruler and protector of her people. Employing the apophatic strategy of "many names" which overwhelm and therefore "unsay" just one name, Johnson names Sophia as "sister, mother, female beloved, chef and hostess" but also "preacher, judge, liberator, [and] establisher of justice."[90] Johnson also proceeds carefully as she elaborates on God as Mother-Sophia. Although pointing to the powerful ability to give and sustain life, motherhood has also been utilized by dominant society as a tool to control women. Johnson does not wish to romanticize motherhood or suggest that it is the only or most meaningful social role for women.[91] Amid this ambiguity, Johnson proceeds with a constructive rendering of the Divine Mother, but only after acknowledging "that speech about God proceeds by way of analogy, God being more unlike than like what we know in the best of mothers."[92] Apophasis, then, is the groundwork for the creative maternal love of Mother-Creator, who sustains life and pursues justice and yet remains infinitely hidden, "her vast freedom forever incomprehensible to our minds."[93]

To articulate the movement of apophasis within the Trinity it is helpful to draw a connection between the unsaying of numbers in the Trinity and the unsaying of gender. When we talk about numbers and the Trinity, we again find ourselves approaching apophasis; God is three persons but not three, one but not one. The play of one and three helps disrupt a literal interpretation of the number three in the trinitarian life. Johnson writes, "These terms are not intended to denote anything positive in God, but to remove something" that is the idea that God is *only* the singleness of one or the unity of three. Rather then understand numbers as a map explaining God, the interchange of three and one underscores God's relationality and "refers to divine livingness."[94] The same could be said of gender in the godhead. God is male and not male just as God is female and not female. When we attempt to speak about Divine gender using male and female images, we are both speaking and not speaking about the number two. Perhaps unsaying the two would open space for a third gender, not specific to one "person" of the Trinity, but mysteriously present in all three. Is God disclosing this third in the lives of transgender and genderqueer folks?

THE LIVING TRIUNE GOD: GENDER IN RELATION

In Johnson's Trinity of Spirit-Sophia, Jesus-Sophia, and Mother-Sophia, wisdom crosses into all three persons. Johnson offers an apt quote by Augustine to illustrate the interrelatedness of wisdom to the three persons: "I know not why Father and Son and Holy Spirit should not be called love, and all together one love, just as Father and Son and Holy Spirit are called wisdom, and all together not three but one wisdom."[95] Wisdom participates with each person distinctly, in the roles of creator, redeemer, and sustainer, but also is active in the relationships between the three. In this interrelationship, as previously stated, no one role is performed alone, but all participate together in each distinctive role. Johnson explains this interrelationship as the principle of relationality.[96] Relationality, for Johnson, is marked by deep mutual friendship and radical equality of the three persons.[97] In her essay in this volume, Kathryn Tanner sharpens this thinking when she argues that the relations of the three persons of the Trinity can be understood as both perfectly unified and perfectly different. If God is always a more perfect being than creation, then the diversity between the three persons must be understood as absolute diversity, a diversity that is only approximated by the diversity of creation.[98] Tanner's explanation of how God achieves simultaneous unity and difference is a helpful illustration of how God's being always exceeds human logic. Pointing, again, to the apophatic dimension of our knowledge of God, Keller writes, "We cannot overcome our ignorance of the infinite any more than we can overcome our finitude."[99]

We have traced the Spirit's excess, Christ's reversibility, and God's apophasis in the triune God. Certainly the three tools are not restrictive to the three persons but, like the persons themselves, interrelate and cross over borders into the other. The three tools are helpful, however, for reading gender in the Trinity as a whole. In part, we can say that gender in the godhead is excessive, a "more" that cannot be contained by the symbols of masculinity and femininity or by our understandings of how these symbols relate to male and female bodies. The "more" of God's gender is something that we can indeed look for and identify, but our naming of it will be partial and incomplete. This is so because of the workings of reversibility. In the three persons, masculinity and femininity intermingle and reemerge in a way that transforms the symbols. Finally, the gender of God can be said to not be there at all, resisting our anthropomorphic tendencies in references to God as "he" or "she" as well as descriptors of masculine and feminine attributes such as Father and Mother. Soskice writes: "God is not a male. Even though God became incarnate in the man, Jesus Christ. God is not a creature at all, far less a male creature."[100] In the same way God is not female, although this construction has had much less play in our historical and corporate theological imagination, which is exactly Johnson's point in writing *She Who Is*. Building on Johnson, this essay illustrates how trinitarian life disrupts our concept of male and female as two because the Divine is always exceeding, reversing, and, simultaneously, undoing the constructions of gender as we know them.

A NOMADIC *IMAGO DEI*

As Johnson's foundational text demonstrates, theology has erroneously mapped onto the godhead the human history of inequality between men and women so that God as male became a literal idol in Christian speech about God. Johnson's reconstruction of Sophia as central to the triune God was an intervention into this idolatrous history. Constructive theology, like Johnson's, has positively worked to affirm the identities of those marginalized by theology. This work, however, has also contributed to a certain reification of identity in our speech about humanity. We sometimes confidently proclaim that gendered imagery for God is metaphorical, as if our own gender were completely understandable. Focusing on excess, reversibility, and apophasis is a way to tell the story of gender differently, to uncover how masculinity and femininity in the godhead are always in play together, each contributing to, constituting, and transforming the other. Further, the formulation of the triune three and one interrupts the dyad of gender, opening up a space for the discussion of a third gender, beyond the constructions of male and female.

Gregory of Nyssa aptly says, "Human nature is not able to contain the infinite, unbounded divine nature."[101] Therefore, the incomprehensibility of gender in the Trinity is mirrored, if feebly, in the mystery of our own gender identities where we continually encounter excess, reversibility, and apophasis in our gendered understandings and performances. Turning to scripture, we find that humans are created in the image of God, "male and female God created them" (Genesis 1:27). Indeed, God may create us as *gendered*, but this is not the end of the story, as our gender, created in the image of Divine mystery, is undetermined enough to keep troubling us as we strive to articulate and express it. Along these lines Keller wonders, "*Am* I simply a gender? Or do I *have* one? As for sex, am I one? More than one? Or is sex what I *do*? Or don't?"[102] Yet we also learn from scripture that our gender is transformed by our life in Christ (Galatians 3:28). Since it is through Christ that we participate in the triune life, it follows that in Christ our own gendered understandings are exceeded, reversed, and receding. Christ queers gender so that in Christ our understanding of our own gender is transformed.[103]

Pursuing a theological anthropology that both affirms and yet undoes gender is one task of the nomadic theologian. Nomadic theological practice asserts that we have too readily constructed God in our image while God has, all along, been beckoning us across such borders, moving us toward a practice of wandering that trinitarian life exemplifies. Each crossing highlights the indwelling of the three as one as much as it defines their distinctiveness as an absolutely diverse three. In God, gender migrates from one to two to three and back again. Human gender identities have borders that are traversed in multiple ways. Like Braidotti's multilingual nomad, the "polyglot," transgender people speak a multigendered language that creatively reforms gender norms. For some transgender folks, there is one crossing over, from the gender assigned at birth to the other gender. This crossing is a coming home. For others who identify as genderqueer there may be infinite crossings. For many, the ambiguous symbols of masculinity and femininity are rearticulated as they overlap with sexual identities including straight, bisexual, gay, lesbian, and queer.[104] For those embodying a "monolingual" gender (or sexuality), the triune God beckons deeper into the mystery of gender, revealing a silence that "opens a visionary space in which unexpected solidarities can form."[105] The more we can defer any final determination of our own gendered understanding, the more space we allow for others to live. "Since," as Butler writes, "life might be understood as precisely that which exceeds any account we may try to give it."[106]

Admitting the partiality of our gendered expressions, we are all "nomadic subjects."[107] Gender is always slipping away from us as much as it also, sometimes, holds together. The mystery of ourselves, however, is like the mystery of God; it is not a threat but an opportunity for deeper reflection. In Johnson's wise words, "The triune God is not simply unknown, but positively known to be unknown and unknowable—which is a dear and profound kind of knowledge."[108] With a nomadic spirit, we pursue the knowledge of the unknowable with passion and grace.

Doxological Diversities and Canticle Multiplicities: The Trinitarian Anthropologies of David H. Kelsey and Ivone Gebara

JACOB J. ERICKSON

> For the designation seraphim really teaches this—a perennial circling around the divine things, penetrating warmth, the overflowing heat of movement which never falters and never fails . . .
> —PSEUDO-DIONYSIUS, *The Celestial Hierarchy*

> Three things that I would be: radiant as Cherubim
> As tranquil as are Thrones, on fire as Seraphim
> —ANGELUS SILESIUS, *The Cherubinic Wanderer*

The grand philosophical tradition examining the problem of the "One and the Many" is not something one learns in elementary school. And yet, I feel inexorably drawn to that very problem—there is something elementary (indeed, elemental) about the infinite relations of the one and the many. It is the quotidianness, the strange ordinariness, of the multiplicity of life that still draws me to reflect on that very problem, whether consciously using the philosophical tradition laid before me or not. One might better say that the "problem" is not a "problem" at all, but a possibility of life and living itself.

From the vantage point of the prairie farm community where I grew up, the "many" of the earth exposes the fragility of humanity daily. Diverse weather patterns shift quickly, and prairies, for all their apparent bare glory, live out one of the most ecologically turbulent and biodiverse ecosystems on the planet. To look upon the multiplicity of prairie grasses as an entangled ecosystem, sometimes as one organism, is simply to see a beautiful reality of life. Indeed, it was such a creative reality that offered the philosophers Gilles Deleuze and Félix Guattari the metaphor for their philosophical writing as "rhizomatic."[1]

In our contemporary age of ecological crises, ecojustice becomes entwined with an everyday problem of the "one and the many." We live in an era where the daily choices, movements, and conceptual delineations of one constructed species—the human—is snuffing out the many in all forms. At this moment, human beings move to control and exploit the rich biodiversity of animals and plants, the multiplicity of climate systems, and the diversities of ecological interactions. Mass extinctions that could never before have been imagined are becoming inescapable realities.

Human technological creation is not in itself morally wrong. New philosophical and theological projects into the technological "posthuman" are remarkably promising (Donna Haraway's work, for example). Yet, traditional theology historically tends toward a vision of anthropological "dominion" which overlooks and often willingly sacrifices the beauty-ridden messiness of planetary life to the false human projects of invulnerability and isolation. In this light, technology becomes dubious when viewed as exclusively human, unambiguously good, used without conscience, and exercised without moral ecological vision and imagination.

It might be asked at this point, if ecology is my concern, why write on theological anthropology in the first place? As an isolatable doctrinal locus, theological anthropology is fairly young—indeed, itself constituted by the project of the Modern (read: White, European, Male, Straight) Individual. Isn't such a theological space already caught up in the midst of an irredeemable project? Would writing about theological anthropology itself contribute to ecological violence?

I'm convinced that to leave theological anthropology in general untouched and untransformed does more harm than good. Theological writing is always implicated in a strange cacophony of voices. Like overgrowing weeds and plants that take back human ruins deep into the soil of the planet, ecological theology must transgress into those doctrinal spaces that traditionally would sacrifice environmental concerns to human interest. To reenvision ecological justice into these spaces is to imagine unexpected blossoms in the midst of scorched places. Consider it the theological version of guerrilla gardening.

Reflecting on theological anthropology entails great risks, then, if we attempt to discern hope even in the midst of our historical failures. This is, of course, an existential commitment to divine incarnation in all messy, graceful forms. Most of all, responsible reflection demands the risky companionship of creeping plants, fluttering birds, and the eyes of cats (Jacques Derrida, among others, knew this well). Too long the human has occupied the space of the "one"; we must rethink the human back into the theological many, and rethink the distinct "oneness" of each creature constituting and constituted by that "manyness." We must reflect our ecological relations, our biomultiplicities. If I might be so bold as to paraphrase a well-known saying from Irenaeus: The glory of God is the cosmos made fully alive, fully queer, and fully entangled.[2]

RETHINKING THE ANTHROPOCENTRISM OF ANTHROPOLOGY

I begin with a blurry textual icon from the history of negative theology. A flock of seraphim, hybrid creatures of six wings, human, bird, and possibly snake. A seraph's wings flutter, blurring sight and vision of the divine, blurring sight and vision of the other circling creatures. The blur, the "penetrating warmth," the "overflowing heat of movement" is an eternal reality, never faltering or failing, signaling a deep relationship of love within the angelic assembly. For this vision of life, all is blurred without erasure of difference among these creatures and among the divine. Indeed, in the ancient hymn, "Let All Mortal Flesh Keep Silence," the seraphim "veil their faces to the presence as with ceaseless voice they cry."[3] In the presence of the divine, seraphim sing a mysterious, simultaneous response and call, illumining a mysterious economy of divinity. These wingéd apophatics find the "presence" of divine relation with Others in a blurred singing of a thrice-times-holy[4] closely associated by many theologians in the Christian tradition with the classical doctrine of the Trinity.

I offer this image of the hybrid, the seraph, as a strange theopoetic proposal for theological anthropology. In the wake of environmental philosophy and ecotheology's criticisms of dangerous anthropocentrisms, we must find new ways of understanding our creatureliness in the midst of our planetary relations to the divine. Resting in the wisdom and wispy rustling of these queer-looking seraphim, my working hunch is that our wrestling with the symbol of the Trinity, divine multiplicity—more than offering a social program or unveiling insight into the life of God—sings an unsaying, a warm blur, of the human, and, as such, exposes fragilities in often falsely constructed creaturely boundaries of life.[5] Talking Trinity in theological anthropology can continuously deconstruct dangerous impulses of anthropocentrism. And, so, what I propose is a circulation around and between some recent work in theological anthropology, David H. Kelsey and Ivone Gebara, mainly, but also other contemporary feminist voices, for a queering of the human creature in relation to the divine. What emerges is a divine relationality that illumines ecologically convivial, *queer* creatures—a blur of human, animal, bird, elements, and divine warmth—where the burning passion of seraphim in all of their suffering and ecstasy might more closely model a contemporary hope for a "posthuman" vision of theological anthropology;[6] for if human beings (and all creatures for that earthly matter) are something akin to what many in the Christian tradition call a "vestige of the Trinity," that blurry mark divests senses of anthropocentrism and exposes our own odd, everyday creatureliness, a creatureliness that sings mysterious stories, doxologies, and canticles of divinity.[7]

DOXOLOGICAL DIVERSITIES

The latter half of the twentieth century positively bursts with new rejuvenations and reconstructions of trinitarian thought in relation to the everyday human creature.[8] Karl Rahner's axiomatic descriptions of the immanent and economic Trinity, for instance, strongly move to the fore a question of theological relevance. Is the Trinity necessary? What meaning does the Trinity hold for Christian theology, if any? And how does the Trinity relate to ordinary life, ordinary experience, ordinary practice? Emblematic of this movement, Catherine Mowry LaCugna, herself following Rahner's work, proclaimed that "the doctrine of the Trinity is ultimately a practical doctrine with radical consequences for Christian life."[9] In this peculiar turn to the quotidian, meditations on the Trinity emphasize economic formulations in the concrete world of the human being. The "radical consequences" surprisingly emerge within the familiarity of human life. That is to say, this new trinitarian resurgence primarily concerns itself with theological anthropology.

One of the more recent of these works is David H. Kelsey's majestic *Eccentric Existence: A Theological Anthropology*. Although he explicitly writes in the doctrinal locus of theological anthropology in this work, Kelsey, too, locates *Eccentric Existence* in the midst of the new discussions and emerging contours of trinitarian theology. And, indeed, the text could almost be read as a long meditation on the economic Trinity. In a chapter titled "The One Who Has to Do with Us," Kelsey turns to the *"taxes,"* the Greek term for the relational patterns of the classical persons of the Trinity. By examining the movement of these "persons," Kelsey proposes to explore divine relation to human being.[10] Fundamentally, he notes that in "God's creating, eschatologically consummating, and reconciling, the pattern of relationships among the three hypostases changes."[11] God's relation to human creatures changes as different sorts of stories are told about that relationality. Kelsey argues that out of the perichoretic whir of the Trinity, three sorts of patterned stories emerge into a complex theological description of the human.

Here, of course, I must risk a disclaimer: I can raise only a handful of particular features from a very precise work that contains over one thousand pages.[12] What I attempt here, however, is to crystallize some of *Eccentric Existence*'s spoken and unspoken trinitarian moves. To that end, Kelsey parcels these three patterned stories first with the relation of creation, "It is the triune God in its threefold dancing around that creates. Formulated abstractly, the plot of scriptural stories of God creating relates the three in a definite pattern: the Father creates through the Son in the power of the Spirit."[13] The divine story of creation emerges out of this particular pattern, while other stories emerge out of the other *taxes*. After explaining some of the particular emphases of this sort of creation, Kelsey argues, second, that, in a very different kind of story, "It is the perichoretic triune God that draws creation—and humankind as part of creation—into an eschatological consummation. Formulated abstractly, the plot of scriptural stories of God drawing creation to eschatological consummation relates the three in a different pattern: 'The Spirit, sent by the Father with the Son, draws creation to eschatological consummation.'"[14] The *taxes* of the Trinity, construed this way, tell a distinctly different story of human being, and finally, "It is the triune God in its threefold *circumcessio* that reconciles estranged creatures to itself. Formulated abstractly, the plot of scriptural stories of God reconciling alienated humankind relates the three in yet another pattern: the Son, sent by the Father in the power of the Spirit, reconciles."[15] With yet another shuffle of the hypostases, a third story emerges about human being.

These perichoretic "snapshots," Kelsey argues, provide three sorts of stories that serve as identity descriptions in theological anthropology, each giving different sorts of answers to the three questions of (1) what and (2) who a human is and (3) how a human is supposed to be oriented toward her or his contexts. These three separate storied *taxes* form what Kelsey argues is a theological triple helix of the human. As such, these plots imprint themselves on the human in quotidian contexts, shaping everyday life and possibility.

Even more, however, these three expose a blur, a peculiar mystery of the divine's relation to us. If theological anthropology implies separate, irreducible stories, we find ourselves confronted with a strange feature of God-talk. Human relation to the divine is described as a narrative multiplicity. "No single monolithic story can be told about God's relating to us. God's mystery eludes that, which means that there can be no single monolithic theological story to tell about what and who we are and how we ought to be."[16] One simple appeal cannot explain away theological anthropology in Kelsey's theocentric construal of anthropology. In speaking of the divine, one finds that other unspoken stories remain just as vital to who one is, and yet we cannot account for them all simultaneously. Kelsey continues, "If the ways in which God relates are irreducibly threefold, theocentric accounts of human persons will be irreducibility threefold. There is no single, simple Christian metanarrative."[17] Theology itself, because of the *taxes* of God, can never be a single story told.[18]

To give an account of the divine is not only a difficult task because of the oft-made finite/infinite binary or the dangers of idol construction, then, but because the divine relates to human beings—each human being—in a multiplicity of ways; no simple testimony can speak the full texture of all that happens theologically in a single human life. I can begin to speak of my life as a created being, how I comprehend the flesh of my body as created, my complicated place in ecological systems, even the infinitesimal reality of my cosmological existence, and yet I have not spoken anything of the other ways God's economy relates to me. I have barely even hoped to fully account for the mystery of my createdness. Multiple narratives, multiple creatures constitute my relationality with the divine. Of the threefold narrativity of what he calls a "systematically unsystematic" theology, Kelsey beautifully observes:

Nor can there be, parasitic on it, any Christian anthropological metatheory about human persons that can, at least in principle, systematically synthesize all relevant true claims about human being, Christian theological claims or otherwise. Human beings are in their own way too richly glorious, too inexhaustibly incomprehensible, too capable of profound distortions and bondage in living deaths, too capable of holiness, in short, too mysterious to be captured in that fashion.[19]

Too mysterious to give an account of ourselves and our bodies, and yet we feel compelled to do so. We sing, encounter mysterious vision. We circle in an attempt to speak a description, and yet no butterfly net we make could capture our full mysterious messiness.[20]

To speak of the divine, to give an account of divine relationality, is to encounter a narrative blur. Such an account is a doxology, a praise-filled response to the glorious mystery of the divine. The mysterious relation of the divine evokes our own thrice-called "holies," wholly meaningful yet wholly inadequate. Indeed, Kelsey's triple helix perhaps offers us an insight into doxology not unlike the theory of giving an account of oneself recently developed by Judith Butler, where "the 'I' can tell neither the story of its own emergence nor the conditions of its own possibility without bearing witness to a state of affairs to which one could not have been present, which are prior to one's own emergence as a subject who can know, and so constitute a set of origins that one can narrate only at the expense of authoritative knowledge."[21] I find myself having to risk speaking differently about myself. For when we are asked to give an account of ourselves as theological creatures, we encounter the difficult, storied, diversity of the economic Trinity. Should we orient our selves to this diversity of stories, giving an account of the *taxes* on our own peculiar lives requires a kind of fiction. Our imaginations burst with accounts of the divine's relation to "us" and the world.

Even while exposing theological openings and diversities in the various narrated doxologies of humans, *Eccentric Existence* might be opened further into a broader narrative multiplicity. Kelsey's work on theological anthropology serves as a sort of innovation on an orthodox theme but leaves certain questions unanswered. First, why is the same, masculine-gendered language used so consistently throughout the text? Kelsey's particular use of trinitarian economy does evoke the classical language in fresh ways, most certainly. But even while the relational terms of Father, Son, and Spirit are qualified as just that—relational terms to each other within the Trinity—patriarchal gender constructions of the Trinity still function to create certain forms and formations of masculinity.[22] In exegeting the perichoretic whir of the classical Christian God, couldn't a great assembly of divine images be proposed?[23]

Another realm of concerns that arises from and about Kelsey's text is that of ecological context and anthropocentrism. In each of the major sections of the work, Kelsey helpfully discusses the deep textures of proximate and ultimate contexts to which we belong; he does great honor to the beauty and glory of our proximate, and also ecological, contexts. Still, such a bifurcation of proximate and ultimate might risk the very "otherworldliness" and supernaturalism of theology that unhelpfully devalues our proximate ecological contexts. Truly, Kelsey's sketching of theo-anthropological contexts under the scrutiny of ecological theory deserves an in-depth treatment elsewhere.

In an excursus from a section on "Our Proximate Contexts as Created," *Eccentric Existence* spends just a brief amount of space exploring the difficulties of anthropocentrism explicitly.[24] Theological meditation of the sort attempted in *Eccentric Existence*, Kesley argues, can never really escape the bounds of human reflection and the human practices that constitute our quotidian lives. Contextually, humans, for him, seem to be bound by certain epistemological limits. Conceptualization is a *human* activity to begin with, and human beings can only really press at the limits of their knowledgeable attentiveness to the ecological worlds around them. Kelsey observes, "It is, we might say, epistemically anthropocentric. Indeed, we might wonder how it could be otherwise when it is human persons who are trying to understand the context into which they have been born as God's creation."[25] Human knowledge, in this view, is circumscribed to human beings in some way. Human persons describing the richness of their contexts cannot fully escape the human limits in describing other creatures and the theological complexities of life. Yet, might ecological relations run deeper? Might not nonhuman ecologies actually *constitute* humanity in a way that a nonanthropocentric epistemology is not only possible, but probable, necessary, and the only way to actually know? That is, how do animals like dogs or giraffes intimately constitute the quotidian of human and other creaturely lives?

Kelsey does argue that epistemic anthropocentrism does not necessarily entail an anthropocentric description of the whole of reality. He asserts that the project "need not be or become ontologically anthropocentric. It does not assume or suggest that other creatures are real and have value only to the extent that they can serve as instruments that extend the scope and power of human persons' practices, rather than being real and valuable in their own right."[26] The ontological reality of creatures in relation to the triune God is not, for Kelsey, anthropocentric in value. Other creatures do indeed lead lives of value independent of human valuing of them. Still, creaturely subjectivities and practices, if we can use those terms, constitute human creatures in ways contemporary thought is just beginning to explore.

Here, finally, from these lines of thought a related question emerges, in this storied multiplicity: Why do just three narratives emerge? Differentiating the three with precision is a helpful move for conceptual clarity, but "three" stories cannot begin to fully account for the different, manifold experiences of divine relationality. To get stuck on just three Christian anthropological stories risks a so-often-occurring taxidermy of the *taxes*. Stories of call, liberation, eros, flesh all can have life and testimony on their own. Perichoresis, if it is a blurry dance with the creaturely, surely contains more than just three snapshots of Christian life, even if such stories are particularly located in creation, consummation, and redemption. To give an account of God's differentiated relation with human beings in a threefold way seems to see only the tip of the divine iceberg. In all of our doxological diversity, we speak the little that we know, veiled to the full presences and absences of the divine and yet part of those manifold stories nonetheless.[27]

CANTICLE MULTIPLICITIES

Even with all of this talk of doxological diversity, rarely do anthropologies rooted in the Trinity coincide with talk about our ecological life. In fact, trinitarian discourse *on the whole* (with regard to anthropology and otherwise) tends to swirl into a mysterious math problem or an enigmatic theological confusion to be ignored. And so, to speak about ecology and the Trinity usually reduces to some vaguely halting statement that, somehow, the Triune God creates. Following that thesis, the traditional metaphoric language people use for the Triune God in everyday speech sounds all too human: God is a communion of three *persons* who create or, at its most eccentric, two men and a bird (with the bird usually forgotten, fluttering about in the background).

The traditional language of the persons of the Trinity, even if theologically functional, presents a variety of difficulties when attempting to talk about everyday human life and ecology. Other theologians have begun to offer exciting proposals for alternatives to classical trinitarian language.[28] In a move with which I'm implicated, a number of theologians have turned to speak of the Trinity as a symbol of divine multiplicity.[29] In tandem to such proposals, another dimension of trinitarian language might prove helpful in "grounding" such language in its ecological context.[30] Trinitarian theologians generally speak of triune life in process, in movement, in circulation with all life. The concept for such language is, of course, perichoresis.[31] As Elizabeth A. Johnson observes, "Divine life circulates, without any anteriority or posteriority, without any superiority or inferiority of one to the other."[32] And the sheer movement of the concept might articulate a nearness to the creativity of life that helps bring trinitarian language back to earth, for to talk about perichoresis is to talk about the movements of the very blurs of life that evoke the doxologies of Creation.

Yet, doxology is never enough, one might say, and never truly remains doxology. Praise does sing at the limits of what we theologically describe. But in singing, music blurs with other music circulating around. To speak those musical stories is to speak a blur of storied flesh. The divine does not simply tell stories of human being and humans sing back obediently. Perichoresis disperses stories that are enfleshed and unruly. Laurel Schneider reminds us that "stories themselves have lives and creative agency. Stories, told in the right season and in a good mind, build and unbuild the world. . . . Honest stories have power and sway, which, once told, are *never* under the control of the storyteller."[33] The stories of divine relationality escape and blur into the world. Stories *occur*, moving created flesh as fingerpaints on wax paper, blending and evoking a number of colors and textures. According to Schneider, "Stories—the ones that get loose, build and unbuild the world—are the real concern of theology precisely because they express the motility of creation."[34] Stories of creatures occur with stories of other creatures, a blending of words, flesh, and spirit.

Divine stories, multiply enfleshed, evoke yet another glance at theological anthropology—that of a *bodied*, relational multiplicity. The work of Ivone Gebara is helpful here. She, too, wrestles with the Trinity's disconnection from the bodies of life and stories of justice. In *Longing for Running Water*, she observes, "The Trinity seems to have nothing to do with abandoned children, landlessness, women's oppression, the neglect of indigenous people and blacks, and the extermination of children and young people."[35] Does language of the Trinity, Gebara asks, intersect with the everyday sufferings of social, racial, gendered, and ecological injustice? Like Lacugna or Kelsey, Gebara is concerned that the Trinity should intersect with the quotidian, but only if we are to get beyond the doctrine's traditional anthropocentric and androcentric language.[36] She continues, "The inquiry includes the following lines of inquiry: exploring what, in human experience, is related to trinitarian language; examining religious language and its crystallization in religious institutions; and reconstructing trinitarian meanings and celebrating life."[37] Rooted in language, what of human experience causes one to speak trinitarianly?

In an evocative meditation, Gebara pauses to give suggestive answers and to speak of the experience of wonder and the human. She urges, "I want to remind readers that human beings are the fruit of a long process in the evolution of life itself. Life evolved for millions and millions of years before the creation of the species to which we belong and which we call human. Within humanity, life continues to be created."[38] Speaking of human life, at the very least biologically, is a remarkable experience of envisioning the complex processes of emergent creativity.

That emergent creativity blurs into human production itself. Humans are not only the strange, complex products of movements of creativity in Gebara's thought; human beings exercise a stunning creativity themselves. She writes, "Participating in the creative evolution of life, we re-create ourselves. This is manifested in our ability to reflect and love, in our ethical behavior, and in all the other capabilities that make us what we are."[39] In a paradoxically open tautology, human beings create out of their creativity. Importantly, Gebara's view does not simply jettison anthropocentrism per se, but includes humanity and gestures toward new ways of being human.

Arguing for this sort of creative newness, Gebara argues that if the threeness of the divine is a symbol instead for the multiplicity of life, we might find more resonances in our everyday interactions: "If we take the number three as a symbol of multiplicity, we will find that, in their lived lives, people experience the awesome multiplicity of things—of their plurality, the great differences among them, their bewildering transformations, their fragility and transience, and the blend of life and death, death and life."[40] This multiplicity of things, in all of their movement, speaks to a human sense of the multiplicity of the divine. For, as Gebara clarifies, "The Trinity is not a being in itself, to be portrayed by us as if we were describing the qualities of an apple or a cashew. The Trinity we worship lives in us and we live in it."[41] The mutual dwelling of the Trinity and world is a relational story where divinity and flesh remain inseparable, and often difficult to distinguish. To speak of our relation to the divine is inevitably to speak about our lives, the other creatures, ecologies, and organisms that constitute those lives. We end up speaking of wings and scales that blur, circulate, and constitute our own flesh. "In speaking of [the Trinity], we speak of ourselves. In attempting to describe it, we describe ourselves. The Trinity is a language, a metaphor that seeks to explain the unexplainable, the ineffable."[42] Our language is of flesh; our stories blur with the creatures around us; and our self-descriptions become hybrid and seraphic.

This similar emphasis on language allows Gebara to break down a God-world binary alongside a human-earth binary. She argues, "The Father, Son, and Holy Spirit are not of divine stuff as opposed to our human stuff; rather, they are relationships—relationships we human beings experience and express in metaphorical language rather than metaphysical terms."[43] These divine bodied relationships, throughout the cosmos, the earth, in human beings, in creatures, open up life as a continuing relational mystery of both destruction and creation, where our lives become enveloped in stories of divinity and therefore stories of divine creatures. "Therefore we need to reaffirm that the Trinity is the expression of the Mystery, both one and multiple, that envelops us, that has made us what we are, and in which we participate ceaselessly."[44] Oneness and multiplicity become expressions of our storied bodies together.

As divine relationships, the human creatures sing out psalmic praise, stories of newness all their own. "We are constantly being invited to return to our roots: to commune with the earth, with all peoples, and with all living things, and to realize that transcendence is not a reality 'out there,' isolated, 'in itself,' superior to all that exists, but a transcendence within us, among us; in the earth, in the cosmos, and everywhere."[45] We sing out of canticle multiplicities, new stories emerging of our life together. An inability to give a full account of who we are related to the divine brings newness. In the blur of the creaturely, we sing new stories that get loose, again retexturing their worlds. As Gebara states, "This transcendence is a canticle, a symphony unceasingly played by the infinite creativity of *life*."[46] The canticles of life illumine a sort of elastic interrelatedness: the multiplicity of Trinity with the multiplicity of earth.[47] All bear some vestige of this multiplicity, this difference in togetherness. This is a panentheistic view, to boot. Talk about the Trinity, then, can serve powerfully to direct theological discourse away from its often caustically anthropocentric convictions—even in the locus of theological anthropology.

In a later work, Gebara speaks about this multiplicity of stories through the concept of the "esse-diversity of God." In *Out of the Depths: Women's Experience of Evil and Salvation*, she argues that the contemporary situation of the earth in both its pluralism and need for ecological consciousness prods us into new modes of speaking and theological discourse. Out of the breakdown of the God-world binary, she observes, "This situation leads us to look for a plural discourse on God or on this mystery that crosses our lives."[48] The search begins for a multiplicity of language that can speak to the mystery of God's multiplicity, of a God that dwells in, with, and under created reality in a depth of relationship. She clarifies further, "To speak of the esse-diversity of God means to speak first of all of life in its extraordinary richness, but a life that unfolds in the complexity of a vital mystery."[49] Like the deep metaphoric language of the Trinity, God's esse-diversity is grounded in the stunning multiplicity of created reality.

For Gebara, the esse-diversity of God points toward God's interpenetrating relationality with the vast and varied life of ecological creatureliness. She asserts that "the concept of esse-diversity favors equally the contribution of all beings, situates them outside hierarchical boundaries, and still does not accentuate any presumed superiority of some over others."[50] Divine esse-diversity attempts to reenvision nonhierarchical relationships throughout the whole of creation. She continues, noting that "the esse-diversity of God is a metaphor based on the relatedness of everything with everything else: all things live in God and God lives in everything. In this sense, God is that reality that penetrates, crosses, and vivifies every other reality."⁵¹ Gebara exposes here a vast theological, cosmological interpenetration of divinity. God is that which binds and vivifies all created life in a deep relationality of "all in all."

There is multiplicity in the divine stories of our flesh. And accordingly, life moves and pulses in a multidirectionality of relationship. The explosive, creative potential of canticles signals something about creation. In a previous, mysterious incarnation of this colloquium of which this book is a part, Kathryn Tanner argued, contrary to some essential human nature in theological anthropology, for the plasticity of the human. She observed that "human beings have plastic power, self-formative capacities."⁵² These capacities create the peculiarity of human beings, a peculiar involvement of self-creation. She continues, insightfully: "When it is the plasticity of human lives before the divine that is the issue, blurring the boundary between spirit and matter is often a primary gambit."⁵³ The plastic multiplicity of matter becomes a serious issue when talking about divine-human relationality. And, beyond the human, "Humans demonstrate that, appearances to the contrary . . . the material world itself is plastic—by extension just as plastic to divine influence, one might hope, as human lives."⁵⁴ Viewing Tanner's statement from another angle, a human being is not simply plastic to the divine stories that relate to her, but to the materialities and creatures that surround her as well.

What the Trinity exposes through my exploration of Kelsey and Gebara is this plasticity of creation that might be more appropriately described as an interplasticity or even an interadaptation.⁵⁵ Elements, waves, molecules, and flesh can all bear the vestige of trinitarian life, trinitarian stories. These creatures sing together of creation, consummation, redemption, liberation, eros, and more. The entire reality of storied-flesh and cosmos is one that participates in and sings impressions of the divine. The interplasticity of the divine interplays with the interplasticity of life. And the interplasticity of life with the divine opens up the mysterious possibilities of planetary existence, an existence where creatures and divinity blur, tell powerful stories inevitably enmeshed together.

The Trinity exposes the mystery of creaturely being with other creatures—creatures with creatures, creatures in creatures, worlds in worlds. When the economy of the Trinity is meditated on as theological anthropology, human beings find themselves inhabiting a larger ecological multiplicity and a fragile relationality. What I am suggesting is that the Trinity exposes a strange *mysterium convivium*, a mystery of life together. We find our doxological attempts to respond to divine stories simultaneously, queerly blurred with the canticle-like eruptions of divine stories and poems—all of them refiguring new textures, new practices, and possibilities in everyday life. To borrow images from Mayra Rivera and Laurel Schneider, respectively, the relocation of trinitarian language in experience illumines the reality that transcendence *touches* and incarnation is *promiscuous*.[56] In a seraphic blur, angelic wings brush and heat our lives daily, flirting and enticing. This sort of trinitarian economy is much more fleshy than we might have imagined!

SERAPHIC VESTIGES: SINGING A MYSTERIOUS CONVIVIALITY OF THE EARTH

Through this blur of trinitarian stories and flesh, one can hear again the fluttering wings of the seraph from where this writing began.[57] What new possibilities for an ecological anthropology might be sung into existence? At first glimpse, the symbol of the angel is an unlikely theological resource for developing a theological anthropology; for a theology attempting to take into account the heterogeneity of bodied experience, seraphim are unlikely companions. Theologians and mystics often describe angels as incorporeal and ethereal, at best. At worst, angels may deceive in their mysterious messages and potentially ominous intentions. For certain conservative, supernaturalistic Protestant factions, fallen angels roam the hillsides beckoning the weak of faith to idolatry and doom.

Nevertheless, some apophatic mystics in the history of Christian theology turned to angelic themes precisely where tradition failed them. In his exploration of this unsaying of God, Pseudo-Dionysius explores "celestial hierarchies" populated with uncommon creatures and relations.[58] And, Angelus Silesius, for example, mysteriously beloved by Jacques Derrida, fashions in *The Cherubinic Wanderer* a Christian life in the image and vestige of angelic mysticism.[59] Silesius's human wanderer desires the burning passion of angelic love for the divine. In the passage quoted at the beginning of this essay titled "What God's Lover Desires," the mystic casts himself as the erotic lover of the divine and strangely desires to be "on fire as Seraphim."[60] The theopoetic flesh of angels is exactly what theological anthropology might need to unpack a queer ecological vision of divine multiplicity, again, a *mysterium convivium*.[61]

In a strange desire to follow this poetic move by Silesius and others, we might begin to say that a seraphic theological imagination involves itself in an angelic conviviality, in *a planetary vision of wandering in divine love*. Angelic relations overflow with the excess of the divine love of Trinity and the divine love connecting each other. Each seraph, complexly dependent on the rest of the angelic host, blurs into the others in the pulsing circulation of a divine love that constitutes each creature uniquely yet knows no bounds. The angels wander in and beyond one another, reveling in divine passion through a long journey of creaturely relations.

These creatures revel in a vulnerability that risks loving possibility, an angelic biodiversity that is upheld by love by and through difference, not in spite of it. Dionysius's angels live polylogical, multidialogical lives together, responding and calling to one another, responding and calling to the divine. Each porous creature sings in an exposed interpenetration of love, queerly gendered and creatured in that pulsing warmth of an erotic divinity.

Imagined this way, if angelic creatures are entangled in their angelic ecologies by love, love itself urges us toward a theo-ethical consideration of our ecological relations as well. In a stunning essay that meditates on the work of Anne Conway, Catherine Keller asks similarly, "Might we now read the interlinkage of complex creatures as the manifestation of a Supreme Conviviality? As another way of translating 'God is love'?"[62] Indeed, a risking of love relationships with all creatures, related in a perichoresis of "trinitarian" life, becomes possible when such planetary conviviality is taken seriously. Realizing that the creative riskiness of love is the basis of our creaturely relations urges us to love relationships with our ecological contexts. To love our ecological contexts because they are so deeply a part of us entails a recognition of the deep mystery of the relations that constitute creaturely life.

I might say further, then, that this love is the basis for the cosmic interplasticity of creation. Planetary ecologies are molded by, wander through, form with, and encompass creatures in remarkably different ways from moment to moment. These promiscuously entangled creatures grow remarkably unique (queer) interpenetrating relationships. As animals, winds, sounds, elements, and other creatures migrate and move, their interactions are constituted and lured by a divine love that pulsates between and beyond them. Each creature wanders in and as a heterogeneous, convivial performance of life, enriched by the risky blurring of our ecological bounds, ecologies continuously perform new relationships for the purposes of flourishing and survival.

Another way of expressing this love would be to say that our multiple creaturely relationships form ecologically interrelated harmonies and cacophonies that become the bio-Spiritual grounds of divine incarnation. The unique performances of vulnerable and resilient flesh are songs of a mysterious response and call. The mystery of this sort of angelic conviviality is that ecological stories become the actual ground for speaking of the divine, even as those songs fail to adequately describe the pulsations of divine love. These songs compose the ecological doxologies and canticles that emerge in the Christian theological tradition. In creaturely conviviality, *flesh evokes, seduces, and disturbs Word*. In that seduction, that divine perichoretic dance, a queer praise-singing emerges that discerns to receive divine love and delights to create open spaces.

The seductive praise-singing of life together occurs in a multiplicity of performances and a queer performativity that one cannot reduce to language. As the critical theorist Karen Barad argues in her rethinking of the concept of performativity, "Discursive practices are not human-based activities but specific material (re)configurings of the world through which boundaries, properties, and meanings are differentially enacted."[63] Discourses pulse (angelic in this case) with the weight of convivial materialities; words do not simply represent passive matter or create regardless of material reality. They make up and move mountains in surprising ways in what Barad calls "agential realism." She continues, "And matter is not a fixed essence; rather, matter is substance in its intra-active becoming—not a thing but a doing, a congealing of agency."[64] Matter congeals as an esse-diversity that exercises a strange agential power in the theology of mattered life.

Queer doxologies and canticles occur throughout theological life, unexpectedly challenging and reforming the cosmologies of worship. For example, it was such a mysterious sense of life, including a vision of a visit from a crucified seraph, that led Saint Francis of Assisi to proclaim his *Laudes Creaturarum*, the "Praise of the Creatures," a canticle for a strange host of creatures—Brother Sun, Sister Moon, Brothers Wind and Air,

Sister Water, Brother Fire, Mother Earth. Francis imaginatively rethinks creatureliness in the oddest of circumstances. Ecological creatures reveal convivial relations.

In the midst of these relations, conviviality finally exposes the mysterious reality of creaturely hybridity. When humans give an account of themselves in doxological narrative or in the canticle multiplicity of the bodied earth, they necessarily must speak of a variety of materialities, fellow animals, and expansive ecologies that form unique creatures. Human animal lives flutter and migrate in ecological relations with other animals. Human earthy lives shift in the midst of the very instabilities of the earth.

To that end, human flesh is a mélange of soil—flesh, bone, cartilage that makes up a few handfuls of mineralic dust. Neurons in the brain, the great electricity that illuminates thinking, cognitive and emotional life, literally fire the body. The digestive system burns food for life. Our very bodies are wind tunnels, nostrils and lungs hollowed out by a cool breeze of oxygen and carbon dioxide. Our bodily being is performed by water, liquid, oceanic in its flux. Rivers of blood flow throughout bodies. Tears wash our faces with joy and sadness. This is Trinity, too.

The queer everydayness of trinitarian life unfolds in a strange blur of doxologies and canticles—indeed, a *polydoxology* that compels one to rethink trinitarian life itself. We experience the beautiful inadequacy of speaking the completeness of divinity we're related to, who we are, the inexhaustible theological mystery of the human that is precisely in Trinity. We are divine stories that have gotten loose in the world, always surpassing ourselves, always blurred stories of divinity and creatureliness.[65] We sing out, realizing that other creatures sing with us as new forms of multiplicity reshape our everyday lives. The blurs and rushing wings of seraphim rightly reveal the circling of these stories, the warmth of their agency, the mysterious "penetrating warmth" or "overflowing heat" (according to Pseudo-Dionysius) of creatures with each other, the mysterious interpenetration of creatures with the divine dwelling in, with, and underneath them. Human, avian, creaturely, all blur together in this queer, perichoretic circulation of life. A seraphic blur nods to our own polymorphous interaction with the Trinity—hidden and revealing, veiled and crying. We rustle wings, too, whether they be the flappings of an actual bird or the brush of angel wings in a gay club or in the blur of a lover's embrace. And those rustlings spin out into the world with the verve of Trinity.

❧ The Holy Spirit, the Story of God

SAM LAURENT

Then afterward I will pour out my spirit on all flesh; your sons and your daughters shall prophesy, your old men shall dream dreams, and your young men shall see visions. Even on the male and female slaves, in those days, I will pour out my spirit.
—JOEL 2:28

My thoughts on the "one and the many," thinking through divine multiplicity, stem from my intuition that the practice of Christianity too often entails an agreed-upon set of doctrines and efforts to generate wider agreement on those doctrines. Christian churches are ever parting ways, breaking the ties of communion over particular beliefs they deem absolutely critical to authentic Christian life. In my own denomination, the Episcopal Church, tensions in the Anglican Communion are higher than ever following years of disagreement about opening the priesthood and episcopacy to people who are not heterosexual men. Phrases like "exclusion from communion" are commonly used, and already American Episcopalians have been denied seats in broader ecumenical conversations in which the Anglican Communion participates, consequent to what are called "innovations" in our practices. I find this to be a shame.

The one and the many, most readily expressed in Christianity via the mystery of the Trinity, offers reason to strive for communion within and among our denominations, and to practice an ethos of love outside the increasingly blurred boundaries of Christianity. The multiplicity in the Trinity is real: Christ's divinity is not incomplete, nor is that of the Spirit. And yet, the unity of the Trinity is also, paradoxically complete. The notion that the Spirit's motion between and beyond the first two persons perfects the community of the immanent Trinity suggests, as Kathryn Tanner does in her contribution to this volume, that unity and difference coexist in the divine life. If our lives are, as closely as possible, to mirror the divine, then our differences of viewpoint are not the obstacles to unity. A reluctance to love across difference is more likely to blame.

To be Christian, in the light of the sense of the Holy Spirit I begin to develop in my essay, is to accept an invitation into a value field in which dogmatic certainty is replaced by an abiding and risky ethos of conversation and respect of difference. This is not meant to diminish proclamations of faith, but to suggest that no single one of them can fully express our relationship to God. The potential schism that looms over the Anglican Communion is a result of centuries of history and sizable cultural and theological difference. To suggest that we simply agree to disagree on certain issues is, of course, a naïve idealism. This debate is a source of pain on multiple fronts. The multiply active Holy Spirit, though, aims to unite us, as it unites the Trinity, not in sameness but in love. This is a simple principle, but one that may serve to hold open lines of conversation and even lead to new understandings of what it means to be in communion.

My suggestion of "story" as a metaphor for Spirit aims, then, to highlight the manifold voices that respond to what Laurel Schneider calls the "occurrence of divinity in the world," and to suggest that God is behind that diversity. A sort of priesthood of all believers, this model might also underscore my beliefs about more formal priesthoods, but the theological models I employ predate these recent debates, being in fact older than the Anglican Communion itself by a millennium. Although ecclesiological differences are inevitable in a world characterized by profound multiplicity, my sense is that the communion to which we are called, the unity for which Jesus prays in John 17, is made manifest by the Holy Spirit, and that a recognition of this communion might hold open spaces for real dialogue and collaboration across the lines of differences that too easily divide us. To talk of the Spirit as a story, as a story that is many stories, might then be a step toward living into the communion the Spirit invokes without taking that move to be an erasure of the difference and diversity of God's creation.

• • •

The Spirit poured out on all flesh, igniting multiple sites of prophecy, calling forth dreams and visions, bypassing established orders of material distribution. This is a Spirit that can seriously shake things up. Indeed the Holy Spirit is a daunting subject precisely because it resists codification, appearing in prophets and poets, imbuing individuals with divine authority outside the machinery of established churches. It is this enigmatic nature of the Spirit's movement, though, that may offer the greatest potential for mobilizing Spirit-talk toward a deeper understanding of divine multiplicity in our world. The Spirit whispers divine love in our ears, reveals God's love to us in time and space. In short, the Spirit tells us the story of God in and for the world. But we hear different stories. We tell different stories. The Spirit is present to each individual, but does not broadcast a unified message to all. Instead, what we receive are variations, the inspiration for our own tellings of God's story. I argue that understanding the Spirit as this paradoxically multiple story of God in our lives offers a conceptual framework for conceiving of divine multiplicity and creaturely diversity not as challenges or threats to faith, but as the very structuring of our lives with God. Spirit as Story represents God's participation in our construction of truths, as well as God's graceful, insistent presence that invites each person into a greater fullness of life. Our own particular stories, viewed as individual constituents of the multiplicity of stories proceeding from God in the Spirit, draw us into greater openness toward divine revelation in unexpected places and emphasize the maintenance of community across—not at the expense of—difference.

The narrative and slippery qualities of the Spirit resist systematization, and yet an infusion of radically egalitarian storytelling might limber up theologies that lack sufficient mechanisms for attending to the wind that blows where She will. This essay offers one such mechanism, in the form of a pneumatology of story. The multiply narrative qualities of the Spirit are not recently discovered or remembered, but run through much of Christian trinitarian thought, and it is through trinitarian theology that the story of the Spirit will be told. Paraphysicality and Incarnationality, terms applied to the Spirit by Eugene Rogers and Kathryn Tanner, respectively, form the central trinitarian characteristics of Spirit as Story. Focusing on these traits opens space for the Spirit to be seen diversifying the world rather than uniting it in sameness. The process of deification, deployed with care by Rogers, will characterize the movement of the Spirit in the world, and in so doing will frame the love of God as active through diversity and difference, themselves reflective of the trinitarian communion. Building on this understanding of deification, which does not make humans divine, but rather shares divine life with the human, the Spirit's procession with and beyond Christ is framed through Tanner's work as an incarnational gesture, God's participation in the affairs of the world via christomorphic variations of the fullness of life. Combined with the paraphysical procession, this incarnationality frames the Spirit's diversification as work carried out by multiple actions. The notion of story helps capture the sense of what Rogers will call the paralogic of the Spirit.

The trinitarian structure established, the work of Laurel Schneider helps to quite literally flesh out the implications of the Spirit as Story. Read through her own interrogation of the logic of the One, Spirit as Story offers a new model for understanding the role of the incarnational Spirit in the diversity of religious views. Schneider's own work with narrative forms of truth-making offers a paradigm for thinking through the ways in which Spirit as story might lead to an anthropology of diversity to accompany a God who acts multiply but is perfected by the love amid the divine manifold. The Spirit's transformative work in telling the story of God offers suggestions for adapting an appropriately flexible theological stance. If the Spirit is the Wind that blows where She will, a flexible theology, one willing to let the Wind shape it, will prove more effective than one so rigid it has no choice but to break. Again, the Spirit's movement as story will couple with the gesture of deification to suggest that our speech about God at best reflects God's revelation to us, which is encountered in time and space, as narrative. To say we participate in divine life via the story of God is therefore a gesture of openness and sensitivity to the manifold contours of that story.

MANIFOLD TRINITARIAN SPIRIT

It abides
  not less than itself,
  one in its manifoldness,

>   unified in its procession,
>   full in its difference,
> By its beyond-beingly apartness from beings,
>   its single bringing up of the whole, and
>   its undiminished flowing of its
>   undiminished gifts.
>
>   PSEUDO-DIONYSIUS, *The Divine Names and Mystical Theology*

The flowing of gifts into the world, God's sustaining act of creation which maintains being and difference, poetically expressed by Pseudo-Dionysius,[1] is the gesture by which a story, or cohesion of any sort becomes possible. Trinitarian thought offers resources for conceptualizing this flow, in particular for understanding the Spirit's activity as the source of stories about God, which may be called a single story only insomuch as that story is "one in its manifoldness."

In his short essay, "The Spirit Rests on the Son Paraphysically," Eugene Rogers offers a retrieval of multiplicity implicit in early Christian understandings of the Spirit. In meditating on the relationship of Son and Spirit in trinitarian models, Rogers is particularly attentive to the procession, or flow, of divine gifts into the Son in the midst of the world. "The Spirit rests on the Son paraphysically because the Spirit gives itself—or in the Syriac tradition, herself—to *accompany* the physical for the Son's sake. The Spirit rests on the Son paraphysically because the Spirit *befriends* the physical for the Son's sake. The Spirit rests on the Son paraphysically because the Spirit *transcends* and *surpasses* the physical for the Son's sake."[2] The Spirit's presence, the accompanying, befriending, transcending, surpassing relationship to the physical world is part and parcel of God's love for the world. Paraphysicality, as Rogers conceives it, implies presence "alongside, in excess of, and in addition to the physical." The physical, by which is implied humanity and not just the incarnate Son, is then awash in the outflow of God's gifts.

According to Rogers, this paraphysical procession of the Spirit denotes the making of "additional sons to the Son, brothers with him and fellow heirs with Christ."[3] Such multiplicity is not beholden to the calculus of salvation. "Why another? Is not the Son enough? Yes, but that is the para-logic, the logic of excess, the economy of abundance."[4] The story of Christ, the communication across ages and seas of the expression of God in human form, is in this model buoyed by the Spirit, seeking, in the terms of trinitarian theology, to perfect the persons it encounters. For Rogers, this principle is established by the analogous continuity of the immanent and economic trinities; the intertrinitarian relationships reflect the relationships of the trinitarian persons to the world, and vice versa. "Each appropriates in the economy what each does in the Trinity. The Father sources the Son and the Spirit. The Word expresses the Father. The Spirit perfects the community of the Three. So the Father sources also the body; so the Son expresses also the body; so the Spirit perfects also the body."[5]

Rogers's insight into the Spirit's role in the immanent Trinity is this: "If, as many patristic authors agree, the Spirit's appropriated activity in the economy is *teleopoiesis*, perfecting or completing, then that can only be by analogous activity among the Three."[6] The communication between Father and Son, the Love that constitutes their relationship, the Spirit in this mode of thinking not only makes possible the perfection of the triune God by extending divine grace to all corners of creation, but also, in accompanying the Son's procession into flesh and from the grave, makes possible the diversity of the Trinity. Cohesion and diversification are dual aspects of this one nature of the Spirit. Following through on Basil of Caesarea's argument that the Spirit completes God's triune nature, Rogers suggests that "the Holy Spirit makes the Trinity, too, a community, completes and perfects it, fills it out as the God that the Trinity is. Because the Holy Spirit diversifies God in the Trinity, so it distinguishes human beings also in the economy. Because the Holy Spirit makes God the God that God is in the Trinity, so it divinizes human beings also in the economy."[7] The Holy Spirit, in this immanent/economic analogy, then provides the identification of the Son as well as the Son's cohesion to the Father, and in the world breathes distinction among humans and yet draws them together in God's love.

Pseudo-Dionysius offers one such poetic understanding of the Spirit's unifying diversification in his versified meditation on his statement that "the divine difference is the good-showing processions of the godhead."[8]

> It is differenced in a unified way:
> being given to all beings
> overflowing the participations of the

totality of those that are good,
singly made many,
non-wanderingly multiplied out of the one.⁹

Athanasius indeed roots diversity in the unity of a transcendent divine viewpoint to instill order and relationality to the creation, by way of arguing against the Epicurean view that all things are self-originated.

> If all things had come into being in this automatic fashion, instead of being the outcome of Mind, though they existed, they would all be uniform and without distinction. In the universe everything would be sun or moon or whatever it was, and in the human body the whole would be hand or eye or foot. . . . This distinctness of things argues not a spontaneous generation but a prevenient Cause and from that Cause we can apprehend God, the Designer and Maker of all.¹⁰

Trinitarian thought, then, offers in the diversity of the triune God a way of thinking through creaturely diversity as "singly made many, non-wanderingly multiplied out of the one." Indeed, trinitarian difference is elsewhere in this volume found to be fundamental to human difference.

The "good-showing procession" of the Spirit from the Father to—and beyond—the Son does not displace the Son as the full expression of divine love in the world. To suggest that the Spirit is the nonwanderingly multiplied story of God is not to diminish the centrality of Christ to a trinitarian understanding of God or to undercut the significance of Christ's work. Rather, positing the Spirit as story is to suggest that our knowledge of Christ is carried forth by the Spirit's paraphysical movement, which supplies both the differentiation required for stories and storytelling, and the cohesive relationships that make community possible.

Rogers has argued, following the analogical deduction of knowledge of the immanent Trinity from the economic Trinity, that the Spirit's primary relationship to human persons is one of deification. He clarifies that by deification he does not mean "the erasure of the boundary of the Creator and the creature," but rather "the crossing of that boundary."¹¹ For Rogers, this deification is an inclusion of humans in the divine life, via the fluidity of the divine and economic Trinity (a fluidity made possible by the procession of the Spirit). "The Spirit, so far from hiding herself, would actually be seeking to make herself known, in the only way possible: by incoporating subsidiary persons, human persons, into the trinitarian life, where alone the Spirit's personhood could be experienced, by reading them into the text, narrating them typologically into the stories she shares with Jesus and the Father."[12] Framing deification as an enfolding, by the Spirit, of humans into the divine life has, for an understanding of the Spirit as God's manifold story, two principal implications: God's gift of Spirit aims toward our deeper understanding of God, and God's gift of Spirit presents us with a God who *wants* to bring the fullness of God's life to our lives. Unfolding these two principles will offer, as a counterpart to a story-shaped pneumatology, an anthropology in which humans seek that fullness of life through a deeper understanding of the grace by which they participate in the divine life.

Deification, in the sense Rogers suggests, is God's self-revelation via the Spirit. 1 Corinthians 2:9–12 offers a scriptural foundation for this move. "The Spirit searches everything, even the depths of God. For what human being knows what is truly human except the human spirit that is within? So also no one comprehends what is truly God's except the Spirit of God." These first two verses highlight Paul's own analogical modeling of divine personhood on human personhood; a kind of reverse-engineering via *imago dei*. The inner workings of a person are private to themselves, unless communicated; likewise, Paul assumes the divine life is not transparent, but can be seen only via a form of communication. The difference in these similarly-structured knowledges, between human and divine, is the exact gap addressed by the self-revelation of the Spirit. "Now we have received not the spirit of the world, but the Spirit that is from God, so that we may understand the gifts bestowed on us by God." It is this understanding facilitated by the Spirit for which Pseudo-Dionysius prays in beginning *The Divine Names*. Similarly, Athanasius's argument for a divine Mind as a result of the seemingly designed differences in the created world falls back on the logic of a uniquely divine knowledge, which can be shared only by gracious divine self-revelation. The gifts we have received from God include the gift of unique identity: a unique role in the world and a unique viewpoint on the affairs of the world. The diversity in creation, in mirroring the diversity of the Trinity, is an expression of divine gift. The Spirit's incorporation of human life into the divine life, historically the calling forth of prophecy and visions, is a fundamentally pedagogical gesture.

The stories we tell about God are Spirit-led attempts to communicate the giftedness of our lives in the light of the divine life.

The second principle I draw out of Rogers's understanding of deification, God's desire that we share more fully in the divine life, underscores the understanding of the Spirit as divine love. Look back to Rogers's words expressing the Spirit's motivation for deification: "seeking to make herself known." God's incorporation of human life into the divine life is born of God's desire that humans enjoy fuller participation in the perfection of divine love. This desire is emphatically not communicated by a removal from the physical world but by a constant entering into it. "Human beings can enter the trinitarian life, only but indeed because the trinitarian life already embraces human beings."[13] Here the popular connotation of "spiritual," operating in opposition to the physical, runs aground. The deification performed by the Spirit is an ongoing gesture of accompaniment, paraphysically communicating God's love to the world in the world, making God's internal life visible so that the world may better reflect it. This desire, as we shall see, does not seek to resolve the diversity of the world into a homogenized unity, but, in keeping with the language of deification, to perfect it. The act of creating identity performed by the Spirit is part of this deification; each person is incorporated *where they are* into the divine life. If the first person of the Trinity is the source of being, and the second is the expression of the first, then the Spirit is the carrying-forth of that expression, the re-creation of that story via the act of differentiation in creation. The divine desire for increased fullness of human life, following this trinitarian logic, is not a desire for a decrease in diversity, but rather for a perfection of it in love. Rogers's deification is an appropriately modest one. It does not confer divine powers or properties on humanity, but makes the human life divine via association with the Trinity. The Spirit's paraphysical procession with and in excess of the Son not only calls forth difference but also aims to perfect that difference in a noncontradictory unity, via love.

God's perennially sharing embrace of the creation can then be seen as the primary work of the Spirit. In all its movements—the primordial creation of diversity, expression through the words of prophets, the descent above the baptismal waters of Christ, the commissioning of God's story in multiple tongues at the Pentecost, and in the ongoing sharing of divine life with human life—the Spirit breathes life into our stories of God by sharing Godself with us. This inherently trinitarian dynamic, in which God shares

Godself through the Son and the Spirit, receives systematic development in the works of Kathryn Tanner. In constructing her theological system around God's sharing of Godself, Tanner deploys the language of Spirit in ways at once classical and postmodern to create space for diverse manifestations of God's love through the Spirit.

Tanner's system is built on two key theological assertions, neither of which diverges from the dynamics of deification discussed thus far, and both of which necessarily invoke the work of the Spirit. One "is the sense of God as the giver of all good gifts, the fount, luminous source, fecund treasury, and store house."[14] God provides the differentiation that makes the relational network of our giftedness possible, and through God's Spirit, facilitates the ongoing creation of that difference such that those gifts might be known and utilized. Second, in line with the anthropological consequences of deification, "in establishing the world in relationship to Godself, God's intent is to communicate such gifts to us."[15] Put differently, in what amounts to a justification of the economic Trinity, "God, who is already abundant fullness, truly wishes to replicate to every degree possible the fullness of life, light, and love outward in what is not God."[16] This move, in short, rephrases God's "yes" such that it is a clear embrace not only of the human spirit, but of the created world. God is at work out of love for the world, seeking to transform it to better reflect the divine life in which it is created.

Tanner extrapolates two key principles from these foundational statements, and those principles will guide the development of a theological system around this core understanding of God's grace. First, and perhaps most centrally to the development of a robust doctrine of the Holy Spirit, God's desire to share God's life with the world manifests as a noncompetitive relationship between God and world. "A non-competitive relation between creatures and God means that the creature does not decrease so that God may increase."[17] The glorification of God does not come at the expense of creatures. Tanner's doctrine here stems from her earlier argument that Christian talk about divine transcendence, in order to avoid a conflict between that transcendence and God's involvement in the world, must avoid a contrastive definition of transcendence, that is, ought to abide "by a rule that prohibits a simple contrast between divine and non-divine predicates when talking about God's agency."[18] God then transcends the differences that form identity, and the oppositional simplicity of a divine/

world duality. Following this rule, Tanner argues, leads to talk of God, who "will become the genuine source of everything that is, *in* all its diversity, multiplicity and particularity, without the need for any indirection."[19] Indeed, the Incarnation, by which God saves humanity, presents an apparent conflict between human and divine attributes, unless one understands divine transcendence as transcending difference. Yet divine action once again proceeds precisely *through* that difference. "God must be incarnate in order to save, but God must be different than us in order to save us."[20] The Incarnational manifestation of divine love and power is indeed a central trope of this theological system, lending a christomorphic contour to talk of Spirit as story.

"Because the shape of Jesus' whole human life is the out-working of God's own trinitarian life, Jesus is not simply the means to what the triune God wants to give us out of its fullness; the shape of Jesus' life is the end or goal of that giving, which we are to receive in union with him."[21] Here the linkage between our experience of Christ and our experience of the Spirit becomes clear. Christ is, within this trinitarian structure, the pattern of fullness of life by which we might also receive God's gifts more completely. That this can be so relies on the paraphysical movement of the Spirit, which performs variations *on that pattern* through its presence at and between each point in the world. "Jesus, as the human version of the Son in his relations with the Father and Spirit, is the means by which we are to receive the Spirit and be transformed thereby in our own humanity, but the Spirit is the Spirit of Christ who therefore works to conform us with the Son."[22] The same Spirit that has been with the world since its inception eternally processes alongside and beyond the Son, seeking to perfect or transform the world in the image of God's full expression in the Son. The story of Christ's life, the shape of the fullness of divine life in our world, transcends the limitations of Jesus' time and mortality precisely in the paraphysical procession of the Spirit. The story of Christ is made known to us by the grace of the Holy Spirit and is told anew as a result of the Spirit's infusion of love into the world. God is present in the world as Spirit and communicates the trinitarian life *through* Spirit. That communication, the story of God in the world, told in diversity and difference, is the work of the Spirit.

The implications of this inclusion in divine life via God's involvement in human life are fairly dramatic within the shape of Spirit talk. In particular, the noncontrastive understanding of God, coupled with divine shaping of the diversity of the world means that the understandings of God brought forth by encounters with the Spirit will not by any logical necessity conform exactly to one another. Within Tanner's system, the finite scope of theological proclamations is one aspect of our own telling of the story of God and the world. "If God usually works with, rather than overriding, the ordinary character of human life, we have every reason to think that God sanctions thereby the limited, fallible, correctable truths typical of it."[23] In a rather poetic passage, Tanner speaks of the human consequences of what Rogers labels deification: "When human processes become Spirit-filled, they are not made more than human themselves. Instead, something about their human character changes. From that chaotic formlessness of many uncoordinated voices or the shapeless convergence of multiple causal trajectories comes a new direction for human processes."[24] The sheer multplicity of the Spirit's movements is hinted at in this passage, and indeed Tanner's chapter on the Spirit in *Christ the Key* is structured as a critical comparison of two paradigms of the working of the Spirit, one in which the Spirit works "immediately . . . in exceptional events rather than in the ordinary run of human affairs" and the other in which "the Spirit is thought to work gradually, and without final resolution, in and through the usual fully human and fully fallible . . . public processes of give and take in ordinary life."[25] In taking seriously both accounts of spiritual movement, those epitomized by the Pentecost, say, and those epitomized by the Spirit's personal revelation of divine life to us, Tanner makes clear that God's sharing through the Spirit does not adhere to a linear narrative. Divine presence in mundane, unexceptional events, and in people whose inspiration is not announced by meteorological phenomena is, on face value, a subversive concept within institutional understandings of religion, and indeed does signify the Spirit's potential to challenge stale or misguided interpretations of divine love through unexpected means. This more broadly conceived notion of spiritual activity is dubbed, by Tanner, "the attempt to bring back the fuller picture in an updated way."[26] It is, to be sure, an unsettling prospect for religious folk who rely on the assurance of doctrines. "The recognition that human processes mediate God's working opens up to question claims to divine validation and in that way threatens to overturn the whole apple cart in which unquestioned assurance and a divine sanction for what one believes typically go together."[27]

By the same token, a not unhealthy dose of humility is delivered in this multivocal Spiritual paradigm, for to insist that our proclamations of our understanding of God might not just be finite, but are in fact subject to correction or even refutation, is to live intellectually into the intuitive knowledge that we still learn from the Holy Spirit's love-filled presence in our life; if the goal is to shape our lives after Christ's then an awareness of the differences between the two ought to condition our willingness to draw rigid doctrinal lines.

The more subtly active Spirit, which expands beyond the "exceptional" mode of Spiritual presence but does not negate it, Tanner points out, is amenable both to scientific ways of thinking through divine presence and to classical trinitarian formulations of the Spirit. Particularly, the Spirit active in and through human processes everywhere reflects the christomorphic shape of the Spirit who accompanies and exceeds the life of Christ, effective via the noncompetitive relationship between God and world. In this account of the christomorphic shape of the work of the Spirit, "God does not evacuate the human or push it aside."[28] The gesture of embrace by God of humanity in Christ, the Incarnation central to Christian narrative, can be seen, then, in the work of the Spirit. "God works in Christ as the Spirit works in us; in and through the human."[29] The interface of human and divine and the noncompetitive relationship between the two is, then, a baseline understanding of incarnation. Again, the extent of the deification that occurs in this process necessarily must not be overstated. The full expression of God in Christ is, as Tanner would say, on a different plane than the expression of God we offer forth in our responses to the Spirit. Our participation in the divine life does not afford us divine powers, but it can, if we have eyes to see, open possibilities for deeper understanding of our gifts.

The full expression in Christ occurs, however, like the love that seeks full expression in the rest of humanity, through the Holy Spirit. The creedal formulations of the early church bear this out with their references to Christ, who "by the power of the Holy Spirit . . . became incarnate from the Virgin Mary, and was made man." The story of Christ is, insofar as it participates in human affairs, told by the Holy Spirit's work of incorporating human life into divine life. Pseudo-Dionysius notes that "the logos attributes in a common and unified way all that pertains to the Father and Himself to the Spirit."[30] Human experience of God occurs through the Holy Spirit, and human proclamations about God are first about the Holy Spirit, God as medium for the experience of God. This assertion is not a construction of hierarchy within the Trinity but an epistemological result of the nature of the trinitarian divine life. The difference that provides identity reflects the creativity of the Spirit, and the experiences of God that the Spirit facilitates to each part of creation are then experiences of God *through the Holy Spirit*. Though the second and third persons of the Trinity are said to proceed from the first, human knowledge of God begins at—and as a result of—the reach of the procession of the Spirit. The immediacy of the Spirit and its role in conveying God's love to us then matches with the paraphysical procession and incarnational dynamic described by Rogers and Tanner; the divinity of Christ is made known through the divinity of the Spirit, who draws humans into the divine life. It is the paraphysicality, the excess, the going-beyond the Son that enables Spirit to do this work.

The creation of diversity patterned on the triunity of the divine life and the incarnational embrace of human life into that perfected triunity—both works of the Spirit—call forth a vision of the Spirit as potentially disruptive of those human practices and institutions that interfere with the patterning of human life on divine life. In particular, the claims to authority made by churches acting as caretakers of the story of Christ are found to be constructed on unstable ground. The Spirit tells the story of Christ through the diversity and multiplicity of the world, not against it. At first blush, this is a highly decentralizing impulse. So Tanner: "Appeals to the Spirit are not a way of taking sides in a controversy between one commonly accepted way of justifying religious authority and another.... Instead, an appeal to the direct working of the Spirit amounts to a fundamental questioning of all of them."[31] Tanner's analysis of the consequences of this broader model of the Spirit's work underscores both the subversiveness of the radical democracy it would seem to suggest and the possible compromise of prophetic force by the very diffusion of authority to make religious claims. In comparison to the supernormal events of the Pentecost or the baptism of Christ, "the second view of how the Spirit works"—the view that the Spirit works *through* human processes—"is not directed with the same force as the first against the usual sources of religious authority; it seems to dull the very attack on those sources that the first appeal to the Spirit makes possible, by now extending the workings of Spirit to the usual sources themselves."[32] Put simply, if the Spirit is in everyone, the Spirit is in *everyone*, including those whose authority would be compromised by more populist claims. The multiplicity of the Spirit's operations, the multiplicity it creates in the world, will not in and of itself lead to changes in already existing institutions if it is lobbed rhetorically as a challenge to their authority. Tanner suggests, in a passage that warrants a lengthy quotation, that the action of the Spirit internal to religious authorities will be the source of institutional transformation to reflect the diversity of divine life.

> Rather than attack the usual sources with unmitigated ferocity from the outside . . . the appeal to the Spirit on the second view would loosen up the usual sources of religious authority by increasing their flexibility, tolerance for diversity of opinion, and openness to change. By talking about the Spirit at work in them, one would be trying to increase the complexity of the usual sources to bring about their greater inclusiveness and internal diversity. More open-ended processes of religious formation would ensue, with stability no longer secured, in a top-down fashion, through enforced redundancy and mechanical repetition of a neat linear sort—that is, by simply insisting others believe what one tells them to believe.[33]

Such is the challenge of seeking to model human life on a divine life that is differentiated in a unified way and singly made many. The metaphor of story, if grounded in this trinitarian structure—that is, as stories nonwanderingly multiplied out of the one—serves to codify the tension between the diversified household of God, which glorifies God in its very differences, and the unity of God, which also seeks expression in the world. The central story to Christian theology is that of the life of Christ. By recognizing that the Spirit, in its paraphysical procession, carries that story to each person uniquely, the manifold story told by the Spirit is in our world a multitude of stories, only united in the triune God. Rogers expresses this relationship eloquently.

> The Spirit does not follow a straightforward logic, you might say, but a logic of its own, a paralogic. What would that mean? Something that accompanies logic, expands on it, embroiders, elaborates, filigrees, celebrates it, . . . What is paraphysical in the economy, accom-

panying the human nature taken on by the Logos, is first paralogical in the Trinity, accompanying the Logos in itself, ready to expand upon its stucture and story.[34]

To speak of the Spirit as the story of God made by its procession the *stories* of God invites a certain cognitive dissonance by design. The language of Spirit as story suggests that discernment of God's movement in the world should be a process of dwelling in that seeming disharmony, where the Story of God is one through God's unity, but is told through God's cultivating of multiplicity in the work of the Spirit. "The Spirit," Rogers offers, "rests on the Son paraphysically, so that she can gather the diverse, and diversify the corporate, to vary and manifest the body of the Son."[35] Christian proclamations about God, shaped by this trinitarian understanding, are transformed from preservations of static truths to variations on a theme, improvisations rather than recitals, a story made living by the incorporation of manifold stories into its grace and depth. This story does not resolve its internal diversity into a homogenizing unity, but rather finds in the irreducible difference of human subjects the driving force for love. Again, the Trinity provides a guiding ethos for theologies; the Spirit, the Love of God, perfects the community of the three divine hypostases, maintaining a unity in their differences by virtue of their shared love. Likewise, the unity intended for human life is not one that will be attained by a rigid conformity or adherence to hierarchical structures. Like the divine life, human life will find its unity in the love that perfects community. If the trinitarian life calls us to reflect the Spirit's presence by diversifying the sources of our religious understandings and claims and committing to unity not in doctrinal detail but in love, then our human lives will necessarily have to adopt an accommodating posture toward diversity in our midst.

MANIFOLD CREATURES, MANIFOLD SPIRIT

The Spirit as manifold Story, creating difference and relationship in and through the christomorphic variations it evokes in the world calls for a human response. Insistence on a hierarchically imposed unity via agreed-upon expressions of faith will not suffice to express the dynamic, paradoxical, incarnational gesture of the Spirit's procession. Religious institutions, in this model of spiritual activity, find themselves creating space for the constant negotiation of belief, for the sharing of stories, and for the cultivation of the mutual love that is the mortar of human unity. As such, the logic of hierarchy requires a transformation to reflect the paralogic of the Spirit. In this paralogic, divine love is expressed through variations and elaborations, through each human life, expressing the divine Logos through difference. The transformation called for is the one Laurel Schneider sets forth in *Beyond Monotheism*, a recognition of the limitations of what she calls the "logic of the one" and a movement toward understandings of the divine expressed through creaturely diversity. By reading a pneumatology of story through the hermeneutic of *Beyond Monotheism*, the shape of human relationships shaped by stories of God's fullness of life is traced out.

Schneider's assessment and deconstruction of the logic of the One focuses on the construction of the narrative of the one God and the requirements of ideological unity perceived as necessary in following that deity. Buried in the sawdust of such a construction are the lives and stories of those at the margins, those rendered voiceless by the drive to consolidate diversity into manageable political unity. "The story of the One denies fleshiness and the stubborn shiftiness of bodies; it cannot abide ambiguities and unfinished business; it cannot speak syllables of earth. But in its failures are openings, for there are always gaps in the story of the One, fissures that widen and crumble at the edges."[36] Indeed, the presumption of a unity that obtains through the perfection of divine love is not misguided, but the presumption of a complete human expression of that understanding is. "The logic of the One is not *wrong*, except, ironically, when it is taken to be the whole story. Rather than false it is incomplete. The logic of the One (and the concept of God that falls within it) is simply *not* One. There is always less, and more, to the story."[37] Schneider posits *occurring* divinity, which unfolds in time, space, and flesh, a pursuance of the incarnation in bodies. Spirit as story, framed in the trinitarian incarnational sense developed on prior pages draws from a similar assumption. The telling of the story, effected through the Sprit's incorporation of human life into divine life, does not occur at a remove from the time and space of creaturely affairs. It happens in the midst of creaturely messiness. A story implies development over time. The manifold story of God multiplies in time as myriad stories, encounters with God in particular places and time. Each story aims toward sharing divine life with the world. Strained allegiance to a singular narrative arc distorts the grace inherent in each moment of life in and with the Spirit. The narrative of incarnation is played uniquely in each life. "Literally meaning 'in the flesh,' incarnation is *about* bodies and so already cannot be reduced to oneness without withdrawing, again, from actual bodies in their necessary particularity."[38]

The incarnational nature of God's relating to the world through Spirit means that claims about God will be made humanly, in narrative threads constructed in time. "The evidence suggests . . . that truth is constituted in story, even in the hypothetical stories that scientists tell in order to make coherent their findings and to guide their investigations. This means that whatever human beings strive to call truth is inaccessible to human life except fleshed in folds of language, culture, and interpretation."[39] Just as humans narrate their lives and probe their world through stories, God's presence in the world, which aims to deepen our understanding of God's gifts to us, likewise is encountered and described as story. Knowledge of God comes through the Spirit, which comes to us as unfolding stories.

For Schneider, the instability of absolute claims leads to a theological methodology that incorporates vulnerability. "We are after theological claims that can be accountable and responsive to the inevitability of our own mistakes in judgment."[40] The present study of the Spirit echoes this value, for the Spirit bears out the particularity of divine relationship to each person and place. The wind that blows where She will, the Spirit tasks theologians with proclaiming God's particular love and with constructing theologies capacious enough to recognize the inevitable change and disagreement that follow. Spirit as story means that theology at its best helps individuals recognize the movement of God in their own lives, and empowers them to share their story with a community ready to learn from it. "It is," Schneider notes, "made easier by doctrinal claims for a trinitarian Spirit that flows throughout creation and is at times embodied in the gathered community of worshippers."[41] As the Spirit brings forth its fresh variation on the love of God exemplified in Christ, what emerges is a story finite in stature and scope, which draws the human into the infinite divine life. The desire to make grand truth claims based on certainty runs deep, but the multiplicity and difference performed by the work of the Spirit in each moment emphasize the particularity of our statements. Our stories, after all, are incomplete. The Spirit's movement is an embrace, and invitation, not a complete revelation, for such knowledge would be beyond the scope of finitude. What does Spirit as story allow us to say, then? The story is only *a* story from the vantage point of the undifferentiated whole. As humans, we are gifted with a multitude of stories of God's incarnational embrace, and with the relationality required to come together in love to share and discuss those stories. Truth is not ruled out by this understanding of Spirit, but absolute certainty is. Spirit as story depicts the truths of our world inasmuch as we are prepared to perceive them.

The preparation to receive these truths, the work of humans in relationship with God, necessarily ought to adapt to the nature of God's presentation of these truths. God, in Schneider's language, *occurs* in the world, and multiply so, thus resisting the instinctive certainty so often accorded theological proclamations. "There is good news in the fact that part of getting it 'right' lies not in getting it right in any absolute or final sense . . . but rather that getting it 'right' lies in a suppleness of posture toward truth and toward the stories that give themselves to be told, again."[42] The good news is the incarnational presence of the Spirit, the extension by grace of a hand to pull us out of the Pelagian dilemma of hoping to perfect ourselves. The persistently dynamic movement of the Spirit does not simply undercut attempts to build knowledge on a metaphysics of divine stasis, but it also offers in each moment a story to tell. The Spirit's enfolding of human life into divine life is not a passive gesture, a divinity waiting for human action. It is a constant hopeful embrace, in which divine love is mobilized to provide the opportunity for growth in love at each moment. The multiplicity of this occurring divinity, from the human standpoint, is not a push toward a rigid orthodoxy so much as a calling to a value field in which the relationships between individuals, if cultivated with love, might become the structure of unity in the world. "Stories," says Schneider, "—the ones that get loose, build and unbuild worlds—are the real concern of theology precisely because they express the motility of creation."[43] An insistence that Christianity has only ever told one story forecloses this motility of creation, and it is the doctrine of the Holy Spirit that, more than any other theological topic, reminds us of the surprising grace of God's movement in the world. The claim, valid until recent decades, that the Spirit was "forgotten" in theological discourse may have something to do with the disruptive potential it always harbors toward closed-off religious talk.

Story, then, serves as an apt metaphor for the Spirit both in the sense that God's creative agency is active through the Spirit, and in the sense that the Spirit, as the source of individual subjecthood, creates the differences that thwart superficial attempts to consolidate our multiple stories of God into one. The triune God transcends difference and unity, always exceeding even Godself in love. "Incarnate divinity is multiple beyond the One-Many divide, opposed neither to oneness nor to unity, but unlimited by both just as the simplest earthworm, in its ever-changing existence from morning till night, is neither an unchanging one nor is it without a certain slant of unity."[44] The Holy Spirit as story implicitly involves movement in time, and is differently present at various moments and places, and yet is participatory in the unity of the Trinity. The Holy Spirit as story means that the flux in the divine economy reflects not imperfection, but the dynamic nature of divine life, which itself unfolds with a love that holds the multiplicity and unity of the Trinity in community. Inasmuch as the Holy Spirit diversifies the world, its work is ongoing, always still unfolding, a story being told. This participation in world processes does not diminish the divinity of God, but rather in its very paradoxical nature as a story that is a vast multiplicity of stories asserts divine transcendence beyond human grasping, as the Spirit processes paraphysically through and beyond each person. The value field established by the story of God is by virtue of its multiplicity a holding open of theological statements to allow room for the movement of the Spirit to shape the stories we piece together to express our diverse experiences of God.

This trinitarian construction, from the core of Christian doctrine, can then be read as an opening for real conversation and learning from outside the particular traditions in which individuals participate. The multiplicity of expressions of the divine through the Spirit/story, then given voice by the diversity of humans diversified by the Spirit signals that sharing across differences, rather than ignoring them with blunt rhetoric or filling them in with trite relativism, is the task to which we are called—to unite the world not with sameness but with love. The multiplicity of God's presence in the world and the differences in experiences of God that follow from that multiplicity are inscribed in the doctrine of the Trinity and glorified by the procession of the Spirit as story. As such, the challenges of talking across religious divides are underscored as challenges worth sitting with, and the divides themselves signals of the diversification of the Story of God, which decentralizes religious authority and tasks each person with constructing their story of divinity.

Story is an intentionally vague, slippery metaphor, joining wind, flame, and a multitude of others as signals of the Spirit's freedom and unpredictability. Story recognizes the threads of narrative with which we knit together our knowledge and also the incompleteness of any such construction. Story recognizes the rich history of God's love for the world and the wide array of such histories that provide meaning for people. The Story that is stories, a unity only in the excess of its multiplicity, the Holy Spirit communicates God's love intimately to each person in each corner of the world and commissions each of us to reflect that love in our grapplings with difference.

Doctrinal Explorations: Trinity, Christology, and the Quality of Relation

❧ Absolute Difference

KATHRYN TANNER

The question of the one or the many, per se, has very little existential traction for me, so I don't expect much on that score from discussion of unity and diversity within the Trinity. As far as I can see, without fleshing out their respective constitutions in greater detail, unity and diversity are mere abstractions devoid of any particular existential import. Worrying over the question of unity or diversity at a high level of generality—for example, fulminating, in the abstract, against the former in order to promote the latter—is therefore a case of misplaced concreteness if ever there was one. Yes, unity that stifles diversity can be suffocating, but would a genuinely encompassing unity, comprehensive of all perfection in the highest degree, do the same? Diversity can be enriching, of course, but what if this diversity were to include grossly unfair extremes of inequality in character or circumstance? And so on. In sum, apart from a more concrete discussion of particulars, I don't see much reason to favor (or be wary of) one or the other, on simply a priori grounds.

I'm more interested in the complex way unity and diversity are held together—for very specific, indeed highly unusual reasons—within the Trinity. I'm more interested, that is, in the exact shape (to the extent it can be made exact) of the way they are found conjoined there. I'm afraid, however, that the very unusual character of these specifics seriously blunts any general existential significance they might have. When so generalized, in other words, the particulars turn into nothing but platitudes: Here is a unity among diverse equals—yeah! But there is nothing very surprising about our preference for that; it's what we're already favorably disposed to, and the Trinity is just an elaborate runaround back to that fact.

Nor do I think unity and diversity within the Trinity have much to contribute in the way of a metaphysics providing practical orientation in the world; that is not its chief existential significance. I don't think as a historical matter that Christian trinitarian speculation originated with general metaphysical questions. (The more specific questions that prompted it had to do with figuring out the implications for divinity of associating a fully fledged divine principle so closely with a suffering and clearly mortal human being.) And, had it been designed to answer general metaphysical questions, the results seem too crude to be more than a philosophical embarrassment (at the very least apart from some enormous effort at further elaboration). Can a unity limited in its internal diversity to three, perforce quite general, metaphysical principles ever be adequate to the mysterious and incredibly robust complexity of the known (and unknown) world? I'd rather just read process philosophy and be done with it. Instead of trinitarian theology, give me, indeed, any philosophy whose explicit intent is to do justice to such complexity, utilizing all necessary means, which obviously lead well beyond the domain of specifically theological competency.

More existentially pertinent, to me at least, is the way Christian trinitarian reflection is a kind of hyperbolic and excessive speculation about the joys and trials of relational existence, particularly as that is manifest for us in interpersonal relationships. Here in the Trinity is relationality taken to an unimaginable extreme, and in the light of it one can reflect, as in a photographic negative, on what so often goes wrong in human lives, sometimes no doubt because of sinful failings, but more often than not as an inevitable concomitant of simple finitude: how one love pushes out another despite an earnest, and often quite innocent, desire to share ourselves more widely; how we are both built up and eventually undone by those who have made us what we are; how the need to carry on without them, and the slow dampening of once visceral ties, lead us to replace those who have meant everything to us; and so on. The Trinity becomes a way of imagining what is impossible for us and therefore of making clear to us both what we are and what we ideally, despite ourselves, aspire to.

PRIVILEGING THE ONE

One of the mysteries of classical formulations of the Trinity is how to reconcile the one and the three, unity and diversity within the Trinity. They appear to be at loggerheads with each and other; and, when push comes to shove, diversity always seems to lose out. Especially in Neoplatonically inflected versions of classical trinitarianism, diversity within the Trinity is qualified to do justice to unity without a similar qualification of unity to respect diversity. Because the Trinity is perfectly one, the persons of the Trinity can only be as different from one another as that unity allows; unity, in other words, sets a limit on how different the persons of the Trinity can be from one another. The unity of the Trinity, however, just because of its perfection, rules out similar qualification by diversity: The Trinity is not any less one by reason of that diversity.

The upshot of this priority of unity over diversity within the Trinity is that the persons of the Trinity do not seem to be as different from one another as other things are. The differences among persons of the Trinity do not, for example, seem to be as extreme as the difference between God and the world or the differences among things within the world. In short, while it is not unusual to say the Trinity is supremely, absolutely, or excessively one—as one as anything could be—it is very unusual in classical trinitarianism to say that the persons of the Trinity are supremely, absolutely, or excessively different—as different from one another as anything can be.

The intent of this essay is to show how diversity and unity can be put on a more equal footing given the assumptions of classical trinitarianism: One should say, for a variety of classical reasons, that the persons of the Trinity are perfectly different. The Trinity is both absolutely one and constituted by absolute differences among the persons, and those claims are perfectly compatible: In fact, what makes the persons of the Trinity supremely different also perfectly unites them.

The sort of short shrift given to diversity within classical trinitarianism, which I have briefly outlined, finds support in a number of assumptions with Neoplatonic pedigree. First of all is the metaphysical presumption that the one is the prior source of multiplicity as that is established by either quantitative or qualitative difference. Multiplicity is subsequent, both logically and causally, to what is one; it presupposes for its intelligibility and therefore actually derives from unity (while the reverse does not hold).

For example, multiple things are each, in and of themselves, one, while what is one need not be itself multiple; and so on. Classical trinitarianism attempts to resist any suggestion of a logical or causal priority of unity within the Trinity by insisting that the unity of the Trinity is always also a unity among the three: The one God does not subsequently become three, nor are the three some supplementary or optional additions to what the one God is essentially or substantially. But the frequent reemergence within Christianity of the so-called Sabellian heresy in a variety of guises at least suggests that something about classical trinitarianism makes this a constant temptation. The claim that distinctions among the persons of the Trinity do not come later and never go away is rarely completely compelling within classical trinitarianism perhaps because it trades, more than it lets on, on such a Neoplatonic heritage.

A second Neoplatonically derived assumption is simply to define divinity as the one and thus account for the difference between divine and nondivine by way of a distinction between unity and diversity. The creation or causal production of the nondivine is, in other words, the very creation of difference: first, the difference between God and the world, and, second, of differences among things within the world. A contrastive account of divine simplicity—that is, one in which simplicity seems opposed to complexity—accentuates this tendency to account for the difference between God and the world in terms of the difference between the one and the multiple. The idea that divine attributes are only conceptually—that is, according to our limited understanding—and not really distinct in God easily suggests that there is no properly divine sense to the term "complexity." Oneness in its proper sense (which we cannot comprehend) applies to divinity, whereas complexity in its proper sense applies to us and not to God.

A third, closely connected Neoplatonic assumption is that created diversity represents devolution, an ontological or moral (or both) decline (and qua moral a fall in the Christian understanding of that). In Neoplatonism the farther one gets from the One, the more different things become: Nous, the first emanation from the One, includes only incipient or virtual differences (for example, between thought thinking itself) which then become full-blown, both quantitatively and qualitatively, farther on down the chain of successive emanations (for example, within a highly diverse material world of multiple things). And although everything has its source in the One, the farther one goes down the chain the less of both being and value one finds ("being" and "value" being convertible terms)—though, given that the One is everything's ultimate source, the degree of being and value never falls to zero or turns negative (that is, even the lowest beings within the material world are not evil).

Christian affirmations of diversity within the world—that view it, that is, not as a product of the fall but as a good thing, a sign of God's beneficence—are nevertheless predicated on an association of diversity with ontological decline. Thomas Aquinas, for instance, argues this way: No single kind of creature, because of the very fact of its limitation to a particular kind of thing, could ever approximate the all-comprehensive perfection of God. Given that God wishes to communicate the perfection of God's own being as much as possible to creatures, God must create a highly diverse world. Diversity, in short, is a way of approximating the unitary or singular perfection of divinity under conditions of ontological limitation or imperfection that define creaturehood—for example, given that no one creature can be everything in the way God is. Thomas summarizes his argument this way:

> God is the most perfect agent. It was his prerogative, therefore, to induce his likeness into created things most perfectly, to a degree consonant with the nature of created being. But created things cannot attain to a perfect likeness to God according to only one species of creature. . . . The presence of multiplicity and difference was therefore necessary that a perfect likeness to God be found in them according to their manner of being.[1]

One finds a Christian association of diversity with not just ontological but moral decline in theologians such as Origen. Before the fall God created multiple rational souls. There were many of them, simply as a manifestation of divine power, one supposes: God created many of them simply because God could (because God has the power to do so and divine power cannot be hindered). But they were exactly alike in both character and capacity, as an exemplification of both divine goodness and fairness. Rational souls are the highest beings of the greatest value that God could create, and therefore a beneficent God would not want any of his creatures to enjoy anything less. And had God given any creature less, that just wouldn't have been fair. If the world as we know it is much more diverse than this—including rational beings of varying intelligence, bodies in addition to minds, and lots of qualitatively different things—those rational creatures positioned in the lower ranks of existence by virtue of such diversity must, of their own volition, have done something wrong to account for their position in the lower ranks. God, in making use of that diversity and confirming it through God's own creative response to the fall, is doing nothing more than justly punishing the prior wayward inclinations of these rational creatures and trying, out of sheer goodness, to get them to turn their lives around by lessons learned from their now diverse characters and circumstances. Origen summarizes the major presuppositions of his account of diversity this way:

> God the Creator of the universe is both good and just and omnipotent. Now when "in the beginning" he created what he wished to create, that is rational beings, he had no other reason . . . [than] his goodness. As therefore he himself, in whom was neither variation nor change, nor lack of power, was the cause of all that was to be created, he created all his creatures equal and alike, for the simple reason that there was in him no cause that could give rise to variety and diversity. But since these rational creatures . . . were endowed with the power of free will, it was this freedom which induced each one by his own voluntary choice either to . . . imitate God or to deteriorate through negligence. This . . . was the cause of . . . diversity, . . . [And] God . . . then felt it just to arrange his creation according to merit, gathering the diversities of minds into the harmony of a single world . . . in which there must be not only vessels of gold and silver, but also of wood and of earth, and some unto honour and some unto dishonour.[2]

Although for Origen a diverse world is still all to the good in that it incorporates a providential response to the fall on God's part, it is hard not to see a kind of Neoplatonically inflected, full-fledged a-cosmism in other Christian interpretations of created diversity. The sort of diversity one finds in the created world as we know it is not a good thing, and if this sort of diversity is simply part and parcel of creation, it would have been better if the world hadn't been created at all. Salvation therefore becomes a kind of de-creation understood as a ridding of things of their diversity. Here, as with Plotinus, one seems to get closer to the One God the more one is able, in a very thoroughgoing way, to contain no more difference—no differences of kind distinguishing one sort of thing from another, no division of kinds into multiple individuals, no composition of individuals into parts, and so on.³ In the Christian version represented by someone like Meister Eckhart (where Nous is collapsed into the One as God's own intelligence), the Christian project is to get back to the sort of existence one had in the mind of God before one was actually created—that is where one's true and perfect self lies. And, in that sort of virtual existence one still enjoys in God, one is no different from God or from anything else. Commenting on Wisdom 1:14, Eckhart makes the point about the essentially devolved character of creation this way:

> By the fact that something is created, it is distinct and is unequal and many. By its descent from the One and the Indistinct the created thing falls from the One and into distinction and hence into inequality. The Uncreated, on the contrary, has no fall or descent and therefore remains and stands in the fountainhead of unity, equality, and indistinction.⁴

This then sets the stage for Eckhart's account of salvation, as in his commentary on Luke 19:12: "A man 'comes back richer' than he went out. Whoever had so gone out of himself would be given back again to himself, more his own, and all the things he had in multiplicity and forsook will be wholly given back to him in unity."⁵ In short, "the further a thing is removed from the many and aims toward the One the more perfect and divine it is;"⁶ and this is to be as one is in the mind of God and as if "[one] did not [yet] exist."⁷

DIVERSITY RESURGENT

There are, however, resources within Neoplatonism for reaffirming the importance of difference within divinity (although these are often underutilized within Christian theology and overlooked in the secondary literature). The major one stems from the Neoplatonic principle that a cause contains its effects in a higher, more perfect fashion.⁸ If God produces diversity, that must mean that diversity exists in a higher, more perfect fashion in God than it does in creatures.

This "higher and more perfect fashion" is very often taken to mean "simpler" in the contrastive sense whereby the difference between God and creatures lines up with a difference between unity and diversity. So, in Thomas's argument above—about diversity making the world better than it would otherwise be—a supporting premise is: "Since the cause transcends the effect, that which is in the cause, simply and unitedly, exists in the effect in composite and multiple fashion."⁹ But even when identified with simplicity and unity, this "higher and more perfect fashion" often also means "in an unlimited, unconditioned, and unbounded way."¹⁰ And in that case divine simplicity and unity, rather than suggesting a contrast with diversity, may just mean that, unlike creatures who are diverse in some limited, partial, or incomplete way, God is diverse in the most intense, unconditional, and fullest fashion possible: God, in contrast to the imperfect diversity characteristic of creatures, contains infinite, excessive, absolute difference.

Although Aquinas (for example) does not draw this inference, it would seem to follow from his general principles regarding the way created goods preexist in God more perfectly.

> The mode of a thing's excellence is according to the mode of its being. For a thing is said to be more or less excellent according as its being is limited to a certain greater or lesser mode of excellence. Therefore, if there is something to which the whole power of being belongs [i.e., God], it can lack no excellence that is proper to some thing. But for a thing that is its own being it is proper to be according to the whole power of being. For example, if there were a separately existing whiteness, it could not lack any of the power of whiteness. For a given white thing lacks something of the power of whiteness through a defect in the receiver of whiteness, which receives it according to its mode and perhaps not according to the whole power of whiteness. God, therefore, who is his being . . . has being according to the whole power of being itself. Hence, he cannot lack any excellence that belongs to any given thing.¹¹

If diversity is some sort of good, then what this passage suggests holds for other created goods should hold for it: The goodness of diversity should be found in the fullest and most intense fashion in God.

And there's the rub—that "if." Although someone like Aquinas goes out of his way to affirm the goodness of diversity, multiplicity, and complexity within the created world, such an affirmation is still strongly tinged by the second principle discussed above, according to which they also represent an ontological devolution. In short, diversity, multiplicity, and complexity are good only for things that are limited and imperfect to begin with. For example, a perfection is instantiated in multiple individuals only when any one recipient is unable to contain the whole of it. This strong association of diversity with limitation and imperfection breaks, for the case of diversity, the usual inference to the hyper or excessive existence within God of perfections that exist in a conditioned and limited fashion within the world.

Ironically enough, given that he is the primary source of arguments like those of Aquinas, Pseudo-Dionysius comes closest to drawing the inference for difference. The divine contains within itself "everything" that comes forth from it, "every mode of being" without exception, in a transcendent, because "uncomplicated and boundless manner."[12] And among the things that come forth from it, diversity is stressed (perhaps almost as much as unity). "This—the One, the Good, the Beautiful—is in its uniqueness the Cause of the multitudes of the good and the beautiful. From it derives the existence of everything as beings, what they have in common and what differentiates them, their identicalness and differences, their similarities and dissimilarities, their sharing of opposites."[13] Thus, divinity is like "the sun . . . acting upon the essences and the qualities of the many and various things we perceive. . . . It establishes the differences between them and it unifies them."[14] The diversity one finds within the created world is, moreover, quite good for it, and is therefore not lessened through salvation: "It is the righteousness of God which orders everything, setting boundaries, keeping things distinct and unconfused"—maintaining them, in short, as a unified multiplicity by "preserving them in their distinctiveness and yet linking them together in an universal and unconfused alliance."[15] And this righteousness is also "praised as salvation," "since it ensures that each thing is preserved and maintained in its proper being and order, distinct from everything else"; the peace that is the hoped-for end of things will continue to "[guard] without confusion the individuality of each."[16]

As the source of such an apparently unqualified good, divinity, one would think, must certainly pre-contain diversity in the usual superabundant fashion; and, despite the fact that for him "in the divine realm unities hold a higher place than differentiations," Dionysius comes right to the edge of flat-out affirmation to that effect: "Since God is a 'being' in a way beyond being, he bestows existence upon everything and brings the whole world into being, so that his single existence is said to be *manifold* by virtue of the fact that it brings so many things to being from itself"; God "transcends the unity which is in beings. He is *indivisible multiplicity*, the unfilled overfullness which produces, perfects, and preserves all unity *and* all multiplicity."[17] Divine differentiations proceed from the One and in this sense seem to hold a lower place, but this does not stop Dionysius from talking about the "differentiated being of God" or about God's "becoming differentiated" in virtue of such processions while remaining one and "without ceasing to be a unity": God "remains one amid the plurality, unified throughout the procession, and full amid the emptying act of differentiation."[18]

Though "one" remains Pseudo-Dionysius's preferred term for divinity, that seems to mean, not that God is more one than many, but that everything in the world—including both unity and diversity—traces its source back to *the same thing*, whose constitution for that very reason must be beyond the usual unity/multiplicity distinction that holds for things within the world. "The One cause of all things is not one of the many things in the world but actually precedes oneness and multiplicity and indeed defines oneness and multiplicity," such that "there is nothing at all lacking a share in that One which in its utterly comprehensive unity uniquely contains all and every thing beforehand, even opposites"—such as unity and multiplicity.[19] "Our song of praise must be for the single complete deity which is the one cause of all things and which is there before every oneness and multiplicity, before every part and whole, before the definite and indefinite, before the limited and the unlimited."[20]

Indeed, it is because the One defines what it really means to be one or many—the perfection of those terms beyond the meanings we ordinarily give to them—that God can be both one and triune.[21] Just as unity and diversity are found harmoniously integrated in the world, so they are supremely in God.

> In the totality of nature all the laws governing each individual nature are gathered together in one unity within which there is no confusion, and in the soul the individual powers providing for all the parts of the body are assembled together as one. So there is nothing absurd in rising up, as we do, from obscure images to the single Cause of everything, even the things that are opposites . . . [including] all unity and intermingling and attraction, all cohesiveness [on the one hand] and [all] differentiation, all definition, and indeed every attribute which by the mere fact of being gives a character thereby to every existing thing [on the other].[22]

DIVERSITY AND UNITY IN GOD

Although he spends quite a lot of time talking about God as supremely "One," Dionysius doesn't say much of anything about what might make God superabundantly different, about the specific way in which God contains a supreme form of diversity, greater and better than anything found in the things God effects. What makes diversity within God different from the diversity of created things?

Dionysius does suggest, in some of the quotations above (notably, the one immediately above), that the way unity and diversity complement each other in creation has a higher analogue in the way the two opposites come together in God. Because unity and diversity in God are unlimited and absolute, they go together: They are integrated in perfect harmony and are rendered perfectly compatible with each other. Might it not be the case, then, that the imperfect character of difference within creation is manifest in the way diversity and unity remain in tension with each other? In the rest of this essay, I develop this idea by suggesting a close connection between the intense relationality of trinitarian persons as that is affirmed in classical trinitarianism (for example, in the idea that the persons are subsistent relations) and the minority report, also found in classical trinitarianism, that absolute difference characterizes the persons of Trinity.[23]

Trinitarian persons are different, for example, from human persons— this will be the specific created contrast case in what follows—in ways that make them more different from one another than human beings can be. And the underlying difference from humans that accounts for excessive difference among trinitarian persons derives, ironically enough, from the latter's unusual relationality. Divine persons, in short, seem much more relational than human beings are or ever could be, and this is what ultimately accounts for their excessive difference.[24]

Human persons can never be as closely tied to their relations with others as persons in the Trinity are commonly thought to be.[25] Thus, it would be very unusual to suggest that trinitarian persons temporally precede in existence the relations among them that make them what they are, in the way this happens in human relations. Human beings exist before the relations with others that decisively shape their characters; I, for example, existed prior to those relationships with duplicitous others that ended up making me a bitter, distrustful old person. But the character of trinitarian persons does not accrue to them subsequently by way of the sort of relations they come to have with one another; rather than qualifying an existence they already have, those relations constitute them as the sort of persons they are from the very beginning. Unlike human persons, trinitarian persons simply *are* their relations with one another.

Character, moreover, in human beings is not as bound up with actual relationships with others. I can be defined by certain general relational capacities before, and whatever the way in which, these capacities are realized in my relationships. For example, my character might be constituted by the tendency to be suspicious before, and whether or not, my relations with others give me good grounds to be that way. For much the same reasons, the character formed in me by virtue of my relations with others remains even when the relations that gave rise to it end: My character remains, despite, for example, the deaths of the people and communities who have contributed most to it. The relational characteristics of trinitarian persons, to the contrary, are much more tightly a function of actual relationships: The first person of the Trinity, for example, is not defined as someone with the general capacity to beget someone, but as the one who is and remains the first person only in begetting just this second person.[26]

The character of a human person, moreover, takes different forms in the course of relations with different people. I always have the capacity to be more or other than I am right now with you, dear reader: I have the capacity, for example, to be enormously engaging and incredibly funny (unlike now) and the capacity to be hateful when made the brunt of ridicule. Consequently, to know a human person in her relations with you is to know her only incompletely. Theologians generally do not want to say anything quite like that about the Trinity. Trinitarian persons are fully themselves in their relations with one another and with us; trinitarian persons are not in themselves, for example, other than the persons they show themselves to be to us—for example, in their working within the world to save us. And trinitarian persons do not become progressively more or other than themselves as their relations are extended, say, beyond themselves to the world; people at all times and places, therefore, relate to members of the Trinity in their same fully realized characters.

Trinitarian persons are, moreover, always themselves in their relations with one another because they relate to one another immediately—without any externality or media that might possibly disguise their true selves. The distinction between existence and character and the general potentials that constitute the latter prevent this from being the case in human relations. Because there is something to human beings prior to their relations with others, what human beings already are must be conveyed through fallible, merely partially adequate media over the course of these subsequent relations with others. The love I already have for you, I fear, can never be adequately expressed. And because the love formed in my ongoing relations with you amounts to a generalized capacity to act on it in the future, I require media—hugs, kisses, cards, presents—to actualize it, media that always bring with them the possibility of hindering or diminishing its character: Oh, no, I've said the wrong thing! I've given you the same birthday present as your previous bad boyfriend! And so on. Thomas Weinandy combines the two points about fallible media in either expressing a prior state or realizing a general potential for future action this way:

> Human beings relate to one another through mediating acts—words, hugs, kisses. While these actions bring about actual relations, the very fact that they are mediating acts means that human beings are never fully in communion with one another as they are in themselves. For example, if two people intensely love one another, their words and acts of love never fully express the whole of their love for the acts, being mediatory, do not fully embody or express the entirety of their love.[27]

Or the fullness (I might add) of what that love already is or has the potential to be.

Just because their relationality is so inimitably intense, trinitarian persons are irreducibly distinct from one another in ways that human beings cannot imitate. Father and Son—to use classical trinitarian language—remain absolutely different from each other, because, unlike the case of human fathers and sons, here the Father has never been a Son—the Father is always Father—and the Son never becomes a Father in turn—the Son is always Son.[28] Terms such as "father" and "son" when used of persons of the Trinity do not, in short, indicate general capacities, which a variety of individuals might exhibit, but are person-specific, person-defining properties. In the human case, I am different from my mother in that I am my mother's daughter, but I can also become like my mother by becoming the mother of a daughter myself; and therefore in being different from my mother I am not absolutely different from her. The human relations that distinguish people never simply define them, and thus one can lose one's primary identification in those relations (one's character as the daughter of a mother, say, once one's mother has been dead for thirty years) and take on others (the identity of a mother to one's own daughter) while remaining oneself. But persons of the Trinity are too tied to their specific relationships—of being, say, Father and Son—to do this. They are too absolutely what they are—e.g., Son or Father—and too absolutely distinct from one another in such a relationship for that to be possible.

Indeed, in the Trinity relations of tremendous intensity never threaten the individuality of the persons in the way relations like that threaten to blur the identities of human beings. Unlike the case of trinitarian persons, the individual identity of humans seems to require a sort of policing of boundaries between themselves and others that often breaks off relationships. I will never be my own person unless I can break away from the incredibly intense relationship I have with my mother. In the Trinity, to the contrary, the persons are absolutely different from one another in the very intensity of the relationships they have with one another. It is because the relationship is so intense for them both, so to speak, that the Father can only be a Father and the Son only a Son. Only in virtue of maintaining their relationship inviolate do they remain absolutely different from one another—the Father without any capacity whatever to be a Son because of it, and the Son nothing like what makes the Father Father in begetting him. They are themselves only if the relationship maintains its intensity for both of them, never themselves by mitigating or somehow attenuating it.

PERFECT DIFFERENCE

Now this sort of absolute difference, even if it is a consequence of intense relationality, might not seem especially perfect to us. Don't we have here, as Virginia Burrus eloquently proclaims, "the perfected security of relational identities put permanently 'on ice,'" identities that are "frozen" and "fixed"?[29] Isn't this sort of hyperdiversity within the Trinity just an exaggerated form, in fact, of the this-worldly "goods" of diversity that Pseudo-Dionysius seems to praise so highly—the good of staying in one's allotted place and never getting out of line, the good of having a clear boundary to one's identity and role, which, even if it needn't be guarded against relationality, prevents all blurring into others? Doesn't all this make one long for the stress on perfect equality for all held up by Origen and Eckhart, even were that stress to bring along with it a disparagement of the ultimate value of difference?

This impression of fixity within the classical trinitarian account of the persons can be alleviated somewhat if one recognizes that the relations that establish identity are themselves dynamic—they involve, for example, processions or generative flows and movements of response.[30] The identities of the persons may not be subject to change, but what defines them may still amount to activities or movements—say, of coming and going, issuing and receiving, giving back what one is getting or carrying it to another, and so on. These relations, indeed, may be so intensely full as to invite a multiplicity of characterizations—the first person of the Trinity gives rise to the second like a father generating a son, or a woman giving birth, or light streaming from the sun, or a word issuing from one's mouth—and be so complex as to overlap in ways impossible for the simpler relations of our world—for example, this issuing forth is at the same time a receiving back of what is issued from the one now receiving it, and so on.

One can also argue that, although the unchangeable character of their identities is no doubt affirmed, incommunicability rather than fixity is more at issue. In general in classical trinitarianism, when defining the persons of the Trinity, one is concerned, not with properties like immutability or eternity that define the one substance or essence of the Trinity and so do not set the persons of the Trinity off from one another, but specifically with what is not shared or communicated among the three. Talk about absolute differences among persons of the Trinity would quite naturally be a way of making that point—not about immutability, which all the persons share and which is usually discussed in connection with divine unity, but about incommunicability, about what the persons do not share or communicate among themselves in virtue of their dynamic interrelationships. They share those relationships, and these relationships involve sharing or self-communication, but the positions they hold in those relationships are not for that reason interchangeable.

If incommunicability is what is at issue, the absolute difference that constitutes divine hyperdifference represents not so much what is beyond imperfect difference marked by change and confusion as a perfect difference of the unique and the irreplaceable beyond all differences among replicable and therefore fungible things. There is nothing else like any of the persons of the Trinity, and thus none of them can be a stand-in or substitute for another. Unlike human relationships, where psychic health (so they say) is a matter of eventually giving up the lost beloved object, no matter how strong the attachment, and moving on, finding a replacement, persons of the Trinity would lose themselves in losing just those specific, albeit different, ones to which they relate in those many different, incredibly intense connections among them that constitute their identities. In short, the persons of the Trinity mean everything to one another, too much to one another, indeed, to ever let one another go. Any loss among the absolutely different would be an absolute, inconsolable one, in other words.

Here the Trinity serves to highlight, by way of contrast, the peculiarities of the present world in which we live: What we perhaps take for granted, especially as contemporary Americans, begins to stand out as strange when seen in the light of a trinitarian form of relationality, a form of relationality that, although beyond our reach apart from God's own work to save us from the tragedies of finitude, many Christians hope will one day, with God's help, become ours. As Americans beset by economic forces encouraging us at least until very recently to consume well beyond our means, we have been led to see the world in which we live as one of complete fungibility, a fungibility that has the effect of detaching us from the unique particularities of seemingly everything to which we relate.[31] Everything, in other words, has become replaceable, preferably as soon as possible, before we even know we've tired of it. How attached can we be to anything, no matter how fulfilling the present experience of it, when we are even now anticipating with pleasure the new model to come? In such a world is there not some good, albeit hard, word in the all-or-nothing, irreplaceable intensity of relations to be found only, classical trinitarianism tells us, in this time between the times, within the Trinity?

Multiplicity and Christocentric Theology

JOHN F. HOFFMEYER

The Christian religion has been implicated in manifold forms of domination, imperialism, and conquest. Powerful historical agents have repeatedly inflated Christian particularity into a false universal. Discussions and movements critical of the soul-scarring and sometimes death-dealing imposition of Christian particularity are always to be welcomed. However, it is tempting for both those who advance such criticism and those who try to defend Christianity against it to operate with a one-sided sense of Christian particularity. Specifically, it is too often assumed that the embrace of Christian particularity entails elevating Christ to the position of the organizing center around which all other creatures must be organized. This essay arises from the desire to reject such christocentricity, as well as from the conviction that christocentricity can be part of the solution rather than part of the problem.

MULTIPLE PERSPECTIVES ON MULTIPLICITY

In most of the conferences that I attend and in much of the contemporary theology and philosophy that I read, multiplicity is "in." It is among a group of semantically related words that generally receive a quick positive response at the academic conferences and meetings to which I am attracted: words such as "other," "difference," "différance," and "poly-" (polydoxy, but not polyester). On the other side of the ledger, words such as "unity," "totality," "same," and "oneness" are liable to evoke suspicion. When Hegel, writing two centuries ago, said that "truth is the whole," he was arguing against the dichotomizing tendencies of the European Enlightenment, warning against claiming too much for one-sided positions. In many circles today Hegel's claim is likely to sound "totalizing," and thus to be primarily something to avoid. Lurking behind the statement that "truth is the whole" might be the mistaken assumption that any one thinker or any one perspective could comprehend "the whole" sufficiently to give it exhaustive articulation. Alternatively, the talk about truth and the whole might betray the elevation of one's own particular perspective to universal status.

Of course, as other participants in this colloquium have persuasively argued for years now, the metaphor of a ledger opposing "good" and "bad" abstract terms will serve only a superficial analysis. I want to focus on two of the reasons why this is the case. The first is that linguistic terms lead an ecological existence. They do not exist in abstract isolation, but in historically evolving webs of relation. An emphasis on multiplicity is a precious and welcome thing in the face of long-standing patterns of imposed unification. To know that there is another option besides that imposed unification is already a blessing. To recognize that there is more than one option, that resistance to the imposed unification need not be the mirror image of that against which we are reacting, is a further blessing. As an example, consider the beautiful book of one of our colloquium organizers, Catherine Keller, on apocalypse.[1] In that book she shows how easily resistance to what she calls the "apocalypse habit" can find itself stuck in apocalyptic patterns. It is all too tempting for the struggle against the apocalypse habit to take on, in turn, the rhetoric and the form of an apocalyptic battle. In the face of this temptation, Keller holds out the hope of being "counter-apocalyptic": opposing the apocalypse habit in a nonapocalyptic way. This is welcome multiplicity.

There are also contexts and uses that make "multiplicity" sound less attractive. Consumer society celebrates multiplicity. Barry Schwartz begins his illuminating study *The Paradox of Choice: Why More Is Less* by recounting how he went to buy a new pair of jeans when his old pair was worn out, only to be confronted with an overwhelming multiplicity of options for cut, color, fit, and style. His book goes on to argue, through a multiplicity of psychological studies, that we who live in consumer society have often falsely extrapolated from (a) the fact that an increase in choice, particularly from a minimal level, can bring an increase in happiness to (b) the assumption that multiplying choice will generally multiply happiness. Closer examination reveals that the multiplication of choices readily leads to (a) unpleasant difficulty in settling on one choice and (b) second-guessing and regret once a choice is made, because of the imagined likelihood that one could have made a better choice. For example, how can one even survey all the available cell-phone plans in order to determine which is the best? Even if it were possible, a new and "improved" plan will surely be coming in the mail this week.[2]

Of course, one can object that the apparent multiplicity of consumer society harbors an illusion. The eighteen-theater "multiplex" at the local mall actually offers only ten different movies, since the blockbusters show in multiple theaters, and the remaining ten actually comprise only three different types of films. In addition, most of the current films seem more or less like minor variations on the films that ran last month. The multiplicity of the multiplex—or of the sixty-seven varieties of breakfast cereal, or of the fourteen brands and sixty-five flavors of toothpaste—is ambiguous.

The recognition that multiplicity is ambiguous and that this ambiguity calls us to careful thought is, if I understand it correctly, one of the basic motivations behind this colloquium. The title focus of our gathering is not so much the multiplicity of prepared breakfast cereals as it is divine multiplicity—although I assume that the two are not unrelated. Divine multiplicity has its own ambiguity. For example, as a teacher at a Christian theological seminary, I frequently hear students talk about multiple divine characteristics in a way that assumes they exist in a balancing act. Most frequently, the balance is between divine justice, on the one hand, and divine grace, on the other. Generally in the conversations at my school, grace has the upper hand—perhaps not surprising for a Lutheran seminary.

This kind of divine multiplicity is not helpful. Despite the weaknesses of the long-standing Christian theological doctrine of divine simplicity, it has the virtue of countering that fragmenting style of multiplicity. If God is simple, in the sense of that traditional teaching, then divine justice and divine love ultimately have to be the same thing. Consider, for example, the thundering announcement by the prophet Amos of God's disgust with beautiful and moving religious liturgies in the presence of chronic injustice.

Thus says the Lord:
For three transgressions of Israel,
and for four, I will not revoke the punishment;
because they sell the righteous for silver,
and the needy for a pair of sandals—
they who trample the head of the poor into the dust of the earth,
and push the afflicted out of the way;
father and son go in to the same girl,
so that my holy name is profaned;
they lay themselves down beside every altar
on garments taken in pledge;
and in the house of their God they drink
wine bought with fines they imposed.

I hate, I despise your festivals,
and I take no delight in your solemn assemblies.
[You can do beautiful liturgies by the book
and claim that it is all at considerable cost to yourselves.
I am not impressed.
Get rid of all those chorales and praise songs and Taizé chants and
    gospel
favorites;
I will not listen to your organs and electric keyboards.]
But let justice [*mishpat*] roll down like waters
and justice [*tsedakah*] like an ever-flowing stream.[3]

This is not the voice of God's justice and anger as contrasted with, or even opposed to, God's grace, love, and mercy. This is the angry voice of God's love for those suffering chronic injustice.

One need not affirm the doctrine of divine simplicity in order to recognize the value of avoiding an interpretation of divine multiplicity that would be tantamount to divine fragmentation. At the same time, fragmentation, tending toward disjointed "manyness," is not the only sense of multiplicity. Already the etymology of "multiplicity" works against such fragmentation. "Multi-plicity" is "many-foldedness." On the one hand, multiplicity is not simplicity ("one-foldedness").[4] On the other hand, multiplicity is not unrelated many-ness. A sheet of paper folded into an origami bird encompasses the differentiation introduced by the many folds, but without the paper being cut apart into many separate pieces of paper. This embrace of differentiation is the etymological background of the word "complexity," from the Latin *complector*, "to embrace, to clasp."

The second reason for being circumspect about overextending initial positive reactions to terms such as "multiplicity" lies, if you will, in the multiplicity of the term. Heraclitus said that *panta rhei*, "everything flows." If everything flows, then the Heraclitean statement cannot function as a fixed description of reality. The claim of the statement undermines the possibility of such fixity. The truth-value of the predication "everything flows" must also flow. Likewise, if everything is multiplicity, then the predication "everything is multiplicity" cannot have a unitary truth-value. Multiplicity cannot be the only valid description of what everything is. Alternatively, any predication of the form "everything is . . ." is, in its universalizing claim, a limitation on the scope of multiplicity, even if the word "multiplicity" completes the predication. If everything really were multiplicity, that very fact would undermine any and every universalizing claim. The universal quantifier "everything" and the singular verb "is" would have no joint projects to accomplish together in such a strictly multiple word. The statement "everything is multiplicity" must itself be subject to all that is entailed in the claim that reality is thoroughly multiple. The statement that "everything is multiplicity" must be a duplicitous claim.

MULTIPLICITY, UNITY, AND THE CONCRETENESS OF CHRIST

Much of the enduring fascination of the relation of unity and multiplicity is that they are not just two important factors that need to be properly balanced. They are mutually constitutive. As a result, complex presentations of that relation are generally open to multiple readings. It would be handy to use the term *dialectical* to describe the complex relation of mutual constitution that leads to the likelihood of multiple readings, but the very pertinence of the term means that it, too, is the object of multiple and contested readings. Some interpreters emphasize dialectic as a philosophical championing of otherness and difference. These interpreters may well note that "dialectical" comes from the same Greek word as "dialogical." For other interpreters, dialectic looks suspiciously like a way of taking otherness and difference captive to a monological sameness.[5]

The extent to which profound meditations on the one and the many give rise to multiple readings is apparent from interpretations of Hegel—to take one influential philosopher of the one and the many. Some of the basic concerns entailed in the theme of Divine Multiplicity mark the space of two divergent ways of reading and appropriating Hegel. Consider, for example, Lévinas's *Totality and Infinity,* by which he means "Totality or Infinity," in which the "or" is exclusive.[6] Is Hegel the crown prince of totality, as Lévinas believes, so that *Geist* is the ultimate "totalizing" metaphysical trump card? Or is *Geist* Hegel's way of talking about what Terry Pinkard calls the "sociality of reason"?[7] Here reason is not itself some unifying trump, but a partly descriptive and partly normative reference to how it is the case that humans live in what Wilfrid Sellars called a "space of reasons, of justifying and being able to justify what one says."[8] On this vision universality is not the imperialistic squelching of difference and the other, but the advocacy that everyone have equal rights of citizenship in the space of giving and receiving reasons. More specifically, it is the advocacy that the next person you encounter always has a legitimate claim to full citizenship in that social space of giving and receiving reasons.

Hopefully, recognition of divergent possibilities and patterns of interpretation does not simply leave the divergent paths juxtaposed. As I understand it, that hope is also part of the motivation of this colloquium. To turn once more to the example of the interpretation of Hegel's thought, the dialogue between Jacques Derrida and the great French Hegel scholar Pierre-Jean Labarrière provides an encouraging model of the possibility of moving beyond stale oppositions and unproductive juxtapositions. In a discussion published in the 1980s under the title *Alterities,* Labarrière acknowledges in Hegel's philosophy a monistic "tendency," if not a monistic "design," that would recuperate the one at the expense of the many. Derrida subsequently lays out an understanding of *différance,* including its difference from Hegelian dialectic. Labarrière then articulates his own attempt to conjoin a "logic of mediation" and a "logic of interruption," so that "irrepressible interruption" occurs "at the very center of a process of mediation." Labarrière concludes by saying that he keeps returning to Hegel because of the latter's intuition—not always consistently maintained—concerning these conjoined logics. Derrida responds: "I agree. That is what I was saying about *différance* a little while ago."[9]

At its best, the Christian doctrine of the Trinity meditates on the dialectic of unity and multiplicity, but it also does more than that. It moves that dialectic off the plane of abstraction. The primary evaluative question in considering unity and multiplicity is not "Unity or multiplicity?" but "What sort of unity and what sort of multiplicity?" Historically, Christian trinitarianism did not develop primarily out of a felt need for a better theory of the dialectic of unity and multiplicity. The development of Christian trinitarianism in the ancient church was inseparable from the development of christology. Both developments, in their inseparability, had to deal with the concrete person of Jesus of Nazareth. The challenge of how to think together the eternal divine and the concrete person Jesus of Nazareth drove both developments. This is by no means to deny that those developments called forth questionable, sometimes bizarre abstractions about that concrete person. It was always possible, though, to evoke the concrete person as a criterion for judging those abstractions.

The historical development suggests a central claim of my essay: Namely, Christian trinitarian thinking about multiplicity and unity is inseparable from the concreteness of the person of Jesus the Christ. Christ functions as criterion in making judgments about multiplicity and unity. Christian trinitarian theology, as I understand it, warns against any unity or any multiplicity that is incompatible with Christ. This is the point, for example, of the first article of the Barmen Declaration of the Confessing Church in Nazi Germany. Barmen rejects a unity dependent upon the Nazi *Führer*. Instead, "Jesus Christ, as witnessed to us in Holy Scripture, is the one word of God to which we have to listen and which we have to trust and obey in life and in death."[10]

It is easy to join Barmen in rejecting the nazification of the German church. But at a conference on "Divine Multiplicities," the emphasis on Jesus Christ as the *one* word of God is sure to raise concern. In any case, it raises my concern—bearing in mind that concern is not rejection, but an impetus to further thought or action. Can there be genuinely respectful and mutual religious encounter and dialogue between Christians and persons of faiths other than Christianity if the Christians involved hold that Jesus Christ is the one word of God? Does the claim that Jesus Christ is the one word of God not belie my claim that the doctrine of the Trinity recognizes the dialectic of unity and multiplicity? In other words, does christocentric unity dissolve this dialectic in favor of unity over multiplicity?

One way to respond to the uneasiness expressed in these questions is to keep one's distance from the christocentrism expressed in the Barmen Declaration. More accurately, one way to respond to the uneasiness expressed in these questions is to keep one's distance from christocentrism more generally, indeed from monocentrism still more generally. Another approach, which I will explore in this essay, is to reconsider the concept of center in the light of, as Barmen puts it, "Jesus Christ, as witnessed to us in Holy Scripture." If Christ plays an essential role of concrete specification in the trinitarian dialectic of unity and multiplicity, it is important to examine concretely the kind of center that Christ might be.

In his 1975 work *God of the Oppressed*, James Cone identifies black experience and scripture as the two sources of Black theology. He goes on to emphasize that each is "a *source* of the Truth but not the Truth itself. Jesus Christ is the Truth and thus stands in judgment over all statements about truth." This is a strong christocentric statement. Cone hastens to add a qualification that does not so much mitigate the christocentrism as specify the kind of center that Jesus Christ is. "There is no truth in Jesus Christ independent of the oppressed of the land."[11] I am going to continue tracing out what Cone's argument suggests about christocentrism by attending to the famous judgment story that concludes the twenty-fifth chapter of the Gospel according to Matthew. In the story the king, the "child of the human being," divides "all the peoples" into two groups: the "sheep" and the "goats." The king praises the sheep for having fed him when he was hungry, supplied him with drink when he was thirsty, showed him hospitality when he was a stranger, clothed him when he was naked, attended to him when he was sick, and come to be present with him when he was in prison. They respond by asking when they had seen the king in those conditions and responded to his need. The king responds, "As much as you did to the least of these my brothers and sisters, you did to me" (v. 40).

This is a well-known text that many Christian sermons have quoted. Yet how is it possible to preach this text in a way that does not contradict the story? With this question I do not mean only the simplistic mistake that too many preachers make, using the story as the grounds for an appeal to go out and do the "Christ-like thing" and feed the hungry. The story does not say anything explicitly about "Christ," but to the extent that Christian tradition has identified Christ with the "child of the human being" and the king in the story, the story in turn identifies Christ not with the person doing the feeding, but with the person being fed.

Beyond that confusion, though, there is a deeper problem. Suppose the preacher follows the story more accurately and tells her hearers that this story promises that, in feeding persons who are hungry, they will encounter Christ. The preacher's act of telling her hearers this has made it impossible for them to be in the position of the "sheep" in the story. In the story they say, in effect, "We didn't know it was you; we never saw you." They were not feeding hungry persons with the idea that thereby they would encounter Christ. They were just feeding hungry persons. This is the action—"just feeding hungry persons"—which receives praise in the story. This is the action in which they turn out to have encountered the "child of the human being" or the king/Christ. How can people who hear a Christian sermon on this text then go out and "just feed hungry persons"? If they approach feeding people as an encounter with Christ, they are doing something other than what the story describes and commends.

To be faithful to the text, the preacher needs to preach in a way that moves people, in a sense, to forget about Christ and feed persons who are hungry, visit people who are imprisoned, attend to people who are sick, and show hospitality to strangers. The encounter with Christ takes place not by making other persons means to the end of encountering Christ, or even multiple instances of the overarching presence of the one Christ. On the contrary, this text from Matthew suggests that encounter with Christ occurs when there are "only" the multiple loving interactions with other persons.

The story of the sheep and the goats demonstrates that the logic of christocentric thought requires decentering Christ. After noticing this about the story, I was pleased to discover a resonance with Catherine Keller's formulation that a "truly christocentric theology will decenter Christology."[12] The resonance lies both in the movement of decentering and in the christocentric grounding of that decentering. At the same time, there is a difference in formulation, since my argument is about decentering "Christ" rather than "Christology." The logic of a christocentric decentering of Christ decenters christology as well, if Christ is the center of christology. Yet this logic is in its own way christocentric. It is a christo-logic, a logic centered on Christ as decentering center.

CHRISTOCENTRICITY AND THE CRITIQUE OF METANARRATIVES

This dialectic of centering and decentering can help orient christological thinking toward one influential contemporary form of the relation between the one and the many: Jean-François Lyotard's distinction between "metanarrative" (or "grand narrative") and "small narrative." Lyotard's most famous claim, of course, is that suspicion toward metanarratives characterizes "the postmodern condition." In postmodernity, metanarratives have lost their capacity to provide legitimation for claimants to the status of knowledge. Postmodernity deals in small narratives or, to use Lyotard's more frequent language, which he picks up from Wittgenstein, regional "language games."

Given the widespread currency of the notion that metanarratives are passé in postmodernity, a Christian theologian might well wonder about the relation between Christian faith and metanarrative. Certainly there are versions of Christian theology with a very big narrative structure: for example, talk of "the Christian story" stretching from creation, through fall (into sin) and redemption, to eschatological consummation. This recognition does not mean that Christianity is passé in postmodernity, even if "metanarratives" are. It could just be that metanarrative versions of Christianity are passé.

What exactly is a metanarrative version of Christianity? How extensive must a story's compass be for it to pass over from the status of "small narrative" to that of "grand narrative"? Suppose that Chris Boesel gives an unusually insightful paper at this fall's meeting of the American Academy of Religion in Atlanta. Afterwards one could tell a specific story about that particular paper presentation. Suppose that Catherine Keller also gives an unusually insightful paper at AAR. One could tell a specific story about that paper presentation. One could also move up one level of generalization and tell a story about the unusual insightfulness of Drew theologians and colloquium organizers, instantiated in both Boesel and Keller. In relation to the first two stories, one could call this last story a "metanarrative." To claim that my example fits what Lyotard means by "metanarrative" would be unfair and wrongheaded. The example does indicate, though, the difficulty in specifying just what postmodernity is suspicious of, if it is suspicious of metanarratives. The move to a "meta-" level is not a move to any fixed logical or metaphysical level. It is a move to a level that is logically beyond the preceding level of the conversation. "Meta-" is a contextually relational term.

The context of Lyotard's use of the term "metanarrative" is, as the subtitle of *The Postmodern Condition* announces, a contemporary "report on knowledge." More specifically—picking up the titles of the book's first three chapters—the field of his inquiry is "knowledge in information societies"; the problem that he is exploring is "legitimation"; and the method of his investigation is "language games."[13] It is in relation to this field, this problem, and this method that Lyotard employs the concept of metanarrative. He is also careful to note in introducing the concept that he is engaging in an extreme simplification.[14] Within this simplification, what Lyotard means by "metanarrative" is more restrained than some of the subsequent invocations of his idea. He is not rejecting large-scale, sweeping stories about cultural and intellectual developments. In *The Postmodern Condition* Lyotard tells such a story to explain how developments in the nineteenth and twentieth centuries led to a crisis in accustomed appeals to overarching narratives to provide a framework for what should count as legitimate knowledge. What Lyotard thinks is incompatible with the postmodern condition is the turn to large-scale narratives of legitimation that reduce local "language games" in their incommensurable multiplicity to second-class status.

The postmodern condition, according to Lyotard, finds the homogenizing logic of such overarching narratives of legitimation unbelievable. Instead of such homogenizing logic, such "homo-logy," Lyotard describes and prescribes a logic of incommensurable multiplicity, a "para-logy." One might wonder how the delegitimation of metanarratives fits into this scheme. If the postmodern condition is one of paralogy, what could be more "paralogical," more adversarial to the logic of the postmodern condition, than a renewed call for legitimation by metanarrative? If the name of the postmodern game is a multiplicity of local language games, why is the appeal to metanarrative legitimation not one such language game? It might be an unstable language game, since it claims to be something more than a local language game. But can the paralogistic condition of multiple local language games admit of a criterion that would weed out unstable language games? If so, stability would emerge as a homologizing force, requiring that the multiplicity of language games conform to a universal standard.

It is possible to argue on ethical grounds against appeals to legitimating metanarratives in those cases where such appeals disguise particular perspectives as universal norms. For example, thinkers from Enrique Dussel[15] to Susan Buck-Morss[16] have rightly criticized the Eurocentric particularity of Hegel's supposedly universal history. This specific criticism of Hegel, appropriate though it is, is not part of Lyotard's project in *The Postmodern Condition*. As far as I can see, this kind of ethical critique of particularlistic metanarratives is not the work in which he is engaged.

Where does Christian theology fit in Lyotard's contest between homology and paralogy? Christian theology certainly can be strongly homological. As noted earlier in the discussion of the Barmen Declaration, christocentric theology of the one word of God can and often has resulted in a clear preference for the one over the many. The story of the sheep and the goats in Matthew 25 suggests that this need not be the case, indeed that a concretely christocentric theology argues against the triumph of the one over the many. At the same time, the logic of the story does not lead to an unstructured field of multiplicity: that is, multiplicity that degenerates into mere "many-ness." It does not drift toward undifferentiated paralogy. The multiple encounters in the story are all encounters with the centering figure of the "king." Yet this is not the one, true, essential content of these encounters, in comparison with which the multiplicity of the encounters would be of only secondary importance. The condition of the possibility of the encounters with hungry persons and imprisoned persons being encounters with the king is that these multiple encounters not be treated as mere instances of, or occasions for, encountering the king.

The king is not the unique organizing center of the story. The king's centrality is inseparable from the centering of compassionate attention on the person who is hungry, the person who is sick, the person who is imprisoned. This complex centering refuses to break the dialectic of the one and the many in either direction. It does, however, provide a normative structure. The norm is not the priority of the king over other persons, but the response of compassion and solidarity with other persons, rather than rationalizations that would elude such a response ("When did we see you hungry and not feed you?"). The story makes clear normative judgments about the multiple possible ways of responding to the hunger, the thirst, the status as stranger, the lack of adequate clothing and shelter, the sickness, and the imprisonment of other people. The story indicates no openness to language games that would result in not visiting the imprisoned, not feeding the hungry, not attending to the sick, and similar actions.

The narrative framework of the story about the sheep and the goats is a scene in which the king pronounced judgment on his subjects. This scene seems tailor-made to reinforce christocentric thinking of a form that belongs to the christology rightly criticized as "exclusionary" by much liberal and progressive theology. The king is the powerful center, lord over his subjects. One way of restating my interpretation of the story is to say that it identifies the king with his supposed subjects in such a way as to undo the hierarchical roles of king and subject. There no longer is a one who rules over the many.

THE DECENTERING CHRIST AS DIVINE REVELATION

Perhaps I can throw some more light upon my christological argument for decentering Christ by placing it within the context of a broad and influential tradition of classical Christian orthodoxy. The council of Chalcedon in 451 C.E. claimed that Jesus Christ was truly God and truly human. Christological thinking has often operated as if this formulation were an attempt to define a unique and obscure metaphysical entity—Jesus Christ as the incarnate word of God—in terms of two better-known realities—God and human being. One could interpret in a different direction. Jesus Christ manifests or reveals the truly divine and the truly human. This manifestation is salutary because we human beings come up with far too many shallow, misguided, or dehumanizing ideas about what it means to be human—not to mention what it means to be divine. The discrepancy between what is manifest in Christ and our many misguided notions is what lies behind Paul's claim in 1 Corinthians that the revelation in Christ is a "scandal to Jews" and "folly to *goyim*" (1 Cor 1:23).

Christian tradition is certainly not without wise theologians who have argued in the second of the two christological directions that I have suggested. Kathryn Tanner's *Christ the Key* is a richly argued model of such thinking.[17] If it is not presumptuous to add my little riff on her leitmotif, my proposal is (1) that we see Jesus the Christ as key to what centrality means in the concept of christocentrism and (2) that the story of the sheep and the goats from Matthew 25 provides an illuminating guide for doing so. The idea that christocentric theology entails elevating Jesus at the expense of other human beings, or indeed at the expense of other creatures in general, depends on a conception of centrality other than that suggested by the Matthean text.

If Jesus is the unsurpassable revelation of God, then this decentering centrality pertains not just to the way in which God appears in Jesus the Christ, but to God's very being. Before exploring this claim, a word is in order about the description of Jesus as the unsurpassable revelation of God. This conception of divine revelation is not a way of reneging on the decentering christology proposed in this chapter. I neither intend nor understand it to be a way of reintroducing a Christian monopoly on truth, or even a controlling ownership of truth. The unsurpassable word is not the only word, in the sense of the exclusionary christology to which liberal and progressive theologies rightly object. The unsurpassable word is not the last word in a sense that would contradict the well-conceived slogan of the United Church of Christ that "God is still speaking." The unsurpassable word is a word that will never be left behind, a word whose criteriological function as question and promise will never become passé. The assertion that Jesus is the unsurpassable word of God is not Christian triumphalism for the reason that Christian triumphalism, as far as I can see, pretends that God has something to say that contradicts what God says in Jesus. If the unsurpassable divine self-identification is with someone who died from state-sponsored torture, then apparently God is not essentially concerned about winning. All Christian visions of a "second coming" in which Christ arrives in power, ready this time to knock heads, put the cosmos in order, and show which religion gets the prize, are rejections of the position that Jesus is the unsurpassable word of God. The unsurpassable word made flesh is the one who is encountered by "forgetting about Christ"—in the sense articulated above—and centering attention on one's fellow creatures.

The unsurpassably revelatory character of Jesus as the Christ means that the divine center is also decentered. Making this point is one of the functions of the doctrine of the Trinity. In the view of Gregory of Nazianzus, the doctrine of the Trinity directs us to the fact that reality is multiple all the way down. We can never leave multiplicity in a subordinate position and center on the one, even if we call that one "God." As Gregory puts it, "No sooner do I think the one than I am illumined round about by the three; no sooner do I differentiate the three than I am borne back to the one."[18]

This point presents a critical conceptual juncture for Christian trinitarian thought. Does the doctrine of the Trinity incorporate multiplicity into the concept of God, but then forget the lesson of christological decentering and make the triune God the transcendent center, "above" and "outside" the multiplicity of creation? Many contemporary theologians have argued against this abstract way of conceiving transcendence as the simple opposite of immanence. For example, Mayra Rivera argues against abstracting the divinely creative gift of life "from materiality by positing an immaterial creator God outside the cosmos," with the result that human "participation in the divine, or getting closer to God, is imagined as a movement away from creatures."[19] To return once more to the story of the sheep and the goats in Matthew 25, one of its basic christological lessons is that the movement closer to God and the movement closer to creatures do not run in contrary directions. As Kathryn Tanner has insistently argued, God's relation to creatures is noncompetitive.[20]

At the beginning of the last chapter of Rivera's lovely book, she writes: "The various models of interhuman transcendence we have reviewed lead us back to explicit God-talk, to divine transcendence—which, of course, we never really left behind."[21] This raises again the question of metanarrative. Some might argue that if divine transcendence is at play in all the multiple, local events of interhuman transcendence, theology is necessarily metanarrative. Are not the multiple stories of all those events of interhuman transcendence also a story of divine transcendence?

I argued earlier that Lyotard's understanding of the postmodern suspicion toward metanarratives can hardly rule out all large-scale stories that move to a meta-level in relation to other stories, since Lyotard devotes a good portion of his book to telling such a story. Lyotard's primary concern seems to be with the demotion of local stories and local language games to second-class status in a hierarchy organized by a controlling metanarrative. In chapter 9, "The Narratives of the Legitimation of Knowledge," Lyotard links important modern metanarratives with the invocation of a "meta-subject."[22] This meta-subject provides the fundamental legitimating framework. If history is at heart the life and becoming of such a meta-subject, then the life of this subject provides the criteria for whatever counts as knowledge, and for the appropriate institutional structures and processes for developing and communicating knowledge. Lyotard does not say that all the metanarratives of which postmodernity is suspicious are narratives of such a meta-subject. But for theology the question quickly arises: Is God such a meta-subject?

If the decentered Christ is the unsurpassable revelatory word of God, then the idea of a divine meta-subject is seriously in doubt. Of course "God" functions as the grammatical subject in myriad theological propositions. The grammatical form of the proposition might suggest a picture according to which the subject, the *sub-jectum*, the "under-lying," is the foundation on which the rest of the statement builds. Yet as Hegel argued, we should not let the apparently foundation place of the subject in propositional grammatical form mislead us into assuming a metaphysics of foundational "subjects."[23] The story of the sheep and the goats in Matthew 25 demonstrates that the apparent status of Christ as meta-subject in christocentric theology is misleading. Christocentric thought issues in an open multiplicity of subjects not subjugated to any meta-subject. To the extent that Christ reveals the divine, theology has good reason to expect to find God no more interested in the role of meta-subject.

AFTERWORD

The preceding essay is a lightly amended version of the essay that I wrote for the colloquium. At the colloquium Michelle Voss Roberts provided a generous and challenging response. A recurrent theme in her questions was whether my decentered and decentering christocentrism might still be a way of elevating a particular position or logic to the status of a universal norm. For all my emphasis on decentering, was I still leaving too little room for difference? For instance, was I turning the function of "decentering the center" into a universal criterion of religious truth?

The terms of the question itself already point to the limits of my essay in relation to the theme of the colloquium. The theme of the colloquium invited explicit wrestling with the complex reality of religious diversity. Religious diversity in the sense of diversity between so-called world religions was a major focus of the colloquium.[24] My essay was not directly about religious diversity. It operated in Christian categories. This was partly because many participants in the colloquium were much better equipped than I to discuss religious diversity, but mostly because my project was to see how far categories of Christian particularity might open out onto vistas of multiplicity and difference. It was not an exercise in comparative theology or in theology of religious pluralism. It would be false, though, to describe my project as an "immanent" Christian one. Specifically, it would be a futile exercise to try to separate out the Buddhist influences in my own Christian thought and practice. It is likely that my christology would not have the same attentiveness to a logic of decentering were it not for how Buddhism has shaped me. Yet my project was to show how much such a logic of decentering is at home in Christian theology.

Attentive to my attempt to articulate a christo-logic, Voss Roberts posed a question that might serve as a bridge to a more direct engagement with the gifts and challenges of religious diversity. She asked: "Can the logic of the decentered center accept the viability of *other* orienting centers"?[25] My discussion of Christ as a decentered and decentering center presents a center that is also not a center. A decentered and decentering center, a center that is not a center, does not need to "get out of the way" to make room for other centers, since its peculiar identity as center is not dependent on clinging to the center space. At this level of abstraction a decentered and decentering center is compatible with other orienting centers. As one introduces a little more concrete content into the picture, some incompatibility appears. Among the "other orienting centers" to which Voss Roberts refers, some could themselves be decentered and decentering, while others could depend on seeing centering and decentering as mutually exclusive, so that a true center cannot be decentered or decentering. Proponents of the second type of center would not be interested in compatibility with a decentered and decentering center. A decentered and decentering christocentrism can regard this second type of center as a viable moment in the dialectic of centering, but not as an adequate expression of the fuller dialectic, which transcends each of its individual moments. Within the complex historical phenomenon of Christianity it is easy to find both types of center represented in christocentric thought and practice. My admittedly limited knowledge of other major religions has not yet given me reason to think that the breadth of each of them, as actually thought and practiced across time and place, does not also encompass proponents of both types of center.

Voss Roberts wonders whether my proposal might unintentionally be "operating in an economy of the same." If I understand correctly, her concern is that, for all the talk of a decentered and decentering christocentricy, it is still *Christo*-centricity. All other centers must be related to Christ; Christ provides the moment of "sameness" to which all difference must relate.

I hold that Christ is as much a diversifying figure as a unifying figure. In the trinitarian repertoire of Christian theology, this diversification is the work of the Spirit—the Spirit who is inseparable from the presence of the resurrected Christ. Perhaps I am mistaken that Christ can be as much a diversifying figure as a unifying one. The fact that I repeatedly use a particular figure—Christ—to identify this dialectic of diversification and unification does not in itself subordinate diversity to unity, or difference to identity. Part of the wisdom of Hegel's claim that *Geist* is the identity of identity and difference is not that identity is more valuable or fundamental than difference, but that the two are mutually constitutive. The alternative phrase, "the difference of identity and difference," would not elevate difference, but would state a commonsense platitude.

I doubt that any of the points in the preceding paragraph directly addresses Voss Roberts's concern. To come a little closer to her point, let me risk saying something after all about religious diversity, despite my confessed lack of expertise. It is important to distinguish between the truth of a decentered and decentering christocentricity and the truth of the Christian religion. My proposal in no way intends to hold the door open in the hope or expectation that the other religious traditions will eventually come over to Christianity. Christocentricity and "Christianity-centricity" are not the same by a long shot. The latter has no hope of being genuinely decentered and decentering.[26] The former, I have tried to show, is centering only to the extent that it is decentering, a center only to the extent that it is decentered.

Divine Relationality and (the Methodological Constraints of) the Gospel as Piece of News: Tracing the Limits of Trinitarian Ethics

CHRIS BOESEL

She was a really cool kisser and she wasn't all that strict of a Christian.
—THE HOLD STEADY, "Stuck between Stations"

The Shepherd leaves the ninety-nine, to go and seek the one who's out walkin' the line.
—PENTECOSTAL BOUFFANT, "Stand in Awe"

While drowning in the all-too-familiar missed-deadline panic, having lost the woods for the trees, I was listening to a story about Imam Feisal Abdul Rauf, the Muslim cleric spearheading plans for an Islamic community center near "ground zero" in New York City, on NPR's *All Things Considered*. During an interview for the story, the imam made the comment that "the real battlefront is not between Muslims and non-Muslims, between Muslims and Jews, between Muslims and Christians" but "between all moderates of all faith traditions and all of the extremists of all faith traditions."[1] This statement cut through the fog of panic and helped me recover the woods, at least for a moment. I of course agree wholeheartedly with the imam's first point: no battles between religions. But the second point is trickier. (a) Because—according to what I assume is entailed *theologically* in his definition—I am one of the religious extremists (though not the kind he was encountering in the "ground zero" controversy). (b) It is precisely the particular content of my religious extremism that constrains me to a pacifist rejection of waging battle against anyone of any religion, of seeing any religious neighbor, whether extremist or moderate, as enemy. So it is precisely as a religious extremist that I seem to be more inclusively for the religious neighbor of any and all stripes than the imam is as a religious moderate.

Wait. That can't be right. What manner of complexity is afoot here?[2]

This is the driving—and open-ended—question of my essay, the goal of which is not to solve this disorienting complexity but to take a brief stab at simply unearthing it, peeling back some of its layers, and hopefully thereby contributing to a better understanding and appreciation of its difficulties and possibilities.

My general interest in the theme of Divine Multiplicity is, rather boringly, the interest of a Christian systematic theologian and is mostly concerned with methodological questions, possibilities, and decisions internal to that disciplinary identity. However, I am also concerned with the ethical dynamics and implications inherent in that internal and sometimes tedious strategic maneuvering. The genesis of the essay, then, arises from my observation of and growing curiosity about the contemporary resurgence in trinitarian thought among Christian theologians, the driving energy of which appears to be the rediscovery of the doctrine of the Trinity as a site for a good, progressive ethics of relationality. Two arenas of relationality seem to be getting most of the attention: egalitarian social ordering and interreligious encounter open to and affirming of the diversity of human religious experience (e.g., discourses of religious pluralism and comparative theology).

What strikes me most immediately is the compelling nature of the arguments and the ethical desire driving them. What's not to like about good progressive ethics? I am, after all, a relatively robust social and political progressive. But as a *theological* extremist I skew traditional on the Jesus business, and these arguments challenge me to do some deep-tissue theological soul-searching. The second thing I observe about the trinitarian resurgence is the necessary theological decisions and moves made in order to rehabilitate traditional formulations of the doctrine of the Trinity sufficiently, so that it might be seen to do this good progressive ethical work in the twentieth and now the twenty-first centuries.

The first of these moves is more of an unstated assumption: A good ethics makes good theology; or as Hegel might have it, in relation to theology, ethics is the highest. Second, although not all the major participants in the trinitarian resurgence are on exactly the same page here, there is a very strong move to reconceive the language of the Trinity and the doctrine itself, along with all theological language and doctrine, in terms of religious symbol. If the Trinity is conceived as one religious symbol among many, then it is deprived of any finally exclusionary particularity in relation to other religious symbols and symbol systems. It is also itself rendered pliable, susceptible to reconstruction to accommodate the demands of contemporary visions of ethical relationality.[3] This, as over against traditional literal, actualist, or accommodationist interpretations of the Trinity that assume that the biblical language and the doctrinal language of the church witness to divine reality and action in a creaturely, limited yet final way. These traditional views are based on the conviction that God has in fact disclosed and given Herself to the creature fully in and through actual, irrepeatable, and unsubstitutable concrete historical occurrence and so also in and through the language of its reportage and witness (in radical self-restriction and self-binding, as we shall see).

Consequently, the first move of liberal, progressive doctrinal reconstruction is methodological. It must take what was and is assumed by traditional practitioners as witness to historical event—for example, God's unique action in history—and translate it into the anthropological register of symbolic expression of universally and ontologically available religious experience, in order for the ethical transformation and reconstruction of traditional doctrinal content to proceed. In most cases that I am aware of, this reconstructive procedure is not seen as a form of interpretive violence that would need to ask for the consent of whatever traditional religious practitioners might be involved or affected before legitimately proceeding, as it is assumed to be so clearly the right thing to do and so clearly for their own—and their neighbor's—good.

And here is where I begin to get curious.

The closer I pay attention, the more it seems to me that the approach to the doctrine of the Trinity as a site for a progressive ethics of relationality cannot quite shake an ethically problematic shadow of its own. In the effort to overcome exclusion and hierarchy, it seems to be constituted by its own forms of these very ethical limitations.

I'll just give two brief "bullet-point" examples here, and then get on with the essay proper.

Egalitarian Social Ordering. The liberation theologian Leonardo Boff argues compellingly that a conception of God's very being as a society of equals constitutes a powerful model for the just ordering of social relations among creatures. Part and parcel of his argument, however, is a withering critique of monotheistic conceptions of God working hand in glove with inherently violent and hierarchical monarchical social ordering: "Strict monotheism can justify totalitarianism and the concentration of power in one person's hands, in politics and in religion," leading to "excessive power on the one hand and submission on the other, to absolutism coupled with dependence and slavery."[4] For all the passionate commitment to egalitarian, nonhierarchical relations, one cannot help but wonder if this analysis is capable of considering the monotheisms of Judaism and Islam, and those who practice them, as being on an equal ethical footing with an appropriately updated trinitarian Christianity; they appear excluded from serious consideration as ethically viable conceptions of the divine together with the socioreligious practices engendered by such conceptions.

Religious Pluralism and Comparative Theology. As I have shown elsewhere, an inclusive embrace of Judaism extended by Rosemary Radford Ruether—"leav[ing] room for the distinctiveness of others," "guaranteeing the integrity of each people to stand before God in their own identities and histories," and affirming "access to God for those who go forward on other grounds"—becomes qualified in a later context wherein the full affirmation of those identities, histories, and grounds appears to be rescinded.[5] In this later context, what she calls the "ethnocentric-cultic" dimensions of Judaism are condemned as a "terrible mandate . . . for later people" to "act out similar patterns of ruthless colonization of conquered lands and extermination or enslavement of their former inhabitants."[6] The harshness of the anti-Judaism here is not entirely distinguishable from the supersessionism and "teaching of contempt" one finds in traditional Christian triumphalism.[7]

This brings us back to the statement by Imam Rauf. The inclusive affirmation of all religions can pack a rather mean exclusionary punch for certain religious practitioners. (And, it might be argued, for very good reasons—which nicely raises the question at the heart of the essay: Are there ever good reasons for certain kinds of exclusion?) Or put differently, what appears to be the inclusive affirmation of all religions appears to be, in fact, an exclusionary affirmation of only certain ethically viable (e.g., "moderate") ways of understanding, inhabiting and practicing religion as such (but viable according to whom?).

It is out of a concern for—and for a better understanding of—the ethical consequences of doctrinal formulation and content that I attempt to unpack this strange complexity and its possible alternatives in relation to the doctrine of the Trinity. But there is a counterintuitive, paradoxical thesis lurking behind this ethically concerned effort (which must await another context to be fully articulated and demonstrated): the nature of Christian faith, and perhaps religious faith more generally, is such that its ethical resources are most robust, available, and efficacious precisely when faith is not confessed and lived—much less, analyzed—for the sake of the ethical itself; that is, precisely when it is religious faith in a sense irreducible to a strategic site of ethical function. The consequence of this thesis, if sound, would be that modern and postmodern reductions of religious faith to the ethical, for example, as a site for ethical relationality, cannot avoid eventually stumbling over a certain ethical limit of their own.

THEOLOGY, THE ETHICAL, AND THE QUESTION OF TWO FORMS OF EXCLUSION

In this essay I suggest that the difference between traditional approaches to the doctrine of the Trinity, on one hand, and various contemporary progressive transformations of Trinitarian theology, on the other, may not be the difference between exclusion in the former case and inclusion in the latter, as the latter has sometimes been known to have it. I ask, rather, if we might be confronted here with two forms, or modes, of exclusion. And if this is the case, then a further question: Why does it strike us as an ethical violation (as we will no doubt experience acutely as soon as I turn to my reading of Karl Barth) to tell the religious neighbor that one thinks they are wrong about the God business, that is, to "exclude" them on *theological* grounds, although it often strikes us as appropriate and even necessary to say the very same thing to them on *ethical* grounds? What are the assumptions in play here about the nature of theology and ethics and their various grounds, and about the varying possibilities of certainty, authority, self-assurance, self-critique, and "dogmatic" fixity in relation to these grounds? How are we to weigh the alternatives in the midst of this complexity? How are we to assess the stakes?

To at least begin to unpack the complexity of what is involved and at stake here, I revisit the initial, traditional problem of exclusion entailed in the Christian particularism of the doctrine of the Trinity (when understood "literally," that is, as response to reports of divine action as actual, intractable historical occurrence, that is, as something that has actually happened in history as a part of history), by way of the preeminent Christian particularist, Karl Barth. My wager is that contemporary theological remedies of said particularism, in prescribing inclusion (on the front end, as it were), inevitably encounter their own problems of exclusion (on the back end); and if this is the case, then perhaps the traditional problem of exclusion (on the front end) might be discovered to have some unexpected resources of inclusion (on the back end)—indeed, even resources not entirely foreign to a progressive ethics of relationality. The goal, despite a generous though hopefully sound and candid reading, is not simply to make a pitch for the tradition, or for Barth. It is, more modestly, to get some clarity on the complexity of the limits—both traditional and contemporary—of trinitarian ethics, such that our decisions in relation to both traditional and contemporary theological voices and resources become more informed, more responsible, and more difficult.

METHODOLOGICAL LIMITS: THE DOCTRINE OF THE TRINITY AS RESPONSE TO GOSPEL NEWS

What *if* the Christian doctrine of the Trinity is not primarily a religious symbolic site for a progressive ethics, one symbol among many of a general relationality, but is fundamentally a response to reports of God's unique, irrepeatable, and unsubstitutable saving action in the person and history of Jesus Christ in the power of the Spirit? Exactly what kind of theological and ethical relationality is excluded here, and to what extent? And what kind of theological and ethical relationality is *included*? Could *this* theological and ethical relationality be found to entail its own form of inclusive embrace of the neighbor, including the religious neighbor?

Taking Barth as a paradigmatic representative of this theological assumption, I focus in this section on the most fundamental limits entailed in and following methodologically from the above "if" when taken as the starting point for a doctrine of the Trinity. In the following sections I will go on to consider what is excluded and what is included, theologically and ethically, in and by the constriction of these methodological limits.

In Jesus Christ: The Christological Constriction of Trinitarian Identity
Let us begin with a very brief primer on Barth's basic methodological assumptions. Barth can be seen as a theologian of radical constriction, of rigorous limitation (which is somewhat paradoxical, as he has also been

called a "theologian of freedom").[8] Barth assumes that all of the church's knowledge of and speech about God and God's relation to the world is made possible only by and so must be rooted in and bound to God's own living, active, self-revealing, and self-giving Word to us about who God is and how God relates Herself[9] to us and the world.[10]

> Theology must begin with Jesus Christ, and not with general principles, however better, or, at any rate, more relevant and illuminating they may appear to be. . . . Theology must also end with Him and not with supposedly self-evident general conclusions . . . as though in the things of God there were anything general which we could know [e.g., divine "relationality"] . . . in addition to and even independent of this particular.[11]

Exactly what this exclusion of the "general" entails for the reality of divine relationality—for God's relationality in Godself, God's relationality to the human creature, and the consequent ethical relation to the religious neighbor—constitutes the central investigative thread of the essay. At this point it is enough to note that, for Barth, a Christian doctrine of God can *only* be about the God who makes Herself known in Jesus through the power of the Spirit; that is, in witness and testimony to God's revealing and reconciling self-giving to the creature in the living, personal reality that is Jesus Christ in the Spirit. It is a doctrine of God, therefore, that can only be *trinitarian*: The church's God can only always already be the God who is for us in the trinitarian life and movement of Jesus and the Spirit. In his own words, all that can be said of God in the doctrine of God "is disclosed only in the name of Jesus Christ," is "wholly and entirely enclosed in Him."[12] Consequently, "we know and have God only in Jesus Christ."[13]

Ouch! Behold, the painful and offensive pinch of exclusivist methodological constraint in all its unrepentant clarity. And here we are already up against the problem in its clearest expression, from the perspective of the ethical desire of a theology of religious pluralism, while simultaneously catching a glimpse of a certain complexity.

The problem is obvious: God *only* in Jesus Christ. The traditional methodological assumptions about the doctrine of the Trinity limit the Christian understanding of God to the God who is for us in Jesus Christ in the power of the Spirit. But seemingly intent on making matters as bad as they could possibly be, Barth drives the point home that this is not merely an *epistemological* limit *for us*, the creature, such that God is *known* only in God's self-communication to the creature in Jesus Christ. Barth goes further, asserting that God *is God* only in Her self-communication to the creature in Jesus Christ in the power of the Spirit. Which means that God's self-communication in Jesus Christ is in fact God's self-giving to and for the creature wholly and without reserve. This allows Barth to say that there is no God behind, before, beyond, or apart from the God who decides in and from the heart of God's eternal triune life to be for and with—and so in radical relation to—the creature in Jesus Christ in the power of the Spirit.[14] The "Subject" of the doctrine of God, then, is "one which in virtue of its innermost being, willing and nature does not stand outside all relationships, but stands in definite relationship *ad extra* to another."[15] This is "a relationship outside of which God no longer wills to be and no longer is God," a relationship that "is irrevocable, so that once God has willed to enter into it, and has in fact entered into it, He could not be God without it."[16]

Here we glimpse the complexity I mentioned above. Appropriately understood, it is *God's* self-limiting and self-binding decision and action to be God "only in Jesus Christ," as the very "beginning of God," that precedes and so constrains *our* methodological "beginning," that limits our starting point, that is, that constrains and binds us to this thing that has *happened*, to this particular thing that God has decided and has done.[17] Which means that, *if* this is the case, if this thing has indeed happened, the exclusionary problem of Christocentric trinitarianism is not *our* problem to correct. Indeed, it is not a problem we *can* correct, as it is primarily the result of intractable divine decision and action rather than of human mythological or anthropomorphic misinterpretation. It is *God* who has anthropomorphized *Herself* in an unconditional and irrevocable self-giving to the human creature for a particular kind of relationship. In other words, don't blame Barth, blame God.

God's Saving Action in Jesus Christ: The Good News of God for Us
For Barth, to know God in Jesus Christ in the power of the Spirit is to know God as Trinity. Likewise, to know God as Trinity is therefore to already know God as Savior and Redeemer (and Judge)—as God *for us*—and so too to know of our salvation. The doctrine of the Trinity, then, is bound to and constrained by the witness to good news.[18]

For surely the news of salvation is *good* news, is it not? News to be received with great rejoicing? Well, yes and no.

Here is the tricky bit. The good news that one is saved entails the bad news that one is in need of saving. And if the predicament we are saved from is called sin, the news may even strike us as an insult, especially if we do not consider ourselves to be in so radical and shameful a predicament. The Gospel is good news *for sinners*. And if one believes that one's own or one's neighbor's religious identity, practice, piety, or devotion exempts one from this category or mediates it in a significant way, then one is bound to take offense at the news. Put differently, as good news for sinners, the Gospel entails bad news for the prospects of religion; it is unimpressed by religion and the religious, assuming religion to be part and parcel of the human condition of sinfulness and not a purified sacred space or transformatory method of enlightenment or escape.

So the ability to demonstrate the goodness of the news of salvation in a way that is publicly recognizable and confirmable, for example, by the neighbor herself, is problematically limited by the fact that this particular news is for sinners. It inescapably implies the sinfulness of the neighbor (as it does my own sinfulness, the believing Christian), a sinfulness that includes their religious identity and practice. It implies they are sinners who have been saved, but not by their worthy and admirable religious commitment and practice (as I am not saved by my Christian belief and practice).

The demonstrable goodness of this news is further complicated by the fact that sin itself is an unfathomable mystery. According to Barth, there is no true knowledge of sin apart from one's confession of one's own sinfulness in thankfulness for being saved from it. Sin is most fully and truly known in the event of hearing and believing the good news of one's salvation from it. There is no neutral ground, therefore, upon which one can invite the neighbor to stand so as to observe and acknowledge the full dimensions of the reality of sin (theirs, yours, ours, the world's), no general anthropological ground of observation this side of confession where one is able to analyze it and take its measure.

A Response to Reports of God's Saving Action in Jesus Christ:
Witness, Testimony, and the Gospel as Piece of News

Given Barth's methodological assumptions, the doctrine of the Trinity must always be about the God who *is* redemptively for us in Jesus Christ in the power of the Spirit because God *has actually acted* redemptively for us in just this way. Which is to say, redemption is not a reality separable from this particular history of divine decision and action and the revelation of divine self-giving that occurs and becomes actual in that history. Which is also to say that the doctrine of the Trinity, for Barth, is not a religious symbol expressing a particular experience of a general divine multiplicity and relationality that can be symbolized just as well if not better in and through other religious or cultural symbols so long as *some* notion of divine multiplicity and relationality as such is communicated. Rather, the doctrine of the Trinity is a response to reports of particular divine saving action in and for the world that has occurred in Jesus in the power of the Spirit.

Consequently, the church's knowledge of God expressed in the doctrine of the Trinity is on some intractable level a (albeit paradoxical) form of historical knowledge. It is knowledge of witness and testimony to something that is said to have happened in the midst of history as a part of history: a singular, unrepeatable, unsubstitutable, and radically contingent event. It is knowledge of a piece of news.

And this is a huge, if not *the* huge, problem for modernity with regard to Christianity (and to any "historical" or "positive" religion). Gotthold Lessing made it quite clear that even the best, most reliable instance of historical knowledge from witness and testimony was simply not reliable enough—was too fragile, questionable—to be considered appropriate to the subject matter of divine reality.[19]

A certain paradox, then. If it is indeed the case that the Gospel is a piece of news, as Barth assumes it is, then Christian knowledge of God and its expression in doctrines such as the Trinity are "bound to what has already happened."[20] Consequently, the fragile "spider's thread" of historical witness and testimony paradoxically functions as an intractable, unbreakable cord that "binds" and so constricts theological construction. We may not like it, but if the Gospel is a piece of news about particular divine action that has actually occurred in history as a part of history—for all of history—there is very little we can do about it.[21] Again, don't blame Barth, blame God. *If* the Gospel is a piece of news.

THE FORK IN THE ROAD REGARDING RELIGIOUS PLURALISM: INTRACTABLE OFFENSE, INESCAPABLE EXCLUSION

I have tried to render the methodological limits of Barth's founding theological assumptions—in general and in particular relation to a doctrine of the Trinity—with some attention to their complexity. But the stark reality that no complexity can avoid or qualify is the way in which these theological assumptions exclude the possibility of religious pluralism or of comparative theology as positive Christian theological positions for Barth. If God is truly and fully known only in the definite trinitarian reality, event, and relation that is Jesus Christ in the Spirit, then God is not truly and fully known elsewhere or otherwise. And this, because there *is* no other God to know. It is not because other religious traditions are inadequate where Christianity, as a religion, is superior in resources and capacity. It is because God has chosen and acted *to be* God only in Jesus Christ in the power of the Spirit and so in this definite relation accomplished and actual in his Person and history.

What is equally clear at this point, then, is that the discourses of religious pluralism and comparative theology, in order to ground and launch themselves, must necessarily exclude the methodological assumption that the doctrine of the Trinity is a response to gospel news. And one of the things I am suggesting is that this may constitute a problematic limit of their own according to their own criteria, for example, in relation to an explicit ethic of inclusion and affirmation of religious difference that understands itself as an alternative to and remedy for Barth's exclusionary methodological assumptions. Alternatively, I am suggesting that Barth's exclusionary methodological assumptions might prove capable of a surprising though very specific and concrete inclusivity.

In what follows I allow the contours of the former suggestion to emerge by highlighting the concrete features of the latter. I focus on what the binding constriction of Barth's methodological limits entail with regard to divine, divine-human, and human-human relationality, and the particular consequences for the religious neighbor. Along the way I occasionally pause to identify and reflect on certain questions this might raise with regard to possible theological and ethical limits entailed in the more methodologically inclusive theological alternatives.

WHAT (THE METHODOLOGICAL LIMITS OF) THE GOSPEL AS PIECE OF NEWS BINDS US TO: UNIVERSAL BREADTH OF PERSONAL RELATION

A quick summary of Barth's methodological limits. We know and have God only in Jesus Christ in the power of the Spirit; God has decided from all eternity *to be* God only in this way, in giving Herself to the creature as Redeemer, divine covenant partner, and friend.

Here I note three concrete dimensions of *theological* relationality that are included in and required by the methodological constriction of this "only." In the concluding section I briefly address the *ethics* implied by and entailed in this theological relationality.

God's Own Trinitarian Relationality: God In Se

If Jesus Christ, as God's revealing and reconciling Word to and for the creature in the power of the Spirit, constitutes the relation outside of which God is not God and so is not known, then, as we have already seen, there is no Christian doctrine of God that is not always already trinitarian. Even more, for Barth, there is no Christian trinitarian doctrine of God that is strictly about God *in se*, God in and for Godself (e.g., the "immanent" eternal processions of the persons known and articulated in isolation from their "economic" missions of revelation, reconciliation, and redemption). As Barth says in *The Humanity of God*, there is no such thing as a strict Christian *theology*, but only "the-anthropology." "For an abstract doctrine of God has no place in the Christian realm, only a 'doctrine of God and of man,' a doctrine of the commerce and communion between God and man."[22]

This aversion to the "abstract" on one hand and the commitment to "communion" on the other will be vital for what follows. For now it is enough to note that Christian talk about God as God is in Godself is no simple matter for Barth, as our knowledge of God is grounded in and limited to the definite relation between God and the human being that occurs and is accomplished in the one human being, Jesus of Nazareth, in the power of the Spirit (according to God's own self-limitation). God has chosen not to be and never to be God without the human being, apart and outside of this definite relation. Is it possible, then, to speak of God as God is in Godself apart from and distinct from the creature with which She is in relation, given this self-limitation to not be God outside of this relation?

Somewhat surprisingly, given what I have just said, it *is* possible, for Barth, and for two reasons. It is *necessary* for at least one. It is *possible* because (a) God remains *God* in this relation. This relation, as intimate and radical as it is, is not a mixture or blending together of the divine and the human in some cosmic alchemy (the divine spark within, etc). It is precisely a relation of persons who are genuinely different and retain the integrity of their difference and particularity within the relation. It is a relation of face-to-face encounter. That is, it remains a relation and does not capitulate to absorption or indeterminate blurriness or the subsuming of one into the other or the *Aufhebung* of both into a higher unity. The Christological formula, two natures in one person *without mixture*, holds firm and fast here. And (b) God truly *gives Herself*, as and who She really is, fully and wholly in and to this relation without reserve, qualification, or equivocation. This, of course, is the whole point of the christological debate that resulted in a formalized doctrine of the Trinity in the first place: Is it really God in Godself, wholly, fully, and uniquely, that is with and for us in Jesus in the power of the Spirit? Barth is orthodox to the extent that his answer here is yes. He is a bit *un*orthodox in pushing to the conclusion that there is therefore no God behind, beyond, above, or beside the God encountered in this Jesus in this way.

Therefore, the God encountered in the trinitarian, divine-human relation that is Jesus Christ in the Spirit is really who God *is*, in *Godself*. This is what Barth feels it is vitally important for the church to be able to say. As we have already seen, the Subject of the doctrine of God is "One which in *virtue of its innermost being, willing and nature* does not stand outside all relationships, but stands in definite relationship *ad extra* to another."[23] Further, the nature of the relation that God gives Godself in and to, and creates and calls the creature for and to, is an expression of God's *own* nature, as not simply relational or relationality in general, but as a very definite kind of relation. God for us in Jesus in the power of the Spirit means "not merely that He creates and sustains the world, but that He works on it and in it by . . . giving Himself to it. It means the will *for fellowship* . . . *which is His very being* and to which the world owes its existence."[24]

Consequently, though the trinitarian relationality of God can never be known and so articulated (e.g., doctrinally) apart from or without the creature, that is, to the exclusion of the concrete divine-human relation of revelation, incarnation, and reconciliation that is Jesus Christ in the Spirit, it *is* nevertheless *possible* to say that God *in Godself* is constituted as trinitarian relation of fellowship and communion. Barth: God is "for him [the human being] *too* the One who loves in freedom."[25] This "too" implies that God is in Herself *already* the God who loves in freedom, the God eternally and so essentially constituted by and as the *particular kind* of relationality determined as fellowship and communion of persons, "prior" to—as the ground for, source of, and goal of—the divine-creature relationality.

Now, why is it *necessary* to say this, and indeed, to say it more strongly: that God in Godself is constituted as trinitarian relation of fellowship and communion *apart from and without the creature*? Doesn't this threaten to undermine the affirmation and assertion that God has chosen not to be God without the creature and so is in fact not God outside of this very definite relation? Well, yes and no.

There is a counterintuitive logic entailed here that I will touch on just briefly.

It is precisely because of and for the sake of the definite *kind* of relation between God and the human being—*as fellowship and communion between persons free for each other in love*—that it is necessary to say that God *in Godself* is relational in precisely this way, as fellowship and communion of loving freedom, apart from and without the creature.

As just mentioned, this apparent severing of God's relationality from God's relation to the creature seems to undermine the extent of God's essential relationality, asserting a kind of "self-sufficiency" of God's relationality that is actual *on its own* and not, in fact, in relation to the creature as an "other." This appears to be a limiting of God's relationality. Indeed it is; but it is a limit of a very particular sort. It is properly understood not as a "limiting *of*," for example, a limiting of the *extent* of divine relationality—its breadth, or depth, or quantity, or universality. Rather, it is a "limiting *to*," for example, a limiting to a specific *quality* of divine relationality, to a particular and definite *kind* of relationality that pertains to God's own life. Divine relationality, for Barth, is specifically *not* a relationality in general.

The reason it is necessary to say that God is essentially and fundamentally relational *apart from and without* the creature is to ensure that God's relationality *to and with* the creature is a very specific *kind* of relationality: a relationality of fellowship and communion in loving freedom as distinct from all other kinds of possible relations. Put the other way around, if God's relationality is a consequence of God's relation to creation such that God cannot be said to be relational in Godself prior to and apart from the creature, then the divine-human relation would not be an event of free divine self-giving. It would rather be one of structural, ontological, and/or metaphysical necessity; God would be related to us whether God liked it or not—whether God wanted to be or not—rather than precisely as an intentional act of loving self-giving. The freedom and contingency of gratuitous, loving self-giving is essential to the specific kind of relationality we refer to as personal fellowship and communion. Consequently, without that divine freedom and contingency neither divine relationality in itself nor divine-human relationality could be fundamentally characterized as this specific kind of relationality. It would rather be fundamentally determined as some form (metaphysical, ontological, cosmological, structural) of nonintentional, co-constitutive necessity.

All that is to say, God's relation with the creature—*as this definite kind of relation, the relation of fellowship and communion of persons*—is only *possible* to the extent that it is *not necessary*; to the extent that it is indeed a contingent act of divine loving freedom, of free divine self-giving. It is necessary to say God is essentially and fundamentally relational apart from and without the creature, then, in order to ensure the goodness of the news about the particular way of God's relation with and for the creature (and also, as we shall see, about the way we as creatures are to then be related to one another as neighbors, as sisters and brothers, as distinct from—or, inclusive of yet above and beyond—being inter-dependent organisms in an ecosystem).

Ergo, a Definite Kind of Trinitarian Divine-Human Relationality: God Pro Nobis

For Barth, the relation of fellowship and communion in loving freedom between God and the human being that takes place in Jesus in the power of the Spirit is a *personal* relation. This means first and foremost for Barth that it is distinguishable from relations characterized by necessity, by the automatic, the mechanical, structural, cosmological, for example, relations grounded in ontological, metaphysical, or cosmological structures and processes, entailing dimensions of generality and neutrality.[26]

As personal, this relation involves and is the result of a specific divine willing, deciding, intending, and acting. It is a living *history*. This means that in this relation as God's action of self-giving, we are dealing with an event and a happening that is most properly a "deed" as distinct from a "mere occurrence" that either happens accidentally or automatically as the necessary unfolding of a cosmological or ontological process or structure or rational program or logic, or according to an inherent nature or instinct that is "hard-wired" into a transcendental category or ontological or metaphysical structure.

The personal relation is one wherein God is not *stuck* with us—or *to* us—as it were, automatically, constitutionally, as if God's relationality with and to creation happens to God as part and parcel of God's ontological constitution. Rather, God *chooses* us, and in choosing seeks and creates a particular kind of relation distinct from relationality by virtue of necessary ontological connection.[27]

There are two key dimensions to God's choosing that I want to tease out.

(a) God chooses across difference. In an act of free self-giving, God chooses that which is and those who are genuinely different. It is precisely as intercourse and encounter across difference and otherness, and for the sake of that which is different and other and not for God's *own* sake—that is, because the different and other is *loved* (in *some* way distinguishable from love of self)[28]—that God's relation with the creature is fellowship and communion. Giving oneself to another in loving freedom is possible precisely to the extent that the other is other above, beyond, and in addition to any automatic, constitutional connection of shared onto-cosmological stuff, structure, or process. Here lies the difference between general connection, neutral touch—sharing stardust—on one hand, and the embrace of loved ones, the kiss of lovers, on the other: the difference between being stuck on the same subway train together and inviting each other over for dinner for no other reason than for the sake of and for the blessing of each other's company.

God's choosing, then, is not based on or made possible by the way or ways we are naturally *similar* to God, especially in terms of ontological or metaphysical or cosmological similarity: shared characteristics or stuff.[29] Relationality based on necessary similarity, as in the case of shared metaphysical categories, ontological structures or cosmological processes (Reason, Being, Creativity, Relationality, Eros, etc.) is relationality to be sure, a kind that can be said to go all the way down, and so be described as radical. But inasmuch as they do not entail and so fall short of approaching the particular *kind* of relationality meant when we speak of persons in the fellowship and communion of loving freedom, they are, for Barth, simply not good enough—not in the sense of the "superiority" of the Christian religion but in the sense of redeeming news for the lost and the least. For Barth, news of relationality by necessary, structural similarity is less good than news of the specific kind of relation between God and the lost human being that the Gospel reports to have occurred in and been accomplished by God's action in Jesus Christ in the power of the Spirit.[30]

Barth suspects someone always gets left out, denigrated, or placed under the shadow of threat when divine and divine-human relationality is conceived in terms of co-constitution according to a shared ontological, cosmological, or metaphysical category. What of those with less of a share? What of those—persons, communities, and religions—who are *differently*-abled in this particular respect? Less creative? Less erotic? Less fundamentally ontological? What of that which or those who appear to oppose and so stifle and threaten the flourishing of said category?

Now we will want to object that this leaving folks (or plants and animals) out business is precisely what Barth's theological assumptions and their methodological limits do. And it is precisely this exclusion that "relational theologies" of ontological and cosmological co-constitution are meant to correct and avoid. None of this is being questioned here. What *is* being questioned are the exact extent and dimensions of Barth's exclusion, on the one hand, and the extent and dimensions of progressive relational and pluralist theologies' inclusion, on the other. Is the latter's ethical desire undermined by the founding assumptions that make it possible? Do they confront an intractable ethical limit of their own here?

(b) God chooses across conflict. The fellowship and communion sought and created by God with and for the human being as a relation of persons free for each other in love is not simply an instance of intentional self-giving to the other across *difference*. It includes self-giving to the other across *conflictual* difference— across conflict, estrangement, and alienation; across not just separation but brokenness. That is, it includes the seeking and creating of friends where there once were strangers and enemies. It is precisely these that God chooses and to whom God gives Herself, for their sake and as an end in themselves, for no other reason than for the blessing of fellowship with them and for them, for their company and embrace. It is for them that God has chosen not only to touch in terms of the fold of a napkin (though *at least* that, certainly), but to kill the fatted calf and throw a banqueting feast in their honor.

For Barth, in the specific kind of relationality determined as fellowship and communion of loving freedom terms like forgiveness, mercy, reconciliation, salvation, liberation, blessing, hospitality, feast, banquet, household—joy in the embrace of those formerly estranged in bitter conflict—constitute a lexicon of *final* significance. Alternatively, if because of their personal and anthropomorphic nature these terms are considered only penultimate and provisional symbols that may be permissible with caution, but less capable than nonpersonal symbols to communicate the kind of relationality (or relationalities) that ultimately pertain(s) between divinity and the cosmos, then, for Barth, there is simply not much to celebrate. No reason to throw a feast. There is no cause for *joy*. Least of all for those who are considered (by their own or their neighbor's respective religion) to be strangers and enemies of God.

Theologically, to Barth's mind, a God signified by nonpersonal symbols is a God less radically—less irrevocably, irreversibly, unconditionally—*for* us, including the least capable, least interested, least interest*ing*, and least deserving among us. And to anticipate, one could argue that the news here is less good *ethically* as well, in that *we* are determined less radically *for* the neighbor—for each and every neighbor, including and especially the least of these, less radically determined for *each other*—across both difference and conflict.

The Breadth of God's Trinitarian Relationality
The "God for us" that takes place in the exclusionary "only" of "*only* in Jesus Christ" means that God is always and only *for* us (never against us). But additionally, for Barth, the "us" of "God for us" means always and only that God is "for *the world*" (never an "us" to the exclusion of the world).[31]

If, in the relation of fellowship and communion with the creature that occurs and is accomplished in Jesus Christ in the power of the Spirit God *chooses* a creaturely partner and friend, and in so choosing, chooses those who are different and other, including the stranger and the enemy, then there is simply no one who is not included as the intended and desired object of this divine choosing, and no one for whom the identity of partner and friend in fellowship and communion with God is not accomplished and made actual in the person and history of Jesus Christ in the Spirit. No one, absolutely no one, can be left outside—or leave themselves outside, remove themselves from—the sphere of God's relation to them in the fellowship and communion of loving freedom.

This radical inclusion of *all* (on the back end) in the radical constriction of the *only* (on the front end) is true first and foremost because this divine choosing, as we have seen, is a choosing of Godself that occurs in eternity as the "beginning" of God and the determining of all God's "works and ways." Just as there is no God outside, behind, above, beyond, or beside God's eternal decision to be God in relation to the creature in Jesus Christ in the power of the Spirit, so there is no creature who falls outside this relation or the one divine will expressed in the decision establishing this relation. Thus, Barth comes to the unheard of conclusion that it is in light of the most despised piece of Christian doctrine (for everyone but hardcore Calvinists), the doctrine of eternal election, that the Gospel is light and only light.[32] God chooses the human being, choosing to be for her too the God who loves in freedom.

Within the context of the doctrine of election the methodological limits of Barth's founding assumptions can conclude only that "that which has been eternally determined in Jesus Christ is concretely determined for *every* individual man [and giving Barth the benefit of the doubt, here, *every* individual *woman*] to the extent that in the form of the witness of Israel and of the Church it is also addressed to him and applies to him and comes to him"; God, "by His Word makes him an elected man. . . . It is for him that this self-giving is effective. . . . He is the object of the divine election of grace."[33]

And as we have glimpsed, that which is eternally determined in Jesus Christ in the power of the Spirit for every individual human being is determined for them and applies to them precisely as stranger and enemy, as *unbelieving* creature. What then are the theological consequences for the religious neighbor? For Barth—obviously no religious pluralist—religious identity, belief, and practice different from and even in resistance to confessing faith in the God who is for us in Jesus Christ in the power of the Spirit constitutes unbelief and therefore a form of being alienated and estranged from God, even conflictually so (note: "correct" belief can also be a form of estrangement from this God). However, it is precisely *as* those who are thus alienated and estranged from God that God chooses the human creature for fellowship and communion. Therefore, having a religious identity other than Christian and so being "outside" the visible church can in no way mean that one is effectively outside of the relation of fellowship and communion between God and the creature that occurs and *is* Jesus Christ in the Spirit (no more than one's Christian identity and one's being "inside" the visible church constitutes the grounds for one's being effectively inside this relation).[34]

But there is more that is included here. If, when, and to the extent to which the religious neighbor is considered wrong about the God business by and according to the assumptions and terms of their *own* religion, or any other religion, this cannot in any way or at any moment place them outside the sphere of God's relation to and for them in Jesus Christ in the power of the Spirit. They are still the partner of God's choosing for fellowship and communion even if their own religion may exclude or diminish this possibility for any of the myriad reasons that religions—including Christianity—do just this, for example, reasons of birth, class, gender, ethnicity, sexual orientation, disability, occupation, education, seriousness of commitment, correctness of belief, refinement and purity of piety, length and disciplinary perfection of practice, level of enlightened wisdom and knowledge. Being a bad Hindu or the wrong kind of Muslim or a failed hunter or warrior or a barren wife or a daughter rather than a son or gay rather than straight can in no way exclude one from the sphere of God's choosing or diminish or qualify the irrevocable and irreversible way in which God is for one in Jesus Christ in the power of the Spirit, despite what anyone's religion has to say about the matter. And the same of course holds true in relation to the assumptions and terms of the religion of the religious neighbor's *other* religious neighbor, to whatever extent that other religion might exclude, threaten, demonize, denigrate, or diminish the reality of God's claiming them for fellowship and communion in loving freedom as it has occurred in Jesus Christ in the power of the Spirit.

For Barth, religion as such, in whatever form it might take and however it might be conceived, simply does not have this power. Which is good news if you're bad at it. Or if you are simply too busy having to work your fingers to the bone feeding, clothing, and housing your children to care or to commit the needed time for appropriate practice, devotion, or disciplined intention. However, it may very well strike one as bad news if one is especially good at it and finds in it one's sense of comfort, security, identity, and social status.

All this is to say that Barth's God of the gospel news is not content to leave the religious neighbor, or the neighbor of the religious neighbor, in the hands of religion, even if it is their *own* religion (indeed, even if it is Christianity). This God does not trust religion enough to take this posture of neutrality, does not trust religion (any religion, perhaps least of all the *religion* of Christianity) to be absolutely, unconditionally, irrevocably, and irreversibly for *each and every one* of its own practitioners, even the least of these, as well as for its nonpracticing, nonbelieving, or alternatively identified religious neighbors. This God of the Gospel does not trust religion to find and affirm each of these as the friend and partner of God in the fellowship of loving freedom for whom God leaves the faithful "ninety-nine" to find and embrace as singularly invaluable and irreplaceable.

THE ETHICS OF THE BOUND: TRINITARIAN FELLOWSHIP AND COMMUNION WITH THE NEIGHBOR AND THE NEIGHBOR'S NEIGHBOR

In what follows I attempt only a sketch of the ethical consequences entailed in the theological affirmations above. What kind of relation are *we* called to seek and create with the neighbor, and the religious neighbor in particular, by the news that God is with and redemptively for us in the trinitarian, divine-human event and relation that is Jesus Christ in the Spirit?

God Chooses Us in Loving Freedom

As bound to who God is and what God has done in Jesus Christ in the power of the Spirit, the church knows no other neighbor or shared world than the neighbor and world to and for whom God is unequivocally and irrevocably committed for the sake of friendship in fellowship and communion. It therefore knows itself in no other way—knows no other church—than as a community already determined by and taken up into such a commitment. It knows itself only as already called to concrete responsibility in precisely this particular, concrete relation to God, neighbor, and world. We are not only to be *with* the neighbor but *for* the neighbor, *choosing* the neighbor and giving ourselves to the neighbor in and for a very specific kind of relation.[35]

Consequently, neutrality and indifference are not possible for the church, either theologically or ethically. As we have already seen, *theologically*, the church is deprived of all neutrality in its methodological stance and approach. It is deprived of all undisturbed reflection and neutral observation. The church is not free in any abstract sense of the term. It does not have the freedom of unencumbered free agency, as if it could begin elsewhere or otherwise than with the very particular beginning God Herself has already, unequivocally and irrevocably made as God's own beginning and so as the beginning of all things, a beginning with and for which God has called the church into being and to its responsibility within and for a very particular kind of relation with God and so with *God's world*, the world it shares with the neighbor. *Ethically*, then, the church cannot live a life of neutrality in relation to the neighbor or the neighbor's neighbor or in relation to our shared world. As bound by and to God's decision for the world in Jesus Christ, the church knows itself *only* as concretely and urgently called to be actively engaged and committed to the welfare of the neighbor and the neighbor's neighbor, and the common social, political, economic, and ecological life we share.

God Chooses Us across Difference
We are called to choose our neighbor as friend and partner in the fellowship and communion of loving freedom. And this means being called to see ourselves as not only "stuck with" and "stuck to" our neighbors in terms of what we share either naturally or culturally, be it sharing chromosomes, blood, ancestry, tribe, history, tradition, nation, culture, geography, planet, or stardust. That is, we are to see our relation with the neighbor above and beyond the ways in which we are indeed part of each other and co-constituted subjectivities by and with each other metaphysically, ontologically, cosmologically, materially, sociologically, culturally.

All these modes of connectivity constitute various forms of intimate and even radical relationality, to be sure. Nevertheless, from the point of view of the Gospel, as Barth understands it, they are still not relational enough. Or at least they do not yet constitute the *particular kind of relation* that we are called into by God according to the report of the Gospel; a relation of intentional choosing and acting toward fellowship and communion between persons free for each other in love.[36] A critical distinction remains between all the radical relationalities of material and structural necessity and that of fellowship and communion. It is the distinction mentioned earlier between the necessity of shared stardust and the contingent, gratuitous invitation to a shared kiss or meal. It is the distinction between, on one hand, the acknowledgment of blood relation (blood of my blood, bone of my bone, dust of my dust: radical connection of co-constitutionality) and with it the necessary granting of the appropriate share of an inheritance according to what is legally, traditionally, or naturally required; and, on the other hand, the killing of the fatted calf for a banquet, or the spending of one's last two *colōnes* for a shared *pupusa* (fellowship and communion!), to celebrate the reunion of homecoming, the finding of what has been lost, the reconciliation of those who were estranged, and embracing them in love.

The radical connectivity of shared stardust and co-constituting subjectivities requires and necessarily includes the former concrete event of blood or legal relation, but it does not necessarily include the latter's gratuitous excess of self-giving and hospitality. Although by no means explicitly preventing or forbidding the latter, the radical connectivity of shared stardust as articulated by relational (onto)theologies keeps open the possibility of the latter's being left out or passed over or lost among the alternatives. Consequently, openness can appear here to be a less radically ethical resource than a certain instance of constriction and closure. For example, a theological stance of openness to possibility (on the front end)—as a value in itself, perhaps *the* value—renders the embrace of fellowship and communion as just that, a possibility, one among many. And can we say with confidence that those "many" possibilities are all necessarily as theologically and ethically robust as this "one"? Are they all constituted by radically gratuitous generosity and hospitality for and with those who are radically different, even the least of these, in a feast of fellowship and communion?

God Chooses Us across Conflict: Strangers and Enemies
Those to whom we are called to be intentionally and actively with and for in Jesus Christ in the power of the Spirit, choosing and inviting as friends and partners in fellowship and communion, includes those from whom we are estranged and with whom we are in conflict. And this means giv-

ing oneself to the enemy and inviting them to give of themselves in like manner.

Enemy, here, cuts both ways, or three (or more) ways, actually. It does not signify only those whom *we* believe to be *our* enemy, either because of experience or because of the indigenous cultural, ethnic, national, political, economic, ethical, and *religious* discourses and forces that constitute our personal and social identity: those whom we believe to be or have demonstrated themselves to be a threat to us and ours. It also signifies those who believe these very things about *us*, as informed and constituted by their own experience and/or cultural and religious and other discourses: those who believe that *we* are *their* enemy, posing a hostile and dangerous threat of harm and destruction. And of course, it also signifies the *other* other, the neighbor of our neighbor (who is also our neighbor), whom our neighbor may believe to be an—or *the*—enemy, a hostile threat of harm and destruction. We are to give ourselves to the neighbor whom my other neighbor believes is its enemy or our shared enemy.[37] A trinitarian ethic, then, entails a certain amount of risk and even danger. What if the neighbor who believes us to be enemies is not compelled by my exchanging of swords for plowshares to do the same?

The pertinent point for us here is that we are not able to content ourselves that our ethical obligation is fulfilled by leaving our neighbor(s) (and their neighbor) to their own self-understanding, religious or otherwise. For it is always possible that this self-understanding of our neighbor, of the "other," may determine us or other "others" as stranger or enemy. To confess and live out of the belief that we are all made partners and friends in and for fellowship and communion is to contest any and all discourses and practices (even experiences? perhaps the most scandalous implication) that determine others as strangers and enemies, both those discourses and practices that hold sway in our own context and those that may be cherished by our neighbor. To confess Christian faith, then, is to contest and resist the myriad of material, social, and cultural forces, discourses, and traditions that constitute and order relations otherwise than as relations of fellowship and communion of persons free for each other in love, that render certain neighbors (or neighbors of neighbors) vulnerable, expendable, and excludable.

More particularly, living out of this kind of trinitarian confession is to contest and resist forces, discourses, and traditions that marginalize and demonize in the name of the well-being of the whole, the community, the common good, the majority, the norm. More particularly still, it is to contest and resist those forces, discourses, and traditions to the extent that they attempt to ground these various orderings of relation in *nature*—in the nature and structure of things, in cosmology and ontology—by arguing that the way things are, is the way things are meant to be.

A trinitarian ethic of the Gospel, then, may constitute a form of revolutionary resistance, albeit as decidedly nonviolent practice. It will be necessarily suspicious of forces, discourses, and traditions that support and defend the status quo of sociopolitical relations and the "established order," especially as that which is said to be natural (i.e., a "conservative" natural [onto]theology, à la Parmenides). But it will also be inevitably wary of discourses that *challenge* the status quo of the "established order" with their own appeals to the natural, for example, a conception of the natural—the ontological or cosmological—as a more primal co-creative "established order" constituted by fluid interconnectivity and interdependence and so by movement, change, and transformation (i.e., a "progressive" natural [onto]theology, à la Heraclitus).[38]

And this goes for *any* force, discourse, or tradition: philosophical, cultural, economic, political, and, of course, religious and theological. For as Mircea Eliade has compellingly argued, religious cosmological myth and ritual are often employed to confirm that the way things are with regard to social ordering—for example, that a particular family rules and should continue to rule the tribe—is woven into the fabric of the very origins of the cosmos, which is to say, the way things are is the way things are meant to be.

INTERRELIGIOUS ENCOUNTER AS APPEAL AND CONTESTATION

The ecclesiological consequences of Barth's theological assumptions gives us (or *should* give us) a church required to *both* appeal to—that is, proclaim—the unequivocal and irrevocable Yes of God to fellowship and communion with the world *and* live out of this Yes in active witness to it, seeking to live in fellowship with and for the neighbor with and for our common, shared creaturely life as an expression of God's desire for, and very nature as, the communion of fellowship. However, as we have already noted, this is admittedly not on the basis of the neighbor's own religious grounds, whatever they may be. This *appeal* to and living out of the gospel news of God with and for us in Jesus Christ in the power of the Spirit involves a certain *contestation* with the religious (or nonreligious, as the case may be: atheist, Marxist, capitalist, philosopher, deconstructionist) neighbor vis-à-vis their religious identity, belief, and practice.

Consequently, the first thing that happens when a theologian such as Barth appears on the scene is that general concepts such as the modern concept of religion are immediately put to interrogation; a rigorous hermeneutic of suspicion is brought to bear. Religious identity, belief, and practice (including Christian, as a religious identity) is understood to be a fully human enterprise among and amid all other human enterprises of individual and social identity, belief, and practice. It does not merit special status; it does not constitute sacred space apart and free from the consequences of human finitude, frailty, brokenness, and sin, or provide a way out of these predicaments. Religion and theology, our own and everyone else's, are as much inscribed in and compromised by these limits as anything else and so are not to be taken at face value or as simple givens or in any way simply benign or positive goods. And this, even when framed in the language that has accrued uncontestable cultural authority in our business: Religion as the "self-understanding of the other."

Barth, then, will not be surprised when told by the sociologist, anthropologist, or historian that religions—as human seeking, desiring, discovering, and constructing—are no stranger to powerful mechanisms of exclusion, demonization, hierarchical marginalization, and unequal distribution of material and cultural resources, both in relation to a religion's own practitioners and to its "others."[39] And when Christianity functions this way, as a *religion* (as it always does), it is to be judged as well. Indeed, it is to be judged first and foremost, such that its hermeneutic of suspicion, if and when it functions in the life of the church, is most powerfully and appropriately a hermeneutic of rigorous and unflinching *self*-critique.

Consonant with this mode of self-critique, the church is free to recognize and affirm ways and instances in which other religious languages, practices, and commitments often witness to the kind of relation between God and the human being that the church confesses has occurred and so is actual in Jesus Christ in the power of the Spirit. The church is free to—and indeed, bound to—recognize the ways in which religions witness to what this relation with God (and neighbor, and the neighbor's neighbor) in the fellowship and communion of persons free for each other in love might look like in the flesh, in the way we live our lives together as creatures. This is a witness that is all too often *not* given but betrayed by the church itself. To put it in the idiom of previous examples, one does not have to be a strictly orthodox trinitarian Christian to be a good kisser or a generous self-giving host. And the good kiss or gratuitous offer of hospitality—*wherever and in whomever it is found*—can witness to the trinitarian, divine-human reality of God with and for us, and us for God and for each other, much more faithfully than a sophisticated orthodox articulation and confession of the doctrine of the Trinity.

This is possible *if* (though for Barth, of course: *because*—) God has indeed *acted* in Jesus Christ in the power of the Spirit, and *if* this self-giving action has indeed occurred and been accomplished *in* the world *for* the world and as such is an actual living reality *abroad* in the world. Barth speaks often of the "parables of the kingdom" to be found in "the world." He gained some notoriety for speaking of socialism and communism in this way, as well as of the work of decidedly non-Christian (in terms of personal confession) thinkers such as Feuerbach and Overbeck (whom he nevertheless *includes* in his survey of nineteenth-century Christian thought). And although he is not as explicit in this way with regard to other religious traditions, there is no reason to assume that this possibility is excluded for us.

Now again, this is obviously no robust religious pluralism; Barth is doing the *religion* of the religious neighbor no favors here. And inasmuch as said neighbor understands his or her relation to divinity or ultimate reality (and to neighbor) to be fundamentally determined by the identity, belief, and practice of that religion, this will no doubt be taken as a personal offense. This trinitarian-christological inclusivism (on the back end) constitutes a kind of interpretive imperialism wherein the neighbor is unequivocally included, affirmed, and embraced within the sphere of God's reconciling action on behalf of the creature for the sake of fellowship and communion, but (on the front end) on terms other than the neighbor's own religious self-understanding.

A fundamental and painful question confronts us here. Does love of neighbor (and of the neighbor's neighbor) exclude the possibility of contesting in any way the neighbor's self-understanding, religious or otherwise? The answer, for Barth, is obviously, no. And by now we should have a pretty good idea of the very specific theological and ethical reasons why.

The question remains as to how and why the discourses of religious pluralism, comparative theology, and relational (onto)theologies answer here.

For Barth's part, he is exclusionary in the very specific way that he is (on the front end) precisely because he believes the goodness of the news to be such that we are constrained to leave no one *out* (on the back end), constrained to leave no one to their fate out in what he believes to be the cold (albeit well-intentioned) arms of a general and neutral religious inclusivism. On the basis of what he believes to be the goodness of the gospel news (about which, of course, he could be seriously and dangerously deluded), Barth simply does not trust religion enough to be willing to leave the neighbor or the neighbor's neighbor in its hands, even if it is in the hands of the neighbor's *own* (or their neighbor's) religion; including in the hands of *Christianity* as a "world religion."

The question for us is: To what extent should *we*? More particularly: To what extent *do* we? Do the discourses of religious pluralism, comparative theology, and relational (onto)theologies—at least in the form of progressive remedies of orthodox trinitarian Christian theology—extend the hand of affirmation and inclusion to the religious neighbor (on the front end) precisely on ethical grounds that themselves entail (on the back end) the inevitable contestation and even exclusion of any and all discourses and practices, religion included, that conflict with those very ethical grounds, assumptions, and convictions? Are these discourses able to appear more ethically inclusive and hospitable to the religious neighbor qua religious initially (on the front end) while holding in reserve (on the back end) the proprietary right and authority to contest, criticize, and exclude that neighbor's religion—or that neighbor, by virtue of his or her particular way of inhabiting that religion—on ethical grounds? That is, in appearing to have methodologically remedied the problem of religious and theological particularism and exclusivity inherent in traditional trinitarian-christocentric *theology*, do these discourses inadvertently hide the pea of exclusion under another, for example, *ethical*, shell?

❧ The Universe, Raw: Saying Something about Everything

CYNTHIA L. RIGBY

Who will interpret the raw universe?
. . . When [theologians] do, they speak the same hard words.
—ANNIE DILLARD, *Living by Fiction*

Every fall semester, in the first couple of weeks of my introductory theology class, something I say in lecture triggers the elephant story. "Oh! You mean like in that story about the elephant and the blind mice!" a student says, as though some kind of light has dawned. And then she looks around at her classmates and explains, in earnest: "One mouse can describe only the elephant's skin, another only the trunk, another only the ear, and still another only the tail. No one mouse alone has a sense for the whole elephant! So each needs the perspective of the others, and each needs always to remember that he or she only knows a 'piece' of the truth."[1]

The other students nod at this wisdom, and I try to register appreciation and count to ten, silently, before saying, "Yes, this makes some sense, when it comes to recognizing that everyone sees things differently. But you didn't come to seminary to learn how to preach only about a trunk, an ear, or a tail—did you? Don't you also want to be able to say something true about the whole elephant?"

And then they look at me blankly, because they think I have been saying we can't know the whole elephant. True enough, I have been lecturing about how we, as people of faith, are not in the business of providing exhaustive answers to metaphysical questions, but are rather always in process of discovery.[2] And I have been teaching that our language for God is not univocal, and not equivocal, but analogical. I have also been suggesting that, even when we have strong convictions, we should find ways of being open to the possibility that we might be wrong.

Why then, they wonder, am I seemingly so quick to renege on what I am trying to teach them?

For reasons I don't understand, my new theology students seem consistently to translate something I say into something I don't say. What I say is: "God cannot be known fully, but only in part." What they hear, somehow, is: "Only parts of God can be known fully." Clearly, these are very different statements, with very different implications for how we engage the theological task. On the one hand, to speak about a God who can never be known fully requires participation in the subject matter and submission to an ongoing process of discovery. To aim to capture what little can be fully known, on the other hand, requires distancing oneself from the mystery of the whole in the name of preserving a particular expertise or vocation. Again, to recognize the provisional character of our attempts to speak of God implies that any metaphysical claims we make are subject to ongoing revision. But to focus on describing "parts" of God aims at mastery of the material, however narrowly focused the material might be.

What drives my writing in this essay is that I want to be able to say something about everything without forgetting that I cannot say everything about everything, and in fact can probably not even say everything about anything. I cannot say everything even about the paper clip sitting on my desk. Certainly, I cannot say everything there is to know about God.

But am I, therefore, confined to describing only God's tail? Or God's skin, or God's trunk? If it is in fact the case that any of us, at best, can describe only a "piece" or a "part" of God, what is to prevent us from conceding that the God we experience as love might actually be more hateful, proportionally speaking, than loving? After all, if our knowledge of God is only a "part" of who God is, perhaps God's loving is the equivalent of only one ear on an elephant. Perhaps we should presume "love" is just a small percentage of whoever or whatever God is.

But we claim love is more than a fractional reality. On what basis do we make such a claim? How do we say, "God is love," for example, in ways that address what we wonder about most without presuming that even this most hopeful of all theological claims is all there is to say?

In this essay I suggest how the doctrine of the Trinity invites us into ways of speaking about all that matters to us that honor—even value—the limits of our theological claims. I do this by exploring what "the one that is three" and "the three that is one" tell us about everything. Most importantly, I argue that the doctrine of the Trinity shows us how our appreciation for a tail, an ear, or the trunk of an elephant can be deepened—not diminished—when the elephant as a whole is spoken of, boldly.

. . .

This essay explores how particularities, diversities, and multiplicities can best be honored and celebrated when they are known in relation to unities and syntheses. It does this, in part, by reflecting on what meaning "looks like" at the interface of particulars and universals. Engaging the Christian doctrine of the Trinity, it considers the kinds of meanings that emerge not only when particulars and universals are upheld as important but distinct realities that exist in tension but also when they are experienced in such ways that the boundaries between them are at one and the same time both maintained and dissolved.

To argue for a simultaneous maintenance and dissolution of boundaries is, as far as I can conceptualize, logically incoherent.[3] This essay suggests that it is precisely our determination to avoid such incoherence that has led us to deprive ourselves of the kind of meaning that comes with recognizing that multiple—even logically conflictual—statements must remain in play if we are in fact to speak of that which matters to us most.[4] It is not in the tension between the one and the three, or in the space between the one and three, or in accepting the fact that the one and the three reside together ever in a relationship that is mathematically incommensurable, that we know that which is most meaningful. Rather, it is in believing that the simultaneity of one and three is *not*, finally, a paradox[5]—even though it appears to be so. It is in baldly asserting that to establish a paradox between one and three, unity and multiplicity, is to have turned away from the goodness of the raw, created universe (the universe created in the image of the [triune] God), and toward a universe that is "cooked":[6] the universe postfall, the actual universe we live in.

Interpreting the raw universe from the limited perspective of the cooked one might entail that we think of the one and three in something like "dialectical relationship,"[7] offering all the appropriate qualifications (such as the reminder that all of our language for God is analogical, or that the dialogue between the one and the three should never be understood as a mere by-product of the relationship between them, but as a way that comes closer to thinking of both at once). But it should never entail—as I think, too often, it has—thinking that the doctrine of the Trinity justifies any settling for the fact that the best we can do is resign ourselves to a lifetime, a history, or even an eternity of negotiating some kind of tension between unity and multiplicity.

Before presenting the problematic I am trying to address, there are four remarks I want to make that I think will be helpful for setting my argument in context.

1. This essay might aptly be described as a gloss on perichoresis: the reality of "mutual indwelling," or the divine "dancing around," that requires universals and particulars to be both and at once in precisely the same and in clearly distinct spaces. This mutual indwelling itself is not a case of particulars uniting together (3 → 1), or a universal manifesting distinction (1 → 3), or a tension between the universal (one) and the particulars (three), but something else: something representing a different kind of meaning altogether, where one *is* three and three *is* one.

2. It will be noted that the category of "mystery" is just under the surface of the exploration undertaken. But it is "mystery" understood not only in terms of the "One," as though our only relationship to it can be a throwing up of our hands, as finite beings, in the face of a God who is beyond anything we can ask or think. Nor is it the mystery that this unknowable one is known in the three (though this certainly is an unfathomable, indispensable, transformative mystery!).[8] Rather, it is the mystery that the words of Christian traditions are attempting to invoke when they testify that the one is the three and the three is the one at the very same time that each of the three is neither of the other two.[9] They are both "of the same stuff" and not the same at all.

Part and parcel of this acknowledgment of mystery is the recognition that words are limited in their capacity to evoke what they are intending to reference.[10] But there are, I think, words that are more limited, and those that are less limited, in this regard. There are "hard words" that don't seem to get very far in saying "something about everything,"[11] words that have given up on indwelling whatever the reality *is* in favor of telling listeners what reality *is all about*. And then there are better words. This essay aims at better words about how the Trinity affects our understanding of multiplicities and diversities. Better words eschew "neither the mystical nor the metaphysical."[12] They participate in the interface of the one and the three, more effectively interpreting "the raw universe."

3. As is evident in the preceding point, I am a realist. I believe there is a reality, "God," and that theological words are sacramental insofar as they participate in (but do not exhaust) the reality that is God.

4. I am inspired, in my quest to use "less hard" words, by the trinitarian debates that took place in the fourth century and specifically those that took place in Alexandria in 362. It was there that the formulation, "one *ousia* in three *hypostases*" was developed, later affirmed at the Council of Constantinople (381). It is often shocking, for those fond of parsing trinitarian doctrine, to learn that *"ousia"* and *"hypostases"* were generally considered synonymous and certainly could not be readily translated as "substance" and "persons." Perhaps even more disturbing, for some, is the fact that the participants at Alexandria were so matter-of-fact about the limitations of their language.[13] The historical theologian J. N. D. Kelly puts it this way: "At the council [of Alexandria, in 362] it was formally recognized that what mattered was not the language used but the meaning underlying it."[14]

This essay assumes there is meaning underlying our words that our words more or less inadequately, but always inadequately, express. It suggests that, following Alexandria, a better route to speaking less inadequately is to refuse either to conflate or to separate truths that seem, logically, to conflict with each other. It further suggests that such words—which I would identify as "confessional," "sacramental," and probably also "absurd"[15]—can actually facilitate our participation in a different kind of meaning: a participation in the indwelling of the one and the three.

Finally, this essay is divided into four sections. (1) First is a section lamenting the loss of meaning that comes with setting aside metaphysical analyses because we think we need to do so if particularities, diversities, and multiplicities are to be honored. (2) Second is a section clarifying the thesis and beginning explorations of it. In short, the thesis is that metaphysics can actually *support* the honoring and celebration of multiplicities and diversities, when the "one" (which we cannot see, but do know) and the "three" (which we can see, but don't always) are understood to exist in perichoretic relationship. This is in part because particularities (and diversities and multiplicities following from them) are best known in the context of relations, which generally rely on appeal to commonalities (both inherent and constructed). (3) Third is a section exploring how saying something about everything can actually help us reflect on three things we wonder about most: (a) perceiving the unperceivable; (b) acting, as finite beings, in a world full of contingencies; and (c) knowing and being known by others. This section attempts, in part, to address a common "liberal" assumption that attentiveness to the universal, in the context of such wonderings, inevitably entails the devaluing of the particular. (4) And fourth is a shorter, concluding section that plays with a recent quote from the *New Yorker* to suggest, once again, that we really need to attend to reclaiming "perichoretic possibilities" if multiplicities and diversities are to be supported by simplicities and unities.

THE NEGLECT OF WONDER

In her 1993 book, *Living by Fiction*, Annie Dillard laments the demise of metaphysicians. She says there is no one, anymore, who seems to say anything about what we wonder about most. There are plenty of people out there who examine "human events and human artifacts," she points out, but what we really want is for someone to say something about *"all we experience, all things cultural and natural, all of the universe that is known, given, made, and changing: the world, and they that dwell therein."*[16] Theologians *should* be able to "interpret the raw universe" (as she puts it), but they have by and large failed us. They have failed us, Dillard says, because they keep on speaking "the same hard words."[17] Words without passion, words without soul, words that dismember the soul from the body as though the body and this world, and our sacramental experiences of it, have nothing to do with our souls, with what really matters. So disillusioned is Dillard with people like us that she says her hope is no longer in theologians, but in poets.

Is Dillard right that theologians are no longer metaphysicians? What are "the same hard words" that theologians keep speaking?

I would identify one category of such words as universalizing to such an extreme that individuals, with their particularities and experiences,[18] are diminished. This is the category that is typically well-identified, analyzed, and eschewed by self-identified "progressive" or "liberal" theologians (including myself).[19] I discern, also, that there are also those words so attuned to particularities they refuse to speak in unqualified ways about anyone but the actual speaker and the specific circumstances. These seem to be more the kind of hard words Dillard has in mind when she expresses that she is weary of endless talk of "events and artifacts." Following Dillard, this essay suggests these words can actually exclude in the name of inclusion; they can isolate in the name of honoring particularities, diversities, and multiplicities; they can cut off those who have been so well described and distinguished from the broader hope being described in particular, diverse, and multiple ways.[20] Words about artifacts can compare and contrast. They can marvel at simultaneities and learn from differences. But they cannot indulge the curiosity of those who yearn to explore experiences, suspicions, and convictions of and about noumena. The most such words could do, perhaps, is acknowledge that the experience of noumena is common and widespread. But speaking words that put forward such acknowledgments may well be unkind, if they are proffered to those who, with Dillard, are not looking for affirmation of their experiences so much as for words that share in these experiences and thereby facilitate our deeper experiences of them.[21]

Let me illustrate these two categories of "hard words" in relation to a single scenario: Imagine the devastation of a spouse who has lost his or her partner unexpectedly. A theologian called upon to offer counsel in this situation (whether a pastor, a churchgoer, or a local seminary professor) might very well try to place the event in cosmic perspective, evoking God's sovereign care and/or God's promise to—somehow—"work all things together for good."[22] But these words could easily become "hard" ones, devaluing the particular people involved, minimizing the extent of their pain.

Or, the "hard words" spoken might take on a different shape. They might emerge so specifically from and be directed so specifically to the circumstances of the death that the spouse and other grieving ones feel completely isolated—as though they and they alone have suffered a particular grief no one else could possibly understand. In such an instance, it could be the case that the listener's intent *not* to speak the "hard words" indicative of the first category but rather to be truly present to the hurting other is, in fact, inadvertently thwarted by the assumption that nothing from the "outside," nothing metaphysical, can be safely introduced (no stories of those who have survived similar circumstances, no evocation of the promises of God). When they connect to nothing beyond the immediate circumstances, however, words attempting to be fully present cannot always heal and can often even perpetuate the brokenness.

In the first category of hard worded-ness, theologians transcend what really matters in the name of what they hope *really* matters. In other words, in the supposed service of ultimate meaning, they inadvertently minimize particular people and circumstances. (Maybe Dillard would say we lose touch with the raw universe whenever particularities and diversities are excluded from the discussion, since these are, in fact, what the raw universe is made of.)[23] In the second category, what really matters risks being lost (rather than known in) the particular, untranscendable circumstances. (Maybe Dillard would say we lose touch with the raw universe in our discussion of particularities and appreciation of related diversities, whenever we fail to treat it as more than the sum of its parts.)

One of the principles I'm finding it useful to remember, in reflecting on how to avoid speaking words out of either of these two "categories," is Kant's "concepts without intuitions are empty; intuitions without concepts are blind." Words that talk about God somehow making good, without attention to the rawness of the particular circumstances, are hard because they are meaningless to the moment; words that wallow in the rawness of particular experiences without evoking a broader relational context cannot see enough to make meaning.[24] Or, putting this in the trinitarian terms that frame this essay: The "oneness" of God without the "threeness" is empty; the threeness without the oneness is blind. Words that evoke the immanent Trinity without referencing God's particular acts are meaningless for creatures. Words celebrating the economic Trinity without remembering that the God who is true to God's acts is, also, never exhausted by them have no insight beyond the created order. Either set of hard words fails to describe (as Dillard puts it) "the raw universe." These words fail to participate in the beautiful, horrible details of peoples' lives. They fail to offer hope beyond this world, in this world; in this world, beyond it.

THESIS AND RUMINATIONS: A DIFFERENT KIND OF MEANING

How might we go about interpreting the raw universe in ways that are not "hard"? In ways that celebrate multiplicities and diversities without reducing them to the sum of their parts; in ways that evoke the metaphysical without forgetting that "no miracle could be greater than the life we are experiencing right now"?[25]

In the remainder of this essay I will experiment with the kind of meaning that is known not in the negotiation or tension between individuation and participation (à la Tillich) or in accepting the paradox established by the simultaneity of the one and the three (à la Tillich's rendering of Barth's position, a position that Tillich rejected), or even simply in recognizing that unity and multiplicity exist in "dialectical relationship" (Barth's own articulation of how he saw things, which I do think has a great deal of merit). Rather, if there is a tension that facilitates our participation in a new kind of meaning, I think it is between contingency and consistency. That is: in the contingency that corresponds to the claim that God is three as well as one;[26] in the consistency evident in the relation of a Father who is not the Son or the Spirit, the Son who is not the Father or the Spirit, and the Spirit who is not the Father or the Son, when all three are equally and at the very same time fully God.[27]

I will explain in more detail what I mean when I say we can find a new kind of meaning in the shared space of such contingency and consistency. But first let me make the perhaps obvious but certainly crucial point that any description of "tension" or "dialectic" in the life of the triune God is not intended to reference the conundrum "three cannot equal one" or "one does not equal three." To think so simplistically about the relation between unity and multiplicity in the life of the Trinity at worst leads to treating God as a kind of mathematical conundrum that begs either to be worked out or to be left uninterpreted; at best (that is, "less bad!") it leads to a laying out of contrasting attributes that characterize "oneness" and "threeness," respectively (for example, one is all-powerful, united, self-sufficient, perfect, whole; three is individuated, particular, open to difference, etc.). Only hard words can emerge from the terms of such negotiation, words that attempt either to override contingency (forgetting that the one is the three) or to overlook consistency (denying that the three are the one). Ironically, navigating *between* the "one" and the "three," though this is a common practice thought to be faithful to the doctrine, actually neglects the trinitarian insight that the one cannot be known apart from the three, and the three without recognition of the one.

That there is no conflict between the unity and the multiplicity of God is something difficult to get our heads around, given the conflicts between the one and the many that abound in our actual world. Although it might well be that we experience moments of harmony breaking through the continual negotiations of this world, it would strike us as absurd to order our lives or make important decisions as though the harmony were the actual reality. In order to survive the place and the dynamics of the "cooked universe," we have to learn to manipulate, to leverage, to strive for a fair balance, and maybe (if we are, for example, kind and faithful Christians) to be peacemakers between those who err on the side of the one and those who err on the side of the three.

Church politics consistently accept such problematic negotiation, evoking the doctrine of the Trinity as justification for their procedures. In the Presbyterian Church (USA), for example, amendments to our constitution are achieved through majority vote: We pray that there will somehow be unity (one), even as diverse views are honored (three) even as we cast our ballots. Theological questions about the afterlife commonly reflect neat application of the "three" and the "one" to the conditions of historical existence. "Will we recognize each other in heaven?" we ask and are asked. And just underneath this question, really, is another: namely, "Will the one beat out the three in the end?" (We radically individualized Westerners, especially, hope not.) Polity such as this and questions such as these suggest we are not adequately influenced, in concrete ways, by the trinitarian convictions we genuinely believe ourselves to hold.

Which is why, again, our words are hard. Finally, it comes down to who wins the vote or whether the one *or* the three is, finally, the more ultimate. The problem comes, of course, when and because we project the daily tensions we negotiate onto the doctrine of the Trinity, understanding the relation between the three and the one as illuminating our struggles rather than throwing their reality into such severe question that we are stopped short in our well-intentioned commitments to live our lives (and do our scholarship, and teach our students, and write our blogs, and preach our sermons, etc.) in a negotiation we had accepted as (at least functionally) eternal.

My suspicion is that the three-in-one and the one-in-three actually de-authorize all this, inviting us to lives and approaches that are founded in a different kind of meaning altogether—a meaning that recognizes that the tension is not between multiplicity and unity but between that which really is (the trinitarian reality) and that which actually is (the tensions/polarities/negotiations of our day-to-day lives). To keep on interpreting the raw universe even as we are living in the cooked one is to insist there is no real conflict between multiplicity and unity even as we recognize, and challenge, the conflict that actually exists. It is to live as those who refuse the hard words that come with negotiating the three *and* the one, and who instead inhabit the space of the three-*in*-one and the one-*in*-three. In this space, metaphysical pursuits are always "impassioned," and mystical reflections are rigorous in their commitment to inquiry.[28] What we wonder about most will, in this space, surely be considered.

In contrast to this idea that there must certainly be tension between the oneness and the threeness of God are the classic words of Gregory of Nazianzus, as quoted by Calvin: "I cannot think on the one without quickly being encircled by the splendor of the three; nor can I discern the three without being straightway carried back to the one."[29] It is striking, in this quote, that the one is not threatened by, but "encircled by" (embraced by, supported by) the "splendid" three. The one and the three are not, here, in tension. On the contrary, they support and lean into one another.

The Trinity names, in a word, the simultaneity of two things that cannot be conceptualized simultaneously—the space of a Life in which a different kind of meaning is claimed, the space in which God is both all-in-all and acts in particular ways. And if the simultaneity of the one and the three cannot be conceptualized, neither can the confession that they live in the same space without any conflict between them. The God who is "all in all" *is*, simultaneously, also who the acts of God reveal God to be. The one *is* the three, and vice versa.

Although speaking of a "tension" between the *one* and the *three* is, then, not useful to the task of interpreting the raw universe, there is value in thinking of the relationship between the *one that is three* and the *three that is one* in a kind of generative tension. Let me explain further. To say the one God is three is to acknowledge that God is with us in concrete ways and in particular acts. It is to say, for example, that "God is with us" in Jesus Christ. To say the God who is three is always and also one is to remember that God is not exhausted by or changed by God's particular acts. Jesus Christ—God with us—is never apart from God, and is integral to the creation of all that is. To put these statements together, affirming that God is known to us in Jesus Christ who is—at the same time—the God who is incomprehensively all-in-all is not a coherent move, logically speaking. It might be considered incoherent because (for example) to be incarnate in flesh implies change, and to be fully God in the flesh implies immutability. In any case, who God is, as the one who is three, is always consistent with God's acts and is, in this very specific sense, contingent on them. Yet at the same time the triune God, as Three-in-One, is always precisely who God is regardless of what God does.

In one of her nonfiction essays, Marilynne Robinson comments that a "conceptual problem . . . lies at the center of all meaning."[30] Robinson says this in the context of lauding Calvin's theological approach, but I think her understanding of the "conceptual problem" is useful for reflecting on what it means to do all theology, as metaphysicians committed to including "artifacts" (in all their particularities, diversities, and multiplicities) in our metaphysical claims. Robinson implies that beautiful words, rather than hard ones, can be spoken when we recognize that "the Creator is, by his reckoning, utterly greater than any conception we can form of his creation, and at the same time free, present, just, loving, and intimately attentive to fallen humankind, collectively and one by one. . . . It is as if we were to propose," Robinson adds, "that that great energy only exists to make possible our miraculously delicate participation in it."[31] In this quote, one can almost feel how it is that the oneness does not compromise the multiplicity, but actually affirms, upholds, and promotes it.

I appreciate Robinson's identification and definition of "the conceptual problem." I think it might be useful in identifying what we are up against, when we work to say words about the one-in-three and three-in-one. And I think there is a sense in which Robinson's assertion that this "problem . . . lies at the center of all meaning" might help shape a response to Dillard's question: "Who will interpret the raw universe?" Those who interpret the raw universe, it seems to me, are those who speak out of, and about, the conceptual problem that lies in the center. In my view, to occupy the space of the three-in-one and one-in-three is to be positioned to say *something about everything*. At the same time, because the three-in-one is the one-in-three, we are also ready to say *some things about everything*. To say both of these are true of the triune God is to acknowledge we are free to speak to what we wonder about most. We are, in fact, free to gather all our artifacts together and wonder about every thing and everything they may very well be about.

DEMONSTRATIONS: THREE THINGS THAT MATTER MOST

In this section I briefly sketch what it might "look like" to interpret the raw universe when the continuity indicative of the fact that the three are one functions to highlight, and never to undermine, the contingency that is part and parcel of the claim that the one is three. Metaphysical speech that resists evoking "unity" apart from unity's participation in multiplicity affirms multiplicity and diversity rather than undermining or trumping it. Without metaphysics, in fact, multiplicities and diversities—celebrated only for their own sake—are without broader influence, transforming voice, eternal life. Consistent with this, I try to illustrate, multiplicities and diversities that are isolated from the whole can be multiplicities and diversities only in a way akin to the triune three being three without the one. Three without the one tells us nothing about the whole, nothing about what finally matters, nothing about the raw universe that is the matrix in which we experience every one, two, and three.

In these demonstrations, I explore each of three things I think we "wonder about most" (Dillard): (1) We wonder whether there is some loving presence beyond what we can perceive and how we might have access to it; (2) we wonder if and how we are really actors in relation to our own finitude, and in relation to the contingencies of this world; and (3) we wonder if it is really possible to know and truly to be known by others. Allow me to consider each of these in turn, in the light of my thesis that metaphysical claims do not dishonor, but actually support, diversities and multiplicities when the unities they espouse are known only by virtue of the indwelling of particulars.

Wondering #1: Perceiving a Loving Presence Behind It All
A story: It is my daughter Jessica's fourth birthday. I am driving her home from preschool, where she is about to be greeted by a stack of presents and a Disney princess birthday cake, when she suddenly asks me: "Mommy, are we going to die?" After I tell her, "Yes, but hopefully only after a long, long, LONG time," she happily and confidently asks me, "When we die, can we hold hands?"

Is there any possible way I can answer "yes" to this question? Is there any way a "yes" can be authorized, given my belief that even death will not sever my connection to my daughter, given the fact that I—a Christian believer—confess the "communion of saints"?

But I don't want to be deceptive. And the last thing I want to do is teach my children theology that denies the embodied realities of this world. So I answer Jessica's question straightforwardly, with the honest words I feel are necessary, spoken as gently as possible. I tell her that it is unlikely we will die together, and that I hope she will live way longer than I will, given that I am older (I add, of course, that I plan on living with her for a long, long, LONG time). And I am surprised by her silence as she thinks through what I have said, and then shocked by her deep, broken sobs.

Calvin recommends "meditation on the wondrous works" of God, which "speak of . . . the glorious splendour of God's kingdom."[32] He notes that it is "fitting . . . for us to pursue this particular search for God, which may so hold our mental powers suspended in wonderment as at the same time to stir us deeply."[33] It seems to me possible that all four-year-olds may know how to do this, and that I have largely forgotten. I forget, in my answer to Jessica, the "conceptual problem" that drives all trinitarian theology—that is, that the God who is three is also one; that the God who "rules over all" (in whatever sense we understand this) is the very same God who calls us particular ones by name. In my answer to Jessica—in my eagerness to avoid those hard theological words that can serve as an escape hatch from this world and its beautiful frailties (particularities, multiplicities, diversities), I leave her completely and utterly alone and demolished.[34]

Since that conversation on my daughter's birthday, less than a couple of years ago, now, I have grown in the realization that Jessica was really asking me a question about *everything*, and I met her only with the same hard words. She was, with her question, standing in wonderment at it all, and I—mother and theologian that I am—discouraged her perception by collapsing the conceptual problem into something that made more sense. Into something that prioritized the distinction between her particularity and my own. Into something that brutally forced forward threeness without remembering the three's common indwelling as one.

You'll be happy to know that Jessica gives me another chance. About two weeks later, again from the backseat of the car, she asks me: "Mommy, when we die, can we hold hands?" And this time I respond: "Yes, Jessica, we can hold hands." And who she is, as a distinct and beautiful creature, is not only left intact, but honored and upheld.

Pastors sensitive to the ways hard theological words have been used to distance human beings from the joys and struggles of this world often ask me what they should say when someone they are visiting in the hospital asks them if they are going to see their loved ones again after they die. So much has rightly been made about the patriarchal narcissism that has shaped theological responses to this question that assert individual human beings will be immortalized. But is our alternative to theological words that are hard because they collapse the particulars into the universal to forgo consideration of the universal altogether? Is the "real" answer to the question about the loved ones (regardless of what might be said at the actual deathbed): "No, you won't see them. There isn't life after death. To think there is would be to dishonor multiplicities and diversities by positing their ultimate collapse into a unified reality, and sorry, but—I'm afraid we just can't do that." As in the case of Jessica, to utter such hard words would be to abandon, to diminish particularities and multiplicities by reducing them to only what can be seen and known—to treat them like "artifacts" that participate in no larger reality.

Another approach to this question might follow along these lines: If the default reality honors, simultaneously, both multiplicity and unity, if in fact "threeness" and "oneness" are, in this reality, not actually in tension or conflict, then there is reason to hope both that we will be able to recognize our loved ones and that we will be united (perichoretically) with one another at one and the same time. Our union will support the celebration of multiplicity that indwells it without compromise to itself.

Wondering #2: Acting as Agents in the Face of Contingency
A second thing we wonder about most is whether we have the power to act in relation to the contingencies of our own lives. As we all are aware, there are plenty of "hard words" that have leveraged metaphysical claims as means to silence particular people and groups of people from naming the ways their agency has been stymied. Christian workers[35] have told starving people that their bodies don't really matter; they should attend to their souls. Families of Holocaust victims, those who were abused by apartheid, survivors of abuse—a myriad of suffering people, and groups of suffering people, have been told they should forgive, because there is a God who has already forgiven. There is no question that imposing the all-in-all "one," apart from remembering this one is also three, has fostered and perpetuated immeasurable quantities of injustice.

So bad is the problem that good Christian theologians have proposed we set aside the metaphysical, at least for a time, in order to prevent ourselves from speaking "hard words" that do further injustice. What happens, though, when the metaphysical "one" is understood ever and also to be "three?" This is, of course, not a new theological question. Its asking and its answering has been well explored, in the last several decades, by theologians such as Jürgen Moltmann and Catherine Mowry LaCugna. When the one is also three, it is not only the case that the world to come is what matters. In the particular acts of God (creation, cross, resurrection, sacramental gifts), this world—and the particular and multiple bodies living in it—matter. Because the one is also three, it is not only the case that God forgives. God also enters in, and is crucified.

A reason not to set aside appeal to the one is that it can help victims and sufferers remember what they wonder about most, and thereby hold onto their status as agents in the world. Recall the spirituals sung by American slaves: "Soon and very soon we are going to see the King" wasn't only about claiming their place, as children, in the Kingdom of God. It was also about remembering their place before God, so they might be empowered to claim their status as God's children here on this earth. Recall the famous question reported by Elie Wiesel, from the time when he was a boy in a concentration camp and forced to witness a gruesome hanging: "Where is God?" To ask where God is, even in the most horrific instance, is to insist that there is more to the raw universe than the gruesome hangings going on before your eyes. And the answer to the question, as Wiesel reports it, is: "There he is—he's hanging in the gallows."[36] A remembering, perhaps, of the contingency God enters into out of God's love for us, particular beings?

From the center of all meaning, in the trinitarian terms of the conceptual problem, there are only certain words, and not others, that should be used to interpret the raw universe with and/or for people who are suffering and want to exercise their agency. First, the God who we cannot see in relation to the particular circumstances is the sovereign God who is all-in-all, so a suffering person has every reason to cry out to God and ask what is going on. Second, the God who is all-in-all has entered into the particularities of existence with us, and in this sense understands the sufferer and has not abandoned the person who is suffering. The productive tension between God's supposed consistency and God's entry into the painful contingencies of historical existence can be maddening, logically and existentially speaking. But say that God is only consistent, without any participation in the contingencies, and we're back to hard words that deny the value of the world by setting God up as a kind of trump card over it. Say that God is stuck in the contingencies, however, with no promise of consistency, and the sufferer is left with a God that is no less a victim than the sufferer is. And take God out of the equation altogether, and we are left with a "cosmodicy"[37] rather than a theodicy. Annie Dillard and I need more help—and hope—than a cosmodicy can give.

Wondering #3: Knowing and Being Known

A third thing we wonder about most is whether it is possible truly to be known and truly to know others. "Knowing," here, is meant to refer to the relational as well as the intellectual. What I have in mind is the kind of knowing Kant said was impossible through "reason alone"—the kind of *knowing* that says something about the *"Ding-en-sich"* (the "thing in itself"), the kind of knowing that can be enjoyed only in the context of relationship.

If reference to the metaphysical is set aside, I suggest, we have no way to speak the right kind of words about what it means to know, and be known by, one another. Now, I understand that reference to the metaphysical has been evoked in the creation of "hard words" that shut off participation in the lives of one another by minimizing the other's particular beauties, attributes, and needs. This gets tricky, since this very minimization is often done in the name of honoring particularities. Let me name an example.

In volume 3, part 4, section 54 of the *Church Dogmatics*, Karl Barth describes the relationship between "male and female." In it, he is ostensibly trying to honor the differences between the sexes, treating "whatever it means to be a man" and "whatever it means to be a woman" as complementary to one another.[38] "We cannot really characterise man and woman in the form of a definition," he insists.[39] But he then goes on to specify that (all) men are "As" and (all) women are Bs," delineating a corresponding list of attributes for each. Any wish an A might have for the attributes on the B list, and any wish a B might have for attributes on the A list is a wish "not to be an 'A'" or "not to be a 'B,'" respectively speaking.[40] Clearly, Barth's self-proclaimed commitment to honoring diversity does not win the day; Barth's commitment to adhering to the "order of creation," as commanded by the one God, overrides the importance of any diversities among men or among women.

As if this weren't problematic enough, from the trinitarian perspective that has been explored here, Barth goes on to reassure his readers that, while "A" is always superordinate to "B," and "B" is always subordinate to "A," it is not the case that women are subordinate to men (even though—remember—all men are "As" and all women are "Bs"). The reason why this is the case, according to Barth, is that women—as Bs—are not asked by God to submit to men, but to the order God has created and commanded. For a woman to subordinate herself to a man does not make her unequal to him, since the one she is actually submitting to is God and not the man.

In Barth's paradigm, mutual indwelling of the life of a man and the life of a woman is rendered impossible, despite his attempts to argue to the contrary. The two cannot become also one because neither is genuinely submitting to the other. Rather, their radical individuation is preserved by their individual submission to the order of God. And the irony, here, is that their individuation isn't in the business of honoring their beautiful particularities, since each must be only an "A" or a "B" with said corresponding attributes. *Because* the two are not one, *because* they cannot submit *to one another as* particular, blessed, multiple, diverse human beings, their particularities can be known only in homogeneous (A or B) ways.

The question is: Is the dishonoring of particularities and multiplicities reflected in Barth's understanding fostered by his metaphysical commitment to one, sovereign (and, by the way, triune) God who has ordered certain things? Is it his commitment to some form of simplicity that prevents him from speaking good words about how we can be known and can know others?

I think, in fact, that it is not. And while I do not have time or space at the moment (not to mention the psychological expertise!) to delve into what Barth's life situation might have contributed to his understanding of male/female relations, I will point out that, in his model, even God is not directly present. Men and women do not, in their submission to their roles, participate in the being of one another. But neither do they, in their submission, participate in the life of God. Rather, according to Barth, they prove faithfulness to "a command" that is seemingly extrapolated from the life of the triune God whom Barth had earlier (and beautifully) suggested invites men and women into the "dialectical dance" of the Godhead.[41] In other words, I think we would be hard put to blame Barth's lack of concern for diversities and multiplicities on his metaphysics. In fact, I bet I could show that it is precisely at the point where he moves away from reflecting on men and women's relative roles in relation to the triune God that his discourse shifts from talking in terms of the "dialectical dance" to talking in terms of a strictly boundaried "A" and "B."[42] Clearly, struggle with the "conceptual problem" is nowhere in evidence in his careful assignment of men and women's roles.

Contrast this to what happens in the story of Eve's presentation to Adam.[43] He does not look her in the eye and say: "You are so different from me! We won't be able to understand each other without the help of some Deborah Tannen books!" Presumably (especially since they are naked), he is at least aware of their differences. But what he says is this: "You are bone of my bones, and flesh of my flesh." They are brought together as "three": different, individuated, multiple. And the first thing Adam does is name the "oneness" of their relationship: bone of bone, flesh of flesh. Both one and three are present, and there is no conflict. And the one, I bet, deepens the appreciation of the three; the shared humanity deepens the appreciation of their differences. It is the sharing of the "one" that makes the differences of Adam and Eve more pondered, and cherished, than they otherwise would be. I imagine them asking, How could one who shares in the very same "stuff" with me be so different? And they—standing smack in the conceptual problem[44]—are left in wonder, knowing each other.

The son of someone very close to me was recently diagnosed with autism. He is a beautiful boy who looks exactly like his father. And I watch my friend teach "Samuel"; I watch him wonder at how Samuel thinks, as he works to maintain connection. And my friend looks at Samuel with the eyes of one who shares the same bones, who shares the same flesh. This is my son, he says. This one whom I can't always understand—this one who is so different from me—the one whom I know, even in my not knowing. My friend does not say this about every particular child with autism he encounters. Samuel's differences matter supremely to him because the two of them share the same substance.

RECLAIMING PERICHORETIC POSSIBILITIES
FOR DIVERSITIES AND MULTIPLICITIES

> The deeper question is whether the uncertainty at the center mimics the plurality of possibilities essential to liberal debate, as the more open-minded theologians like to believe, or is an antique mystery in a

story open only as the tomb is open, with a mystery left inside, never to be entirely explored or explained.

ADAM GOPNIK, "What Did Jesus Do?"

In this comment made by the *New Yorker* contributor Adam Gopnik,[45] at the close of a strong article about different approaches to understanding Jesus, readers are offered a choice. In the face of multiple faces of Jesus, will they succumb to the reality composed of all sorts of contingencies, deciding to forgo continuity in order to preserve and uphold multiplicity? Or will they cling to a metaphysical claim—to the mystery that, somehow, God is one and consistent—never to be adequately explained and therefore only to be minimally explored?

This essay has rejected the idea that mystery (metaphysics, unfathomable all-in-allness) must be set aside if we want to engage the "plurality of possibilities essential to liberal debate." It also rejects the easy correlations between: (1) *embracing uncertainty* and *welcoming a range of voices* and (2) *embracing mystery* and *being whatever is the opposite of an open-minded liberal.*

Liberal theologians can and do, in fact, bear witness to the divine mystery even as they lobby for more diversity, more attention to multiplicities. In this essay, I have tried to show that reflection on the character of the triune life—the perichoretic relationship of the one and the three—offers some justification for resisting the common dichotomization reflected in Gopnik's quote. I have also suggested that attention to the mystery, glossed in this essay as the "conceptual problem" or the "tension between contingency and consistency" can actually draw us into deeper appreciation of particularities, diversities, and multiplicities. Certainly, trinitarian mystery invites the articulation of uncertainties. The one is three; you will bear God to the world: "How can this be?"[46] The three is one; the God you seek by making particular idols is the God "in whom you live and move and have your being"; what strange "new teaching" is this?[47]

More work needs to be done by theologians interested in reflecting on metaphysics and mystery without speaking the kind of "hard words" that overlook artifacts and other particulars in the name of evoking the whole. I am grateful that this volume, and the conference that precipitated it, has space for such reflection. More spaces are needed; they must be claimed and created if indeed they are to become generative spaces for us all. They must be claimed and created because, as is evidenced in Dillard, Gopnik, and others, it is being decided *for* us at least as much as *by* us that we theologians who care about making space for multiple voices aren't interested in speaking much, anymore, about the one "who by the power at work within us is able to accomplish abundantly far more than all we can ask or imagine" (Ephesians 3:20).[48] I guess a relevant question to ask, at this point, is: Are they right? I myself don't believe they are.

A little midrash on Psalm 139, to bring this essay to a close: Each of us—distinct, particular, multiple beings that we are—were knit together in our mother's wombs. And our days play out. And what happens this afternoon will have an impact on the next week, and so forth. And the God who is three has entered into all this, into the contingencies of these happenings. But this God also knows every day of our lives before one of them comes to be. Here is the trinitarian, perichoretic tension: How can God at once both enter into the conditions of historical existence and know each one of us, and every detail of our schedules? Multiplicities, diversities, and particularities, if never known, would only be lost in the negotiations of historical existence. Even the God who enters in, acting alongside of us, would be lost: rejected, despised, crucified, forgotten. Apart from the one, the three is only crucified, crucified only. It is the consistency of the fact that the three is one that ensures, however, that the three are not only lost. For they are remembered; they are known; and they are joined. Each and every one who is knit together in the mother's womb matters not just because he or she exists as a particular individual, but because he or she is known as that individual, and not another. We need the one, and whatever metaphysical approaches help us remember the one, to affirm this. And we need then to go on to speak about what these beloved, particular, and multiple ones wonder about—and care about—most.

NOTES

THE GOD WHO IS (NOT) ONE: OF ELEPHANTS, BLIND MEN, AND DISAPPEARING TIGERS | PHILIP CLAYTON

1. Stephen Prothero, *God Is Not One: The Eight Rival Religions That Run the World—and Why Their Differences Matter* (San Francisco: HarperOne, 2010).
2. For an excellent summary, see Paul O. Ingram, *The Modern Buddhist-Christian Dialogue: Two Universalistic Religions in Transformation* (Lewiston, Maine: E. Mellen Press, 1988).
3. John Hick, *An Interpretation of Religion* (New Haven: Yale University Press, 1989).
4. See www.ClaremontLincoln.org.
5. Catherine Keller and Laurel Schneider, eds., *Polydoxy: Theology of Multiplicity and Relation* (New York: Routledge, 2011).
6. I made the epistemic case in a previous essay for the Drew series. See Philip Clayton, "The Infinite Found in Human Form: Intertwinings of Cosmology and Incarnation," in *Apophatic Bodies: Negative Theology, Incarnation, and Relationality*, ed. Chris Boesel and Catherine Keller (New York: Fordham University Press, 2010).
7. J. Wentzel van Huyssteen, *Essays in Postfoundationalist Theology* (Grand Rapids, Mich.: W. B. Eerdmans, 1997).
8. John Rawls, *A Theory of Justice*, 2nd ed. (Cambridge, Mass.: Harvard University Press, 1999); idem, *Political Liberalism* (New York: Columbia University Press, 1996); idem, *Justice as Fairness: A Restatement* (Cambridge, Mass.: Harvard University Press, 2001).

9. Among innumerable publications see esp. Jürgen Habermas, *The Theory of Communicative Action*, trans. Thomas McCarthy, 2 vols. (Boston: Beacon Press, 1984–87).
10. The debate on coherence theories in Anglo-American philosophy goes back to W. V. O. Quine and J. S. Ullian, *The Web of Belief* (New York: Random House, 1970). Key works include Laurence BonJour, *The Structure of Empirical Knowledge* (Cambridge, Mass.: Harvard University Press, 1985), and Keith Lehrer, *Theory of Knowledge*, 2nd ed. (Boulder: Routledge, 2000).
11. See, e.g., Donna Haraway, "Situated Knowledges: The Science Question in Feminism and the Privilege of Partial Perspectives," *Feminist Studies* 14, no. 3 (1988): 575–99; Luce Irigaray, *To Be Two*, trans. Monique M. Rhodes and Marco F. Cocito-Monoc (New York: Routledge, 2001); idem, *The Irigaray Reader*, ed. Margaret Whitford (Cambridge, Mass.: Basil Blackwell, 1991).
12. Robert Brandom's appropriation of Hegel has been a notable exception; see Robert Brandom, *Making It Explicit: Reasoning, Representing, and Discursive Commitment* (Cambridge, Mass.: Harvard University Press, 1994); idem, *Between Saying and Doing: Towards an Analytic Pragmatism* (Oxford: Oxford University Press, 2008). When analytic philosophers move in this direction, one usually finds contemporary Continental philosophy or feminist theory among the causes. For a great example in the analytic tradition, see Karen Warren, *Ecofeminist Philosophy: A Western Perspective on What It Is and Why It Matters* (Lanham, Md.: Rowman and Littlefield, 2000).
13. See Richard Rorty, *Philosophy and the Mirror of Nature* (Princeton: Princeton University Press, 1979); John R. Searle, *The Construction of Social Reality* (New York: Free Press, 1995).
14. Philippa Foot, *Virtues and Vices and Other Essays in Moral Philosophy* (Oxford: Clarendon Press; New York: Oxford University Press, 2002); Martha C. Nussbaum, *The Fragility of Goodness: Luck and Ethics in Greek Tragedy and Philosophy* (Cambridge: Cambridge University Press, 1986).
15. See Franz Rosenzweig, *The Star of Redemption*, trans. of the 2nd ed. [1930] by William W. Hallo (Notre Dame, Ind.: Notre Dame Press, 1985); Gershom Scholem, *Major Trends in Jewish Mysticism* (New York: Schocken Books, 1995); and (more controversially) Martin Buber, e.g., Martin Buber, *Tales of the Hasidim*, 2 vols., trans. Olga Marx (New York: Schocken Books, 1991).
16. See Emil L. Fackenheim, *To Mend the World: Foundations of Post-Holocaust Jewish Thought* (Bloomington: Indiana University Press, 1994). In particular, the Kabbalistic narrative of bringing together the divine sparks from the *En Soph* through human community, observance, and the quest for justice combined

metaphysical narrative with the distinctives of Jewish observance in a way that is paradigmatic of the type of work I am defending.

17. It's not that the simple solutions are wrong; narratives can express ethical and political commitments and ideals, and thus encourage powerful prophetic action within society.

18. Marjorie Suchocki, *God, Christ, Church: A Practical Guide to Process Theology* (New York: Crossroad, 1989), 33.

19. Philip Clayton and Steven Knapp, *The Predicament of Belief: Science, Philosophy, Faith* (Oxford: Oxford University Press, 2011).

20. See Jürgen Moltmann, *The Crucified God: The Cross of Christ as the Foundation and Criticism of Christian Theology*, trans. R. A. Wilson and John Bowden (New York: Harper and Row, 1974), esp. chap. 6.

21. I happily acknowledge the leadership of John Thatamanil in this project. Not only has John made the case in *The Immanent Divine: God, Creation, and the Human Predicament* (Minneapolis: Fortress Press, 2006), but he has also brought it home effectively in numerous lectures, blogs, and videos.

22. http://www.iucnredlist.org/news/following-flex, accessed May 14, 2012.

23. Visit http://www.greenmuze.com/animals/wild/2058-wild-tigers-disappearing.html, accessed May 14, 2012. Or just google "disappearing tigers."

GOD'S VITALITY: CREATIVE TENSION AND THE ABYSS OF *DIFFÉRANCE* WITHIN THE DIVINE LIFE | ERIC TROZZO

1. Notable figures within this group would include Mark Heim and David Ray Griffin, and Laurel Schneider. While there are clearly differences between the proposals and projects of these theologians, they share an interest in the role of multiplicity within divinity.

2. See John Hoffmeyer's essay in this volume, "Multiplicity and Christocentric Theology."

3. Lewis S. Ford, "The Appropriation of Dynamics and Form for Tillich's God," *Harvard Theological Review* 68 no. 1 (1975): 37.

4. Paul Tillich, *Systematic Theology*, vol. 1 (Chicago: University of Chicago Press, 1951), 179. Tillich distinguishes between *me on* (relative or potential nonbeing) and *ouk on* (absolute nonbeing). *Me on* is the dynamic potentiality of that which does not exist but might and so could burst into the realm of being, whereas *ouk on* is the absolute not existing that stops all being.

5. Ibid.

6. Ibid., 41.

7. Ibid., 156.
8. I am specifically referring to Tillich's understanding of the Spirit offered up in this passage of the first volume of his *Systematic Theology*. He deals with the Spirit in other ways in other places, notably the third volume of the *Systematic Theology*, that lie outside what can be addressed within the current discussion.
9. Tillich, *Systematic Theology*, 1:156.
10. Ibid., 247.
11. Paul Tillich, *The Interpretation of History*, http://www.religion-online.org/showbook.asp?title=377, 1:1b.
12. Tillich, *Systematic Theology*, 1:242.
13. Ford, "Dynamics and Form," 42.
14. Tillich, *Systematic Theology*, 1:246.
15. John J. Thatamanil, *The Immanent Divine: God, Creation, and the Human Predicament* (Minneapolis: Fortress Press, 2006), 144.
16. Ibid., 146.
17. Tillich, *Systematic Theology*, 1:243.
18. Ford, "Dynamics and Form," 46.
19. Daniel J. Peterson, "Jacob Boehme and Paul Tillich: A Reassessment of the Mystical Philosopher and Systematic Theologian," *Religious Studies* 42, no. 2 (2006): 231.
20. Here I have in mind not just the ideas coming from Boehme and Tillich but also Richard Kearney's more recent concern for the potential coming of the monstrous in the messianic expectation of deconstruction. See Kearney's *Strangers, Gods, and Monsters: Interpreting Otherness* (New York: Routledge, 2002).
21. David Ray Griffin, "Religious Pluralism: Generic, Identist, and Deep," in *Deep Religious Pluralism*, ed. David Ray Griffin (Louisville: Westminster John Knox, 2005), 3–38.
22. Filip Ivanovic, "De potential Dei: Some Western and Byzantine Perspectives," *European Legacy: Toward New Paradigms* 13, no. 1 (2008): 1–11, 7.
23. William of Ockham, *Quodlibet*, VI, q. 1, art. 1, in *Opera Theologica* IX (St. Bonaventure, N.Y.: St. Bonaventure University Press, 1980), quoted and translated in Ivanovic, "De potential Dei," 7.
24. Harry S. J. Klocker, *William of Ockham and the Divine Freedom* (Milwaukee: Marquette University Press, 1996), 77.
25. See Luther's engagement with this doctrine in *On the Bondage of the Will*, particularly in *Luther's Works*, vol. 33, American edition, ed. Philip S. Watson (Philadelphia: Fortress Press, 1972), 190.
26. Luther, *Luther's Works*, 33:25.

27. Ibid., 33:139.
28. Quoted in James Luther Adams, "Paul Tillich on Luther," in *Interpreters of Luther: Essays in Honor of Wilhelm Pauck*, ed. Jaroslav Pelikan (Philadelphia: Fortress Press, 1968), 322.
29. Tillich, *Systematic Theology*, 1:168.
30. Jacob Boehme, *Of the Election of Grace, or Of God's Will toward Man*, ed. Martin Euser, trans. John Sparrow, http://www.scribd.com/doc/15427076/Jacob-BoehmeElection-of-GraceElectronic-Text-Edition, 1.6.
31. Ibid., 1.10.
32. Ibid., 1.12.
33. Edward Allen Beach, *The Potencies of God(s): Schelling's Philosophy of Mythology* (Albany: State University of New York Press, 1994), 71.
34. See Daniel J. Peterson's, "The Hidden Heterodoxy of the Hidden God: An Analysis of the Deus Absconditus in Classical and Contemporary Christian theology" (PhD diss., Graduate Theological Union, 2005), 126, for a more in-depth discussion of the complexities on this point in Boehme's thought.
35. Paul Tillich, *Mysticism and Guilt-Consciousness in Schelling's Philosophical Development*, trans. Victor Nuovo (Lewisberg, PA: Bucknell University Press, 1974), 93.
36. Ibid.
37. Ibid.
38. Schelling, quoted in Tillich, *Mysticism*, 93.
39. Tillich, *Mysticism*, 99.
40. Ford, "Dynamics and Form," 45.
41. Tillich, *Systematic Theology*, 1:242.
42. See Plato's *Timaeus*, trans. Benjamin Jowett, http://classics.mit.edu/Plato/timaeus.html.
43. Jacques Derrida, "How to Avoid Speaking: Denials," in *Derrida and Negative Theology*, ed. Howard Coward and Toby Foshay, trans. Ken Freiden (Albany: State University of New York Press, 1992), 107.
44. John D. Caputo, *The Prayers and Tears of Jacques Derrida: Religion without Religion* (Bloomington: Indiana University Press, 1997), 36.
45. John D. Caputo, "Abyssus Abyssum Invocat: A Response to Richard Kearney," in *A Passion for the Impossible: John D. Caputo in Focus*, ed. Mark Dooley (Albany: State University of New York Press, 2003), 127.
46. For more on Thatamanil's argument, see Mark Heim's responses in his essay in this volume, "Differential Pluralism and Trinitarian Theologies of Religion."

POLYPHILIC PLURALISM: BECOMING RELIGIOUS MULTIPLICITIES | ROLAND FABER AND CATHERINE KELLER

This essay was previously published in *Religions in the Making: Whitehead and the Wisdom Traditions of the World*, ed. John Cobb (Eugene, Ore.: Cascade Books, 2012). It is used by permission of Wipf and Stock Publishers, www.wipfandstock.com.

1. See David R. Griffin, ed., *Deep Religious Pluralism* (Louisville: Westminster John Knox Press, 2005).
2. Unfortunately, such an understanding of postmodernity has also befallen theological reflection. See Graham Ward, ed., *The Postmodern God: A Theological Reader* (Oxford: Blackwell, 1998).
3. See John Cobb, *Spiritual Bankruptcy: A Prophetic Call to Action* (Nashville: Abingdon, 2010).
4. Alfred North Whitehead, *Religion in the Making* (Cambridge: Cambridge University Press, 2011), 50.
5. See Roland Faber, *God as Poet of the World: Exploring Process Theologies*, trans. Douglas W. Stott (Louisville: Westminster John Knox, 2008).
6. Alfred North Whitehead, *Process and Reality: An Essay in Cosmology*, corrected ed., ed. David Ray Griffin and Donald W. Sherburne (New York: Free Press, 1978), 22.
7. Ibid., 7.
8. See John Cobb, *Christ in a Pluralistic Age* (Eugene, Ore.: Wipf and Stock, 1998).
9. Alfred North Whitehead, *Adventures of Ideas* (New York: Free Press, 1933), 168.
10. See Catherine Keller, *The Face of the Deep: A Theology of Becoming* (London: Routledge, 2003).
11. See Gene Reeves, "Divinity in Process Thought and the Lotus Sutra," *Journal of Chinese Philosphy* 28, no. 4 (2001): 257–369.
12. Catherine Keller and Laurel Schneider, eds., *Polydoxy: Theology of Multiplicity and Relation* (New York: Routledge, 2011).
13. See Gilles Deleuze, *The Fold: Leibniz and the Baroque* (Minneapolis: University of Minnesota Press, 1993).
14. See Gayatri Chakravorty Spivak, *Critique of Postcolonial Reason: Toward a History of the Vanishing Present* (Cambridge, Mass.: Harvard University Press, 1999).
15. Cf. Catherine Keller, Michael Nausner, and Mayra Rivera, eds., *Postcolonial Theologies: Divinity and Empire* (St. Louis: Chalice Press, 2004).
16. Whitehead, *Adventures of Ideas*, 277.
17. See Faber, *God as Poet*, Postscript.

18. William James, *A Pluralistic Universe* (New York: Longmans, Green, 1909), 130–31
19. Ernesto Cardenal, *Pluriverse: New and Selected Poems*, ed. Jonathan Cohen (New York: New Directions Books, 2009), 212.
20. William Connolly, *Pluralism* (Durham, N.C.: Duke University Press, 2005), 92.
21. Alfred North Whitehead, *Modes of Thought* (New York: Free Press, 1938), 84.
22. See Roland Faber, "Theopoetic Justice: Toward an Ecology of Living Together," Inaugural Lecture for the Kilsby Family/John B. Cobb, Jr, Chair in Process Studies, April 22, 2010, Claremont School of Theology.
23. Whitehead, *Process and Reality*, 21–22.
24. Ibid., 8.
25. See Roland Faber, Review of M. Hampe, *Die Wahrnehmungen der Organismen: Über die Voraussetzungen einer naturalistischen Theorie der Erfahrung in der Metaphysik Whiteheads* (Göttingen 1990), *Process Studies* 25 (1996): 124–28.
26. See Roland Faber and Andrea Stephenson, eds., *Secrets of Becoming: Negotiating Whitehead, Deleuze and Butler* (New York: Fordham University Press, 2010).
27. Whitehead, *Adventures of Ideas*, 296.
28. Deleuze, *Fold*, 82.
29. Ibid., 81.
30. Gilles Deleuze and Felix Guattari, *A Thousand Plateaus* (Minneapolis: University of Minnesota Press, 1987), 25.
31. Deleuze, *Fold*, 81.
32. Whitehead, *Adventures of Ideas*, 274.
33. See Faber, *God as Poet*, §36.
34. *Jeong*, a Korean word for attachment, is developed as theological trope in Anne Wonhee Joh, *The Heart of the Cross: A Postcolonial Theology* (Louisville: Westminster John Knox Press, 2009).
35. For the trickster figure as a device for postcolonial hermeneutics, see Marion Grau, *Of Divine Economy: Refinancing Redemption* (New York: T & T Clark International/Continuum, 2004).
36. Monica A. Coleman, *Making a Way Out of No Way: A Womanist Theology* (Minneapolis: Fortress Press, 2008).
37. Jean-Luc Nancy, *Being Singular Plural*, trans. Robert D. Richardson and Anne E. O'Byrne (Stanford, California: Stanford University Press, 2000), 29.
38. Whitehead, *Process and Reality*, 350. See Roland Faber, "God in the Making: Religious Experience and Cosmology in Whitehead's *Religion in the Making* in Theological Perspective," in *L'experience de Dieu: Lectures de Religion in the Making d'Alfred N. Whitehead. Aletheia*, ed. M. Weber and S. Rouvillois (Janvier: Ecole Saint-Jean, 2005), 179–200.

39. Deleuze, *Fold*, 81.
40. See Roland Faber, "Bodies of the Void: Polyphilia and Theoplicity," in *Apophatic Bodies: Negative Theology, Incarnation, and Relationship*, ed. Chris Boesel and Catherine Keller (New York: Fordham University Press, 2010), 200–223.
41. Gilles Deleuze, *Desert Islands and Other Texts, 1953–1974* (Los Angeles: semiotext(e), 2004), 304–5.
42. Gene Reeves, *The Lotus Sutra: A Contemporary Translation of a Buddhist Classic* (Boston: Wisdom Publications, 2008), 95, our emphasis.
43. Ibid.
44. See Steve Odin, "Peace and Compassion in the Microcosmic-Macrocosmic Paradigm of Whitehead and the Lotus Sutra," *Journal of Chinese Philosophy* 28, no. 4 (2001): 371–84.
45. Reeves, *Lotus Sutra*, 36.
46. See Steve Odin, *Process Metaphysics and Hua-Yen Buddhism: A Critical Study of Cumulative Penetration vs. Interpenetration* (Albany: State University of New York Press, 1981).
47 Whitehead, *Process and Reality*, 348.
48. Ibid., 215, 28.
49. Ibid., 348.
50. Ibid., 214–15.
51. Cf. Whitehead, *Religion in the Making*, 47–57.
52. Ibid., 68–70.
53. Cf. Ibid., 90.
54. Whitehead, *Adventures of Ideas*, 134. See Roland Faber, "Immanence and Incompleteness: Whitehead's Late Metaphysics," in *Beyond Metaphysics? Explorations in Alfred N. Whitehead's Late Thought*, ed. Roland Faber, Brian Henning, and Clinton Combs, Contemporary Whitehead Series, vol. 1 (Amsterdam: Rodopi, 2010).
55. Alfred North Whitehead, *Science in the Modern World* (New York: Free Press, 1953), 179.
56. See Roland Faber, "'The Infinite Movement of Evanescence'—The Pythagorean Puzzle in Plato, Deleuze, and Whitehead," *American Journal of Theology and Philosophy* 21, no. 1 (2000): 171–99.
57. Whitehead, *Process and Reality*, 5.
58. Ibid., 8.
59. Cf. Ibid., 346.
60. Laurel Schneider, *Beyond Monotheism: A Theology of Multiplicity* (New York: Routledge, 2007).

61. See Roland Faber, "'Gottesmeer'—Versuch über die Ununterschiedenheit Gottes," in *"Leben in Fülle": Skizzen zur christlichen Spiritualität*, ed. Th. Dienberg and M. Plattig, Theologie der Spiritualität 5 (Münster: LIT, 2001), 64–95.
62. Whitehead, *Process and Reality*, 3.
63. Ibid., 348.
64. Whitehead, *Modes of Thought*, 174.
65. Cf. Whitehead, *Science in Modern World*, chap. 8.
66. John Archibald Wheeler, cited in John Horgan, *The End of Science* (Reading, Mass.: Little, Brown, 1997), 83.
67. Judith Butler, *Giving an Account of Oneself* (New York: Fordham University Press, 2005), 136.
68. See Faber, *Poet*, §32.
69. See Joseph Bracken, *The Divine Matrix: Creativity as Link between East and West* (Maryknoll: Orbis Books, 1995).
70. Therefore, if Jews and the Muslims will recognize that they need not take our Trinity as a personalist tritheism but as the "identity, equality and connection" of the infinite to itself; if Hindu polytheists will admit that in each of the gods and goddesses "divinity itself" is being worshipped—then we have "one religion with many rites"—not religious pluralism, but the opening of the door to a dialogue of difference, an agonistic respect, that would make a heartier pluralism eventually possible. But as Simone Weil points out, Cusa represents the lost possibility for an alternative modernity for Europe, which would have obviated the endless religious war. The negative theological background for an affirmative corporeality of nonseparable differences in Cusa unfolds in a new apophatic ecumenism. It cannot go all the way to the polydox pluralism that we need—and that Christianity also needs and is in its academies at least rehearsing.
71. William Connolly, *Capitalism and Christianity, American Style* (Durham, N.C.: Duke University Press, 2008), 128.
72. See Faber, *Poet*, §40.
73. See Roland Faber, "De-Ontologizing God: Levinas, Deleuze, and Whitehead," in *Process and Difference: Between Cosmological and Poststructuralist Postmodernism*, ed. Catherine Keller and Anne Daniell, University of New York Series in Constructive Postmodern Thought (New York: State University of New York Press, 2002), 209–34.
74. See Roland Faber, "Ecotheology, Ecoprocess, and Ecotheosis: A Theopoetical Intervention," *Salzburger Zeitschrift für Theologie* 12, no. 1 (2008): 75–115.

ABHINAVAGUPTA'S THEOGRAMMATICAL TOPOGRAPHY OF THE ONE AND THE MANY | LORILIAI BIERNACKI

1. Benjamin Lee Whorf, "The Relation of Habitual Thought and Behavior to Language," in *Language, Culture, and Personality: Essays in Memory of Edward Sapir*, ed. Leslie Spier, A. Irving Hallowell, and Stanley Newman (reprint; Santa Barbara, Calif.: Greenwood Press, 1983), 197–214. Also online at http://en.wikipedia.org/wiki/Benjamin_Lee_Whorf#External_links.
2. Abhinavagupta, *Parātriṁśikāvivarṇa*, downloaded from S. D. Vasudeva's Indology E-text webpage: http://gretil.sub.uni-goettingen.de/gret_ree.htm#ParTri, p. 275: PaTrim24ab: yathā nyagrodhabījastha śaktirūpo mahādrumaḥ / PaTrim24cd: tathā hṛdayabījastham jagad etac carācaram//.
3. Kanti Chandra Pandey, *Abhinavagupta: An Historical and Philosophical Study*, 2nd ed. (Varanasi: Chowkhamba Sanskrit Series Office, 1963), 21.
4. Abhinavagupta, *Īśvara Pratyabhijñā Vivṛti Vimarśinī (IPVV)*, ed. Paṇḍit Madhusudan Kaul Shāstrī, 3 vols. (Delhi: Akay Reprints, 1985), IPVV 3:260: "When those [beings] belonging to *Māyā*—even down to an insect—when they do their own deeds, that which is to be done first stirs in the heart." "Māyīyānāṁ kīṭāntānāṁ svakāryakaraṇāvasare yat kāryaṁ purā hṛdaye sphurati."
5. Bhartṛhari, *Vākya Padīya*, 1:22: "tad vyākaraṇam āgamya paraṁ brahmādhigamyate." Downloaded from GRETIL—Göttingen Register of Electronic Texts in Indian Languages and related Indological materials from Central and Southeast Asia via "Yves Ramseier's page on Bhartṛhari and other South Asia and Sanskrit documents: http://gretil.sub.uni-goettingen.de/gretil.htm#Gram.
6. Ibid., 1.1: anādinidhanam brahma śabdatattvaṁ yad akṣaram | vivartate 'rthabhāvena prakriyā jagato yataḥ || 1.1 ||."
7. Ibid., 1.14: "tad dvāram apavargasya vāṅmalānāṁ cikitsitam." "That [grammar] is the door to the final state, the end of transmigration; it is the cure for the impurities of speech."
8. Ibid., 1.1b-1.2: "vivartate 'rthabhāvena prakriyā jagato yataḥ || 1.1 || ekam eva yad āmnātaṁ bhinnaśaktivyapāśrayāt | apṛthaktve 'pi śaktibhyaḥ pṛthak-tveneva vartate || 1.2 ||." See also *Padīya*, 1.120, where Bhartṛhari tells us that the world evolves from the word—this the "wise" (*amnāyavido*) know.
9. The mantra here is *"sauḥ."*
10. These three levels are Śiva, the highest God, Śakti, the Goddess, and Nara, the human.
11. Indeed, this idea of speech is resonant with Bhartṛhari's understanding of speech as foundational to the identities and consciousness of beings, "the in-

ner consciousness of beings, acting both inside and out . . . without the word, things would be like a stone or piece of wood, without life." See *Vākya Padīya*, 1:126–27. See also Natalia Isaeva's discussion of Bhartṛhari in Natalia Isaeva, *From Early Vedanta to Kashmir Shaivism* (Albany: State University of New York Press, 1995), 110–19. It is, of course, the condition of sentience itself which characterizes the highest level, *parā* that makes the third level more consonant with the thought of Butler or Whorf.

12. Loriliai Biernacki, "Words and Word-Bodies: Writing the Religious Body," in *Futures of the Religious Past: Words* (New York: Fordham University Press, forthcoming).
13. Abhinavagupta, *Parātriṃśikāvivaraṇa*, downloaded from S. D. Vasudeva's Indology E-text webpage: http://homepage.mac.com/somadevah/etx/PaTri Viv.txt, p. 210: śravaṇākhyayā sattayā tiṣṭhantī śravaṇasampuṭasphuṭakramika svaspandamaya varṇarāśi niṣṭham aikātmyāpād anarūpasaṃkalanānusaṃdhā-nākhyaṃ svātantryam / tena hi vinā kalakalalīnaśabdaviśeṣaṃ śṛṇvann api na śṛṇomīti vyavaharati pramātā /
14. Ibid., pp. 190–91.
15. Ibid.
16. Ibid., p. 196: evaṃ tāvat tu syāt, avivakṣite pratiyogiviśeṣe tamapprayogaḥ, pratiyogiviśeṣāpekṣāyāṃ tu tarap / "However, it should be understood in this way: the superlative suffix *-tama* is used without a specific counterpart, an other that mutually defines it. However, the comparative suffix *-tara* implies a counterpart, an other."
17. Abhinavagupta, *Īśvara Pratyabhijñā Vivṛti Vimarśinī*, 3:312: "iti kākākṣivat."
18. Abhinavagupta, *Parātriṃśikāvivaraṇa*, downloaded from S. D. Vasudeva's Indology E-text webpage: http://homepage.mac.com/somadevah/etx/PaTriViv .txt, p. 193: svayam anargalānapekṣaprathācamatkārasāratvāt.
19. Ibid., pp. 193–95. His exegesis on this single word, giving sixteen different meanings takes two full pages of Sanskrit text. The number 16 is also significant, symbolic of the full moon, and with this the idea of completion.
20. Loriliai Biernacki, *Renowned Goddess of Desire: Women, Sex and Speech in Tantra* (Oxford: Oxford University Press, 2007), 129.
21. Abhinavagupta, *Parātriṃśikāvivaraṇa*, downloaded from S. D. Vasudeva's Indology E-text webpage: http://homepage.mac.com/somadevah/etx/PaTriViv .txt, p. 215: garbhīkṛtānantasṛṣṭyādikoṭiśato yasmāt prasṛta etad eva tad anut-taram / yad uktam/ yataḥ sarvam.
22. Ibid., p. 214 / śrītantrasamuccaye 'pi
    Q: naraśaktiśivāveśi viśvam etat sadā sthitam /
    Q: vyavahāre krimīṇāṃ ca sarvajñānāṃ ca sarvaśaḥ.

23. Ibid., pp. 211–12: naraśaktiśivātmakaṃ hīdaṃ sarvaṃ trikarūpam eva / tatra yat kevalaṃ svātmany avasthitaṃ tat kevalaṃ jaḍarūpayogi mukhyatayā narātmakaṃ ghaṭas tiṣṭhatītivat / eṣa eva prathamapuruṣaviṣayaḥ śeṣaḥ / yat punar idam ity api bhāsamānaṃ yadāmantryamāṇatayā āmantrakāhaṃbhāvasamacchāditatadbhinnedaṃbhāvaṃ yuṣmacchabdavyapadeśyaṃ tac chāktaṃ rūpaṃ tvaṃ tiṣṭhasīti / atra hy eṣa eva yuṣmacchabdārtho āmantraṇ atattvaṃ ca / tathā hi yathāhaṃ tiṣṭhāmi tathaiva ayam apīti tasyāpy asmadrūpāvacchinnāhaṃbhāvacamatkārasvātantryam avicchinnāhaṃcamatkāreṇaivābhimanvāna āmantrayate yuṣmadarthena madhyamapuruṣeṇa vyapadiśati / seyaṃ hi bhagavatī parāparā / sarvathā punar avicchinnacamatkāranirapekṣasvātantryāhaṃvimarśe ahaṃ tiṣṭhāmīti parābhaṭṭārikodayo yatrottamatvaṃ puruṣasya.
24. Ibid., p. 212: narātmāno jaḍā api tyaktatatpūrvarūpāḥ śāktaśaivarūpabhājo bhavanti, śṛṇuta grāvāṇaḥ [cf. Mahābhāṣya 3.1.1; cf. Vākyapadīya 3 Puruṣasamuddeśa 2], meruḥ śikhariṇām ahaṃ bhavāmi [Bhagavadgītā 10.23].
25. Ibid., p. 212: vicchedito 'pi yuṣmadartha evam eveti / ata eva aliṅge yuṣmadasmadī gīte. "Even though the meaning of "you" also contains an idea of separation, it is like [the "I"]. As it is sung, 'the you and the I are genderless.'"
26. Ibid., p. 198: Q: api tv ātmabalasparśāt puruṣas tatsamo bhavet [Spandakārikā 1.8].
27. Ibid., p. 213.
28. See Diana Eck, *Darśana: Seeing the Divine Image in India* (New York: Columbia University Press, 1998).
29. Abhinavagupta, *Parātriṃśikāvivaraṇa*, downloaded from S. D. Vasudeva's Indology E-text webpage: http://homepage.mac.com/somadevah/etx/PaTriViv.txt, p. 212: sarvaṃ hi sarvātmakam iti.
30. Ibid., p. 204: prakāśasya hi svābhāvikākṛtrimaparavāṅmantravīryacamatkārātm a ahaṃ iti / yathoktaṃ Q: prakāśasyātmaviśrāntir ahaṃbhāvo hi kīrtitaḥ / [Ajaḍapramātṛsiddhi 22cd] iti / tad eva guhyam atirahasyam.
31. Ibid., p. 214: na hṛdayaṃgamagāminī gīḥ.

ONE AND THE MANY: THE STRUGGLE TO UNDERSTAND PLURALITY WITHIN THE INDIAN TRADITION AND ITS IMPLICATIONS FOR THE DEBATE ON RELIGIOUS PLURALITY TODAY | S. WESLEY ARIARAJAH

1. Panikkar began Christology-based explorations in his *Unknown Christ of Hinduism*, where he depended mainly on reinterpreting the Logos Christology (see Raimundo Panikkar, *Unknown Christ of Hinduism: Toward an Ecumenical*

Christophany [London, UK: Darton, Longman and Todd, 1964]). In his later writings, especially with his concept of Cosmotheandrism, he moved toward a more trinitarian exploration of the issue.
2. Karl Rahner developed this in his *Beyond the Impasse: Towards a Pneumatological Theology of Religions* (Grand Rapids, Mich.: Baker Academic, 2003).
3. First argued forcefully in his *Salvations: Truth and Difference in Religion* (Maryknoll, N.Y.: Orbis Books, 1995), Heim develops this thinking with painstakingly detailed explorations in *The Depth of the Riches: A Trinitarian Theology of Religious Ends* (Grand Rapids, Mich.: Eerdmans, 2000).
4. See Mādhava Acharya, *Sarva-Darsana-Samgraha, or Review of different systems of Hindu Philosophy* (Toronto: University of Toronto Libraries, 2011).
5. These are *Sāṁkhya, Yoga, Nyāya, Vaiśeshika, Purva-Mimāmsa* and *Uttra-Mimāmsa (Vedanta)*.
6. The discussion of the Sāṁkhya system is based on the *Sāṁkhya Kārika* as summarized by M. H. Harrison in his *Hindu Monism and Pluralism—As Found in the Upanishads and in the Philosophies Dependent on Them* (London: Oxford University Press, 1932), 249–82.
7. The possible evolution of the universe from un-manifest prakṛti is compared in the *Sāṁkhya Kārika* to the transformation of water into ice or steam (stanza 16) or of clay into pots (stanza 67) in Īśvara Kṛṣṇa, *The Sāṁkhya Kārika* (Charleston: Bibliobazaar, 2001).
8. Ibid., stanzas 12, 13.
9. Ibid., stanzas, 61–67.
10. The Śaiva Siddhānta appears to have originated in North India and had a long process of development. It was, however, systematized into a philosophic system in the twelfth century in Tamil Nadu by Meykandar and his disciples. There are fourteen texts related to Siddhānta. The discussion here is based on Meykandar's *Śivajnanabotham*.
11. Anantanand Rambachan, "The Value of the World as the Mystery of God in Advaita Vedanta," *Journal of Dharma* 14 (July–September 1989): 292.
12. Ibid., 293–94.

DIFFERENTIAL PLURALISM AND TRINITARIAN THEOLOGIES OF RELIGION | S. MARK HEIM

1. S. Mark Heim, *Salvations: Truth and Difference in Religion*, Faith Meets Faith (Maryknoll, N.Y.: Orbis Books, 1995); S. Mark Heim, *The Depth of the Riches: A Trinitarian Theology of Religious Ends*, Sacra Doctrina (Grand Rapids, Mich.: W. B. Eerdmans, 2001).

2. This is a tendency in Raimundo Panikkar's trinitarian theology, and one I see more faintly in John Thatamanil's proposal.
3. Wesley Ariarajah, "One and the Many: The Struggle to Understand Plurality within the Indian Tradition and Its Implications for the Debate on Religious Plurality Today," a paper delivered at the Transdisciplinary Theological Colloquium at Drew University, Madison, N.J., 2010, and revised for publication in this volume.
4. If some contrasting religious ends are attainable, then those in such states of attainment need not necessarily know or acknowledge that others exist.
5. Hick started his career as a philosophical apologist for the meaningfulness of Christian theological propositions. His pluralistic hypothesis extends this concern to the religions collectively, narrowing the front to be defended to a few generic claims and consigning to cognitive irrelevance the complicating differences. The religions gain in validity what they lose in specificity.
6. Hence the critiques of pluralist theologies of religion that are advanced from socially engaged progressive perspectives in addition to those advanced from traditionalist ones.
7. See Francis X. Clooney, *Comparative Theology: Deep Learning across Religious Borders* (Malden, Mass.: Wiley-Blackwell, 2010); Francis X. Clooney, ed., *The New Comparative Theology: Interreligious Insights from the Next Generation* (London: T & T Clark, 2010).
8. The rise of "pluralistic" theologies of religion, insofar as they focused on assumed commonalities in all religion, was itself not a strong impetus toward interest in the differential qualities of the traditions. See the discussion of Griffin below.
9. David Ray Griffin, ed., *Deep Religious Pluralism*, 1st ed. (Louisville, Ky.: Westminster John Knox Press, 2005), 5.
10. Ibid., 3.
11. Ibid., 24.
12. He summarizes these criticisms in arguments that identist pluralism "falsely claims a neutral universality, that it is not really Christian, that it is not even truly pluralistic, and that it entails a debilitating relativism." Ibid., 4.
13. I see Griffin's point, in this context, when he objects that I fuel this confusion by calling myself an inclusivist. However, I think Griffin has not considered the extent to which the terms of his generic definition of pluralism may be affected by the developments he recounts. He seems not to register that both of his propositions in generic pluralism operate only in the plane that is shared in the battle between identist pluralism and traditional exclusivism and inclusivism—the assumption that there is only one real religious end. Once

that has been changed, what does it mean to deny that Christianity is the sole constitutive vehicle of salvation (the Christian end)? Or for that matter, what does it mean to affirm that other religions are affirmatively vehicles of salvation (as opposed to their own religious end)? Thus, though Griffin is certain I am a differential pluralist, it is not clear that I qualify as a generic pluralist, since I would *not* deny that Christianity is the sole constitutive vehicle of salvation.

14. David Ray Griffin, ""Religious Pluralism: Generic, Identist and Deep,"" in *Deep Religious Pluralism*, ed. David Ray Griffin (Louisville: Westminster John Knox, 2005), 24. Griffin uses both "differential pluralism" and "deep pluralism" but prefers the latter. He sees such pluralism as pioneered by John Cobb and advanced in Heim, *Salvations: Truth and Difference in Religion*.
15. Paul F. Knitter and John Hick, eds., *The Myth of Christian Uniqueness: Toward a Pluralistic Theology of Religions*, Faith Meets Faith (Maryknoll, N.Y.: Orbis Books, 1987), viii.
16. Only much later did I become aware of the work of Jacques Dupuis, who can count as another major example of this dynamic.
17. I say "trinitarian thought," because the affinity does not apply to Christian theologians who simply defend the Trinity as a Christian distinctive rather than engaging it as a guide for their own thinking.
18. See John Cobb, "Beyond Pluralism," in *Christian Uniqueness Reconsidered*, ed. Gavin D'Costa, Faith Meets Faith (Maryknoll, N.Y.: Orbis Books, 1990).
19. A good survey of recent work in this area is Veli-Matti,Kärkkainen, *Trinity and Religious Pluralism: The Doctrine of the Trinity in Christian Theology of Religions* (Aldershot, Hants, Eng.; Ashgate, 2004).
20. John Thatamanil, "Religious Diversity after Religion: Rethinking Theology of Religious Pluralism," a paper presented at a Luce Seminar, 2010, 11.
21. S. Mark Heim, *Is Christ the Only Way?: Christian Faith in a Pluralistic World* (Valley Forge, Penn.: Judson Press, 1985).
22. For example, see John J. Makransky, ""Buddha and Christ as Mediations of Ultimate Reality: A Mahayana Buddhist Perspective,"" in *Buddhism and Christianity in Dialogue*, ed. Perry Schmidt-Leukel (Norwich, Norfolk, Eng.: SCM Press, 2005); Kristin Beise Kiblinger, *Buddhist Inclusivism: Attitudes towards Religious Others*, Ashgate World Philosophies Series (Aldershot, Hants, Eng.: Ashgate, 2005).
23. Raimundo Panikkar, *The Trinity and the Religious Experience of Man: Icon-Person-Mystery* (Maryknoll, N.Y.: Orbis Books, 1973), 41.
24. John Thatamanil, "God as Ground, Contingency and Relation: Trinity, Polydoxy and Religious Diversity," in *Polydoxy: Theology of Multiplicity and Rela-*

tion, ed. Catherine Keller and Laurel C. Schneider (London: Routledge Press, 2010), 17.

SPIRITED TRANSFORMATIONS: PNEUMATOLOGY AS A RESOURCE FOR COMPARATIVE THEOLOGY | HOLLY HILLGARDNER

1. Sharon Betcher elaborates on Catherine Keller's specifically nonfoundationalist metaphor of "grounding the spirit" (Catherine Keller, *Face of the Deep: A Theology of Becoming* [New York: Routledge, 2003], 233) as Betcher works toward an ecofeminist pneumatology in "Grounding the Spirit: An Ecofeminist Pneumatology," in *Ecospirit: Religions and Philosophies for the Earth*, ed. Laurel Kearns and Catherine Keller (New York: Fordham University Press, 2007), 315–36.
2. Francis X. Clooney, "More or Deeper? What Should Be Next in (My) Hindu-Christian Study?" *Journal of Hindu Christian Studies* 21 (2008): 65.
3. The Comparative Theology Group of the American Academy of Religion, "2006 Statement for the Comparative Theology Group for the AAR," 2. This statement was presented at a gathering of the Comparative Theology Group during the annual meeting of the AAR, November 2006, Washington, D.C.
4. For further reference see John Hick et al., *More Than One Way? Four Views on Salvation in a Pluralistic World* (Grand Rapids, Mich.: Zondervan Press, 1995); Paul F. Knitter, "A New Pentecost? A Pneumatological Theology of Religions," *Current Dialogue* 19 (January 1991): 32–41; Karl Rahner, "Aspects of European Theology," in *Theological Investigations*, vol. 21, trans. Hugh M. Riley (New York: Crossroad, 1988).
5. David Ray Griffin's defense of John Cobb's pluralist methodology helpfully elucidates Cobb's pluralism as having more room for some of the challenges of postmodernity. See Griffin's *Deep Religious Pluralism* (Louisville, Ky.: Westminster John Knox Press, 2005), part 1.
6. David Tracy, "Comparative Theology," in *Encyclopedia of Religion*, ed. Mircea Eliade, vol. 14 (New York: Macmillan, 1987), 454.
7. Peter C. Hodgson, *Winds of the Spirit: A Constructive Christian Theology* (Louisville, Ky.: Westminster John Knox Press, 1994), 280.
8. Keller, *Face of the Deep*, 232.
9. Ibid.
10. Laurel C. Schneider, *Beyond Monotheism: A Theology of Multiplicity* (New York: Routledge, 2008), 166.
11. Ibid., 171.
12. Ibid., 167.

13. Hodgson, *Winds of the Spirit*, 285.
14. Keller, *Face of the Deep*, 233.
15. Schneider, *Beyond Monotheism*, 115.
16. Ibid., 203.
17. Hodgson, *Winds of the Spirit*, 171.
18. Schneider, *Beyond Monotheism*, 162.
19. Ibid., 205.
20. Keller, *Face of the Deep*, 230.
21. Ibid., 232.
22. Robert Cummings Neville, *Behind the Masks of God: An Essay toward Comparative Theology* (Albany: State University of New York Press, 1991), 71–72.
23. Francis X. Clooney, *Theology after Vedanta: An Experiment in Comparative Theology* (Albany: State University of New York Press, 1993), 187.
24. Catherine of Siena, *The Letters of St. Catherine of Siena*, vol. I, trans. Suzanne Noffke, vol. II (Tempe: Arizona Center for Medieval and Renaissance Studies, 2000), 601–2.
25. Michelle Voss Roberts, "Worldly Advaita? Limits and Possibilities for an Ecofriendly Nondualism," *Religious Studies Review* 34, no. 3 (2008): 142.
26. See Rita Gross, "Feminist Theology as Theology of Religions," in *The Cambridge Companion to Feminist Theology*, ed. Susan Frank Parsons (Cambridge: Cambridge University Press, 2002).

EXCESS, REVERSIBILITY, AND APOPHASIS:
REREADING GENDER IN FEMINIST TRINITIES |
SARA ROSENAU

1. Laurel Schneider, however, cautions against too easily collapsing and understanding "one" as "sameness" and "many" as "diversity." See Laurel C. Schneider, *Beyond Monotheism: A Theology of Multiplicity* (New York: Routledge, 2008).
2. Judith Butler, *Giving an Account of Oneself* (New York: Fordham University Press, 2005), 81.
3. Anne Fausto-Sterling, *Sexing the Body: Gender Politics and the Construction of Sexuality* (New York: Basic Books, 2000), 51.
4. Judith Butler, *Undoing Gender* (New York: Routledge, 2004), 197.
5. Heidi Beirich, "New Intelligence Report Finds Gays Most Targeted for Violent Hate Crimes," *Southern Poverty Law Center*, November 22, 2010. http://www.splcenter.org/blog/2010/11/22/new-intelligence-report-finds-gays-most-targeted-for-violent-hate-crimes (June 9, 2011). Although the article references LGBT people, the FBI report analyzed data from 1995 to 2008 and did not in-

clude gender identity. Gender identity was included in the Matthew Shepard and James Byrd, Jr. Hate Crimes Prevention Act passed in 2009, and violence against transgendered individuals is now tracked by the FBI. See http://www.fbi.gov/about-us/investigate/civilrights/hate_crimes/shepard-byrd-act-brochure (June 13, 2012).

6. National Center for Transgender Equality and the National Gay and Lesbian Task Force, *National Transgender Discrimination Survey*, November 2009. http://www.transequality.org/Resources/NCTE_prelim_survey_econ.pdf (June 9, 2011).

7. Elizabeth A. Johnson, *She Who Is: The Mystery of God in Feminist Theological Discourse* (New York: Crossroad Publishing, 1993). For other early feminist trinitarian explorations see Catherine Mawry LaCugna, "The Trinitarian Mystery of God," in *Systematic Theology: Roman Catholic Perspectives*, vol. 1, ed. Francis Schüssler Fiorenza and John P. Galvin (Minneapolis: Fortress Press, 1991), 149–92; and Asphodel P. Long, *In a Chariot Drawn by Lions: The Search for the Female in Deity* (London: Women's Press, 1992).

8. Johnson, *She Who Is*, 104. For a condensed account of the apophatic foundation of Johnson's argument see Elizabeth Johnson, "The Incomprehensibility of God and the Image of God: Male and Female," in *Freeing Theology: The Essentials of Theology in Feminist Perspective*, ed. Catherine Mowry LaCugna (San Francisco: Harper, 1993), 115–37.

9. Johnson, *She Who Is*, 5.

10. Ibid., 55.

11. Ibid., 5.

12. Luce Irigaray, "Divine Women," in *Sexes and Genealogies*, trans. Gillian C. Gill (New York: Columbia University Press, 1993), 70.

13. For foundational second-wave works on feminist theory and race see bell hooks, *Ain't I a Woman: Black Women and Feminism* (Boston: South End Press, 1981), and Angela Y. Davis, *Women, Race, Class* (New York: Random House, 1981).

14. Irigaray is the forerunner of this development in continental feminist philosophy. See Luce Irigaray, *This Sex Which Is Not One*, trans. Catherine Porter and Carolyn Burke (Ithaca, N.Y.: Cornell University Press, 1985).

15. Rosi Braidotti, *Nomadic Subjects* (New York: Columbia University Press, 1994), 4.

16. Judith Butler, *Gender Trouble: Feminism and the Subversion of Identity* (New York: Routledge, 1999), 173.

17. Ibid., xi.

18. Butler, *Undoing Gender*, 4.

19. Johnson, *She Who Is*, 57.

20. Janet Martin Soskice, "Trinity and Feminism," in *The Cambridge Companion to Feminist Theology*, ed. Susan Frank Parsons (Cambridge: Cambridge University Press, 2002), 146. This is not to say that Johnson's work is simply one of gender essentialism. She undertakes a nuanced deconstruction of patriarchal masculinity, and her reconstruction of female imagery does not slip easily into feminine stereotypes.
21. Marcella Althaus-Reid, *Queer God* (New York: Routledge, 2003), 49–50.
22. Ibid.
23. Gloria Anzaldua, *Borderlands/La Frontera: The New Mestiza*, 2nd ed. (San Francisco: Aunt Lute Books, 1999), 103.
24. Braidotti, *Nomadic Subjects*, 14.
25. Ibid., 22–23.
26. Ibid., 29.
27. Jenny Daggers, "The Prodigal Daughter: Orthodoxy Revisited," *Feminist Theology* 15, no. 2 (2007): 199–200.
28. Ibid., 198. Regarding a critique of feminist methodology and orthodox doctrine see Kathryn Greene-McCreight, *Feminist Reconstructions of Christian Doctrine: Narrative Analysis and Appraisal* (Oxford: Oxford University Press, 2000).
29. Daggers, "Prodigal Daughter," 200.
30. Johnson, *She Who Is*, 127.
31. Ibid.
32. Ibid., 131.
33. Ibid., 129.
34. Ibid.
35. Ibid., 128. For this reason Johnson begins her constructive trinitarian work with Spirit.
36. Ibid., 130.
37. Butler, *Undoing Gender*, 217.
38. Daniel Boyarin, *Border Lines: The Partition of Judaeo-Christianity* (Philadelphia: University of Pennsylvania Press, 2004), 115.
39. Johnson, *She Who Is*, 97.
40. Quoted in Johnson, *She Who Is*, 98.
41. Johnson, *She Who Is*, 98.
42. Ibid.
43. Elizabeth Schüssler Fiorenza, *Jesus: Miriam's Child, Sophia's Prophet* (New York: Continuum Publishing, 1999), 138. Schüssler Fiorenza suggests that Philo's working with Sophia may have been in response to the attraction of many Jews to an existing wisdom tradition that personified a Divine Sophia. Other theorists have gone further, theorizing that Philo is reacting to the popular

Isis cults in the first century. See Martin Scott, *Sophia and the Johannine Jesus: Journal for the Study of the New Testament* (Sheffield, Eng.: JSOT Press, 1992). For an overview of Wisdom's role in theology see Burton L Mack, "Wisdom Myth and Mythology: An Essay in Understanding a Theological Tradition," *Interpretations* 24, no. 1 (1970): 46–60.

44. Boyarin, *Borderlines*, 113,
45. Ibid., 112. Quoting Erwin Goodenough. Boyarin notes that the patristic scholar Virginia Burrus also argues that Logos theology emerged from scriptural interpretation of worshipping and scholarly communities rather then from philosophical Platonism. See Virginia Burrus, "Creatio Ex Libidine: Reading Ancient Logos Differently," in *Other Testaments: Derrida and Religion*, ed. Kevin Hart and Yvonne Sherwood (London: Routledge, 2004).
46. Johnson, *She Who Is*, 133.
47. Ibid., 136.
48. Ibid., 143–44, 148.
49. Ibid., 148.
50. Gregory of Nyssa uses metaphors of water and the light of the rainbow as examples of the Trinity. See Sarah Coakley's discussion of his trinitarian thought in Sarah Coakley, *Powers and Submissions: Spirituality, Philosophy and Gender* (Oxford, UK: Blackwell, 2002), 121.
51. Soskice, "Trinity and Feminism," 144.
52. Johnson, *She Who Is*, 96. For further work supporting a feminist interpretation of John see Alison E. Jasper, *The Shining Garment of the Text: Gendered Readings of John's Prologue*, JSNTSup 165; Gender, Culture, Theory 6 (Sheffield, Eng.: Sheffield Academic Press, 1998); Sharon H. Ringe, *Wisdom's Friends: Community and Christology in the Fourth Gospel* (Louisville, Ky.: Westminster/John Knox Press, 1999); and Michael E. Willett, *Wisdom Christology in the Fourth Gospel* (San Francisco: Mellen Research University Press, 1992).
53. Johnson, *She Who Is*, 97.
54. Ibid., 88. Johnson outlines Wisdom's work in Proverbs, particularly 9:5: "Come, eat of my bread, and drink of the wine I have mixed."
55. Ibid., 97.
56. Ibid., 151.
57. Ibid., 152.
58. Ibid., 98.
59. Ibid., 151.
60. Ibid., 99. The fourth-century christological controversies are of particular theological importance in further investigating the work of reversibility in traversing gender's borders in the Trinity. Although Johnson doesn't give as

much attention to this time period as she does to the gospels, recent feminist studies of the controversy complicate the story of Sophia's repression by demonstrating how masculine and feminine reversibility are at work even in the theorization of male dominance. See Virginia Burrus, *"Begotten Not Made": Conceiving Manhood in Late Antiquity* (Stanford, Calif.: Stanford University Press, 2000).

61. Johnson, *She Who Is*, 99.
62. Cited in Virginia Burrus, *Sex Lives of Saints: An Erotics of Ancient Hagiography* (Philadelphia: University of Pennsylvania Press, 2004), 76.
63. Shoshana Felman, *What Does a Woman Want?: Reading and Sexual Difference* (Baltimore: Johns Hopkins University Press, 1993), 55.
64. See Rosemary Radford Ruether's treatment of this question in *Sexism and God-Talk* (Boston: Beacon Press, 1983). The contemporary relevance of this question is striking in the light of the controversy over the installation of the sculpture "Crucified Woman" at the University of Toronto. See Doris Jean Dyke's account of the controversy in *Crucified Woman* (Toronto: United Church Publishing House, 1991).
65. Johnson, *She Who Is*, 156.
66. Ibid., 163.
67. Ibid., 157–60.
68. Ibid., 157.
69. Ibid., 161. For a contemporary feminist account of Christ's kenosis see Anna Mercedes, *Power For: Feminism and Christ's Self-Giving* (New York: T&T Clark, 2011).
70. Ibid., 162.
71. Ibid., 165.
72. Sarah Coakley, *Powers and Submissions*, 127–28. Coakley expands on the Trinity and the erotic in "The Trinity, Prayer, and Sexuality," in *Oxford Readings in Feminism: Feminism and Theology*, ed. Janet Martin Soskice and Diana Lipton (Oxford: Oxford University Press, 2003).
73. Ibid., 129.
74. Johnson, *She Who Is*, 62.
75. Ibid., 105. During the conference that inspired this volume, comparative theologian John Thatamanil helpfully clarified the difference between the Kantian noumena, which proposes that we are fundamentally cut off from all of reality, and apophasis. Apophasis, he argued, claims that God always exceeds every disclosure, but this doesn't mean that we can't attempt to describe the disclosure of the Divine. This argument fits well within this essay where the excess and apophasis of the Divine might be conceived of as two sides of the same coin.

76. Ibid.
77. Ibid., 108. Augustine writes, "In loving, we already possess God as known better than we do the fellow human being whom we love. Much better, in fact, because God is nearer, more present, more certain." Johnson also expands on Aquinas's account of the mystery of God.
78. Ibid., 170.
79. Catherine Keller, "Apophasis of Gender: A Fourfold Unsaying of Feminist Theology," *Journal of the American Academy of Religion* 76, no. 4 (2008): 912.
80. Johnson, *She Who Is*, 117–18.
81. Ibid., 174.
82. Keller, "Apophasis of Gender," 905.
83. Ibid., 909.
84. Ibid.
85. Johnson, *She Who Is*, 65.
86. For a more recent elaboration of this point see Kathryn Tanner, "In the Image of the Invisible," in *Apophatic Bodies: Negative Theology, Incarnation, and Relationality*, ed. Chris Boesel and Catherine Keller (New York: Fordham University Press, 2010).
87. Johnson, *She Who Is*, 61.
88. Ibid., 66.
89. Ibid., 71.
90. Ibid., 87.
91. Ibid., 176.
92. Ibid., 178.
93. Ibid., 186.
94. Ibid., 204–5.
95. Quoted in Johnson, *She Who Is*, 212.
96. Ibid., 216.
97. Ibid., 218.
98. See Kathryn Tanner's essay in this volume, "Absolute Difference."
99. Keller, "Apophasis of Gender," 913. Here Keller is inspired by Nicholas of Cusa's *De docta ignorancia*, in which he admits a "knowing ignorance" about God.
100. Soskice, "Trinity and Feminism," 139.
101. Quoted in Coakley, *Powers and Submissions*, 122.
102. Keller, "Apophasis of Gender," 918.
103. For an elaboration on Christ's queer aspects see Patrick Cheng, *From Sin to Amazing Grace: Discovering the Queer Christ* (New York: Seabury Books, 2012).
104. For recent work in transgender theology see Justin Tanis, *Trans-Gendered: Theology, Ministry, and Communities of Faith* (Cleveland, Ohio: Pilgrim Press, 2003);

Lisa Isherwood and Marcella Althaus-Reid, eds., *Trans/formations* (London, UK: SCM Press, 2009). For a brilliant new overview of queer theology from a systematic perspective see Patrick S. Cheng, *Radical Love: An Introduction to Queer Theology* (New York: Seabury Books, 2011).
105. Keller, "Apophasis of Gender," 911.
106. Butler, *Giving an Account of Oneself*, 43.
107. Butler, *Undoing Gender*, 203.
108. Johnson, *She Who Is*, 205.

DOXOLOGICAL DIVERSITIES AND CANTICLE MULTIPLICITIES: THE TRINITARIAN ANTHROPOLOGIES OF DAVID H. KELSEY AND IVONE GEBARA | JACOB J. ERICKSON

1. See Gilles Deleuze and Félix Guattari, *A Thousand Plateaus: Capitalism and Schizophrenia*, trans. Brian Massumi (Minneapolis: University of Minnesota Press, 1987).
2. Speaking of entanglements, thanks for those who have encouraged me along the way in this essay: Catherine Keller offered vital feedback, and Natalie, Jack, and Oscar Williams offered insightful responses prior to and at the initial Drew conference itself. For their unwavering support and the conviviality of friendship, this piece is, with love, for William Lynam, Noah Niermann, and Emily Moen.
3. *Evangelical Lutheran Worship* (Minneapolis: Augsburg Fortress, 2006), 490.
4. From John of Patmos's Revelation, picking up on Isaiah's vision of the seraphim.
5. Patrick S. Cheng observes that the doctrine of creation, for example, takes on new vitality in queer perspective. As he writes in his book, *Radical Love: An Introduction to Queer Theology* (New York: Seabury Books, 2011), 63: "Another way in which the doctrine of creation can be understood as God's outpouring of radical love is that it dissolves the dualism, or hierarchical relationship, of human beings and the rest of creation."
6. There is a risk involved in merging queer theory and ecological theory, as not much work has been done into their interrelationships. My hunch is these fields of thought are not isolated discourses, as we might commonly imagine. Emerging discourses on "queer ecology" rethink the heterosexist implications of human constructions of culture *and* nature in an integrated fashion. See the growing works of queer ecology: Catriona Mortimer-Sandilands and Bruce Erickson, eds., *Queer Ecologies: Sex, Nature, Politics, Desire* (Bloomington: Indiana University Press, 2010) and Noreen Giffney and Myra J. Hird, eds., *Queer-*

ing the Non/Human (Burlington, Vt.: Ashgate, 2008). For earlier attempts at a queer ecotheology see, for example, the multiple trends of ecofeminism and ecowomanism, as well as J. Michael Clark, *Beyond Our Ghettos: Gay Theology in Ecological Perspective* (Cleveland, Ohio: Pilgrim Press, 1993) and Daniel T. Spencer, *Gay and Gaia: Ethics, Ecology, and the Erotic* (Cleveland, Ohio: Pilgrim Press, 1996). My own project is particularly inspired by the work of Karen Barad and Timothy Morton. See Karen Barad, "Nature's Queer Performativity," *Qui Parle: Critical Humanities and Social Sciences* 19, no. 2 (2011): 121–58; and Timothy Morton, "Guest Column: Queer Ecology," *PMLA: Publication of the Modern Language Association of America* 125, no. 2 (2010): 273–82.

7. With similar sentiment, whales speak and tigers prowl the edges of Philip Clayton's article for this volume! For a contemporary gesture toward the vestiges, see, for example, Wolfhart Pannenberg, *Systematic Theology*, trans. Geoffrey W. Bromily, vol. 1 (Grand Rapids, Mich.: William B. Eerdmans, 1991), 287. The concept of the "vestige" is an oft-neglected topic from Catholic theology. A corollary to the *imago dei*, the vestige of the Trinity marks created reality. Pannenberg argues that the vestige can't connect to an explicit doctrine of God: "There may be a vestige of the Trinity in every creature, but it is impossible to deduce from this the divine Trinity of persons." Earlier in the history of Christian theology, Bonaventure explicates the concept of the vestige. And Karl Rahner, nostalgic for Bonaventure, refers to the concept of the vestiges, lamenting the loss of the Trinity's relation to Creation. See *The Trinity* (New York: Herder and Herder, 2005), 13–14. One might suspect the concept of vestiges offers nothing of God, but in an anthropological direction I suspect the vestige is actually a beautiful blurring, a queering of flesh and divine stories.

8. See, for example, the work of Catherine Mowry Lacugna, Robert W. Jensen, Jürgen Moltmann, Leonardo Boff, Miroslav Volf, and Kathryn Tanner. There is also a marvelous rejuvenation in the study of "everydayness" and everyday practices. See, for example, work as varied as that of David H. Kelsey, Emilie M. Townes, and John Caputo.

9. See Catherine Mowry LaCugna, *God for Us: The Trinity and Christian Life* (New York: HarperCollins, 1993), 1.

10. Kathryn Tanner looks at these *taxes*, too, in her work. See *Christ the Key* (New York: Cambridge University Press, 2010), 148.

11. David H. Kelsey, *Eccentric Existence: A Theological Anthropology* (Louisville, Ky.: Westminster John Knox Press, 2009), 121.

12. Kelsey is not known for wasting words!

13. Kelsey, *Eccentric Existence*, 122.

14. Ibid., 125.

15. Ibid., 128.
16. Ibid., 130.
17. Ibid., 131.
18. Later, Kelsey turns to root these narratives in Christology, and that singular focus possibly upends the beautiful multiplicity of narratives.
19. Kelsey, *Eccentric Existence*, 131.
20. Indeed, capturing a seraph in a butterfly net might be just as awkward.
21. Judith Butler, *Giving an Account of Oneself* (New York: Fordham University Press, 2005), 17.
22. On this point, see, generally, Virginia Burrus, *"Begotten Not Made": Conceiving Manhood in Late Antiquity* (Stanford, Calif.: Stanford University Press, 2000).
23. Kelsey's affinity for the biblical wisdom tradition holds tremendous possibility here for visions of Sophia and otherwise.
24. He is addressing a potential criticism that "construing creation, and with it human creatures, as the quotidian, and then construing the quotidian, and with it human creatures, in terms of human practices, privileges a particular model of the human person and a particular conceptual scheme with which to describe it." See Kelsey, *Eccentric Existence*, 199–200.
25. Ibid., 200.
26. Ibid.
27. See Mayra Rivera's meditation here on doxa, in "Glory: The First Passion of Theology?" in *Polydoxy: Theology of Multiplicity and Relation*, ed. Catherine Keller and Laurel C. Schneider (New York: Routledge, 2011), 167–85.
28. John J. Thatamanil, for example, offers the triad of Ground, Contingency, and Relation as a proposal for a new polydox understanding of God. See "God as Ground, Contingency, and Relation: Trinitarian Polydoxy and Religious Diversity," in *Polydoxy: Theology of Multiplicity and Relation*, ed. Catherine Keller and Laurel C. Schneider (New York: Routledge, 2011), 238–57.
29. These works include those by Gebara and, recently, Laurel Schneider's *Beyond Monotheism: A Theology of Multiplicity* (New York: Routledge, 2008).
30. I'm evoking this "grounding" metaphor for the particular function found in Catherine Keller, "Talking Dirty: Ground Is Not Foundation," in *Ecospirit: Religions and Philosophies for the Earth*, ed. Laurel Kearns and Catherine Keller (New York: Fordham University Press, 2007), 63–76.
31. Scholars generally point to John Damascene as an originator of the language of perichoresis. For LaCugna's treatment, see *God for Us*, 270–78.
32. Elizabeth A. Johnson. *She Who Is: The Mystery of God in Feminist Theological Discourse* (New York: Crossroad, 1992), 220.
33. Schneider, *Beyond Monotheism*, 124.

34. Ibid.
35. Ivone Gebara, *Longing for Running Water: Ecofeminism and Liberation*, trans. David Molineaux (Minneapolis: Fortress Press, 1999), 138.
36. And patriarchal language.
37. Gebara, *Running Water*, 139.
38. Ibid., 140.
39. Ibid.
40. Ibid., 147.
41. Ibid., 149.
42. Ibid., 149.
43. Ibid., 153.
44. Ibid., 153.
45. Ibid., 166.
46. Ibid., 167.
47. I'm also thinking of Alfred North Whitehead's idea of "mutual immanence" here. See, for example, Alfred North Whitehead, *Adventures of Ideas* (New York: Free Press, 1967), 197.
48. Ivone Gebara, *Out of the Depths: Women's Experience of Evil and Salvation* (Minneapolis: Fortress Press, 2002), 172.
49. Ibid.
50. Ibid.
51. Ibid.
52. Kathryn Tanner, "In the Image of the Invisible," in *Apophatic Bodies: Negative Theology, Incarnation, and Relationality*, ed. Chris Boesel and Catherine Keller (New York: Fordham University Press, 2010), 125. I'm not convinced by the term "plastic," but the metaphor works somewhat in the right direction.
53. Ibid., 126.
54. Ibid., 127
55. Alfred North Whitehead also argues for a kind of plasticity of nature in *Adventures of Ideas* (78).
56. See Mayra Rivera, *The Touch of Transcendence: A Postcolonial Theology of God* (Louisville, Ky.: Westminster John Knox Press, 2007), and Laurel Schneider, "Promiscuous Incarnation," in *The Embrace of Eros: Bodies, Desires, and Sexuality in Christianity*, ed. Margaret Kamitsuka (Minneapolis: Fortress Press, 2010), 231–46.
57. Catherine Pickstock is another theologian who picks up, to some extent, angelic doxology, invoking the sound-image of "seraphic voices" in *After Writing: On the Liturgical Consummation of Philosophy* (Malden, Mass.: Blackwell, 1998).

Her writing, however, takes on a form of orthodoxy with which I cannot align myself.

58. Pseudo-Dionysius, *The Complete Works*, trans. Colm Luibheid (Mahwah, N.J.: Paulist Press, 1987).
59. Angelus Silesius, *The Cherubinic Wanderer*, trans. Maria Shrady (Mahwah, N.J.: Paulist Press, 1986).
60. Ibid., 79.
61. A queer theological anthropology must envision using both angelic and demonic resources without equating one as good and the other as evil. This essay focuses on angelic possibilities; another work would home in on exploring the potential beauties of the "demonic." For their ambiguity, angels can be terrifying themselves.
62. Catherine Keller, "Be a Multiplicity: Ancestral Anticipations," in *Polydoxy: Theology of Multiplicity and Relation*, ed. Catherine Keller and Laurel Schneider (New York: Routledge, 2011), 95. For more on conviviality see Roland Faber and Catherine Keller's contribution to this volume.
63. Karen Barad, *Meeting the Universe Halfway: Quantum Physics and the Entanglement of Matter and Meaning* (Durham, N.C.: Duke University Press, 2007), 183.
64. Ibid., 183–84.
65. I'm riffing off of Laurel Schneider's language here, as alluded to earlier in this piece.

THE HOLY SPIRIT, THE STORY OF GOD | SAM LAURENT

1. Pseudo-Dionysius Areopagite, *The Divine Names and Mystical Theology*, trans. John D. Jones (Milwaukee, Wisc.: Marquette University Press, 1980), 127.
2. Eugene Rogers, "The Spirit Rests on the Son Paraphysically," in *The Lord and Giver of Life: Perspectives on Constructive Pneumatology*, ed. David H. Jensen (Louisville, Ky.: Westminster John Knox Press, 2008), 87.
3. Ibid., 88.
4. Ibid.
5. Ibid., 89.
6. Ibid.
7. Ibid.
8. Pseudo-Dionysius, *Divine Names*, 126.
9. Ibid.
10. Athanasius, *On the Incarnation: The Treatise De incarnatione Verbi Dei*, trans. Penelope Lawson, 1st ed. (New York: Macmillan, 1981), 4–5.

11. Eugene F. Rogers, *After the Spirit: A Constructive Pneumatology from Resources Outside the Modern West* (Grand Rapids, Mich.: Wm. B. Eerdmans, 2005), 47.
12. Ibid., 46.
13. Ibid., 47.
14. Kathryn Tanner, *Jesus, Humanity and the Trinity: A Brief Systematic Theology*, 1st ed. (Minneapolis: Fortress Press, 2001), 1.
15. Ibid.
16. Ibid., 2.
17. Ibid.
18. Kathryn Tanner, *God and Creation in Christian Theology: Tyranny or Empowerment?* (New York: Blackwell, 1988), 47.
19. Ibid., 48.
20. Tanner, *Jesus, Humanity and the Trinity*, 10.
21. Ibid, 20.
22. Ibid.
23. Kathryn Tanner, *Christ the Key* (New York: Cambridge University Press, 2010), 280.
24. Ibid., 281.
25. Ibid., 274.
26. Ibid., 276.
27. Ibid., 281.
28. Ibid., 296.
29. Ibid., 297.
30. Pseudo-Dionysius, *Divine Names*, 118.
31. Tanner, *Christ The Key*, 288.
32. Ibid., 290.
33. Ibid., 291.
34. Rogers, "Spirit Rests on the Son Paraphysically," 90.
35. Ibid., 95.
36. Laurel C. Schneider, *Beyond Monotheism: A Theology of Multiplicity* (New York: Routledge, 2008), ix.
37. Ibid., 1.
38. Ibid., 142.
39. Ibid., 108.
40. Ibid., 114.
41. Ibid., 115.
42. Ibid.
43. Ibid., 125.
44. Ibid., 198.

ABSOLUTE DIFFERENCE | KATHRYN TANNER

1. Thomas Aquinas, *Summa Contra Gentiles*, bk. 2: Creation, trans. James F. Anderson (Notre Dame, Ind.: University of Notre Dame Press, 1975), chap. 45, sec. 2, 136–37.
2. Origen, *On First Principles*, trans. G. W. Butterworth (Gloucester, Mass.: Peter Smith, 1973), 134.
3. See Plotinus, *The Enneads*, trans. Stephen MacKenna (London: Penguin Books, 1991), Sixth Ennead, Ninth Tractate, sec. 8, 545: "Thus the Supreme as containing no otherness is ever present with us; we with it when we put otherness away."
4. *Meister Eckhart: Teacher and Preacher*, ed. Bernard McGinn, Classics of Western Spirituality (Mahwah, N.J.: Paulist Press, 1986), 154.
5. *Meister Eckhart: The Essential Sermons, Commentaries, Treatises, and Defense*, trans. Edmund College and Bernard McGinn, Classics of Western Spirituality (Mahwah, N.J.: Paulist Press, 1981), 190.
6. Ibid., 165.
7. Ibid., 200.
8. See Fran O'Rourke, *Pseudo-Dionysius and the Metaphysics of Aquinas* (Notre Dame, Ind.: University of Notre Dame Press, 1992), 126, 155–56, 159–60, 190, 192–96.
9. Thomas Aquinas, *Summa Contra Gentiles*, bk. 2, chap. 45, sec. 2, 136–37.
10. See O'Rourke, *Pseudo-Dionysius*, 155–56, 159–60, 192–94.
11. Thomas Aquinas, Summa Contra Gentiles, bk. 1: God, trans. Anton C. Pegis (Notre Dame, Ind.: University of Notre Dame Press, 1955), chap. 28, sec. 2, 135.
12. Pseudo-Dionysius, "The Divine Names," in *Pseudo-Dionysius: The Complete Works*, trans. Colm Luibheid, Classics of Western Spirituality (Mahwah, N.J.: Paulist Press, 1987), chap. 1, sec. 7, 56; and chap. 5, sec. 8, 101–2.
13. Ibid., chap. 4, sec. 7, 77.
14. Ibid., chap. 5, sec. 8, 101–2.
15. Ibid., chap. 8, sec. 7, 13; chap. 10, sec. 2, 122.
16. Ibid., chap. 8, sec. 9, 114; chap. 10, sec. 3, 123.
17. Ibid., chap. 2, sec. 11, 66, 67; my emphases.
18. Ibid., 66.
19. Ibid., chap. 13, sec. 2, 128.
20. Ibid., chap. 13, sec. 3, 129.
21. Ibid.
22. Ibid., chap. 5, sec. 7, 100.

23. For examples of this minority report, see Athanasius, "Four Discourses against the Arians," in *Nicene and Post-Nicene Fathers*, trans. John Henry Newman and Archibald Robertson, 2nd series, vol. 4, ed. Philip Schaff and Henry Wace (Grand Rapids, Mich.: Eerdmans, 1957), Discourse 1, sec. 21, 318–19; and his *The Letters of Saint Athanasius concerning the Holy Spirit*, trans. C. R. B. Shapland (London: Epworth Press, 1951) Epistle 1, sec. 16, 99–103, and Epistle 4, sec. 6, 187–88. See also Gregory of Nazianzus, "Third Theological Oration," trans. Charles Gordon Browne and James Edward Swallow, in *Christology of the Later Fathers*, ed. Edward Hardy (Philadelphia: Westminster Press, 1954), sec. 5, pp. 162–63.
24. For an expanded treatment of differences between divine and human persons, see my *Christ the Key* (Cambridge: Cambridge University Press, 2010), chap. 5. My discussion here follows the discussion in that chapter quite closely.
25. See Thomas G. Weinandy, *Does God Suffer?* (Notre Dame, Ind.: University of Notre Dame Press, 2000), 115, 118, 119, 128, 134–35, 140, 207–8.
26. See Giles Emery, "Essentialism or Personalism in the Treatise on God in Saint Thomas Aquinas?" in *Thomist* 64 (2000): 551–53.
27. Weinandy, *Does God Suffer?* 207n62.
28. See, for example, Athanasius, *Letters concerning the Holy Spirit*, Epistle 4, sec. 6, 187–88; and Gregory of Nazianzus, "Third Theological Oration," sec. 5, 162–63.
29. Virginia Burrus, *"Begotten Not Made": Conceiving Manhood in Late Antiquity* (Stanford, Calif.: Stanford University Press, 2000), 55.
30. See Fergus Kerr, *After Aquinas: Versions of Thomism* (Oxford: Blackwell, 2002), 199–200.
31. See William T. Cavanaugh, *Being Consumed: Economics and Christian Desire* (Grand Rapids, Mich.: Eerdmans, 2008), 33–58; and Vincent J. Miller, *Consuming Religion: Christian Faith and Practice in a Consumer Culture* (New York: Continuum, 2004), 118, 128.

MULTIPLICITY AND CHRISTOCENTRIC THEOLOGY | JOHN F. HOFFMEYER

1. Catherine Keller, *Apocalypse Now and Then: A Feminist Guide to the End of the World* (Boston: Beacon, 1996).
2. Barry Schwartz, *The Paradox of Choice: Why More Is Less* (New York: HarperCollins, 2004).
3. Amos 2:6–8, 5:22–24; the portion in brackets is, of course, a loose paraphrase.
4. This sentence corrects the mistaken etymology included in my original presentation for the colloquium. There I described simplicity as "folded-with-

ness." This etymology would work if the word were "symplicity," using the Latin prefix *sym-*, meaning "with." The actual prefix *sim-* apparently derives from *semel*, meaning "once."

5. For a subtle reflection on the one and the many that refuses both the triumph and the rejection of dialectic, see Catherine Malabou, *La plasticité au soir de l'écriture: Dialectique, destruction, déconstruction* (Paris: Léo Scheer, 2005).
6. Emmanuel Lévinas, *Totalité et infini: Essai sur l'extériorité* (Paris: Livre de Poche, n.d.).
7. Terry Pinkard, *Hegel's "Phenomenology": The Sociality of Reason* (Cambridge: Cambridge University Press, 1996).
8. Wilfrid Sellars, *Empiricism and the Philosophy of Mind* (Cambridge, Mass.: Harvard University Press, 1997), 76.
9. *Altérités: Jacques Derrida et Pierre-Jean Labarrière* (Paris: Osiris, 1986), 66, 81–90.
10. "Barmer Theologische Erklärung," http://www.ekd.de/glauben/bekenntnisse/barmer_theologische_erklaerung.html; accessed 6/12/2012.
11. James H. Cone, *God of the Oppressed*, rev. ed. (Maryknoll, N.Y.: Orbis, 1997), 31.
12. Catherine Keller, "Forces of Love: The Christopoetics of Desire," in *Who Is Jesus Christ for Us Today: Pathways to Contemporary Christology: In Honor of Michael Welker*, ed. Andreas Schuele and Günter Thomas (Louisville, Ky.: Westminster John Knox, 2009), 124.
13. Jean-François Lyotard, *La condition postmoderne: Rapport sur le savoir* (Paris: Minuit, 1979), 11, 17, 20.
14. "En simplifiant à l'extrême, on tient pour 'postmoderne' l'incrédulité à l'égard des métarécits" (ibid., 7).
15. Enrique D. Dussel, *Método para una filosofía de la liberación: superación analéctica de la dialéctica hegeliana* (Salamanca: Sígueme, 1974).
16. Susan Buck-Morss, *Hegel, Haiti, and Universal History* (Pittsburgh: University of Pittsburgh Press, 2009).
17. Kathryn Tanner, *Christ the Key* (Cambridge: Cambridge University Press, 2010).
18. Gregory of Nazianzus, *Orations*, 40:41, *Patrologia graeca*, vol. 36 (Paris: J. P. Migne), 417.
19. Mayra Rivera, *The Touch of Transcendence: A Postcolonial Theology of God* (Louisville, Ky.: Westminster John Knox, 2007), 131–32.
20. See Kathryn Tanner, "Is God in Charge?: Creation and Providence," in *Essentials of Christian Theology*, ed. William C. Placher (Louisville, Ky.: Westminster John Knox, 2003), 116–31, and, more extensively, Kathryn Tanner, *Jesus, Humanity and the Trinity: A Brief Systematic Theology* (Minneapolis: Fortress, 2001).
21. Rivera, *The Touch of Transcendence*, 127.

22. Lyotard, *La condition postmoderne*, 54–62.
23. G. W. F. Hegel, *Phänomenologie des Geistes*, Philosophische Bibliothek (Hamburg: Felix Meiner, 1988), 17–18.
24. This is not the only important form of religious diversity. More than one participant in the colloquium remarked that interreligious encounter and dialogue are sometimes easier than intrareligious encounter and dialogue.
25. Michelle Voss Roberts, typed response to my essay, kindly shared with me by the author.
26. My understanding—though not the terminology—of the distinction between christocentricity and Christianity-centricity owes much to Robert W. Jenson, *A Religion against Itself* (Richmond, Va.: John Knox Press, 1967).

DIVINE RELATIONALITY AND (THE METHODOLOGICAL CONSTRAINTS OF) THE GOSPEL AS PIECE OF NEWS: TRACING THE LIMITS OF TRINITARIAN ETHICS | CHRIS BOESEL

1. Feisal Abdul Rauf, in "Creating a New Vision of Islam in America: Interview with Imam Feisal Abdul Rauf," by Terry Gross, *Fresh Air*, NPR, May 9, 2012.
2. I am aware of the riskiness of using this piece of recent personal experience in this way, as it can be read as dangerously complicit in a long history of Christian competition with and demonization of Islam. Here I can be read as suggesting that my *Christian* religious and theological resources are more ethically robust and efficacious than the imam's *Islamic* religious and theological resources. First, I want to say that I am deeply offended by this history of Christian competition and demonization, and just as deeply troubled by this possible complicity. Second, although it is not possible to absolutely avoid the risk of this possible complicity, if one looks closely at my rendering of the complexity of the encounter, I trust that one can see that there is something else at work here. What I am suggesting for consideration is the extent to which the resources of a very specific kind of "religious extremist" may be more ethically radical and far-reaching than the imam's resources as a "religious moderate," resources that by definition he shares as common ground with moderates of *other religions* (the assumption of a shared foundational core of religious and ethical common ground across religions being central to the position and identity of a religious moderate, as I understand that position and identity). The imam's religious and theological resources in question here are therefore precisely *not* those particular to Islam, but are in principle shared with moderates of all religions. Neither, then, is the encounter that takes place here strictly between two different religions and religious identities, but rather

between two different *ways of inhabiting* religious identity. Finally, the fact that it is the Christian who is the theological extremist and the Muslim who is the moderate in this encounter confounds and overturns—rather than reinforcing and so being complicitous in—the prejudiced dynamics and assumptions fueling the contemporary public discourse on the relation between Christianity and Islam in the West.

3. An example of this doctrinal pliability offered by thinking in terms of the religious symbol surfaced several times throughout the colloquium. It took the form of questions regarding the Christian doctrine of the Trinity: "Why three? Why stop there? Why not more?" If the theological and ethical significance symbolized by the doctrine of the Trinity is the general principle of multiplicity and relationality, both creaturely and divine, couldn't this be communicated by any number of persons or things in various kinds of relation? So not only is the doctrine, as symbol, not tied to the notion of persons, it is not tied or bound to the number three, that is, to the three specific persons witnessed to in the biblical literature and the church's liturgical and creedal formulas. Neither the persons themselves nor their exact number are essential to the theological or ethical content of the doctrine of the Trinity when taken as religious symbol. Rather, it is the principles of multiplicity and relationality as such that they symbolize, a mulitiplicity and a relationality that can be got at—perhaps more effectively—by other means, other symbols. *If*, however, the doctrine of the Trinity is intended to bear witness to God as just these three persons in the very particular relation of fellowship and communion based on witness and testimony to their very particular work and action in history, then the question "Why three?" seems misplaced. It would be like asking why we say "three" when we talk about the Three Stooges. We say "three" because there were, in fact, three (though the midcareer personnel change complicates this example somewhat). If we replaced "three" with "five" or "eight" or "an infinite complexity," we would be changing the subject; we would no longer be talking about Larry, Curly, and Moe. (I am of course trusting that God has a sufficient sense of humor, and reservoir of grace, to appreciate this rather backhanded—and all male!—illustration.)

4. Leonardo Boff, *Trinity and Society* (Maryknoll, N.Y.: Orbis, 1988), 20.

5. Rosemary Radford Ruether, *Faith and Fratricide: The Theological Roots of Anti-Semitism* (New York: Seabury, 1974), 237, 239, 248. See Chris Boesel, *Risking Proclamation, Respecting Difference: Christian Faith, Imperialistic Discourse, and Abraham* (Eugene, Ore.: Cascade, 2008).

6. Rosemary Radford Ruether, *God and Gaia: An Ecofeminist Theology of Earth Healing* (San Francisco: HarperSanFrancisco, 1994), 119.

7. A similar shadow of an ethically grounded hierarchical denigration of "the religious other" haunts Elizabeth Johnson's argument for the inclusion of a limitless multiplicity of theological and trinitarian images and symbols in affirmation of the diversity of religious experience, based on the fundamentally symbolic nature of all theological and religious language. This opening up of inclusionary embrace beyond the exclusionary strictures of Christian orthodoxy seems to entail a censure of its own.

> A religion . . . that would speak about a warlike god and extol the way he smashes his enemies to bits would promote aggressive group behavior. A community that would acclaim God as an arbitrary tyrant would inspire its members to acts of impatience and disrespect toward their fellow creatures. On the other hand, speech about a beneficent and loving God who forgives offenses would turn the faith community toward care for the neighbor and mutual forgiveness. (Elizabeth Johnson, *She Who Is: The Mystery of God and Feminist Theological Discourse* [New York: Crossroads, 1992], 4)

Is it possible to read Johnson here as attempting (paraphrasing Ruether) to "leave room for the distinctiveness" of the first two religious communities in this example? As attempting, in the name and for the sake of those two communities, to "guarantee the integrity of each people to stand before God in their own identities and histories" and have "access to God on their own grounds"?

8. See, for example, Clifford Green, ed., *Karl Barth: Theologian of Freedom* (Minneapolis: Fortress, 1991). For Barth, Christian theology is not an exercise in free thought. A working principle would be "bound to God's Word," which also means to be bound to God's action. Because of this concrete particularity of God's Word in action, we are in the grips of a binding constriction that, at least in Barth's mind, because binding us to *God*, is for the sake of genuine expansiveness and freedom. As Bob Dylan says, "You gotta serve somebody." For Barth, *not* being bound to God in this way does not mean freedom from constriction; it just means that we are bound to something or someone else that or who is *less* radically and truly *for us* than God in God's self-giving in Jesus Christ in the Spirit.

9. My reason for using feminine pronouns for God throughout the text is simply that I find feminist critiques of the idolatrous captivity of the church's theological *imagination* to male-gendered images of God—despite the church's explicit theological *doctrine* of God, as Spirit, being neither male nor female—to be

convincing. It seems obvious to me, then, given that idolatry is to be avoided if we can at all help it, that the employment of feminine language and images for God that are consistent with the biblical witness to who God is and how God is for and with us constitutes a form of faithful Christian practice and theological method. Although I believe that arguments contra this usage based on, for example, the authority of biblical language for the church (e.g., Jesus taught us to pray, saying "Father") should not simply be dismissed, I find the urgency of idolatrous captivity the more compelling claim at this time. Similarly, it could appear that my use of feminine language for God flies in the face of Barth's argument that God gives Godself fully and truly in the man Jesus Christ and the human witness to his life and history and the consequent methodological constraint on the church's theological knowledge. I am happy to let the awkwardness of this contradiction—if it *is* a contradiction—stand, for inasmuch as Barth would insist that said argument and methodological constriction binds the church to exclusively employ male-gendered language for God, I would simply disagree with him. Above and beyond the Bible's own occasional use of feminine language, I would disagree with him on the basis of his own Reformed theological insistence that in the mystery of the incarnational union of God with the man Jesus from Nazareth, God *remains God*—without commingling. Therefore, the characterstics of Jesus' distinctively human gender and genitalia do not "bleed back" to determine the nature of God *as God* in the mystery of that union. The argument that it is precisely this kind of divine "transcendence"—immune to the risky, messy, "relational" immanence of "commingling"—that is essentially masculine needs to be taken seriously. In doing so, one needs to interrogate both the limits of its possible essentialism and the way in which it itself is often employed for the sake of immunity from risk: immunity from the risky messiness of the "scandal of particularity" entailed in the radical singularity of God's full incarnation once for all in the one human, Jesus of Nazareth. It could be suggested that what offends here is precisely *too much* divine self-commitment to the limiting particularity and vulnerability of embodied creaturely finitude; that is, ironically, there is *not enough* "transcendence" assumed proper to the incomprehensibility, ineffability, mystery, depth dimension, excess, and so on, of divine nature. Finally then, from my perspective at this time, although the human male/masculine remains, of its own nature and capacity, as equally *bereft* as the female/feminine with regard to any *natural* similitude to God's reality or capacity to signify or symbolize sufficiently for the sake of theological knowledge or the knowledge of faith, God is equally free and able to use either as an act of self-disclosing and self-giving grace according to Her good pleasure.

10. In his mature doctrine of revelation Barth says, "In relation to God man has constantly to let something be said to him, has constantly to listen to something which he constantly does not know and which in no circumstances and in no sense can he say to himself" (Karl Barth, *Church Dogmatics*, vol. 1, pt. 1, ed. G. W. Bromiley and T. F. Torrance, trans. G. W. Bromiley et al., 3rd ed. [Edinburgh: T&T Clark, 1975], 61). And again: "Only when and to the extent that such a Word of God is spoken by God Himself to the Church is there any right or sense in speaking about God in the Church" (Barth, *CD I/1*, 43). Barth's concern here is that in any other grounding of the church's knowledge of and speech about God—all of which falls under the category of what he calls "natural theology"—God becomes a passive object, lying inertly before the active knowing human subject like some kind of "pillow queen." One consequence of which is that the capacities, agencies, and activities of *human* knowing, interpretation, philo-theo-poetic construction—the linguistic opening of space for new subjectivities, etc.—become the site for what traditional theology assumed to be the provenance of unique *divine* activity, e.g., revelation, creation, salvation, reconciliation, liberation. In short, theology becomes anthropology.

11. Karl Barth, *Church Dogmatics*, vol. 2, pt. 2, ed. G. W. Bromiley and T. F. Torrance, trans. G. W. Bromiley et al. (Edinburgh: T&T Clark, 1957), 4.

12. Ibid., 5.

13. Ibid., 7.

14. Ibid., 95. Barth leaves no doubt as to the radicality of his position: "Before Him and above Him and beside Him and apart from Him there is no election, no beginning, no decree, no Word of God" (Barth, *CD II/2*, 95). As the "Word of God . . . in whose Truth everything is disclosed," Jesus Christ "is the decree of God behind or above [or beside] which there can be no earlier or higher [or other] decree . . . He is the election of God before which and without which and beside which God cannot make any other choices" (Barth, *CD II/2*, 94).

15. Ibid., 6.

16. Ibid., 7. When Barth says that Jesus Christ is the Word of God, he means that Jesus Christ "is the beginning of God," such that God has decided from all eternity to be God "only in this way and not in any other" (Barth, *CD II/2*, 94, 6). In a later passage, Barth adds an important qualifier in this regard. "He was not at the beginning of God, for God has indeed no beginning. But He was at the beginning of all things, at the beginning of God's dealings with the reality which is distinct from Himself" (Barth, *CD II/2*, 102). Consequently, Barth concludes, "The voice of Jesus Christ" is "the *only* voice which can reign

in the Church . . . as the source and norm of all truth" (Barth, CD II/2, 4). It is important to note here that Barth assumes that the voice of Jesus Christ is as such irreducible to and can never simply be identified with the voice of the church or the Bible or of any creature, but always finds us and addresses us in unpredictable and unanticipatable freedom, "absolutely from without."

17. Karl Barth, *Church Dogmatics*, vol. 2, pt. 1, ed. G. W. Bromiley and T. F. Torrance, trans. T. H. L. Parker et al., 2nd ed. (Edinburgh: T&T Clark, 1964), 7–9. For Barth, then, "theology must begin with Jesus Christ," such that what is revealed to the church in the name of Jesus Christ is "the beginning and end of all our thoughts" (Barth, CD II/2, 4–5). Again: "The knowledge of God is bound to the God who in His Word gives Himself to the Church to be known as God" (Barth, CD II/1, 7).

18. And as a piece of good *news*, it is to be addressed to the religious neighbor. They too are among its intended addressees. Just as the church never ceases to be addressed—and judged (an especially important point for Barth)—by the Gospel, neither does the church become its sole proprietor, as exclusive sphere or audience. The Gospel is good news for *the world*. Therefore, interaction and engagement with the religious neighbor cannot be avoided by some retreat behind the walls of a so-called fideistic ghetto. Neither can said interaction and engagement be ultimately hostile and destructive to the religious neighbor. For if the news is genuinely *good*, its content, articulation, and communication cannot be destructive for its intended addressees. Truly good news would need to be able to articulate itself and enflesh itself as *some* form of Wesley Ariarajah's simply and powerfully crafted conviction, "not without my neighbor" (S. Wesley Ariarajah, *Not without My Neighbor: Issues in Interfaith Relations* [Geneva: WCC Publications, 1999]).

19. And it certainly doesn't help matters that the particular reports of these particular witnesses are utterly unbelievable (then as now), both rationally and ethically. For example, that God is fully and uniquely incarnate in Jesus; that Jesus takes the place of all humanity on the cross; that Jesus was raised bodily from the dead. The mystery we are dealing with here is clearly of a different sort than the incomprehensibility of divine nature. It is one of incomprehensible, paradoxical divine *behavior*.

But this is not just a modern problem. The DNA of this problem—the doctrine of the Trinity as response to historical witness and testimony—is inherent in the ancient debates of the church and written into its patristic doctrinal formulas. *If* the doctrine of the Trinity is such a response, then its content is to be judged according to how it corresponds to the reports of said witness and testimony. And the problem from the very beginning was that these particular reports of divine activity flew squarely in the face of the most fundamental assumptions about the nature of divine being held by the best minds and inherent in the prevailing wisdom of the day as assumed philosophical and cosmological givens. This contradiction between the reports of witness and testimony and the philosophical assumptions about what is possible—and impossible—for divine nature and its engagement with the cosmos according to the demands of reason and necessities of logic was especially aggravated for much of the ancient tradition of the church given its own prevailing theological assumption that the truths of reason available to the best philosophical thinking could provide reliable and even revelatory knowledge of divinity. Thus, even in its internal doctrinal struggle (as distinct from apologetic contest with extant philosophical systems and their cosmologies and attendant religious forms) the prevailing philosophical givens of divine impassibility and immutability were shared by the opposing positions of the internal doctrinal debates. For example, if the reports say that Jesus suffered and died, then either God could not have been fully, hypostatically present with us in the human Jesus (Arius) or if so present, it could not have been the divine but only the human nature of Jesus that suffered and died (Athanasius).

This is often cited as an example when the christological and trinitarian debates are critiqued as an accommodationist project from top to bottom, an "extreme make-over" of the biblical Jesus in order to fit him snuggly into the metaphysical and cosmological world of Western culture, wherein the biblical Jesus disappears into the logos of Greek philosophy and biblical Christianity becomes a product and possession of Western culture. But those debates, at their core, often involved theologians breaking open existing philosophical language and concepts, giving them content and employing them in ways determined by that which appeared necessary according to the reports of witness and testimony, precisely *against the grain* of their content and use as embedded in the philosophical and cosmological systems from which they were borrowed. Nevertheless, the church has always winced at the pinch of limitation entailed in accountability to particular witness and testimony recorded in the Bible, and the contradiction to prevailing, and often overwhelmingly compelling, winds of extant wisdom that this involves. The need to resolve the contradiction between the biblical reports and the demands of the prevailing philosophical and cultural wisdom of the day—involving either all manner of intellectual gymnastics or a judicious shaving of the rough and inconvenient edges of the reports to accommodate the demands of philosophical plausibility—has always inhabited the trinitarian inheritance of the church.

20. Barth, *CD II/1*, 8.
21. One person who did not like it was G. W. F. Hegel. He objected precisely on ethical grounds, and more particularly, on grounds decrying this binding and constriction from the outside as the violence of imperialistic imposition, of foreign aggression. He articulates his offense at this imperialistic violence thusly: "Is Judea the Teutons' Fatherland?" And here again we get a glimpse of the anti-Judaism that lies inescapably at the heart of modern ethical desire. The "spider's thread" cum constrictive cord is, after all, a piece of predominantly if not wholly Jewish news. It is this Abrahamic stranglehold on Christian faith that Hegel, and virtually every other modern thinker of import, assumed to be the cause of a poisonous and distorting violence that was not indigenous to Christianity itself.
22. Karl Barth, "Evangelical Theology in the 19th Century," in *The Humanity of God*, trans. John Newton Thomas (Atlanta: John Knox Press, 1960), 11.
23. Barth, *CD II/2*, 6. My emphasis.
24. Ibid., 26. My emphasis. Doctrinally, of course, this is an issue of God's trinitarian nature and activity that goes beyond creation and providence. For Barth, the doctrine of the Trinity *precedes* the doctrine of God. This is another way in which Barth thinks against the grain of the theological tradition.
25. Ibid., 3.
26. The debate about if, and in which way, and to what extent God is person or personal or ultimately nonpersonal is old and worn. For many, as John Thatamanil reminds us, this is not only old and worn but settled, in favor of the nonpersonal. In what follows I bring nothing new to the debate, but risk rehashing what has been hashed over and over again in many other contexts because *this* context's specific concern with the ethics of relationality seems to call for the reminder. Put differently, the way I hear contemporary theological discourse about divine multiplicity (e.g., trinitarian theology) as a valuable site for an ethics of relationality seems to bring the personal/nonpersonal issue quite urgently back to the center of what is at stake in this concern. It relates precisely to what I hear as the possible limits entailed in many of the contemporary theological attempts to remedy the ethically problematic limits of the Christian tradition. For example, discourses that assume the old debate has been settled in favor of a nonanthropomorphic and so nonpersonal divinity as the only philosophically plausible alternative for good moderns often seem to do so for the sake of and according to assumptions inherent in an ethics of personal relationality and responsibility, and so appear to be at odds with their own best intentions.

27. Note the counterintuitive logic: The goodness of the news depends on what modernity can only experience as the bad news of divine election, of God's choosing. One can see here Barth's unapologetic, albeit supersessionist, Abrahamic commitment. The theme of God's choosing—of divine election—is essential to Barth's understanding of God as living and personal. Indeed, perhaps Barth's most innovative doctrinal move in his *Church Dogmatics* is the inclusion of the doctrine of election within the doctrine of God. One can see Barth's commitment to the Hebraic theme of election as central to the way he is problematic to the best ethical desires of liberal, progressive remedies of tradition, such as the discourses of religious pluralism and comparative theology. This also suggests, however, that an anti-Judaism might inevitably inhabit said ethical desire, and so to some extent, these discourses. To exclude or quarantine Barth's exclusionary particularity is of a piece with an exclusion of the Abrahamic tradition. As I have argued elsewhere, at the heart of the modern ethical desire is a dark necessity: Abraham must die. See Boesel, *Risking Proclamation*.
28. I am aware of all the complications here, for example, around the concepts of divine love as *agape*, that is, selfless love, as distinct from *Eros*, and so on. Many of these complications were very helpfully articulated at an earlier Transdisciplinary Theological Colloquium at Drew, precisely on *Eros* (see Virginia Burrus and Catherine Keller, eds., *Toward a Theology of Eros: Transfiguring Passion at the Limits of Discipline* (New York: Fordham University Press, 2006). Although this requires a whole conversation and argument in itself, I am not intending to deny or refuse these complications, but to suggest that what is at stake here is not exhaustively accounted for and dismissed by said complications. I could be wrong, of course; the argument would have to be made and assessed.
29. This would also apply to a theological anthropology that assumes the *imago dei* in the human being to be the natural, constitutional possession of the logos in terms of the capacity for speech, for semantic communication, for example, for hearing and understanding a word of communication (in general) and so too *the* Word (in particular) communicated in revelation as personal divine address. This is what Barth understood to be the essence of Brunner's methodology of eristics, an attempt to redeem some viable form of natural theology in the wake of Barth's relentless "ground-clearing" in his commentary on Romans. It was this attempt that bore the brunt of Barth's unequivocal "Nein!" in their highly public falling out. Note here a possible resonance between Barth's "nein" to Brunner and Derrida's critique of the philosophical distinction of the human from the animal according to the former's assumed possession of the logos.

30. Barth, of course, simply denies that there is any necessary similarity between God and the creature on the basis of an overall general ontological category or metaphysical structure or cosmological process. God's act of creation itself, as an act distinct from incarnation and reconciliation, is, like them, an act of sheer gratuity, of free choosing, and so is itself a gesture of seeking and creating fellowship. This is the whole point of the doctrine of creation ex nihilo, for Barth. It is not primarily cosmological description, but a theological assertion that the meaning and goal of creation is the relation of fellowship and communion and nothing less. "Less," here, means any other kind of relation—for example, the radicality of ontological and/or cosmological co-constitution—wherein God is less radically *for* the creature in loving freedom, wherein God may be with the creature but in a way and according to assumptions and concepts unable to prevent and reject any and all possibility of neutrality, inevitability, or ontological necessity. There is a strong resonance here with the argument of Mark Heim's, *The Depths of the Riches: A Trinitarian Theology of Religious Ends* (Grand Rapids, Mich.: Eerdmans, 2000). Within this general agreement, I would want to distinguish what I am trying to do with Barth, here, from the extent to which I believe Heim is still making some form of argument for the "superiority" of Christianity as a religion over other religions. Barth's view of the Gospel as commissioned human witness and testimony to free and redeeming divine action in history as a part of history places all of what is today called "religion" under the lens of critical judgment, including the religion of Christianity. Regarding the competitive discourse of "superiority" among religions, then, the church (and its theologians) simply has other fish to fry: witnessing to the Gospel in word and deed by attempting to live into the relationality of fellowship and communion into which all have been called and for which all have been redeemed. The church is not called to argue or demonstrate that Christianity is the "superior" religion.
31. Barth, *CD II/2*, 25–26.
32. Ibid., 13.
33. Ibid., 309–10. My emphasis.
34. This constitutes what is both hailed and contested as Barth's christological universalism, which receives its most explicit statement in his innovative doctrine of election. Employing the traditional and biblical language of election and rejection, Barth asserts that whatever negative consequences may be thought to entail upon unbelief or alternative belief can only be seen as "borne and cancelled by Jesus Christ" (Barth, *CD II/2*, 306). It is a negative reality that has "reached its goal," the "execution" of God's judgment upon it having been

fulfilled in the person and history of Jesus Christ such that "eternal damnation" can no longer "be their [the unbeliever's] concern" (Barth, CD II/2, 319). Consequently—*and most troubling to the conservative Christian evangelical heart*; I should know, these are my people—any divine rejection of unbelief, then, has no eternal future and so cannot be a genuine eschatological future awaiting the creature as final destination. The consequences of unbelief or alternative belief can only ever constitute a past that has run its course. And this is what keeps conservative evangelicals up at night: the possibility of an empty hell.

35. The notion of a creaturely free choosing here is not assumed to be one that is immune from or undisplaced by a critical interrogation like that of deconstruction. That is, it is not assumed to be the absolutely free choosing of the absolutely free, autonomous agency of the individual modern subject. A robust doctrine of sin organic to Barth's theological assumptions would see to that, perhaps more radically than deconstruction. In any case, inasmuch as it is still possible, "after" deconstruction has done its work, to speak of intention and decision as distinguishable from and indeed opposable to a more thoroughly automatic, mechanical unfolding of programmatic action—and I believe it is fairly obvious, though depressingly underreported, that Derrida says it *is* possible and is in fact necessary—*that* is what I'm referring to here. See Jacques Derrida, "Signature Event Context," in *Limited Inc*, ed. Gerald Graff, trans. Jeffrey Mehlman and Samuel Weber (Evanston, Ill.: Northwestern University Press, 1988).

36. Again, I am using these problematically loaded terms with the assumptions that (1) they can be—and have been—run through both the confessional-theological and deconstructive critical mills wherein their content and structural limits are determined very specifically, and (2) there is still a viable if radically qualified employment of these terms that "remains," whereby this point can be meaningfully made sufficient to my humble purposes here.

37. The implications of these multiple and apparently conflictual obligations are obviously painfully and perhaps impossibly complex. How to give ourselves to those who are in conflict with each other? Especially when our own ethical and religious discourses and so on include very particular visions of justice that pertain to these conflicts? For example, what if they are *behaving* very much like enemies? What if one has and employs an overabundance of material and cultural power, and so on? As Emmanuel Levinas has put it: "What have they done to one another? Which one passes before the other?" (Emmanuel Levinas, *Otherwise Than Being, or Beyond Essence*, trans. Alphonso Lingis [The Hague: Martinus Nijhoff, 1981], 157). This all demands a careful unpack-

ing, case by case, in concrete contexts of multiple relations, that takes us well beyond the limits of this already overly long essay.

38. Might this include ecological and ecotheological discourses about the radical interconnectivity and interdependence of ecosystems? For example, the interconnectivity and interdependence articulated by these discourses are radical indeed, yet nevertheless allow for and even require sacrifice of the weak and vulnerable—for example, the (naturally selected, nonpersonal) culling of the one weak and vulnerable who strays from the herd of ninety-nine—precisely to sustain an ecological web's necessary and delicate balance of interdependence between organisms and/or communities of organisms.

39. In this, Barth's theological method shares (for better or worse) a similarly critical hermeneutic of suspicion regarding religion with certain social science folks such as Russell McCutcheon. See Russell T. McCutcheon, *Critics Not Caretakers: Redescribing the Public Study of Religion* (Albany: State University of New York Press, 2001).

THE UNIVERSE, RAW: SAYING SOMETHING ABOUT EVERYTHING | CYNTHIA L. RIGBY

1. One version of this story is given in Ed Young, *Seven Blind Mice* (London: Puffin, 2002).
2. As we Presbyterians like to put it, we are "reformed and always reforming, according to the Word of God" (*ecclesia reformata semper reformanda secundum verbum dei*).
3. Although a scientist in one of my theology classes once tried to explain to me how a molecule of water could be, at one and the same time, both liquid and ice. He insisted his argument was logical, and it might have been. But I didn't understand it.
4. This is another allusion to Annie Dillard's *Living by Fiction*. See Annie Dillard, *Living by Fiction*, rev. ed. (New York: Harper Perennial, 1988). This book will be discussed further in the next section of this essay.
5. If the definition of a paradox is putting two things together that we have already decided are incommensurable. (The absurdity I think we are compelled to live into is the fact that the one and the three *are* commensurable; the conflict between them is, in a "cooked" world, completely understandable.)
6. My term, playing off of Dillard's "raw" universe. While I think she means more than "good, created, hope-full" universe by "raw universe," I think this is part of what she means.
7. A good "Reformed theology" approach, in the tradition of Karl Barth (also my tradition).

8. Discussion of the nature of mystery, or aspect of the mystery, has been prevalent in theological discourse on the Trinity in recent decades; see (for example) Barth, Moltmann, LaCugna, Jensen, Tanner.
9. One of the ways this is classically put is: The Father is not the Son or the Spirit; the Son is not the Father or the Spirit; the Spirit is not the Father or the Son.
10. Note that the doctrine of the Trinity does not espouse that the God who is one is both one and "many," but that this God is one and "three." Unlike "many" (which is a general term), "three" conveys God's "scandalous particularity"—the truth that God engages the world in specific, as well as general, ways.
11. These are phrases used by Annie Dillard in *Living by Fiction*. They will be engaged in greater detail below.
12. This is a phrase used by Marilynne Robinson in her discussion of the "conceptual problem" that is at the heart of John Calvin's theology ("Preface," *John Calvin: Steward of God's Creation*, ed. J. F. Thornton and S. B. Varenne, xvi). This will be discussed further, below.
13. I have in mind, for example, some of the contributors to the volume *Speaking the Christian God: The Holy Trinity and the Challenge of Feminism*, ed. Alvin Kimel (Grand Rapids, Mich.: Eerdmans, 1992). Kimel is among those contributors to the volume who seem to think the relationship between our words and the reality they mean to convey is at times univocal, rather than analogical (consider the very title of his essay: "The God Who Likes His Name," 188–208).
14. J. N. D. Kelly, *Early Christian Doctrines* (New York: Harper and Row, 1958), 253.
15. I have in mind here Kierkegaard's use of the term as he uses it in reference to the "knight of faith," who not only "expects what is possible" (and is therefore "great"), but "expects what is impossible" (and is, therefore, "the greatest of all"). Kierkegaard insists that the one who expects what is impossible has "hope that takes the form of madness" (*Fear and Trembling*, ed. H. Hong and E. Hong [Princeton: Princeton University Press, 1983], 36–37).
16. My emphasis.
17. Dillard, *Living by Fiction*, 145–46.
18. And the beauty of every detail—not beautiful details, in general.
19. I have in mind, if I may be so bold, most of us whose work is included in this volume.
20. Because the words spoken in response are not being spoken in relation to what is really meant.
21. This reminds me of a dynamic I have experienced where a student asks me a question that is weighing heavy on her or his heart and I say: "That's a very important and commonly asked question. But we really can't get into that right

now." Such an answer is, I think, actually "hard," even if it is so completely unintentionally and—even—necessarily (practically speaking, given that there is other material that needs covering).

22. See Romans 8:28.
23. Dillard is attentive to particulars in all of her work, but especially in her Pulitzer Prize–winning book, *Pilgrim at Tinker Creek*. Here, she invites us to meet mountains and peaches, muskrats and daffodils, desert rocks and water bugs. (See Annie Dillard, *Pilgrim at Tinker Creek* [Norwich UK: Canterbury Press, 2011].)
24. This is illustrated by the "elephant story" example given in the preface to this piece.
25. These are unpublished words of Marilynne Robinson, as I jotted them down at a conference. They continue to affect how I think and live.
26. Here we remember that who God is is known in God's acts.
27. Here we remember that who God is cannot be reduced to God's acts.
28. I borrow this usage of "mystical" and "metaphysical" from Marilynne Robinson, in her discussion of the strength of Calvin's theological approach. Specifically, Robinson writes that for Calvin "mysticism [is] a method of rigorous inquiry" and "metaphysics . . . an impassioned flight of the soul" (*The Death of Adam* [New York: Picador, 1995], 188). Note that Robinson does not explicitly tie the "mystical" to the three-in-one and the "metaphysical" to the one-in-three as I do here.
29. John Calvin, *Institutes* I.13.17, ed. J. T. McNeil and F. L. Battles (Philadelphia: Westminster Press, 1960), quoting Gregory of Nazianzus, *On Holy Baptism*, oration XL.41.
30. Robinson, "Introduction" to *John Calvin: Steward of God's Creation*, xvi.
31. Ibid.
32. From Calvin's commentary on Psalm 145:5, 11–12.
33. Calvin, *Institutes*, I.5.9.
34. Since I know, from my experience of telling this story, that the reader might want to know what happens next, I'll tell you: I pull off the road and into a Walgreen's parking lot, take Jessica out of the car seat, and embrace her. She will not be consoled (I have never seen her this upset, before or since). After about a half hour of sobbing, I finally bring her into the Walgreen's and down the toy aisle, where I purchase a $10 plastic Disney Princess tea set. That helps a lot, though I haven't had the courage—yet—to analyze the purchase of the tea set via the theological suggestions made in this essay!
35. I recognize that not all missionaries have done or are doing this.

36. See Elie Wiesel, *Night* (New York: Hill and Wang, 2006).
37. This is an important idea developed by William Greenway. See William Greenway, "On Evil and the Problem with Cosmodicy," *Insights* 121, no. 2 (2006): 36–50, http://www.austinseminary.edu/page.cfm?p=541.
38. Karl Barth, *Church Dogmatics*, vol. 3, pt. 4, ed. G. W. Bromiley and T. F. Torrance, trans. G. W. Bromily et al. (Edinburgh: T. & T. Clark, 1961). See especially §54, 150–52.
39. Barth, *CD III/4*, 150.
40. Ibid., 168–72.
41. Ibid., 120–21, where Barth describes the relationship between a man and a woman as "the truly breath-taking dialectic . . . of difference and affinity, of real dualism and equally real unity, of utter self-recollection and utter transport beyond the bounds of self into union with another, of creation and redemption, of this world and the next."
42. See, for example, what directly follows the citation I included in the preceding footnote, on page 120 of *CD III/4*. Notice that Barth pulls away from describing our participation in the life of the triune God, as men and women in relation (which, he thinks, comes too dangerously close to seeing ourselves as God). In order to avoid the danger, he moves instead to discussion of obedience to God's command.
43. I think it is important to mention that I understand this text to be parabolic, not paradigmatic. In other words, I don't think the point of it is to endorse heterosexism (though it has, of course, been used this way countless times). Rather, it reflects that knowing one another with the kind of knowledge that is participatory requires attentiveness to the oneness that is inherently shared as well as to the particulars that are brought.
44. Otherwise known as, "the Garden."
45. Adam Gopnik, "What Did Jesus Do?" *New Yorker*, May 24, 2010, 77.
46. This is an allusion to Mary's response to Gabriel's news, as the story is told in Luke 2, by way of the Chalcedonian insight that Mary is *theotokos*, the "bearer of God."
47. This is an allusion to the story of Paul's sermon on the Areopagus, as it is told in Acts 17.
48. Paul is referencing Jesus. But, more important for my purposes here, he is naming an instance of three being also one, of Jesus participating perichoretically in the life of the Trinity.

CONTRIBUTORS

S. Wesley Ariarajah is Professor of Ecumenical Theology at Drew Theological School. His most recent book is titled *The Bible and People of Other Faiths*.

Loriliai Biernacki is an Associate Professor in the Department of Religious Studies and Director of Graduate Studies at the University of Colorado, Boulder. She is the author of *Renowned Goddess of Desire: Women, Sex, and Speech in Tantra*.

Chris Boesel is Associate Professor of Christian Theology at Drew Theological School. He is the author of *Risking Proclamation, Respecting Difference: Christian Faith, Imperialistic Discourse, and Abraham*.

Philip Clayton is the Ingraham Professor of Theology, Vice President of Academic Affairs and Dean of Faculty at Claremont School of Theology, and Professor of Religion at Claremont Graduate University. His most recent book is titled *Transforming Christian Theology: for Church and Society*.

Jacob J. Erickson is a doctoral candidate in Theological and Philosophical Studies at Drew University. He is currently working on his dissertation, an ecotheology of planetary conviviality that engages the discourses of political ecology, queer theory, apophatic theology, contemporary continental philosophy, and theologies and philosophies of divine immanence.

Roland Faber is the Kilsby Family/John Cobb, Jr., Professor of Process Studies at Claremont Theological School, Professor of Religion and Philosophy at Claremont Graduate University, Executive Co-Director of the Center for Process Studies, and Executive Director of the Whitehead Research Project. He is the author of *God as Poet of the World: Exploring Process Theology*.

S. Mark Heim is the Samuel Abbot Professor of Christian Theology at Andover-Newton Theological School. His most recent book is titled *Saved from Sacrifice: A Theology of the Cross*.

Holly Hillgardner is a doctoral candidate in Theological and Philosophical Studies at Drew University. She is working on her dissertation, which explores theologies of yearning through a study of passionate nonattachment in the medieval writings of Hadewijch and Mirabai. She is the 2012–13 Renner Visiting Scholar at Bethany College, Bethany, West Virginia.

John F. Hoffmeyer is Associate Professor of Systematic Theology at Lutheran Theological Seminary at Philadelphia. He has published on G. W. F. Hegel and Friedrich Schleiermacher and is currently working on a book on trinitarian theology and consumerism.

Catherine Keller is Professor of Constructive Theology at Drew Theological School. Her most recent book is titled *On the Mystery: Discerning God in Process*.

Sam Laurent has a PhD from Drew University. His areas of research include aesthetics, pragmatism, pneumatology, and ecclesiology. He is currently revising his dissertation for publication. It is titled "Incarnational Creativity: A Pneumatology of Improvisation."

Cynthia L. Rigby is the W. C. Brown Professor of Theology at Austin Presbyterian Theological Seminary. She is the author of *The Promotion of Social Righteousness*.

Sara Rosenau is a doctoral candidate in Theological and Philosophical Studies at Drew University. She is currently working on her dissertation on theological method and political theology, arguing for an alternative strategy for progressive theo-politics to either the communitarian political argument of postliberal theological method or the liberal political argument of liberal/correlational theological method.

Kathryn Tanner is Professor of Systematic Theology at Yale Divinity School. Her most recent book is titled *Christ the Key*.

Eric Trozzo is Lecturer of Theology at Sabah Theological Seminary in Kota Kinabalu, Malaysia. He is currently working on a manuscript tentatively titled "Rupturing Eschatology: Divine Glory and the Silence of the Cross."

TRANSDISCIPLINARY THEOLOGICAL COLLOQUIA

Laurel Kearns and Catherine Keller, eds., *Ecospirit: Religions and Philosophies for the Earth*

Virginia Burrus and Catherine Keller, eds., *Toward a Theology of Eros: Transfiguring Passion at the Limits of Discipline*

Ada María Isasi-Díaz and Eduardo Mendieta, eds., *Decolonizing Epistemologies: Latina/o Theology and Philosophy*

Stephen D. Moore and Mayra Rivera, eds., *Planetary Loves: Spivak, Postcoloniality, and Theology*

Chris Boesel and Catherine Keller, eds., *Apophatic Bodies: Negative Theology, Incarnation, and Relationality*

Chris Boesel and S. Wesley Ariarajah, eds., *Divine Multiplicity: Trinities, Diversities, and the Nature of Relation*

www.ingramcontent.com/pod-product-compliance
Lightning Source LLC
Chambersburg PA
CBHW031231290426
44109CB00012B/245